The 49ers II

Also by the same author

The 49ers – THE TRUE STORY

and published by Book Guild

The 49ers II

THE REST OF THE STORY

John Warham

Book Guild Publishing

Sussex, England

First published in Great Britain in 2015 by
The Book Guild Ltd
The Werks
45 Church Road
Hove, BN3 2BE

Typesetting in Times New Roman by
Ellipsis Books Ltd, Glasgow

Printed in Great Britain by
CPI Antony Rowe

A catalogue record for this book is available from
The British Library.

ISBN 978 1 910508 87 9

Especially for Don, Klaske and the BoBs.

But also for the many, many others
who continued to believe,
kept the faith and travelled the long road with us
to our final destination.

Preface

This is the sequel to my first book; *The 49ers – The True Story*. It relates events that occurred after that first book was published. If the reader is not familiar with the first book, some of the events related herein may prove difficult to follow. For ease of reference, the following is a brief summary of events leading up to the present story.

➢ On 9th July 2001, following a protracted industrial dispute, Cathay Pacific Airways sacked 49 of its pilots;

➢ The dismissal notices gave no reasons for the sackings, but Cathay subsequently made statements about the pilots in the world's media that were unfounded, malicious and defamatory;

➢ These statements destroyed the pilots' careers and effectively blacklisted them in the world of commercial aviation;

➢ The pilots filed legal actions against Cathay in Hong Kong, the UK, the USA and Australia;

➢ The UK case went all the way to the House of Lords which ruled in the pilots' favour in 2006;

➢ In the Hong Kong case, the pilots filed three causes of action:
  ▪ Breach of the Employment Ordinance Section S21B, which provides protection against anti-union discrimination,
  ▪ Breach of contract,
  ▪ Defamation;

➢ In November 2009, the High Court in Hong Kong ruled in the pilots' favour on all three legs of their case and awarded them damages of HK$3.45 million, plus one month's salary, each;

➢ Cathay appealed this judgment and the case came to court in July 2010.

Chapter 1 of this book plunges the reader straight into the deep end of the complexities of employment law and the machinations of the Court of Appeal hearing. Some of it may be heavy reading for a first chapter of a book: not an ideal way to capture the interest of a first-time reader. Perhaps it is an indication of my shortcomings as a writer that I have been unable to find another way to tell the story in a logical manner. I can only ask for the reader's forbearance and perseverance. Now read on.

John Warham
February 2015

Contents

Prologue   1

1. Court of Appeal   5

2. Judgment 1   45

3. LTC   55

4. Renaissance   77

5. Cost Benefit Analysis   87

6. Training   105

7. Navigation   127

8. RTB   145

9. Interlude   163

10. Court of Final Appeal   173

11. Judgment 2   201

12. Bertha   233

13. Money   247

14. Justice   267

15. Negotiation   273

16. Settlement   297

17. Lessons   315

Epilogue   351

Afterword   359

Glossary of Terms   361

Index   365

Sources   369

Acknowledgements

Once again my thanks go to all the people who helped me to take this second book from a concept to reality. Carol Biss, Jessica Hampton and all of the team at Book Guild Publishing. I am particularly grateful to my editor, Imogen Palmer, for her patience and skill in dealing with my sometimes unorthodox style. Thanks also go again to Ho Ting Pong and Lawrence Bird for their help with the proof reading and Andy Tiffany for the cover design. My special thanks go to Barry Dalton for his expertise in helping me to polish my initial drafts into something suitable to be released into the public domain.

And, finally, my heartfelt thanks and gratitude go to everyone who lent their help and support, initially to *The 49ers* and, later, to the 'Band of Brothers' throughout our odyssey in the pursuit of justice.

Prologue

Tuesday 21 October 2014, 18:16 hours local time. I was sitting with Klaske in the Pineapple Beach Bar on the southwest coast of Koh Samui for sundowners.

I had HK$125k left in my deposit account in Hong Kong and an overdraft of HK$500k on my current account. With some US$ and GB£ deposits and 10,000 Cathay Pacific shares that I'd kept for old times' sake (and so I could continue go to the AGMs to get in their faces and ask awkward questions), I still had a further HK$120k line of credit on the overdraft. I was HK$150k in hock on my two credit cards and down to just paying the minimum monthly instalments. I had personal liabilities of HK$6.5 million from funding the court cases and I owed HK$1.2 million to a close friend who'd lent me money over the last four years to keep me going. I had some investments in the US worth about US$250k that were due to mature more than three years ago but, because the Securities and Exchange Commission had got involved, they were tied up until who-knows when.

My work as a flight simulator instructor for Oxford Aviation Academy in Hong Kong had dried up over a year ago. We were taken over by CAE and it was a cock-up from the outset. In the space of a few months our new managers managed to transform a vibrant, busy, productive and profitable cash generator into an empty shell. The accountants farmed out our work to Korea and Malaysia because the instructors there were paid less. The trainees still had to take their exams in Hong Kong though. The average pass rate dropped from 82 per cent to around 40 per cent and the airlines cancelled their contracts. Big surprise and red faces all round. But don't worry, they moved the instructors' desks from the front of the office to a pokey corner to make room for the three new salesmen and the HR woman they brought in to address the business and morale problems. So that's all right then. The last I heard they were decommissioning the simulators because they were made by Thale, one of CAE's main competitors, and they wouldn't grant them licences or updates for the software that's needed to run the boxes.

1

My only source of income left was the pub I owned in the UK, The Red Lion in Great Offley; the last asset that I'd managed to hang on to from my previous life. Well, I say I 'owned'. It was actually owned by a company, Jasper Leisure Ltd, but I had 98 per cent of the shares and Klaske had the other 2 per cent. It brought in about GB£25k per annum after tax. At least our house in Taling Ngam was bought and paid for, so we had a roof over our heads. All in all I reckoned we'd got enough cash on hand to keep us going for another three months then we'd be broke. Plan B was to sell the pub and live off that. For the last seven months I'd been playing the final hand of poker and I was all in.

They hadn't got any Heineken so we were drinking bottles of Leo. It was a beautiful evening and we were in for a stunning sunset. Five yards away from where we were sitting, the water was gently lapping up onto the beach and a couple of kids, about four or five years old, brother and sister I guessed, were playing in the surf. The boy had bright red matching shorts and top on with some kind of design on them. I couldn't see what it was without my glasses but I could see he was overweight; unusual for Thai kids generally.

'Oh look, there's a tubby Thai,' I remarked.
'So there is.'
'Too much sugar and junk food I suppose.'
'Yes, fed up.'
'He might want to rethink his clothes size. Bit tight.'
'Yes, but nice and bright though.'
'What's that design?'
'It's Angry Birds.'
'What?'
'Angry Birds. It's the latest thing with kids.'
'What, like Mr Men you mean?'
'Yes, but now it's Angry Birds that are in.'
'Why are they angry?'
'I don't know, it's just what they're called.'
'Well why can't they have Happy Birds or just Slightly Pissed-Off Birds? Why have they got to be angry?'
Just then my old Nokia started ringing in the pocket of my shorts.
'Bollocks. Who's this bothering me now?'
The caller ID said Don Fraser so I answered it.
'Captain Fraser, how are you doing?'

2

'Congratulations.'

'What?'

'I just called to congratulate you.'

'What for?'

'Haven't you seen the email?'

'No, I'm sitting on the beach in Koh Samui having a couple of sundowners with Klaske'

'They've agreed to your counter-proposal.'

'Say that again.'

'They've agreed to your counter-proposal, you've closed the deal. Well done.'

We talked some more. I thanked my closest friend and ally, my brother, for everything he'd done to support me and look after my back over the years. More than thanked him. My gratitude towards him lay deep in my heart and always will be there. He tried to give me the credit but it was a team effort; more than a team effort. I couldn't have done it without him. And I couldn't have got through the last three and a half years without Klaske. She was always there for me, never doubting me, never questioning, just total support and commitment. True belief.

For a few moments the tears came. Then the joy, the relief, the happiness, the euphoria. We partied long and hard into the early hours of the morning. After 13 years, 3 months and 20 days, it was finally over. I'd played the last hand and come away from the table with a good result.

1

Court of Appeal

'In case of dissension, never dare to judge until you have heard the other side.'

Euripides, *Heracleidae*

'Judges are but men, and are swayed like other men by vehement prejudices. This is corruption in reality, give it whatever other name you please.'

David Dudley Field II (1805–1894)

I had not been entirely happy about the Court of Appeal hearing from the outset. To begin with, because he was engaged on another case, we were not able to field our senior counsel, Clive Grossman. If we wanted to wait until he was available, it probably would have entailed a further delay of six months or more. Given our advice that Judge Reyes' original High Court judgment was 'virtually un-appealable', we made the decision to go in with Kam Cheung [KC] and Priscilla Leung alone. Not that I harboured any lack of confidence in the abilities of either of them. Far from it. They both knew the case inside out, were extremely well qualified and more than competent. In addition, Clive's name would also be on the written skeleton submissions to the court thus endorsing our counsels' position. No, that wasn't it. What made me feel uncomfortable was that there was a lot riding on this hearing and we were going into the match without our star opening bowler. It was a judgment call. Either get straight back onto the field as soon as possible and try to finish them off while they were still reeling from their last defeat or wait, possibly for another year, and give them time to regroup. Well, we made the call and went for the early hearing. Of course, when I say early, it was still not scheduled to be heard until the end of July 2010, more than eight months after the original High Court judgment was handed down.

The first day of the hearing, held on 27 July, did nothing to allay my concerns; in fact rather the opposite. It just served to heighten them. The bench consisted of three judges: Hon. Justice Frank Stock VP [FS], Hon. Madam Susan Kwan Shuk-hing [SK] and Hon. Justice Johnson Lam Man-hon [ML]. As well as being a justice of the Court of Appeal, the Hon. Mr Justice Stock was also listed as a non-permanent judge of the Court of Final Appeal. As such he was relatively senior in the legal hierarchy, came with a reputation generally for fair play and we felt comfortable with him. The Hon. Madam Justice Kwan, on the other hand, whilst being a permanent member of the Court of Appeal, came with a reputation for being somewhat 'difficult', given to eccentric behaviour and fits of temper; a reputation that she was to live up to during the course of the hearing. The Hon. Mr Justice Lam, however, was not a member of the Court of Appeal. Rather he was a justice of the Court of First Instance in the High Court 'acting up' as an appeal judge in our hearing. We felt him to be something an unknown quantity in his new role. Things did not start well when the chairman of the bench addressed counsel.

[FS]　　We have read the two judgments of course. We have read your submissions and we have read the submissions of your [learned friend]. As to how much else we've read, that will vary from member to member of the court. I for example haven't read any of the transcripts. So that's the position as far as how far we are, to one degree or another into the case or familiar with the issues in other words, and what the contending arguments are in relation to them.

Oh great. So they hadn't read the papers or the transcripts. They'd just read the judgments. Perhaps we had been spoiled by Justice Reyes at the original trial. With his reputation for hard work and diligence, he was fully conversant, not only with all of the papers, but also the issues under dispute and demonstrated this repeatedly throughout the course of the trial. We were in a different arena with this new bench; a fact that our opponents' counsel was to exploit fully over the next three days.

The opposition kicked off first and almost immediately engaged in some very dirty pool. Adrian Huggins [AH], senior counsel for Cathay, put forward the postulate that, since Brian Keene was not sacked until 11 July 2001, some two days after the other 48 members of our group received notices of dismissal on 9 July, his clients' allegedly defamatory remarks could not possibly be taken to refer to Brian since they were made two days prior to his dismissal rather than after the fact, as in the case of the rest of us. This was news to us. At no time during the main trial did he ever try to field such an argument. The rules of procedure mandate that the Court of Appeal is only to hear arguments and pronounce upon matters and evidence that were presented in the original trial. Only in exceptional circumstances is new evidence permitted to be entered into court. This wasn't new evidence per se. It was an acknowledged fact by all parties that they had waited for Brian's sick leave to finish on 10 July before serving his notice of dismissal, otherwise they could be found to be in breach of the Employment Ordinance. Perish the thought! Now here was Mr Huggins putting forward an argument that had never been raised at all in the High Court in an attempt to exclude Brian from the defamation claim. The bench should have stamped on it there and then. But they didn't.

It is perceived wisdom in legal circles that it is perfectly permissible to criticise a judgment should one consider it to be in error. Indeed, the purpose of articles in many legal journals is to do exactly that; to analyse and critique judgments where they might be found to be flawed. What apparently is not considered good form, however, is to criticise the judge or judges who handed down the verdict. This seems to me to be somewhat perverse. In my own profession of commercial aviation, pilots frequently come in for criticism of their conduct in the event of an incident or accident. Similarly in the medical profession, doctors often are criticised for their conduct when mistakes are made. Why then should the legal profession be immune to similar treatment? Surely the sensibilities of the judiciary are not so fragile that we must treat them as a special case and put them in a cotton wool-lined protective box? Whilst we must be mindful of potential contempt of court charges, I think not.

On that first morning of the appeal hearing, instead of putting a stop to Mr. Huggins' malarkey, the bench appeared to encourage it by debating the point. When our counsel refuted their arguments later in the hearing by pointing out that this matter had never been raised in the original trial, Kam was treated to the first of a number of outbursts that he was obliged to endure from Madam Kwan. The transcript makes for interesting reading.

[KC] Before I move on I should deal with the case of Brian Keene. If this court is under the impression that he is an odd-man-out, let me make it clear that he is not and it has never been considered that he was an odd-man-out... the learned judge set out 21 questions that he had to deal with. Those 21 questions set out all the live issues.

[ML] Is there a document?

[KC] It is not in the bundle but the, all the questions they are reproduced in the body of the judgment, the 21...

[ML] Is that a document called 'agreed list of issues'?

[KC] Yes, that is a list of issues drafted by the defendants; I can reproduce it if that is necessary.

[ML] I can take it from you unless Mr Huggins says otherwise.

[AH] Well my Lord, it's not quite as simple as that but perhaps rather than me interrupting, I'll just let my learned friend say whatever he likes and I'll deal with...

[ML] I see.

[SK] Yes, let him finish first.

[ML] Yes.

[KC] As is apparent from the judgment, we can see that that is not an issue before the trial judge...

[SK] Sorry, what was not set out as an issue? What do you say was not set out as an issue?

[KC] The fact of Brian Keene being served a notice of termination on the 11th of July 2001.

[SK] That's recited in the judgment, the fact is he was not among the 49 pilots who were dismissed. I mean that is a fact, right, that I think you accepted, isn't that the case?

[KC] If I may invite this court to look at that fact in the light of the evidence of the defendant, the first document that I would like to ask this court to look at is the original statement of...

[ML] But Mr Cheung, the, I think the point relates to the defamation aspect, and the defamation statements clearly refer to the 49ers.

[KC]   I agree.

[ML]   And the persons who are subject to those defamatory
statements would be the 49ers; once you accept that Mr Keene
was not one of the 49ers, how can he have a claim in
defamation?

[KC]   The answer to that should be apparent after we have a chance
to look at the original statement of the defendant, the answer
is contained… in an early witness statement of Mr Rhodes…
Mr Keene was always a plaintiff in these proceedings,
paragraph 52, on the 9th of July 2001, CPA [Cathay Pacific
Airways] and USAB [USA Basing] issued letters of
terminations to 49 air crew officers selected by the review
team including the 23 plaintiffs… there was no attempt to
distinguish Mr Keene, and if we look at…

[SK]   Sorry, so the 23 plaintiffs referred to here would include Mr
Keene you say, because he is among the 23 plaintiffs?

[KC]   Yes he was always one of the plaintiffs in these
proceedings… and the statement by Mr Rhodes [shows]
exactly what happened… Mr Keene was in fact amongst the
49ers selected for dismissal at the review meeting, it was only
because he was on certified sick leave on the 9th that,
presumably to avoid further complications, they wait for two
days until sick leave expired…

[SK]   Well in that case the number of people selected for dismissal
wouldn't have been 49, it would have been 50, right, I mean
the fact that he was on sick leave only meant that he got the
letter late, but when we refer to 49 pilots, the 49 doesn't
include Mr Keene, that is a fact.

[KC]   Perhaps we should look at the evidence of Mr Rhodes… on
the 9th July CPA and USAB issued letters of termination to air
crew officers selected by the review team including all the
plaintiffs except Mr Keene… Mr Keene's employment by
USAB was terminated… to take effect from the 11th, the
termination of Mr Keene was delayed because he was on sick
leave on the 9th and 10th of July.

[SK]   It didn't mention here the number of people to whom letters of
termination were issued on the 9th of July. I mean if you
accept on the 9th of July, only 49 people got termination letters
that would not include Mr Keene.

[KC]   I cannot say to this court that there is any evidence to show that on the 9th only 48 of them received the letter…

[SK]   No, 49, sorry 49 – on the 9th of July 49 people were terminated, that would not include Mr Keene because he did not receive the letter that went out on the 9th of July.

[KC]   I can't argue against the fact that he did not receive the letter on the 9th of July, it's a plain fact, what I'm trying to elicit from this paragraph is that the company had a meeting…

[SK]   Well never mind how many people they decided to get rid of by the review committee, the fact is the 49 people, well, they don't include Mr Keene.

[KC]   I can't do the other, the wordings of the witness statement…

[SK]   But that's a fact.

[KC]   Yes it is, and that's why I didn't argue with your Lady that it's nothing but a fact, but if we look at the evidence…

[FS]   I wonder if we can start again, because I'm getting a little confused, let's go to… the statement of claim to see how the matter was put and how the matter was answered.

Yes, no wonder you're confused. If you'd taken the trouble to review all the papers before stepping into court you'd know that this whole thing is a red herring being fielded by the opposition to muddy the waters.

[KC]   In relation to Mr Keene it should be non-core bundle A.

[FS]   Yes.

[KC]   Mr Keene, he is the third plaintiff.

[FS]   Yes.

[KC]   As my learned friend Mr Huggins rightly pointed out in their defence, they…

[FS]   No, how's it pleaded on Mr Keene's behalf.

[KC]   It is the amended statement of claim, in bundle C, page two.

[FS]   Yes we have five plaintiffs in that action.

[KC]   It says by letters dated 9th July 2001, USA Basing purported pursuant to clause 35C, to give notice of termination to the plaintiffs, not distinguishing any of the plaintiffs.

[SK]   Well was Mr Keene employed by USA Basing?

[KC]   Yes.

[SK]   He was employed by USA Basing?

[KC]   Yes, he [was one of] those based outside Hong Kong.

[SK]   I know there're three of them, there're three companies, so Mr Keene's employer was USA Basing?

[KC]   Yes, in fact in this action, we...

[SK]   All the plaintiffs were employed by USA Basing?

[KC]   Yes, for convenient purpose we call them the US plaintiffs.

[SK]   Yeah, all right, fine.

[KC]   We say that... it is rightly pleaded... that under sub-paragraph 4 the third plaintiff was given notice of termination on the 11th July by USA Basing.

[FS]   All right but how, what I was interested in was how is the defamation claim framed in these pleadings in favour of Mr Keene?

At this point, Huggins decided to butt in.

[AH]   Paragraph 20, my Lord, on page 67 that we looked at yesterday or the day before... denied it referred to the plaintiffs.

[FS]   Paragraph 20 of this pleading?

[KC]   Yes of this defence...

[SK]   Sorry?

[FS]   Of the one we've just been looking at... all right, what is pleaded is that the statements actually referred to and were understood to refer to the plaintiffs.

[KC]   Yes, if we look at the defence, the wording of the defence carefully, it says that...

[FS]   Where, page, page...

[KC]   Page 67.

[FS]   Just give us a moment please... Yes?

[KC]   It says that it is admitted that insofar as the statement... makes reference to the officers selected for termination on the 9th of July 2001, [they are] capable of being understood as referring to [all] the plaintiffs...

[AH]   Read on.

[KC]   It is specifically denied that the statement... actually referred to the plaintiffs, [but] then saying that it's *capable* of being understood as referring to the plaintiffs.

[FS]   All right, now, the question I have is this; was this ever, as I understand it, the way in which the matter might have been run on behalf of Mr Keene? But I don't know if it was, was

11

something along these lines, that people would have known
that Mr Keene was one of the, was a person dismissed by
USA Basing or Cathay whatever, it doesn't matter, and, they
might not have made a fine distinction as to whether he was
one of the 49 or not because he was dismissed at about the
same time. Now, my question is, was the question of whether
Mr Keene was a target or might have been understood to have
been a target of the statements made by Cathay ever an issue
in the court below?

Again, if you'd read the papers, you would already know the answer
to that question. But never mind. Let's continue with your education.

[KC]   It was never argued before the judge, in fact…
[FS]   Am I correct in assuming that the case proceeded below on
       the understanding that if the statement was defamatory… that
       it was also defamatory of Mr Keene?
[KC]   I say yes, subject to what Mr Huggins is going to say.

That was exactly correct. The opposition had never tried to raise this
point at the original trial and, therefore, it shouldn't be a matter for
debate here. But now Huggins was on his feet again.

[AH]   It simply wasn't – as I said to you the other day, it simply was
       missed by everyone – it wasn't run on that basis at all, no one
       focused upon it, when I say no one, I'm beginning to wonder
       now whether they had focused on it but kept quiet about it,
       because we had not known what the purpose was of this
       bundle that my learned friend had referred to, the reason it's
       in a separate bundle with the other statement of Rhodes and
       not in the appeal bundle because we said 'Look, why do you
       want that in the appeal bundle?'

Oh yeah right. Throw *your* red herring in the water and then try to
imply that *we're* pulling a fast one.

[FS]   Well, what we need to know at the end of the day is whether
       this is an issue or not, because the one view that might be
       taken is that people reading this statement would have focused
       on the 49 and asked themselves who the 49 were, another

view would be that they would, it could be capable of including Mr Keene as being defamed in the sense that the reader would have known or might have known that he was one of the people who was dismissed whether it was 49 or 50 and would have attached the sting of the statement to him as well.

[AH] My Lord, one can see that what, exactly what your Lordship's saying it would depend entirely on anyone knowing who the 49ers were, none of the statements, all the statements said was that the 49 people, so the only way you would know who, you'd have to know who the 49 were who were terminated on that day... Just step back one moment, this document which was never in evidence...

[FS] Which document?

[AH] The Rhodes first statement which has been referred to.

[FS] Was not in evidence?

[AH] No.

[FS] Well then, we shouldn't be looking at it.

[AH] Exactly, I didn't want to jump up and interrupt my learned friend, it was, wasn't nor was it adopted because, and not only that, the 23 plaintiffs that are referred to in paragraph 52 isn't including Keene, it was a different action.

[FS] All right, anyway, all right, what is it you, Mr Huggins, are inviting us to do in relation to Mr Keene and the defamation?

[AH] In relation to Mr Keene, having focused, and I said it was for the first time, as far as we are concerned, I am, I wonder whether, or when they focused on it, we had denied that that statement ever referred to him.

[FS] To individuals?

[AH] To individuals and to any of the plaintiffs, we can see from the statements themselves of Tyler and Chen that they referred specifically to the people who were terminated that day, so as to...

[FS] Say again.

[AH] They, the statements, referred to the 49 people who were terminated on that day by letters which were sent out that day, Tyler referred specifically to the fact that letters had been sent out earlier that day to 49 people who were terminated, so we say, when, and we take part responsibility as long as, along

13

with counsel for the other side for not having focused on this
before the learned judge.

[FS]   You say the statements were not capable of being defamatory
of Mr Keene?

[AH]   We were saying that in order to award judgment in favour of
Mr Keene, the learned judge would have needed to find, make
a finding that that referred to him, or would have been
understood by at least a substantial number of people as
referring to him.

[FS]   All right, thank you. Now Mr Cheung, just as succinctly as
you can, just state why, your answer to Mr Huggins.

[KC]   I have just asked those who instruct me to dig out the list of
issues that the party placed before the court, as soon as I get
those list of issues, it should help to clarify the matter then I
may come back to that again to see whether there was in fact a
concession that it was not an issue, and at the moment I'm
referring...

[SK]   Sorry, is it your submission that anything that is not on the list
of issues, being the 21 questions, that would not be an issue, is
that what you are saying?

[KC]   I'm setting up the background to explain why the matter was
not taken up by anybody during the trial.

[FS]   All right, but granted that, I don't think we need to go through
the history of why it was not picked up, the question was
where, we're seeking assistance from both sides on this, the
question is where does that leave us, and on the one hand one,
of course one doesn't want to be unfair to Mr Keene, on the
other hand one has to act in accordance with law, and so we
are concerned to know by what route Mr Keene is justifiably a
plaintiff and whether the judge has made a finding in relation
to Mr Keene and if not, where does that leave us.

[KC]   Yes, if I may go back to the defence, at page 67 of non-core
bundle A... in paragraph 20 they refer to the officers selected
for termination on the 9th July 2001, they are not talking about
officers terminated on the 9th July 2001.

[SK]   Sorry I'm afraid I really can't read it that way, the 9th of July
relates to termination and how possibly could you read it that
way?

[KC]   The reason for me reading it that way is in fact from the old
evidence of Mr Rhodes... where [he] explained that the only

reason for delaying the letter of termination in relation to Mr Keene was that he was on sick leave on the 9th and 10th of July, and the implication must be that, had he not been on sick leave, he would have, like the rest of the plaintiffs been served with a letter of termination on the 9th.

[SK]   Well he wasn't selected for termination on the 9th of July, that's a fact.

[KC]   The selection process must...

[SK]   *<angrily>* No but the burden is, it's really on you, I mean you being the plaintiff, I mean you must put your house in order, when the other side came back with a defence pleading specifically, look, this chap got the letter two days late, I mean you should have looked at your pleading and see, look, the statements that we complained of referred to the dismissal of 49 people, those 49 people didn't include Mr Keene, if we are saying that somehow that statement could be taken to refer to Mr Keene, we must plead the matters that would enable the public, or reasonable member of, or reasonable reader to understand that could refer to Mr Keene, it's incumbent on you to plead your case properly, to frame it properly, you hadn't done so... the burden is really on you and nobody else.

[KC]   It must be right I have to say, but I can't go further than that, save that I rely on what is said in the statement of the defendant... [the] defence seems to have accepted that what Tyler and Chen said... in the press release... my submission is that the letter of termination served on Mr Keene was no different from the letter of termination served on others.

This whole exchange demonstrated clearly to me that Madam Kwan, and her colleagues for that matter, had come into the court under-prepared and with scant knowledge of the factual matrix contained within the court papers. She didn't even seem to be aware that it was accepted as a matter of fact that *The 49ers* had been selected for dismissal at the Star Chamber meeting held over the weekend of 5 to 7 July before the dismissal notices were sent out. The hit list supplied by Ian Wilkinson clearly evidenced that Brian's name was amongst those selected at that meeting despite Huggins' attempts to paint a different picture. The actual date of the dismissal letters was irrelevant when it came to identification.

15

In the face of her tirades, Kam's conduct was exemplary. He maintained his cool and continued to press home his point. Shortly after this debate, the court adjourned for lunch. Upon resumption the following exchange took place.

[FS] Can we go back to Mr Keene. The second question which arises in relation to him is the libel issue.

[AH] Yes, now in relation to that, if I may respectfully say so, your Lordship's intervention this morning got us off to the right start because you start by going to see what, if anything, we had omitted in relation to that.

Yes, well, you would say that, wouldn't you? It means that you might be able to turn it into a live issue when you know damned well it's not. But he was in for a surprise.

[SK] Yeah I think I was wrong there Mr Huggins, and I had a change of mind. Let me just try to run it through you, I thought Mr Keene had no case because it didn't refer to him and it wasn't properly pleaded, but when I think about this and I looked at the pleadings again, I think they... we can't leave Mr Keene out, I think he would probably have a case

[AH] My Lady, that's why I'm raising it because I'm going to ask you to consider this as being an answer which we didn't quite get to this morning and I'd like if you would in due course to give it consideration... in the pleading, by us in the defence and we can turn it up I think it was in paragraph 20 and perhaps my learned junior will get it so I don't get it wrong, but my recollection of the pleading was an acknowledgement that the statement was capable of referring to the plaintiffs but then denied that it did, now...

[SK] It's not so much your pleading, it's the way they pleaded reference to Mr Keene, because as I understand it to refer to a plaintiff for defamation purposes, reference does not have to be the correct reference, you do not have to be factually correct in referring to somebody, the test is whether it could reasonably be understood to refer to that person and they have pleaded particulars in their statement of claim, facts which could be read in that light could be understood as reasonably referring to Keene, one of them being that there were a lot of

16

people dismissed in July, so regardless of the fact that 49 is a misnomer, he was not in fact the 49, he was number 50, fact that he was dismissed, he was one of those dismissed in July and that date is fairly close, it could be reasonably understood to mean he was also included in the group that was mentioned in the statement, so I think possibly they may have a case there.

Eureka! Finally she got it. Perhaps the chairman had had a word with her during the break. If so, at least it might mean that he had a better handle on the factual matrix than his colleague (after all on, current evidence, it couldn't be much worse). We could but live in hope. But none of this should ever have been an issue in the first place. If they'd briefed themselves properly before coming into court they would have known what were, and what were not, the live issues.

Not that Kam was the sole subject of Madam Kwan's wrath during the course of the hearing. Far from it. She dispensed her tongue-lashings in equal measure to our opponents' counsel as well. Shortly before lunch on the first day of the trial, Mr Huggins was in the middle of a long dissertation on where Judge Reyes had got it wrong in his judgment (just about everywhere according to him), when Her Ladyship exploded at him and administered what can only be described as a severe bollocking.

[SK] *<angrily>* Mr Huggins, what I disagree with you profoundly is the way you read this judgment. I don't think we should be skipping paragraphs 61 to 64, I think paragraph 65 should be read in the light of paragraph 61 to 64, I mean that's the way how I understood what the judge meant by 'predominant'. I mean, he's not dealing with a matter of percentages at all, if those earlier paragraphs are looked at then one can see what he was driving at when he used the word 'predominant', he was really referring to a true reason, a real reason – I'm sorry, I've been keeping very quiet but the way you've dealt with an invalid reason, and look, your argument on predominance is not something that I can accept.

After gawping at her open-mouthed for some seconds, Huggins switched into his most obsequious Uriah Heep mode.

[AH]   My Lady, may I first of all thank you for the intervention and
       if you'd given me that indication earlier I would immediately
       have done it differently. I am conscious of the fact and I must
       now slow down. I am very… have been worried all along
       about the amount of material that has to be covered and I can
       assure you that the reason I have been doing it in this way is
       in somehow trying to curtail it. Your Ladyship is entirely
       right, too much haste is going to lead me to do it in a way
       which does not help you and I apologise for that, and can I
       now therefore go back to 61, and do it in the way your
       Ladyship would like?

But the chairman was clearly getting fed up with his time-wasting
waffle.

[FS]   Can we do it after lunch, please? Well, before we break for
       lunch what I'd like to canvass with you is the time factor to
       see if we're going to need to take shorter lunches or
       something like that. What is your estimate in terms of when
       you're going to finish the employment issue, do you think? As
       best you can. I know it's difficult.
[SK]   Can we finish by today Mr Huggins, today?
[AH]   Certainly the employment issues, yes, but I am worried as to
       whether I get past that today. I'll try.
[FS]   And the defamation issue, how long do you think that will be?
[AH]   I fear that it's probably into tomorrow afternoon.
[FS]   We'll resume this afternoon's session at 2:15 then.

So that was to be his tactic. Waffle on as long as possible and so give
Kam minimum time for his response. Our case had been set down for
three days only and, if an extension was required, it would lead to
further delay because of the court calendar; so courts generally are
very reluctant to grant extensions.

   After lunch, the next subject he turned his attention to was the
Employment Ordinance (EO) *vs* the terms of the contract of
employment. He repeated his previous argument that the EO gave an
employer an overriding right to terminate a contract of employment at
any time on payment in lieu of notice, irrespective of any and all
terms designed to give an employee security of tenure that may be
included in that contract. We thought that he was banging his head

against a brick wall on this particular point. Judge Reyes had been very clear and unequivocal in his judgment: it does not. In summary, the arguments being debated yet again went as follows.

In scenario one, the employment contract does not have additional protections over and above the EO. In this case, everyone agrees that an employer has a unilateral right to dismiss an employee on notice with no reason given. Not that we as employees agree it is fair. All it does is highlight the archaic, one-sided labour laws in Hong Kong. You can be fired at any time with no reason given. Of course the employers love this. Hire and fire at will. What dictatorial Victorian mill owner wouldn't love it?

In scenario two, the employment contract has additional protections, like the Discipline & Grievance Procedure (DGP) that was in our contract, in the event of dismissal for disciplinary reasons. The argument put forward by Mr Huggins was that, despite this, the employer still has the overriding EO right to dismiss on notice with no reason given. But what if the true reason is disciplinary? Well, all the employer has to do is keep quiet and fire the employee anyway. Alternatively, he could run a DGP, find the employee cleared of all charges, and then fire him anyway under the EO. (This is exactly what Barley did in Dave Clapson's case. Dave was another pilot who, in June 2001, was subjected to a DGP, exonerated of all charges levelled against him but, immediately thereafter, was called into the office next door where Barley was waiting to hand him a dismissal notice.) According to Huggins, that's OK. But, as Judge Reyes said in his judgment on the preliminary issues, this would posit bad faith and there must be an element of mutual trust and respect in any contract; especially employment contracts, it is an implied term. Perish the thought that that same dictatorial Victorian mill owner would act in bad faith.

In the third and final scenario, the employer actually does act in bad faith and/or simply ignores the DGP provisions but then, like Cathay management, just can't keep its trap shut and goes out in public and admits that the real reasons were disciplinary and then goes on to describe the employee as 'unprofessional'. Well, according to this argument that's all right too, because the employee still has the remedy of defamation. It was worrying to see one member of the bench nodding in agreement. What kind of remedy is that for the general public? We were a group of organised professionals with substantial financial backing from our union and, here we were, nine years on from our dismissals, still fighting this in court with the possibility that we may still have to go to the Court of Final Appeal even if we won this round. What could an ordinary working man or woman in Hong Kong do if they were to find themselves in a similar situation to ourselves? What could a cleaner, a bus driver, a dock worker, a typist, a waitress or any other 'normal' working man or woman do in the face of intimidation by an unscrupulous employer? To date, we had spent more than HK$14 million in legal costs. Who else in the general community could afford that? Some remedy!

Clearly Huggins' arguments ignored any concepts of common sense and natural justice, just as they had in the lower court. We'd been advised that it would be very unusual for an appeal court to overturn such a clear ruling as Judge Reyes' and believed we were on firm ground. Subsequent events were to demonstrate that our confidence was misplaced.

The first session of the morning of the second day started out with Huggins pontificating on which specific statements made by Tyler and Chen were being complained of as defamatory. In particular he tried to get a letter written by Chen excluded from consideration under qualified privilege. It was more dirty pool and, initially, he was successful in leading the bench up the garden path resulting in another outburst by Madam Kwan.

[FS]   The real question is whether we should be considering the letter at all, and really it might be helpful for us to know at this stage what the plaintiffs' position is, so if we could hear from Mr Kam Cheung at the moment.

[AH]   I'm so sorry m'Lord, I didn't realise that I was batting on when you were really asking me to sit down and my friend to get up.

[FS]   I hadn't asked you to sit down, but I am now.

[KC]   My Lord, first of all the press release must be something within…

[FS]   Forget about the press release, we're not interested in the press release.

[SK]   No, no, no, just the letter.

[KC]   Yes, in fact not only have…

[FS]   Is the letter a live issue? Let me ask you to deal with that in two stages. The judge found that the letter was written on an occasion of qualified privilege – well, he proceeded on that basis. On the face of matters, there would seem to be a clear correlation of duty and interest by which I mean a duty on the airline to communicate with its staff on this matter and for the staff to receive that information, so it would be difficult it seems to us to argue that the letter was not covered by an occasion of qualified privilege, but even if it were arguable, there is no cross-appeal on the judge's finding and there we have it. Now, if qualified privilege applies and if this court is bound because of the judge's finding and the absence of a cross-appeal on that finding to proceed on the basis that qualified privilege applies, given the absence of any defence of malice, how do you say – if you do – that the letter is a live defamation issue before us?

[KC]   Well m'Lord, my reply is, since we didn't file any respondent notice… the only implication must be that we accepted the presumption made by the judge that the letter, being a letter issued to the employees, must be a letter issued on privileged occasion. We are not seeking to challenge that, but your Lordship will see that it's not the end of the matter and his Lordship went on to say that you have to act reasonably and whether or not…

[SK]   No, act responsibly, that only applies if the Reynolds defence governs the situation of the letter, which it does not.

[KC]   Exactly and that's why when I stood up I raised that the letter was not the end of the matter, there are other things said by Chen…

[SK]   Sorry that's not your complaint, the defamation is limited only to two statements, one is the press statement the other is the letter. We are not concerned with any other utterances of Mr Chen, not the subject of this action.

Oh please. You really haven't read any of the papers, have you?

[KC]   If I may take the court to the judgment which should be…

[SK]   Look, please Mr Cheung, you are digressing, we are concerned in the defamation course of action with only two segments; one is the letter, the other is the press statement, anything else said by Mr Chen, you may choose to bring in action elsewhere, but we are not concerned with any other statement of Mr Chen in this appeal. Can we have an answer to the question? Is the letter a live issue?

[KC]   … If I may, in relation to what the learned judge found in his judgment…

[FS]   No, no we won't shut you out in due course, the only purpose of the exchange Mr Kam Cheung was to find an answer to because we need to know what the ambit is of what it is we're addressing when we hear submissions on defamation, your clients brought an action in defamation.

[KC]   Yes.

[FS]   That action said that the defamatory comments were made in two different places; one was the press release, the other was the letter, end of story, all, we realise fully that the press release is very much a live issue in this appeal, what we found difficulty in understanding in the absence of a plea of malice is how the letter could be a live issue in defamation, that, that, and my question to you was do you accept that you are bound to fail, given the absence of a plea of malice, that you are bound to fail in relation, insofar as you rely on the letter as being defamatory?

[KC]   I said that in relation to the letter and the letter only.

[SK]   That's all we want from you at this stage, I mean you could develop your argument on Reynolds and other matters later on.

[FS]   If you want to say later that the letter is relevant to defamation in the press statement or in relation to the employment issue, of course you can.

[KC]   Yes, perhaps before I sit down if I may be allowed to give the page references to one important matter, and it is page 163 of core bundle A, which refers to a statement made… by Mr Philip Chen and reported in the press.

[SK]   <angrily> What's the relevance of this? What's the relevance of this? What's the relevance of this in relation to what?

[KC]   The relevance of this is referred to in the body of the judgment and…

[SK]   Well what does it show, look, in relation to what issue? Why should we be looking at this letter?

[KC]   It relates to the issue as to what has been said of the plaintiffs.

[SK]   Look, the court is not concerned with what Mr Chen said, unless you tell us the relevance of this we're not going to be looking at this. Is it relevant to Reynolds, is it relevant to the other press statement by Mr Tyler, if it is not why should we be bothered with this?

[KC] I promise that I will [show it] is wholly relevant, if I'm not convinced it has some relevance, it's not my…

[SK] Well then, show me the relevance.

[KC] And just, only because I haven't finished, I'm not trying to argue with the…

[SK] Well tell me the relevance.

He would do if you'd stop bloody interrupting and let him speak.

[KC] It should be apparent if we go to the judgment as well, it is page 30 of the bundle, paragraph 12 of the judgment; we have tied up the press statement, which is produced as appendix 1.

[SK] The judge was reciting the background in those paragraphs, you have not made any specific complaint about that public statement of Mr Chen as part of your course of action in defamation, Mr Cheung.

Yes we bloody well have. Read the fucking papers.

[KC] My Lady, it is in the pleadings.

[SK] Well I don't care but it is not, it doesn't form part of the statements complained of in your defamation, you may put all sorts of things relevant or otherwise in your pleading, the court is not bothered with those statements, sorry.

[KC] If I may, I need to come back to this later when it's my turn to make submissions but at this stage I'm just giving the page references.

[SK] Well I can't see the relevance, if you don't satisfy me of the relevance I won't allow you to develop anything on this, you better make sure it is relevant when it comes your turn to address the court.

[KC] Yes, I will do that.

For me, sitting there listening to all this without being able to say or do anything to refute her nonsense, it was not just frustrating – it was extremely worrying. It was all there in the pleadings if only she and the rest of the bench had taken the time to read the documents and arrive in court aware at least of the basics of the case. But they hadn't and they were falling for Huggins' bullshit, hook, line and sinker. To me, they were derelict in their duty. In my profession, if I'd ever reported for duty as ill-prepared as they were, I'd have been out on my ear. During the coffee break at 11:00, I talked with Kam and told him I was not at all happy with how things were going. I wanted him to be more forceful, cut through the crap, refute what they were saying and make his points clearly and succinctly. Kam was a model of calm and serenity. He told me this was all standard practice with m'Lady Kwan. It's pointless arguing with her when she's in one of these moods. Don't worry, he'd sort it out later when she's calmed down. It'll all come out in the wash. He also told me that there was a standing joke amongst his colleagues about her marriage status. She didn't have one. I could see why. After the coffee break, the following exchange took place.

[SK]   Before you carry on Mr Huggins, I think I owe Mr Cheung an apology.

[AH]   My Lady, I was going to deal with that very thing and say, my Lady…

[SK]   Yeah, because I read the statement of claim over the break and I did discover that the cause of action pleaded in defamation actually covered a total of five statements so they would include not just the letter of Mr Chen but the public statement made by Mr Chen, and that was what Mr Cheung had been trying to refer to, but it does seem, I mean that being a public statement, qualified privilege in the traditional sense would not apply, so it would not be covered by the Reynolds privilege.

[AH]   My Lady, that's very gracious of you.

[SK]   I owe you an apology. I'm so sorry, Mr Cheung.

Well that's all right then. Pity she didn't take the time to read the statement of claim before the trial. And bloody 'gracious' of Huggins to accept her apology on Kam's behalf.

The rest of the morning of the second day of the hearing was taken up with our opponents attempting to portray us as a bunch of hard-line trade unionists determined to bring Cathay management to its knees, thereby destroying the company and causing irreparable damage to Hong Kong. Mr Huggins trotted out the same old stuff that we had to endure at the trial. We had the temerity to support our union in its aims. We admitted as much because we attended union meetings and voted on motions and resolutions. We said so in our evidence! We supported our union!! In Mr Huggins' submission, clearly a heinous crime deserving of instant dismissal without recourse.

It was during this diatribe that we were treated to one of his am-dram cameos. He was talking about the union's advice that we should simply respond, 'I'll do my best' when called out from standby duty by crew control. He leaned across his lectern, legs akimbo, backside sticking out, neck at full stretch, moustache bristling, chin in hand and fixed the bench with his beadiest of stares.

[AH]   ... 'I'll do my best'. That's the answer you should give to any and all questions regarding your travel time to Cathay City. What, when will you arrive? Oh I'll do my best. How long will it take once you're ready? Oh I'll do my best. Can you catch the next bus? I'll do my best. My Lord, it's the sort of thing which if a schoolboy behaved at school he'd be thoroughly reprimanded and in my day thrashed for what is clearly, *clearly* impertinent and uncooperative behaviour.

So that's it then. We all deserved a damned good thrashing.

It was also during this diatribe that he put forward the view that attending union meetings should not be a protected activity under the terms of the ordinance. In fact the ordinance provides protection for two types of activity; activity within the workplace and activity outside of the workplace.

Activity within the workplace is only protected where it takes place with the consent of the employer. Thus, attending a negotiation meeting with the employer is a protected activity as it is an agreed meeting between the employer and union representatives. They can't sack you for being involved in such a meeting; well, not in theory anyway. Activity within the workplace without permission is a different matter and Cathay management had used this as a threat in the past. One of the pilots was caught on a CCTV camera in the crew room posting union flyers in the pilots' mailboxes. They wrote a letter to the AOA (Aircrew Officers' Association) stating that any such activity in the future would make the miscreant subject to dismissal. This was just another petty ruse designed to try to disrupt our communications. We got around it by sending future written communications through the mail. Even then though, we had to put them in different types of envelopes and post them from different places so that they could not filter them out in the mailroom.

Activity outside of the workplace is exactly what it says; attending meetings etc. on one's own time. Even under Hong Kong law, you cannot be fired for being a member of a union and taking part in its normal day-to-day activities in your leisure time. According to Mr Huggins' submission, however, this should be a proscribed activity subject to notice and dismissal. He did not venture to suggest what activities actually *should* be protected under the terms of the ordinance, only rather what shouldn't. It seemed to us a bizarre hypothesis. Under such draconian provisions, perhaps he would like to see the medical and bar associations banned as well with doctors and lawyers subject to swingeing penalties for participating in the activities of their unions. On the other hand, perhaps calling them associations rather than unions makes it OK. Well, in that case he fails again. We were members of the Hong Kong Aircrew Officers' Association.

It was during this harangue that Mr Huggins was pulled up short by the chairman of the bench when he asked a simple question.

[FS]   The point you're going to have to address in due course…
       there was something like 900 people or so who voted for this,
       so, the real question becomes if this is evidence of not acting
       in the best interests of the company, what distinguishes the
       others from these?

Huggins went into goldfish mode for a bit and then started out on possibly the biggest load of waffle and bullshit that he delivered throughout the trial.

[AH]   Well my Lord, can I deal with that straight away? I think
       we've addressed it in the skeleton but let's just look at it now,
       the learned judge and one of the things which we complain of
       with respect is that he said, as your Lordship was putting to
       me, 'Well, look Mr Huggins, if everybody else was doing the
       same thing, why don't you sack the whole lot?' You can't
       have regarded this, how can the court…

26

[FS]   No... that's one way of putting it. Another way of putting it is that the airline was saying 'We are selecting these men as people who cannot be relied upon to act in the interests of the company... ' The clear implication is that the others can be relied upon to act in the interests of the company in the future so I'm wondering to what extent this helps you.

[AH]   Well my Lord, the way the learned judge put it was if Cathay don't regard, Cathay can't regard this as being not acting in the best interests of the company otherwise they would have sacked the 90, the whole lot, the 90 per cent, that's the way he put it, he's saying because Cathay didn't sack the whole lot, therefore how can the court begin to consider that this sort of attitude in relation to the plea of justification could justify the statements made by Tyler and Chen? To which we say that's simply a non sequitur because the reality is at the time that Tyler and Chen made those statements we are, the airline, I'm not saying that they had all the evidence which we now have to justify those statements but the issue of justification is determined at the trial so that the trial judge looked at the statements that Tyler and Chen made, looks at the evidence now before the court because they've now come and given evidence and have been cross examined and, on their own evidence have been supplying material which was not available to Tyler and Chen, namely that they voted in favour of all this, because Rhodes had said, specifically I took you to it the other day, on day six, we didn't know who'd voted in favour, we didn't know all of that, now they've come along later and have actually provided material to the effect that yes they did, were in favour of this, they voted in favour of it, they were in favour of it and so on and we say and we respectfully submit as a matter of law it's right that on the issue of justification the judge doesn't have to say well, Tyler and Chen didn't know that or what would Tyler and Chen have done if they had known that, he has got to look objectively at the evidence now before him and decide whether or not we are right.

[ML]   Yes but I think the focus of my Lord's question perhaps can be demonstrated by... look[ing] at paragraph 198 sub-paragraph 4 of the judgment, where the judge seems to read the statements as having this effect, namely that these 49 people were selected because the statement implied they were the persons behind the union's selfish acts and... they are the ones who have been doing their best to disrupt Cathay's operation.

[AH] Well my Lord, if your Lordship is saying to me that the words, they are in front of persons, he meant the only persons, he's taking the statement to mean the only persons behind the union's selfish acts then I can see your Lordship's point but, with respect, well, I'm bound to say I hadn't looked at it in quite that way before, certainly he was saying look these are... the statements would be taken to mean these people were behind it, but I would respectfully ask the court to reconsider whether or not in truth if you look at those statements that is really saying these are the only people behind it, if your Lordships were to say that, well, that is the effect of it.

[ML] Because the learned judge seems to emphasise the juxtapositions of the measure of dismissal together with the early part of the statement about these disruptive actions.

[AH] It seems to me then that my response has to be this, that you would then be saying that there was a meaning, namely that they were the only ones and that everybody else was...

[ML] Or the main instigators.

[AH] Well, you see again that revolves a... a... a... a change already, you see I respectfully submit that it doesn't mean they're the only ones, obviously I'm happier with the interpretation... well, they're the main ones, but already you'll see there's a difference between main and the only, and where all this would get us I think is that if the court were to feel that there is this implication that we were saying they were the only ones who were doing this, then that is a defamatory meaning which we can't justify.

[FS] Well, it hasn't been pleaded anyway.

[AH] No, but certainly that would be a meaning that we didn't attempt to justify because it, well, as you say it wasn't pleaded, but it would still leave open the central point that I'm making that in relation to these 49ers, insofar as they were in support of these, this industrial action, we respectfully submit that in relation to them and they're the ones complaining that they've been defamed, it was in substance true in relation to them.

[ML]   No, let's forget about whether they are the main instigators or the only ones, just take it on it's face value, the judge read into the statement this meaning at the very least... they are the ones who have been doing their best to disrupt Cathay's operations through tactics described in the first part of [the] press statements. This is what the judge finds to be the meaning, and then coupled with his finding... [that] there's no evidence that the plaintiffs carried out their work in any particular instance with a destructive intent... that seems to me to explain why the judge thinks the statements are defamatory of the plaintiffs and you fail in your justification.

Huggins persisted with his waffle for another few minutes until the chairman put a stop to him.

[FS]   Look – I'm sorry in the event that I interrupted your flow because I think we ought to press on, the intent of my interruption was to say merely this, and I don't want to further the debate, the sting of the press statement was to differentiate between these men and others who had taken part in industrial action and that's what you're going to, now, it's all very well to say that this conduct contract compliance is intended to disrupt and is not in the best interests of the company, that may or may not be so, let's assume for the sake of argument it's so, one has to go further then and say... these men were particularly deserving of dismissal because, that's what we're going to have to come to in due course.

And of course, he could neither answer the question nor prove any justification. They had provided not one shred of evidence to show that any of us had done anything whatsoever that could be remotely construed as not having the best interests of the company at heart. Judge Reyes had made a point of that in his judgment and it seemed that the chairman of the bench shared his view. The whole point was that all the supposed evidence of what the union did, its actions and intentions were totally irrelevant to the proceedings. It was *our* actions that were in question, not the union's, and they had no evidence to show that we had done anything at all to justify dismissal.

It just served to demonstrate that this was an attempted union-bust, plain and simple.

Having dealt with the breach of contract and Employment Ordinance issues, Huggins then turned his attention to the defamation award and it was then that we saw their true colours flying in the wind. It was all about the money. No surprises there then. He first tried to postulate that, because the media statements had been made after the dismissal notices had been sent out, they did not in fact refer to the dismissals themselves since they were made after the fact! This argument was bizarre in the extreme. Disregarding for the moment the fact that the words in the media statements clearly referred to the dismissals and the supposed reasons for the dismissals, how we were supposed to believe that the two were unrelated because they were separated by around four hours, (the time between the dispatch of the DHL packets and the press conference held on the afternoon of 9 July), was completely beyond any logic or reason. Nevertheless, Mr Huggins pressed on with his argument.

We thought we were doing well on the damages issue until a couple of warning bells sounded loudly. The first one rang out when Huggins was discussing quantum. He, of course, was trying to use personal injury awards as a measure of 'reasonable' quantum. This is a tried and tested tactic in defamation cases. In personal injury cases there are guidelines laid down to quantify damages that a court should award. In simple terms it could be summarised as: Loss of an arm; x dollars. Loss of a leg; y dollars. Loss of two arms; $2x$ dollars. Loss of two legs; $2y$ dollars. Loss of all limbs; $2(x+y)$ dollars, etc. So the argument goes, if a man receives only, say, $100k for losing an arm, why should another man receive anything like that in a defamation case just because someone hurt his feelings? It is an accepted principle in case law that the two are not related in assessing damages. One of the reasons for this is that personal injury is physical and very specific. Defamation is not. The results of defamation can be many and varied and, therefore, difficult to specifically define and quantify. That's not to say that lawyers don't try to compare the two as a tactic and that's what Huggins was doing when the bench intervened with the following exchange.

[ML]   And what, what do you say to be the appropriate figure in the present case?

[AH]   My Lord, in this case I would respectfully submit on the evidence that's given, not more than 750,000 dollars, now…

[ML]   750?

[AH]   My Lord, can I, you may be surprised that I have even been bold enough to give that because at the trial, at the hearing below, the learned judge said to me, and to Mr Grossman, I can't actually remember what Mr Grossman's answer was, it was probably pretty massive, but he said to me, 'Well, right, well what award do you say?' I took the view, rightly or wrongly, I didn't think it was actually very, necessarily particularly helpful, because, it might be said, 'Well he would say that, wouldn't he? Look who he's acting for,' so you know what counsel for the defendant says it should be probably isn't worth too much, but what I therefore preferred to do, and I said to the judge, 'Let us look at *Yakoob*, it's got to be way below that,' never mind what I personally think – if I were to say 500,000 or 750,000 or whatever – what does it matter what Huggins thinks? But what I submit…

[ML]   Yes, but you have a duty to assist us.

[AH]   Well, yes I do, but my Lord, I hope it's not immodesty to say I don't know that, how much weight can be attached to what I say, except that the figure…

[ML]   But you can tell us how far down below *Yakoob* you think should be…

[AH]   My Lord, I would say within whatev–, within the parameters of 500 to 750,000 dollars, absolute maximum.

The next remark by Madam Kwan was destined to have massive significance, as we shall see later.

[SK]   We'll be very careful in our judgment, Mr Huggins, we'll make sure whatever amount we arrived at, it is not because of any suggestion made by counsel that we do feel sure it is an appropriate award.

[AH]   My Lord, well my Lady perhaps, I hope it's not impertinent to say this, if you thought, if you thought on either way, if you thought 800,000 were right, then what does it matter that Huggins says 750?

[SK]   Yes, yeah.

[AH]   And again, if your Ladyship having looked at those awards thought that 400,000 was appropriate, one wouldn't say 'Well Huggins conceded it should be 500 or 750 so give him that,' and that's why we got so agitated about the approach of the learned judge in saying 'Well I'm going to put aside *Yakoob*,' when we had used that as the clearest indication that it should be below, below a million dollars, to say 'Oh well, counsel only asked for one million dollars'.

[FS]   All right, I think we're in danger now of encroaching too much on Mr Cheung's time, 'cause time is rushing on.

So there it was. Bald faced. They asked Huggins to nominate what he thought was an appropriate quantum. But don't worry. They'll make sure that whatever they decide upon will not be influenced by his suggestion. So why the fuck did they ask him the question then?

The other exchange on quantum that set off a whole peal of bells, not just a single chime, happened when Kam was addressing the court during the afternoon of the third day.

[FS]   Just remind us, we see at page six of that report we see the – what was alleged against this entirely innocent lady that she was suspected of cheating her clients' building funds, and that she had disappeared with two million dollars.

[KC]   Yes.

[FS]   And that her firm as a result had closed down and that the police had gone to her residence but were unable to make contact with her, in other words a suggestion that she was running from the law, this was, I note the apology section, this was a lady who in terms of the consequences to her, we've had them read out – I'm not going to read them again, but she suffered acute depression, she had nightmares and most seriously, she had this dreadful problem with the birth of the child who is left in a critical condition. Now let's be realistic, in your submissions, and I would like to think that they were not drafted by you because what is said in the original submission at paragraph 24... the *Apple Daily*, award of three million dollars in compensatory damages was made, it is submitted that the plaintiff's case, that's in this case, the statements were of a far more serious nature... now we are in, in silly land aren't we when we're saying that?

[KC]   My Lord, the next sentence that says the statement went to the root of the reputations and employability as professional pilots, this is the impact of the...

[FS]   'Thus branded with the mark of Caine on their foreheads'. I would like you to convey to the draftsman of this document that he's not addressing a jury, but there we are, that's an aside.

[KC]   Yes... and what, the reasons for me to ask your Lordship to look at the apology is that there was an apology in the... I'm trying to distinguish the cases on the basis that an apology was tendered, which obviously would be of help...

[FS]   I'm sure it was of great comfort to the lady concerned.

[KC]   Yes, not only is it a great comfort...

[FS]   No I'm being sarcastic, I don't think it was of any comfort to her whatsoever.

[KC]   My Lord but at the very least, the unfortunate lady being defamed can refer people to the apology...

[FS]   I really don't think you're helping your case by suggesting that this case, I'm not, if defamation is proved, I am not demeaning the feelings of the pilots who were defamed if defamation be proved, and I'm not suggesting for a moment that attacking somebody's professional reputation is not a serious matter, but to compare these two cases is with great respect plain silly, it is, we are in silly season if we're comparing these two cases.

So there we hit the nub of the problem we faced. Our situation could not possibly be compared to that of the unfortunate solicitor, one of theirs, despite the fact that she had her reputation and business fully restored to her whereas the defamation against us had been repeated continuously for more than eight years and no public apology of any sort had ever been given, even to this day. How could he make the comparison? He did not know what damage had been caused to us. He did not know the extent of each individual's pain and suffering. He did not know the effects on our careers, our partners and our families. He did not know because he hadn't read the transcripts of the trial. But he went ahead and came to his conclusion anyway. I'd had the feeling all through the three days of the trial that there was an undercurrent of predisposition coming from the bench. This last exchange did nothing to quell my anxiety.

There was one final exchange that reinforced my unease that they hadn't prepared properly for the trial.

[ML] Mr Cheung, can you explain for my benefit what is the reason why the judge, in awarding aggravated damages, he put down an exception in the case of Mr England?

[KC] Mr England, he died after the dismissal, and their claim for defamation did not survive the death. It's not that the estate can claim on behalf of a deceased person, and that's why the claim of England must go.

[ML] I see... so that applies to the other awards as well?

[KC] Sorry, excuse me?

[SK] He wasn't awarded general damages either, Mr England, as I understand it.

[KC] No, not under the defamation because the estate simply cannot claim that, cannot maintain defamation as a course of action, the cause of action died with the deceased.

If he'd taken the trouble to read the papers, he would have been aware of this most basic of facts; that there had been a royal cock-up on our part in filing the original defamation action. Defamation 101, the action dies with the death of the plaintiff. Greg was already dead when it was filed. We could have filed an alternative cause of action, malicious falsehood, which survives the death of the plaintiff. But we didn't know about that until it was too late.

At the end of the three days I walked out of the court feeling deeply troubled by what I had witnessed. Kam had done a good job under difficult circumstances. Huggins had done a great job of obfuscating, clouding the issues and planting seeds of doubt in the judges' minds. Unlike Judge Reyes' court, he had been allowed to get away with all sorts of red herrings and waffle so as to limit the time available for Kam's rebuttal of their appeal. Compared with our experience in Judge Reyes' court, this had been a circus. Perhaps my feelings could be best summed up in a series of somewhat irreverent emails that Doug had sent out to the BoBs (Band of Brothers) at the end of each day.

Day 1.

Greetings from soggy Hong Kong.

I'm taking it upon myself to send you a very brief message about today. John will be too busy to do this until it's all over.

It's late here, I have to up early for day 2, so, unusual for me, I'll keep it short!!

3 judges: Chairman is from Rhodesia, plus Chinese Lady and Chinese Man.

Apparently the bad people did their usual and sent masses of documents at the 11th hour.

Mrs Miggins has centre stage and just like last October is intent on dragging this out by using 5,000 words when 8 will do!

He is on a mission to make this overrun the 3 days allotted which would incur yet more delay.

The chief judge is aware of this and has made noises about getting on with things.

There is no doubt that Muggins will use all of tomorrow giving Kam only Thursday to do his thing. Kam reckons that that will suffice.

Basically Buggins has spent all day telling the three judges that everything written in Reyes' verdict is wrong and they totally disagree with it.

He started by banging on about his old chestnut of: there is no requirement under Hong Kong law to give a reason for termination of employment, and CX [Cathay Pacific] didn't give a reason because they wanted to be 'kind'!!! The fact that liar and dickhead told the world otherwise is, according to him, irrelevant! This went on for a long time with the odd question coming from the bench.

Then he set off on the employment ordinance thing, (S21B 2b, union activity thing) and the thrust was that the Rodent's testimony was clear and, without a doubt, honest (!) regarding nobody being fired for union activity.

Immediately before the lunch recess while he was in the middle of cherry picking certain aspects of JR's verdict Her Ladyship pretty much exploded at him! It was a bollocking and a half and it left Noggins standing mouth agape looking like the proverbial deer in the headlights.

Priceless!!

After lunch a rather more careful Wiggins finished off his attempt at bashing the EO assessment, but he appeared to be getting bad vibes from the bench, so he quickly wrapped up.

The last 40 minutes was spent with him starting on the defamation bit. Apparently, according to him, when liar and dickhead called us unprofessional it was obvious that they were not referring to our ability to fly and operate big planes! (Well, that's alright then!!)

Impossible to assess what the 3 judges are thinking. It's very different from observing Reyes.

To be continued tomorrow.

Obviously you'll get a fuller, more erudite version from the Brigadier when it's over.

Suffice to say, our team are unfazed by the bullshit, but they do have some work to do on Thursday.

Time for bed.

Standby for episode 2!!!!!!!!

Regards.

Day 2.

Greetings again.

The day started off a bit wobbly!

Before Bilbo Huggins got started the chairman, Judge Stocks, asked our man Kam whether Chen's letter to CX staff was still considered a live issue, (don't ask, legal stuff).

Kam got to his feet and began his response, whereupon Madam Judge, aka Dragon Lady, made like a rabid, hormonally imbalanced, killer Pekinese and started berating him.

Very curious and, for me and the Brigadier, slightly worrying, although as we were subsequently informed this is how she is 'normally'!

All credit to Kam, he was not fazed or intimidated by her tirade and he plugged on with what he had to say, in between her snarling and barking at him.

At the mid-morning break our team entered the huddle room all smiles as if nothing had happened. This is when Kam, Priscilla and Ben all said that this is normal behaviour for her, and Kam assured us that she had got hold of the wrong end of the stick, would eventually realise it and apologise to him.

It certainly didn't look like it was going to happen to me.

Then, upon resumption of the session, before anybody could sneeze, fart or cough the Dragon Lady announced in a loud non-threatening bark that she must apologise to Mr Cheung, (that's Kam to us), as she had been quite wrong!

Well… bugger me!

Meantime Boring of the Bailey had been doing more of what he does best, talking drivel and lots of it.

He was continuing to attempt to convince the panel about how liar and dickhead were justified in making their various statements to the press.

It all hinged on his 'respectful submission' that by admitting in court last October that we had voted in favour of the AOA resolutions on contract compliance, MSS [maximum safety strategy] etc. we had shown that we were not to be relied upon to act in the best interests of the company.

Now he banged on and on and on about this and associated stuff UNTIL the chairman, Judge Stocks, stopped him in his tracks and said, words to the effect of: 'I'm somewhat confused here, so I'd like you to answer this question for me, Mr Huggins. Approximately 900 pilots voted in favour of LIA [limited industrial action] etc, so what EXACTLY singled out these 49 pilots for dismissal when the others also could be said to be 'unreliable' etc. etc, (you get the gist).

Picture, if you will, the face of your neighbour's mongrel when caught in the act of shagging your prize winning thoroughbred poodle, because that's exactly how Buggerlugs suddenly looked!

Did he answer the question?

What do you think?

He waffled and danced around the question until Stocks stopped him and basically told him that he wasn't being very helpful, so he asked him the exact same question for a second time.

Did Higgins answer it?

Nope!

BINGO!!!!!!!!

So the justification thing was put away quite swiftly.

Then we came to what this is really all about… MONEY.

Keeping it short, (I need to get off to beddy-byes), he started off by telling the bench that the amount of money which Reyes had awarded us was totally disproportionate and outrageous.

I couldn't agree more, only he meant way too much.

So he spent an interminable amount of time trying to show that other awards both in HKG and the UK were nothing like as 'huge' as ours whilst also trying to discredit the way Reyes dealt with the assessment as a whole.

He finally shut up at 15:30 which gave Kam one hour on his feet.

He obviously began with the breach of contract D&G aspect and was immediately set upon by all three Judges, albeit one at a time, regarding the statutory right in HKG for an employer to fire an employee for no reason *vs* having a D&G clause in the contract.

At first I thought that this was an indication of the way they were thinking/likely to vote, but K, P and B later explained that this is how things are done at appeal because whatever comes out of this WILL become HKG law and the panel have to test the arguments being put forward with the barristers concerned. This is especially important with this aspect because it could very possibly have a serious effect on current and future HKG employment law.

Anyway, Kam fielded everything that was thrown at him without faltering and even survived another attack from the raving Pekinese and put her back in her kennel!

Kam expects to be done by lunchtime tomorrow.

Unless the Brigadier does a number on me in 'The Office' tomorrow afternoon/evening I shall dispatch Episode 3, (the Final Episode) to you all tomorrow.

Yours etc. etc.

Day 3.

Greetings fellow BoBs.

Play resumed at 09:30 with our man Kam continuing where he had left off yesterday.

The usual suspects were in attendance for the good guys, namely Chris Lawrence and Kevin and Teresa Hoban, The Brigadier and yours truly.

A matter of some concern was the wellbeing, or otherwise, of our Dear Leader who was clearly under the weather and, as it transpired, suffering from a virulent virus, which originated in Scandinavia and is known locally as the 'Carls Berg Virus'!

Kam continued his submission regarding the breach of contract/ D&G procedure and was immediately set upon by all three Judges with searching questions.

Clearly this is, and is going to be, a very significant issue in Hong Kong.

Dragon Lady had not only got out of bed on the wrong side she had obviously had a hearty breakfast of razor blades to boot as she was off and running in no time and all over Kam like a bad rash!

The issue being Mr Keene, or 'Keener' to us.

The bad people, in the form of you-know-who, had previously proposed that because Brian had not been terminated until the 11th July then he could not be considered to be a 49er in the strict sense of the term, with all sorts of ramifications as a result.

Every time Kam attempted to explain the falsity of this proposition, the Dragon Lady started foaming at the mouth and shrieking at Kam, who somehow kept his cool and resisted the temptation to tell the bitch to 'shut the f%%k up and listen'!!

Madam Judge was convinced in her mind that 49 pilots were fired on 09 July and Brian was number 50. (All this due to the smoke and mirror tactics, also known as lies, from Muggins and co.)

The Brigadier, it has to be said, was less than impressed with Kam's response or, as he saw it, lack of response and combined with his 'fever' this made him rather agitated.

So Kam received a bit of an ear wigging at the break, but to give him his due he pointed out that there was no point trying to hammer home the Keener thing because Dragon Lady wasn't in the frame for listening, so it would be dealt with in writing later.

Well, stone me if, after the lunch break, Dragon Lady didn't apologise, yet again, for getting it wrong with respect to Keener and she was at pains to point out to Kam and Muggins that obviously because he had been selected over the weekend of 5,6,7 July then Brian, by definition, MUST be considered to be a 49er.

At that point I thought the Brigadier was going to launch himself headlong across the court room and give Madam Judge a wet kiss!!

The afternoon progressed from there in what I, and the Brig, considered to be a positive fashion.

Kam finished at 15:00 and Motor Mouth was given the opportunity to respond, which he did in spades!

He made it quite clear that, for them this is all about money, (now there's a surprise!)

So he had his say on the quantum issue, followed by his response to the D&G issue and finally the defamation issue finishing up digging himself a nice hole with regards to the issue of Qualified Privilege, i.e. the possible protection afforded to liar and dickhead for the statements which they made to the press about us.

This is all about having the right to inform interested parties, i.e. the travelling public, about what CX was doing to deal with the perceived problems which LIA would have incurred.

Once again the chairman, Stocks, having let Huggins babble on and on, stopped him in his tracks and asked: 'But why was it necessary for CX to tell the public WHY it had terminated 49 pilots?'

You could have heard a fish fart!!

Huggins was totally lost for words, (although not for very long!) Anyway, my friends, at close of play we felt infinitely happier than we had been feeling prior to lunch.

Now we must sit and wait, yet again, for the verdict to be drafted.

The judiciary go on holiday for August so my guess is that we are unlikely to hear anything before the end of October.

As for what we might hear… our team are confident that the 3 judges are unlikely to find fault in Reyes' judgment on the points of law, however they think that it is possible that they might, and I emphasise might, reduce the quantum slightly.

Kam pointed out that Appeal Court judges are known to be very cautious in what they do.

Needless to say we all owe JSW BIG TIME for yet more months of dedication and hard work in assisting the lawyers in putting this case together.

I personally reckon that they, the expensive help, did as good a job as could have been done.

That's all folks!
Regards,

Doug.

And, of course, Doug was right. All we could do now was to sit and
wait. And wait we did.

2

Judgment 1

'"Contrariwise," continued Tweedledee, "if it was so, it might be; and if it were so, it would be; but as it isn't, it ain't. That's logic."'
Lewis Carroll, *Through the Looking-Glass*

It's like sitting outside the headmaster's office waiting for the green enter light to go on. No, it's worse. At least with the head you've got a timescale. It might be 5 minutes or it might be 30 minutes but at least the end's in sight. Worrying about the outcome is the same, but the timing's different. That's one of the many tortures of the civil justice system. The bench reserves judgment with no indication of timescale and sends you packing. They only let you know two days before when they're going to hand down the judgment. They don't even give you a hint. Not even, 'We think it'll be about three months.' Nothing at all. A week goes by. A month goes by. Three months go by. A whole year could go by.

And you worry. And you can speculate as much as you like. 'Well, the issues are cut and dried, aren't they? Surely it can't be that long?' But when it stretches out, 'Well, they admitted themselves that they hadn't read the papers. They're taking time to read through everything. That's good for us, isn't it? It means they'll see the falsity of the opposition's arguments.' But it makes no difference. Whatever you do, it's always there nagging away in the back of your mind. After going through this so many times, you'd think you'd get used to it. Develop some coping strategies. But it's not like that. With something so monumental that's going to affect the rest of your life, whether you're going to have enough money to live on in retirement,

45

whether you're going to be able to provide for your family, whether you're going to lose the pub as well as the house that's already gone. That's what the waiting is like. After three months with no end in sight, I had to do something. Just get away.

When Jill Robinson and I first set up the Animals Asia Foundation in the spare bedroom in our house in 1998, we had no money to fund it. Jill had come back from China with some horrific pictures of Asiatic moonbears. They were being kept imprisoned in crush cages in appalling conditions on 'farms'. They had been surgically implanted with crude, excruciatingly painful catheters to milk them for their bile for use in Chinese medicine. She said she wanted to do something about it, and I agreed. At the time she was working for the International Fund for Animal Welfare (IFAW), an organisation originally set up by a Welshman, Brian Davies, dedicated to ending the annual slaughter of seal pups in northeast Canada for use in the fur trade. She approached them and asked for funding to start doing something about it. They only offered nominal help so, one evening sitting in the garden, she told me she wanted to set up her own organisation. We agreed to mortgage everything we owned to raise the money we needed to make a start. We had no idea how much we'd need, no idea how we'd go about it, no specific aims, no strategy, no tactics. In other words just about the worst, riskiest business model you could envisage. But we went ahead anyway. We called it the Animals Asia Foundation (AAF) and set about trying to find people who might donate money to support the project. The story of how that fledgling operation set up in our spare room has metamorphosed into the global organisation that it is today is a book in itself. But back then we needed money.

People who know me well will tell you that tact and diplomacy are not two of my strong suits. Mea culpa. A reviewer of my first book, under the pseudonym of 'Pegasus', described me thus:

References to 'the Squadron' and 'the Chaps' beggar belief and are presumably intended to create the impression that Warham is some sort of military pilot leading his pilots to victory over a cynical enemy. In fact, Warham is a bluff, pint of beer, meat and two veg. type more likely to be at home in a Wanchai bar than in the Hong Kong Club.

Fortunately, the overwhelming majority of reviews the book received were far more complimentary than that of Pegasus, but his description of my character is not that far wide of the mark. He was wrong about one thing though. I am actually equally at home in both the Hong Kong Club and a Wanchai bar. But if there's a choice, give me a Wanchai bar every time.

But the Hong Kong Club is exactly where I ended up on numerous occasions when Jill and I were trying to raise money for AAF in the early days. Lunches with the great and the good, black tie dinners and fundraisers where I had to hone my limited tact and diplomacy skills trying to prise open their wallets. In the end, we were successful and we found a generous benefactor who gave us the seed money to get started.

At the time we lived in Lobster Bay on Clearwater Bay Road. There was a couple living up the hill, Steve and Sue Dullard, who got in touch and said they'd like to make a donation. We'd never met them before but, since they were neighbours, Jill suggested we invite them down to the house. I had severe reservations. Animal charities attract all sorts of different people. I have always loved animals; in fact when I was younger I had aspirations to be a vet. Fortunately those aspirations came to nought because, since I have come to know many, many vets and watched them at work, I know now that I would have made a terrible vet. So I am an animal lover and a conservationist but I am not a tree-hugger. (Or a bunny-hugger come to that!) In my view, the extremists do such causes a great disservice. Now talking to such people in a neutral venue is one thing but inviting them into your home is something altogether different. Who was to say which category these Dullard people might fit into? So despite my better judgment, Jill talked me into it and we invited them down.

They arrived around six in the evening. Sue was a Geordie and, being a northerner, that was a good start. Steve was a true blue Okker from Victoria and we eyed each other cautiously. I thought I should break the ice.

'Fancy a beer?'

'Oh yeah, mate. Is the Pope a Catholic?'

'Haven't got any of that coloured water you Aussies call piss, it's Sapporo or Sapporo.'

'That'll have to do then.'

Some hours later we were sitting in the garden pissed as farts and that was the start of a firm friendship that has lasted to this day. It turned out that, like me, Stevo is a huge cricket fan. He'd had the same reservations as me about coming to the house. He was worried he was going to have to spend the evening making small talk with a couple of animal rights loonies. Being an Aussie of course, we didn't exactly see eye-to-eye on the subject of the Ashes.

Fast forward to 2005, the year of Freddie Flintoff's Ashes. When the Aussies arrived in the UK, instead of the meek submissive England team they'd come to expect, they ran into a man who could bowl faster, hit the ball further and drink more beer than them after the close of play. He had an earring as well. Of course, Stevo and I had debated the outcome of this series long and hard before it started. We had a bet on it. A case of champagne. Well, that was how the bet started out. One night we were having a beer together and he was berating me yet again about how the Poms didn't stand a chance.

'Oh really? If you're so confident, you should give me odds on the bet,' I responded to his taunting.

'No problem, mate. No worries,' he replied.

'OK, how about 5 to 1 then?'

'Done.'

That was just the first escalation. By the time we'd finished the negotiation he'd given me 18 to 1. It was a bit naughty of me because, as he'll openly admit himself, despite being of convict heritage, Stevo doesn't hold his beer all that well. So when the series was over and Flintoff and his men had demolished the Aussies, he owed me 18 cases of champagne. Being a nice sort of guy, I went to my local wine store and negotiated a 20 per cent bulk purchase discount for him and awaited the arrival of said victuals. They started arriving in dribs and drabs. I knew Steve was a bit short of funds at that time so, after six cases had arrived, I offered to call the bet settled. Sue would have none of it.

'He made the bet, he can pay for it.' Hard but fair.

Fast forward again. I'd always wanted to go to the Boxing Day Test match in Australia. Stevo comes from a big family and one of his brothers was a member of the Melbourne Cricket Club.

'Mate, here's the deal. You get me two tickets behind the bowler's arm at the MCG test and we'll call the bet settled.'

'Done.'

And that was how I ended up on Boxing Day 2010 at the first day of the 325th Ashes Test match at the MCG to watch England bowl out Australia for 98 runs in their first innings and then see Strauss and Cook put on 157 without loss by the close of play. It was a magnificent display of cricket in one of the greatest sporting arenas in the world. I had my seat behind the bowler's arm and, even though Chris Tremlett took 4 for 26 off 11.5 overs, a remarkable feat on its own, for me James Anderson was the pick of our bowlers taking 4 for 44 off 16 overs. He swung the ball in both directions and, at times, was simply unplayable. England went on to win the series and retain the Ashes on the Aussies' home ground – the first time we'd managed that for 24 years. Not only that, we beat them by an innings defeat in three separate matches of the series, aided in no small part by Alastair Cook's magnificent batting. His performances were a glory to behold and, for Ponting's men, it was a rout. My enjoyment of the day's play might have been overshadowed by the dark cloud that was looming after the news I'd received on Christmas Eve morning, but I forced it to the back of my mind, determined that nothing would mar the achievement of one of my bucket list ambitions. I'd got away.

I'd already had an excellent holiday in Australia. We'd started out by staying at Steve and Sue's property in Jilliby, just over an hour's drive north of Sydney. It was still under construction so I helped Steve out a bit by felling a couple of trees on the hill behind the house late one afternoon. It might have been the two or three slabs of Crownies that we'd consumed between us that day since breakfast but, despite liberal applications of Start Ya Bastard, the chainsaw proved to be troublesome so I reverted to basics. Not realising quite how hard the wood of a spotted gum can be, my first blow resulted in the axe flying out of my hands. It missed Stevo's head by a good two feet so no worries. By this time my Sheila was standing well back so when one of the gummies didn't quite drop where I'd planned, there was no harm done. The next day we took the ute for a drive down to Terrigal for a spot of lunch and then up the coast road through The Entrance to stop off for a dip in the ocean, off a beach near Budgewoi. Other than a bloke in a wetsuit, fishing in the surf, as far as the eye could see we had the whole place to ourselves. That kind of alerted me to the water temperature, but I had to try it anyway. After my gonads had re-emerged from my abdominal cavity, we jumped back in the ute and took the Pacific Highway route home in time to join Stevo on the veranda for a couple of Bloody Mary sundowners. He'd had a hard day mowing the paddock on his ride-on and, to avoid dehydration, he'd already done a slab or two so we called it a night soon after and were in bed by ten.

The next day we said au revoir to Steve and went to meet Don Fraser and his partner, Kelly, in Sydney for a couple of days. We stayed at the Shangri-La Hotel and had a room on a high floor overlooking the harbour. It was in stark contrast to the rustic delights of Jilliby but we didn't miss the cicadas which, at times, almost drowned out sensible conversation – not that there had been much of that going on in reality. After leaving Sydney and spending three days in Melbourne, where we met up with Steve and Sue again for the cricket, I returned home to Hong Kong on 28 December to face the gathering storm that had started forming on Christmas Eve.

When I'd decided to get away, I also took the decision not to take my laptop. This, coupled with the fact that I have resisted the modern de rigueur requirement to be in constant contact 24/7 and don't have an iPhone (or any other 'i' thing come to that), meant that I was out of email contact. Deliberately so. But Don was not. He received an email on the 22nd to say that the Court of Appeal's judgment would be handed down on the 24th. Someone was going to get a Christmas present, good or otherwise. Thus it was I found myself standing outside the hotel in Melbourne at 6:45 on the morning of Christmas Eve calling our lawyer, Benedict Chiu, on my Nokia.

'Hi Ben, how's it going?'

'We lost.'

'What?'

'We lost.'

'What, everything?'

'Yes.'

'I can't believe that, let's go through it a step at a time. How did we do on the breach of contract?'

'No, we lost that. They overturned it.'

'Shit. What about the S21B thing?'

'They upheld that.'

'OK so we're good there. Are you telling me that they overturned the defamation ruling as well?'

'No, they upheld it but they've reduced the damages to 700,000 dollars. Do you want me send you a copy of the judgment?'

'Well, you can Ben but I'm not on email 'til I get back. I'll have to deal with it then.'

'OK, we'll talk then. Happy Christmas.'

'Yeah thanks Ben, same to you.'

At that time in the morning, there was no one else around to see my tears. I smoked a couple of cigarettes, pulled myself together and went back inside to give my partner the bad news. I told her what had happened.

'Well? What does it mean?'

'It means that we're broke. They've awarded costs against us as well so they're going to come after me personally for those. I'll probably have to go bankrupt.'

I had previously taken what is described in polite circles as asset protection measures. Having lost my house, I wasn't going to lose the last asset that I had, the pub in the UK. This was owned by a company so they couldn't come after me for that. I might have to resign as a director but my shares would be in the hands of people I could trust. But they could come after me for what I owned in Hong Kong. My plan was to make sure that I only had a dollar left in my bank account there, give them that, file for bankruptcy and go travelling in South America until I could get discharged. It would mean that the bastards had finally achieved their objective; to run me out of money and drive me out of Hong Kong. I'd played the game and lost. Well, if you're not prepared to accept the consequences of playing high-stakes poker, don't sit down at the table. But that wasn't the end of the story though because if they couldn't get the money out of me, they'd go after the other plaintiffs, my BoBs. Some of them were overseas residents so they'd have trouble with them, but some were still in Hong Kong. I had spoken to them previously about taking similar measures to myself but I had no idea if they'd done anything about it. It was a complete mess. Well, there was nothing I could do about it right now until I got back to Hong Kong, so I resolved to keep quiet, say nothing to the others and enjoy the rest of my time in Oz. I did speak to Don and he agreed with my plan.

I got back to Hong Kong and read the judgment. Then I read it again. And then I read it again. And again. I was completely bemused. I couldn't follow the logic of their arguments. They didn't flow, one to another, towards the conclusions they drew. It reminded me of the way the court had been conducted. Semi-organised chaos. The best word I could find to describe this judgment was perverse. I am the first to admit that I have no formal legal qualifications but, over the previous nine years, I had read enough to be at least a well-informed layman. It had got to the point with our counsel that, rather than explaining a point of precedent to me, they just gave me the references to the case law to read for myself. But, nevertheless, this judgment defeated me.

I spoke to Don about it. He felt the same. I talked to Benedict and to our counsel. They felt the same as well. It didn't make sense. Not only that, but some very serious implications arose from the judgment. In overturning the breach of contract leg of the original judgment, and reversing one of Judge Reyes' answers to the preliminary issues, they had opened a massive hole in the labour protection laws in Hong Kong, weak as they already were. What they were effectively saying was that, irrespective of any protections that may be written into an employment contract to give the employee additional protection over and above the basics of the EO, the employer still retained an overriding right to dismiss the employee on notice at any time with no reasons given. We had heard this argument from Huggins during the trial and had almost laughed at how preposterous such a proposition would be. But these clowns had agreed with him. Just think of the implications.

If you want to work for Cathay Pacific, you have to up-sticks and move to Hong Kong. You have to uproot your family, move them halfway across the world, organise schooling for your children, set up home and apply for residence here. The contract of employment itself contains numerous provisions to give you security of tenure. It is very clear from the wording that it is intended to form a long-term relationship between the parties. There is a whole section on career progression; with a starting rank of Second Officer progressing through the ranks to Junior First Officer, First Officer, Senior First Officer, Captain, Senior Captain and ultimately to Check & Training Captain. On the promotion rates that were common when I joined Cathay in 1985, that progression would take around 10 to 12 years. Similarly, the provident fund. Rather than having a pension at the end of your career with monthly payments in retirement, we had a provident fund into which both the employee and the employer make monthly contributions. At the end of your career, this is paid out to do with as you choose to fund your retirement. The fund is managed by a board of trustees and bound by a set of specific rules on calculation of final payout. In the early years, the payout gives very little return on investment but, as the years progress, the multiplication factors increase so that, at year 17, the factor reaches its maximum and the return is very good. Now, clearly, such an arrangement is, again, designed around a long-term relationship between the parties to the contract. There are many other such examples of terms in the contract which demonstrate the intent of 'permanence' including a section on redundancy which specifies the 'last in, first out' principle. So it would seem that this is a pretty solid contract offering the employee protection and security of tenure. Well, it did.

But not any more. According to the judgment of Hon. Stock and his crew, despite what may be written in the contract, despite the clear intent of a long-term relationship, despite specific discipline and grievance procedures being included, in fact despite just about anything, the employer retains an overriding right to simply dismiss the employee at any time with no reasons given. Doesn't matter about the DGP. Rather than waste time giving the employee a fair chance to explain his side of the story, you can just sack him. Even if you do give him a chance and he is exonerated, it doesn't matter, you can just sack him anyway. Perverse is really too weak a word. Lunatic might be better. Or insane. Or just plain wrong. Or how about unjust? Now there's a word. If this was allowed to remain as case law, it would affect every man and woman working in Hong Kong all the way from the blue collar workers through the white collar ranks to the professional people, even to university professors, consultant medical practitioners and, dare I say it, senior judges (if only). Basically what they were saying is that your contract of employment is not worth the paper it's written on. You might as well hang it on a nail in the wall of the nearest lavatory.

And there was another thing about this judgment. In reducing the defamation award from HK$3.3 million to HK$700k, there was a lot of waffle about previous cases such as *Chu* and *Yakoob* that had been quoted as case law at the trial and we'd witnessed the court's predisposition at the time. But, unlike Reyes' judgment, other than to say that the defamation in our case was 'not nearly as serious' and that the original damages awarded by the judge were 'manifestly excessive', there was no indication whatsoever of how they had come to calculate a figure of HK$700k. Well, we know exactly where it came from, don't we?

There was nothing for it. We couldn't let this stand. We'd have to file for leave to take it to the Court of Final Appeal (CoFA), the highest court in Hong Kong, equivalent to the House of Lords (now the Supreme Court) in the UK. At least they'd done us one favour. One of the criteria for granting leave for a case to go to the CoFA is that the matters to be disposed of must be of significant public interest. This certainly was. If it was allowed to stand, everyone in Hong Kong just had their employment rights flushed down the toilet. I'd call that a very significant matter of public interest.

In September 2012, the Hon. Justice Anselmo Trinidad Reyes resigned from the bench and took up the post of Professor of Legal Practice, Faculty of Law, University of Hong Kong. Whether or not this had anything to do with the way Hon. Stock et al had massacred the original judgment in our case is a matter of conjecture. If it had, who could blame him?

3

LTC

'Perhaps he knew, as I did not, that the Earth was made round so that we would not see too far down the road.'
Baroness Karen von Blixen-Finecke, *Out of Africa*

The first thing we had to do was deal with the costs award from the Court of Appeal, which had gone against us. We applied for a stay of execution pending the outcome of a further appeal to the Court of Final Appeal. It was granted. First financial catastrophe averted. The next thing was to get leave to go to the CoFA. That was granted as well and we were given a date of 27 August 2012. More than a year and a half away. More waiting. Oh well, we'd come this far, what was another 20 months? A bloody long time actually but we'd just have to wear it. I was worried about the BoBs as well. Some of them hadn't taken the reversal in the Court of Appeal very well. Understandably so. I was worried that some of them might be ready to call it a day and move on with their lives. I worried unnecessarily. These were the 'hard bastards', as George Crofts had described us. Despite the fact that I received some pretty angry and critical phone calls and emails, they still stuck together as one man.

I didn't say anything to anyone but it had deeply affected me personally as well. The black dog came to visit and I started having some very bad periods when I just didn't want to interact with anyone. It affected my relationship with my partner as well. I had put my trust in the impartiality of the civil justice system and felt it had let me down badly. I had never subscribed to the cynical view that a lot of these decisions are taken behind closed doors in the private rooms of the Hong Kong Club or that the old boys' network would never let us succeed. But now I was beginning to wonder. Hong Kong is run by big business, and it was one of the biggest hongs that we'd taken on. And the judgment just didn't make any sense, unless you looked at it from the big business perspective. It was exactly what they wanted.

As always, if I had been on my own, if it had just been me, it wouldn't be so bad. But it wasn't just me. I had led another 17 men, their wives and partners and families down this path and put them at risk. As Don always said to me, 'We're not in the military, they didn't have to follow your orders, they came along of their own free will and they knew the risks.' Whilst that was true, it didn't make me feel any better about it. I was still the leader and I felt that burden of leadership very strongly. With responsibility comes accountability.

I'd also had to move house in October 2010. On the list of stressful things to do, it was right up there. And then in February 2011, I noticed I was running out of money. I had a Premier account with HSBC. This was one of those arrangements where you can put everything in one account; current account, deposit account, foreign currency, stocks, shares, commodities, CDs, credit cards etc. which made it easy to manage them all in one place. With internet banking you can log on and it gives you a summary of your available balance at the top of the page. This was what I used to keep an eye on my general financial situation. I didn't really check each account individually, just looked at the big picture. One of the reasons for this was because I had been keeping my head above water by forex and commodities trading. And I didn't just make small investments. If you want to win big, bet big. The result was that, sometimes, if a currency deal went against me, I'd see a big drop in the overall balance available; sometimes up to HK$100k or 200k in one month. Usually I'd just wait for it to turn around and close down the position. I don't believe in stop-loss. It's the quickest way to lose your money in a volatile market. These were short- to medium-term trades.

But I went online to pay my rent in February and noticed that I was running short of cash. This was strange because my forex trading had been going generally well. I checked through each account individually and found that six cheques had been cashed out of my current account in the previous month for a total of HK$116k. I had no idea what they were for. I hadn't written any cheques. I do all my banking online and only ever write a couple of cheques a year to pay my car licence tax and the odd occasion where someone specifically asks for a cheque. That had actually happened when I moved house last October. I bought some garden furniture and they'd asked for a cheque. I'd gone to my chequebook in my study and found it was empty so had to apply for a new one before I could pay them. I looked at it now. There was only that one cheque used. Then I looked at the numbers on the cheques that had been cashed. They weren't from this book. It looked like they were from the previous book. I went back through the stubs of the old book. The last one I'd written was on 9 June 2010 and that was when my records for that book stopped – 25 cheques before the end. What the hell was going on? I started going back though the previous statements for my current account. There were 24 cheques that had been cashed in all, starting on 1 September 2010, and they all came from my old chequebook. They came to a total of HK$324k – 324 grand! It had been going on for five months! How the hell had I missed that? I printed off the statements, highlighted the withdrawals, and went down to the HSBC branch in Sai Kung to report that someone had been taking money from my account without my permission. They told me that they'd go back through their records, retrieve the cashed cheques and that, in the meantime, I should go to the police station to report the theft.

I went there to make a statement and they were incredulous. How could you miss such a large amount for so long? Don't you check your statements every month? What were you thinking of? Given the amount of money these guys are on in the police force, I could understand their incredulity. I looked like a total dickhead. And then they asked me THE question. What do you do for a living? I told them I was retired but I used to be a Cathay Pacific captain. Oh, that explained it all. Cathay captain, more money than sense. Overpaid playboy, blah, blah, blah. The bullshit and propaganda that CX management had been pushing out over the last ten years during salary negotiations had its effect. We could never be rid of that stigma. Just then my phone rang. It was the bank.

'Do you know someone called Martin Lau Lap-yan?'

'Yes I do. He's a close personal friend of mine. Why?'

'We've recovered the last five cheques and they're all written out to him.'

'What? That can't be right.'

'Well, it is.'

'Hang on. I'll be right over.'

The police wanted me to stay to finish my statement first, but I told them I'd be back later. I needed to get to the bottom of this.

I'd known Martin and his brother Jimmy for more than 15 years. They were both Chinese but had been brought up in Lancashire where their father, Jimmy Senior, had owned a takeaway. They came back to Hong Kong to live when their father sold up his business. Their first language was English, which they spoke with a broad northern accent. As brothers, they couldn't have been more different in personality. Jimmy worked in the supply and construction industries and was the solid, dependable type with a strong work ethic and a long-term steady girlfriend. His brother had trained as a ballet dancer and travelled the world performing in that role. His last real full-time job had been with the Hong Kong Ballet and, after his career was over, he'd turned his hand to a variety of jobs, some to do with the arts, others not. Unlike his brother, he was extrovert, gregarious and unreliable, and a serial womaniser. Despite the fact that Martin was 20 years younger than me, we became very good friends.

For more than five years we played together in a band that a bunch of us formed in Sai Kung, called SKiNC. He was lead vocalist and I played keyboards, sang backing vocals and grunted some blues numbers. The two of us sometimes rehearsed together, outside of our main band practises, working on timing and harmonies. For a time we had some regular gigs at weekends in the bars in Sai Kung and Wanchai and the whole band got really tight. We didn't have any original stuff but, instead of just playing the easy numbers like most pub bands, we used to try and pick the more difficult numbers and put our own arrangements on them. It was a lot of fun and good while it lasted but then, one by one, the other guys got full-time jobs which made it more difficult for us to practise and play as regularly as we had been.

But Martin and I were more than friends. I treated him like a son. When he got into various scrapes, which he did often, he'd come and talk to me for help and advice and I gave it freely. When he broke up with one of his girlfriends in the middle of 2010, he'd been staying at her place and had nowhere else to go, so I let him stay in my spare room. I gave him keys to the house so he could come and go as he pleased. I did this for another good friend as well when he broke up with his wife. That's how my spare room came to be known as 'the crying room'.

But money was always an issue with Martin. He had a reputation for borrowing from people and not repaying them. Just about everyone in our social circle in Sai Kung had a story to tell. In my case I'd lent him quite a lot of money over the years. At one point, he was being chased by the debt collectors over a credit card that had gone unpaid. He asked me to pay it off for him. I told him to ask his family but he told me that his father had flat refused to help him. In retrospect, perhaps I should have followed his father's lead, but I didn't. I paid it; HK$37k. When it eventually got to the point that he owed me more than HK$100k, I put a stop to it and told him that, if he wanted our friendship to continue, not to ask me to lend him money again until he paid what he owed. He agreed and never asked again. Maybe I should have read the warning signs.

As I walked from the police station back to the bank, the first thought that came to my mind was: why would someone write cheques from my account to Martin? Why would they try to involve him? Were they using his account to launder the money without him realising it? I got to the bank and they showed me the cheques they'd pulled out of the records so far. None of the signatures looked anything like mine, which is quite distinctive, but every single one had his name on it and his mobile phone number on the back from when they'd been paid into his account. The penny started to drop but, at first, I just couldn't believe it. He might be bad with money but he's not a thief. Especially not with me. There's no way he'd do something like that to me, surely? There's got to be some mistake somewhere. It just can't be true! But then things started to fall into place.

At home, there was a small wicker basket on top of a cabinet just inside the door. When I came in, I'd throw my keys and the contents of my pockets in there. I don't carry a wallet. A wallet is the quickest way to lose everything if it gets nicked. So I just carry my cash in a fold. I'd throw that in the basket as well. At the start of each week I'd get enough cash for spending money out of the ATM. That would normally last me through until the next week. But during one period I'd noticed that I was running out before the weekend and had to go back to the ATM. I thought it odd because my spending habits hadn't changed. My partner at the time had two teenage boys. I actually asked her if it was possible that one of them might be helping himself from the basket. She was horrified that I would even ask. What I didn't think of at the time was that this happened when Martin had keys to my house. And what about my chequebook? I kept that in a sort of wire cage attached to an IKEA desk in my study. It was in a black and red plastic cover that HSBC had given to me when I opened my first bank account with them after I arrived in Hong Kong in 1985. When I went to write the cheque for the garden furniture, the chequebook was still there in its cover, but there were no cheques in it. They'd all been torn out. The only person who had access to my study other than me, my partner and her boys was Martin. As the realisation of what he'd done came over me, I felt physically sick. It was like having a panic attack. I felt helpless and disorientated. But then the anger began to grow. I went back to the police station to finish my statement. When that was done, I went to my local pub, The Duke, and there he was. Standing there, bold as brass. He greeted me with open arms like the old friends we were, as if he'd done nothing. He'd been stealing from me for five months and carried on as normal without a care in the world, just like he was doing now. It would have been easy to confront him there and then. But no, I needed the police to gather the evidence against him first and put the fucker away where he belonged, so I acted the same way as him and pretended nothing had happened. I was seething inside but, for once, I controlled my temper. Let the cops do their job, get him up in front of the beak and get him banged up in the big house. Then the world would see him for what he truly is and that would be the end of it. I didn't know then how wrong I was. This was only the start of what was yet to come. This was only the beginning of a sequence of events that would put me back at the bottom of the deep, dark pit that I had last visited during 2004.

I felt as though things were spiralling out of control and I had no idea what was coming next. I needed to get organised and regain control of the situation. OK, try the problem solving models you've been trained to use. Break the big problem down into smaller, more manageable ones. Analyse the situation, identify the individual issues, develop solutions, act on them, review performance and start the cycle again. Do the why, the how and the what.

First thing I needed was cash. The bank had recovered all 24 cheques now and every one had the same fake signature, payee account and mobile phone numbers. They admitted they should never have been cashed. They admitted liability, refunded the money and repaid the interest that had been charged because of the withdrawals. Sounds easy, doesn't it? Well it wasn't. It took six weeks to achieve.

First they wanted me to shut my account completely and open a new one. That didn't sound like a problem until they insisted that I should first cash all my investments into HK$. That would have closed down some of my forex and commodities positions at a loss at that time. I declined their kind offer. Then a security bod, who I had never met, suggested to me over the phone that, to increase security, I should change my signature. The conversation went along the following lines.

'Mr Warham, you must change your signature for security.'

'Mr Chin, I don't know how old you are, you sound very young to me, but I'm 58 years old and I've been signing my name like this for the last 43 years and it's never been a problem before.'

'Ah, I see, well you should think about using your middle initial as well.'

'Have you looked at my signature Mr Chin?'

'Ah, no.'

'Well if you'd taken the trouble to look, you'd see that I already do use my middle initial.'

'Well, perhaps you should stop using your middle initial instead.'

'Mr Chin, have you compared the signatures of the forged cheques with my signature?'

'Ah, no.'

'Well, again, if you'd taken the trouble to look before calling me, you'd see that the two bear no resemblance to each other at all.'

'Oh.'

'So here's my suggestion, Mr Chin. Instead of bothering me with your futile attempts to mitigate the blame, you improve your security precautions with the simple expedient of checking the validity of the fucking signature before cashing the cheque. Thank you for your call Mr Chin, I trust we won't be speaking to each other again.'

There were more Kafkaesque conversations like that with various other departments of the bank. I did eventually get the money refunded; but I had to sign an undertaking that I would appear as a witness in any prosecution that the bank might bring. Show me the paper. Couldn't wait.

The next thing I needed to deal with was the 'why'. Why had he done this to me? I couldn't speak to him directly because the police warned me off doing so and, anyway, I wasn't sure I could trust myself to control my temper. Instead I called his brother Jimmy and asked him to come round to the house. When he arrived I showed him the evidence of what his brother had done. He was absolutely devastated. He started asking the same question as me. Why? What had possessed him to do such a thing? And especially to me; his closest friend and ally.

We talked for a while. I filled him in on the progress of the police investigation and then he said, 'John, even though what he's done is very, very wrong, he's still my brother and I'm going to do everything I can to protect him and keep him out of jail.'

'I know Jimmy and I wouldn't expect anything else of you, but you also need to know that I'm going to do everything I can to make him pay for what he's done.'

'OK, but so long as you understand my position.'

'I do mate and I hope you can understand mine.'

As I mentioned earlier, the two brothers were chalk and cheese. I didn't want to lose Jimmy's friendship as well as a result of all this. If I'd only had the slightest inkling of what was going to happen in the next few months, that would have been the least of my worries but, as they say, ignorance is bliss. The meeting wasn't without humour. As he was leaving, Jimmy turned to me and said, 'Do you want to search me before I go?'

I'd like to say that the police investigation was fast and efficient. I'd like to but, to me, it took forever for them to charge him. I spoke to a friend in the force and he told me that they needed to do forensics on the cheques to see if they could prove he wrote them. I didn't realise that, but there were other questions they asked me that seemed to me to be somewhat bizarre. They asked me if I could give them a copy of his ID card. In Hong Kong, we are all required to have identity cards issued by the immigration department. As part of the application process, you have to give your fingerprints. The civil liberties people in the UK would scream infringement of right to privacy. For me it's never been a problem. In fact, in my experience it's a good thing. The card can be used for identification in banks, shops and so on and also to enter and leave Hong Kong. If you have an ID card you don't need your passport to cross the border. But for the Big Brother brigade, my experience with the police might go some way to dispel their worries. They had his name, so surely they could get his ID card out of the computer? No, they couldn't, which is why they asked me if I'd got a copy. As it happened, I did have a copy. A couple of years earlier we'd set up a company when we were thinking of going into business together. It actually came to nothing, which was probably just as well because he'd have stolen from that as well. But in setting the thing up I'd needed a copy of his ID card, which was still on my computer. I gave it to the police. Next they asked if I knew were he lived. What? Surely with a copy of his ID card they could just go into the computer and get his address? No, they couldn't. So I gave them his address. Then they asked me if I'd got his mobile phone number. I drew the line at that. It was written on the back of all the cheques! After what seemed like an interminable wait, during which he continued to behave as if nothing had happened, as though he hadn't a care in the world, he was finally arrested and charged.

John Graeme Hagon hails from Alnwick in Northumberland. I first met him when I moved to Sai Kung in 1986. He is a criminal barrister who, for many years, specialised in defending triads. His expertise lay not in getting them acquitted; rather he is very good at mitigating the sentence. For him, a win was not a 'not guilty' verdict; it was getting the sentence reduced from five to three years. And he made a good living out of it. Graeme, like me, likes a cold beer on a warm day. There the similarity ended. We did not see eye-to-eye on any number of subjects that had been hotly debated between us over the years. In particular, he thought Cathay pilots were overpaid playboys who needed taking down a peg or two. He especially didn't like unions and, since I was the president of the AOA, that added further fuel to the fire. But in the small community of the watering holes in Sai Kung, we tolerated each other.

Our relationship might best be summarised by an exchange we had one day when he said to me, 'Let me tell you something, you'll never get a fucking invitation to come round to my house.'

'Oh really? Well let me tell you something. If you ever did invite me round, I wouldn't fucking come.'

Hagon agreed to defend Lau in the upcoming trial.

I had stopped drinking in my usual local The Duke, because the man who stole from me and betrayed me was still going in there, bold as brass, still refusing to acknowledge that he'd done anything wrong. In fact, rather the contrary. He was doing something he was very good at as part of the grooming process for his next victim; playing the 'poor me' sympathy card. From what I heard around the traps, it was meeting with some success and he was gathering around him a cabal of sympathisers. I decided it was best to stay away and moved my custom to another bar round the corner called Agua Plus. I was sitting outside there one afternoon when Hagon appeared and sat down at my table. This was a first. He never came into Agua.

'Hello John.'

'Hi Graeme, how're you doing?'

'OK thanks. I suppose you've heard that I'm defending Martin?'

'Yes, I've heard that.'

'I'm only doing it on condition that he pleads guilty.'

'I don't see how he's got much choice. His name and phone number are on all the cheques. He's bang to rights.'

'Yes, but what I'm saying, John, is that I'm only doing it on that condition. If he pleads not guilty, I wouldn't touch him with a barge pole.'

'Look Graeme, as far as I'm concerned you're just doing your job. If it wasn't you it'd be someone else. I hold no malice towards you, if that's what you're asking.'

'Well, I just wanted to tell you that.'

'OK, fine. So how's the defence going? Has he told you why he did it?'

'No. It's almost as if he doesn't think he's done anything wrong. I've talked to Jimmy and it's the same with him. He won't even talk about it. It's like he's in complete denial.'

'That's what I heard. I think he's got mental problems.'

'Yeah and there's something else. He's got previous.'

'What? What for?'

'Last year he was convicted of three counts of theft. He took money out of the account at that health club he was working at. Said it was for unpaid wages. He went to court without representation and got a community service order. Kept it quiet.'

'Fuck me Graeme, I never knew that. He told me he'd been laid off because the club was moving to a new place. That's bad for him, isn't it?'

'Yes it is. We've got the first hearing in the magistrates' court in three weeks. It'll probably get sent straight up to the district court and he's looking at two or three years. If we can keep it in the magistrates' court it might be less 'cause the maximum they can give is two years. But either way he's definitely looking at doing time.'

This was a complete revelation to me. This had happened at the time when he'd split up with his girlfriend and come to stay at my place.

He told me that the club was moving premises and they'd got a new business manager who decided that he was surplus to requirements. I felt really sorry for him. Losing your job and your girlfriend at the same time is right up there on the stress count. It didn't even occur to me that the two events were in any way related. But, some time later, I found out the truth. I met his ex at a social event and we sat down to chat. She told me that the health club was owned by a friend of hers and that she'd got him the job there. She went to the UK for a couple of weeks to see her family and came back to find her friend was livid. He'd been stealing money from the club's bank account. His girlfriend kicked him out on the spot. But there was more. She also told me that the health club had been getting complaints from some female members that money was going missing from their handbags in the locker room while they were using the gym. Guess who was in charge of the locker room security.

Then some more pieces started falling into place. When I was working for Monarch in Luton in the early eighties, I met a lady called Sally Chaston who worked for McAlpine Aviation. We were both part of the same social set of party animals that was around at the time. Sally and her husband Jeremy moved to Hong Kong around the same time as I did and we continued to socialise together. She's a long-standing friend. A couple of years before the current events, Lau had been going out with one of Sally's daughters. Everything seemed to be moonlight and roses until the relationship suddenly broke up. I was surprised by the split but more surprised to find that Sally started behaving a bit coldly towards me. Of course, I was seen as a great buddy of the jilted lover and I suppose it was assumed that I'd take his side. It wasn't just me though. It affected some others in our community who were seen in the same way. It was a forewarning of what was to happen later. When the latest revelations became common knowledge, Sally sought me out and told me what had happened. When he was going out with her daughter, he borrowed money from her. No surprises there then. But then, one day when the family were out of the house, he went round there and made a telephone call. Sally had left an envelope containing HK$1,900 on the sideboard to pay the gardener's wages. When she got back to the house the envelope was gone but the gardener hadn't collected it. The fucker had stolen the gardener's wages. That was the cause of the sudden split in the new romance. A pattern was emerging.

There was something else that happened between him and me though that really took the biscuit. In December 2010, he told me that he had picked up some work and was going to Singapore for the month. I thought, great, it's time he got a break. Of course I found out later that there was no work. He just went down there to swan around for a month. He could afford it because he'd already stolen HK$187k from my account, but I didn't know it at the time. Just before the New Year I got a phone call from Singapore.

'Hi, it's me.'

'Hi, how's it going down there? How's the job? Having a good time?'

'Yeah it's going well. Job's great but it's finished in a couple of days and I'm coming home.'

'Good. Look forward to seeing you for a few beers.'

'Me too but I've got a bit of a problem. They haven't paid me yet so I haven't got enough for my ticket back. I was wondering if you could stump up for it 'til I get paid.'

'Mate, we've been through this before. We don't do that anymore.'

'Yeah I know. I know. But I'm really stuck, mate.'

'Well, just wait 'til they pay you.'

'I've only got the free housing 'til the end of the contract. If I wait I'll have to pay for a hotel. Mate, honestly, I wouldn't ask if I wasn't really stuck.'

'I'm not happy with this. Not at all. How much do you need anyway?'

'Five grand.'

'Now listen, if I lend it to you, when will you pay me back?'

'I can do it next Thursday. I'll have been paid by then, no sweat.'

'Look, I've got major problems with this. If you say Thursday, it has to be Thursday on the nail. No delays, no excuses, no bullshit, right?'

'I promise you mate. Next Thursday.'

And, like a twat, I sent him the money. But he was as good as his word. He met me on the Thursday and paid me HK$5k. Of course, what I didn't know was that, two days earlier, he'd cashed a cheque for HK$25k out of my account. The fucker paid me back with my own money.

I went to the first hearing in the magistrates' court and sat in the public gallery. It was listed for a mention, which means that it was just a preliminary hearing where the magistrate reviews the basics of the case, gives directions to counsel and sets a date for the trial proper. Hagon was there to represent Lau and, whilst no plea is taken at that stage, he gave an indication that the defendant would plead guilty when the time came. During the various exchanges whilst reviewing the case, my name got mentioned as the prime witness for the prosecution at which point Hagon said, 'Well, I believe that Mr Warham is in the court today.' The magistrate gave a double take.

'What's he doing here?'

'I suppose he's taking an interest.'

'Well it's an open court and he has every right to be here but I hope he's not attempting to contact the defendant. That would be most improper,' he said, looking at me. It was obvious who I was. I was the only *gweilo* sitting in the gallery. I had no intention of contacting him but what was I supposed to do? The police weren't telling me anything and neither was the prosecution. They'd got an open and shut case, he was pleading guilty and they could chalk up another successful prosecution on their CVs so why would they need to keep me in the picture? After all, I was only the victim.

A few days later, Hagon approached me again in Agua. He gave me a lot of waffle about how he thought poor old Martin needed help. Apparently he still wouldn't come to terms with what he'd done. Wouldn't accept responsibility. Didn't seem to realise the seriousness of his situation. He wasn't a betting man. Hadn't got a drug habit. What did he need the money for? And anyway, what sane person would put his own name and phone number on the cheques? It's almost as if he was begging to get caught. Perhaps it's a cry for help. I began to smell a large *Rattus norvegicus*. And then he dropped a hook in the water.

'He says in his witness statement that he found your chequebook on the floor of your car when you lent it to him.'

'Oh really, Graeme? Let me tell you something. As well as refusing to show any remorse for what he's done, your client's lying through his teeth to you.'

I went on to describe to him how he'd really got hold of the cheques. How he'd gone into my study, torn the cheques out of the book and put it back in my desk. I was actually trying to be helpful by letting

Hagon know he couldn't trust his client to tell the truth but it was a mistake.

It was shortly afterwards that the whispering campaign started. I began to hear rumours of what people in the local community were saying about me. 'What's John's beef? He can afford it, he's loaded, we all know that. Bloody Cathay pilot for fuck's sake. And he's got his money back so why's he being so vindictive? There's no real harm done. Think of what a prison sentence will do to Martin's family. His parents are getting on and his dad's not well. What will it do to them? I don't think Martin could survive in prison. What if he does something stupid? Didn't he have a brother that committed suicide? If he does that, Warham will have that on his conscience. He should just drop the charges.'

I got some text messages from Jimmy asking me to do just that. I couldn't. It was now out of my hands and, to get my money back, I'd signed an undertaking with the bank. And anyway, why should I? He'd stolen from me, completely betrayed my trust and refused to apologise or show any sign of remorse. All of this culminated in a conversation I had one night in The Duke with one of my oldest friends, Pete Bissell.

I first met Pete in 1984 in a pub near Gatwick called The Lamb at Lamb's Green. I'd arranged to meet an old mate there from Hamble, Fred the Bike, so called for his penchant for motorcycles. We were standing at the bar and I was telling him I'd got an interview with Cathay coming up in Hong Kong. All of a sudden the barman interrupted our conversation.

'I've got an interview with Cathay as well.'

'What, who the fuck are you? You're a barman.'

'No, I'm a pilot as well. I work for BIA (British Island Airways) but the pay's so bad I have to do this to get more money.'

Pete and I ended up joining Cathay together on the same day in March 1985 and we became firm friends. We came from different backgrounds. I'd done the BA cadet thing but he came up through the so-called self-improver route. He paid for his PPL (private pilots licence), got a job instructing to build his hours and then took the CPL (commercial pilots licence) exams; all under his own steam. The induction course at Cathay, like most airlines, was geared around people who'd done formal training courses such as Hamble or the air force. It was high pressure and a lot of exam technique was involved. When we first arrived in Hong Kong, we were put up at the Regal

Airport Hotel, five minutes down the road from the old Kai Tak airport. There was a bar called the Skylight Lounge on the top floor and it had a great view over the airport. At night you could sit there and watch all the long-haul 747s taking off; 747s that we'd come here to learn to fly. About a week into the course, I knocked on his door at 10 o'clock at night. He opened the door and I told him we were going for a beer.

'No, I can't. We've got an exam tomorrow and I've got to study for it.'

I went into his room and stared. Over the mirror he'd taped a large paper print-out of the flight deck of the 747 that we'd been given as part of the training course. He'd coloured in all the indicator lights with felt-tipped pens.

'What the fuck's that?'

'It's the only way I can learn. I have to write everything out. I can't come for a beer, I've got to study.'

'The only thing you need to study is this paper I've got in my hand.'

'What is it?'

'It's a copy of sample questions from tomorrow's paper.'

'Where did you get that?'

'From the guys sitting at the back of the class who're converting off the Tristar.'

'Why did they give it to you?'

'Because I bought them lunch and asked them nicely.'

From then on, that's how we did our study. A couple of hours alone with the books and an hour or so in the bar, going over the sample questions. Exam technique.

Twenty-five years later we were sitting together in The Duke with a problem. Pete broached the subject.

'I want to talk to you about Martin.'

'I guessed you might. Go ahead,' I replied.

'Don't you think he deserves a second chance?'

'No I don't. I think he's had plenty of chances and now I think he needs to pay for what he's done.'

'He's paid the money back so you haven't lost anything.'

'No he hasn't. His family has had a whip-round and paid about 170 grand into court to try to reduce his sentence. He hasn't paid me anything.'

'But you've got your money back from the bank.'

69

'What's that got to do with it? I treated him like a son and in return he completely betrayed my trust. He hasn't made any attempt to apologise or even acknowledge what he's done. I'd just like to know why he did it. Has he told you?'

'No, he won't say. We think he needs help, not punishment.'

'Well, maybe the nick is the place he could get some help.'

'What about all the kindness he's shown you over the years? Don't you think he deserves credit for that?'

'What kindness? D'you mean the kindness of stealing my chequebook and emptying my bank account?'

'What about when you were in hospital when he looked after your dog?'

A few months earlier when my partner was away on holiday with her youngest son, I'd had an operation to put a stent in the artery in my left leg. It was when I took her to the airport and was pushing her baggage trolley up a ramp that I got bad cramp in my left calf. It went away when I rested, but came back as soon as I did any exercise. I didn't mention it to her at the time. Just grin and bear it. I went to the doctor the next day. He couldn't find much of a pulse in my left ankle and a scan showed a partial blockage in my femoral artery. 'Intermittent claudication' is the medical term. I had it fixed straight away. The scan also showed I'd got an abdominal aortic aneurism. Only a minor one but there all the same. It was yet more bad news in a year that was dealing me all black cards.

'Oh, so feeding the dog for a couple of days entitles him to 324 grand, does it?'

'That's the trouble with you. You're always so bloody opinionated. It's always got to be your way, hasn't it? Have some sympathy for god's sake.'

'Wait a minute. Where the fuck's this coming from? Since when were you the judge and jury?'

'The general consensus is that you're being far too harsh and pursuing a vendetta against him. Think of what you're doing to his family.'

'Me? Me? I'm not the one who's hurting his family. He's the bastard that did the deed. He didn't think of his family then, did he? He didn't think of his family 24 times. And what consensus? You mean all the piss-heads in here?'

'I mean the general opinion in Sai Kung. With what you're doing you're going to split the community. You're causing a lot of trouble.'

'I'm causing trouble? I didn't do anything. I'm the fucking victim here, not him.'

'Well, he's asked me to write a character reference for him and I'm going to do it. He deserves a second chance.'

'Pete, that's your decision. It's up to you but before you do it, what about his previous chances?'

'What d'you mean?'

'I mean his previous convictions for theft.'

His jaw dropped.

'Yeah, didn't think he'd told you about that. He got done for nicking money from that health club he was working at. Went to court without a brief, pleaded guilty and got a community service order. He's still on it. That's why his girlfriend kicked him out. Kept that one quiet, didn't he?'

'Who told you that?'

'Hagon. And what about the money he nicked from Sally Chaston?'

'You've only got her word for that.'

'Yeah and you've only got his word. I know who I trust. So think again before you start writing character references.'

This was the first time that Pete and I had had a real row in all the years we'd known each other. I was devastated by what he said to me. Not just devastated; heartbroken. He was taking his side against me. And it sounded like he wasn't alone in his opinions. You read stories in the news about people injuring burglars whilst trying to defend their homes and property getting prosecuted for GBH and manslaughter. The victim turned criminal. It's difficult to comprehend the emotional impact until it happens to you personally. And that's exactly how I felt. All of a sudden, instead of being the victim, I was now the Antichrist. And it got worse. I already knew that I'd made some enemies over the years that I'd been in Sai Kung. I'm the first to admit that I can have an abrasive personality when I'm that way inclined. I'm a great piss-taker and sometimes people take it the wrong way. It's not meant to be vindictive. It's just a bit of fun. Sometimes in a pub debate I'll argue the counterpoint just for the sport of it even though I don't agree with the argument I'm making. But for the last nine years since I was sacked, I'd been living with an anger deep inside me for the injustice I'd been done. I'd learned to control it but it was always there, bubbling away. It didn't make my temperament any more amenable. I suppose that's the reason for what happened next. That and the fact that some people just revel in others' misery. All sorts of horrible stories about me started circulating. I won't repeat them all here because they were very hurtful. I'd always tried to help people when they needed it. If they came to me with problems or for advice, I'd always do my best to help. I lost count of the number of people I'd lent money to over the years to help them through difficult times. Amongst the younger members of my social circle I'd earned the nickname Papa John because of my paternal approach to helping them with their problems. But all of that counted for nothing now. One of the most hurtful stories that did the rounds was that I had given my partner an STD after sleeping with a prostitute. It was spiteful, malicious and totally untrue, but that didn't matter to some. There was a small coven of middle-aged, fat-arsed, *gweipor* divorcees that congregated regularly to rail against everyone and everything. As they stirred their cauldron they lapped it up, as did the committee of vultures that circled overhead, sniffing out carrion.

In such a situation, you don't know how you'll react until it actually happens to you. On the plus side, there were some people who came to me quietly and told me they supported me. That they thought what was happening to me was totally wrong. That they knew who the bad guy was in all this and it wasn't me. It was comforting to know, but they tended to keep their own counsel and not get into debate with the lynch mob. I began to question myself. Were they right? Was I being too hard? Should I just let it go? I was in complete turmoil so I turned to another old friend for advice. His name is Tony White. He was born in Chelsea, is only a year younger than me, and speaks with a broad cockney accent. I first met him in 1986 when I moved to Sai Kung and we'd been through a lot of scrapes together over the years. I called him up and told him I needed to come round to his place for a chat. We sat in his garden, him with his wine box and me with a six-pack. I poured my heart out to him and asked what he thought. What was his advice?

'Mucker, there's only one word to describe that facker. He's a facking thief. And there's a place for facking thieves. It's called the facking nick. And that's where that facker belongs.'

I thought his words summarised the situation clearly and succinctly. It was the best advice I'd received throughout this whole sorry mess. I now knew for sure which path I should tread. No more self-criticism and soul searching. Just get on with it. It made me feel a lot better but it still didn't dispel the desperate feeling of isolation. I was wading through treacle. If I walked into a bar, the conversation would pause for a moment. I saw the looks people gave me. Were they sympathetic or hostile? Difficult to judge sometimes. I put a brave face on it but, inside, I was screaming out for a kind word; for someone to tell me that they'd got my back. And to top it all, the whole thing was affecting my relationship with my partner. That was going even further downhill.

Another call-over hearing was held in the magistrates' court before the trial itself. That was when Hagon showed his hand. He announced that he was removing himself from the case and that another counsel was taking over. This new man typified all the characteristics of the sleazy lawyers you see depicted in Hollywood movies. The stained, ill-fitting, pin-stripe suit. The slicked-down hair, too long at the back. The obsequious, self-ingratiating approach to the bench. He filed various character references. That was when I found out who was who. Pete had provided one and so had Hagon himself, as well as others, some of whom really surprised me. I'd previously thought of them as friends. Clearly my judgment was wrong again. Then an amendment to the defendant's witness statement was quietly slipped in which removed the reference to him finding the chequebook on the floor of my car. That could have been very damaging at trial. If the defendant was shown by the prosecution to still be lying, even to the court, it would weigh heavily against him. So that was the game. Under the pretext of being a concerned friend, Hagon had played me to get as much information as possible that might be useful to the defence before making his exit. Some might think that this amounted to unethical behaviour. Should counsel for the defendant even be communicating with the main prosecution witness at all? But hell, what do ethics count for in the criminal justice system?

At the trial itself, I sat and listened to each of the 24 charges of theft being read out one-by-one and him pleading guilty to each of them in turn. And then it began. The mitigation submissions by Sleazebag.

This was all a terrible mistake made under the pressure, the trauma, of the breakdown of a long-term relationship with his girlfriend. It was completely out of character. This man is an artiste.

He works with children. He does charitable work. He is a pillar of his local community, respected and loved by all. He acknowledges his fault and has tried to make amends by repaying the money. A custodial sentence would be completely inappropriate in this case. A more deserving case for leniency is unlikely to come before the court.

If it's so out of character, enquired the magistrate, what about the CSO he's already serving for theft from his previous employer? Under the terms of that, he should go straight to prison for a repeat offence.

Well, although that was imposed prior to his being charged for the current offences, it was not actually due to take effect until later in February, after the current charges were laid. These events were all part of the same terrible emotional trauma he went through because of the break-up of his long-term relationship. Surely the court could use its discretion and consider the whole series of events in the round? As I said, he is an artiste. He works with children. He is truly remorseful as is shown by his making reparations; and so on and so on, over and over again.

It was the biggest load of bullshit and lies I'd heard in a long time. He'd only been going out with the girl for three or four months. She kicked him out when she found out he'd stolen from her friend. It wasn't done in a moment of emotional anguish. The series of thefts from me were clearly premeditated and executed over more than five months. He'd shown no remorse whatsoever. In fact, the reverse. He was still swanning around, cocky as ever. He hadn't repaid the money. His family had paid it to try to save his arse. It wasn't 'totally out of character'; he'd got plenty of previous. The whole thing was sickening to listen to. And, all the while, the prosecution sat there and said not a word to refute any of these lies.

And that was the beauty of the guilty pleas. No witnesses would be called. I wouldn't be asked to get on the stand and tell the court what really happened; to refute the lies that Sleazebag was feeding the magistrate. In some jurisdictions there are things called victim impact statements. These have two purposes. Firstly to make the perpetrator meet his victim face-to-face so he or she is not just some anonymous statistic and, secondly, for both the court and the defendant to listen to the damage and trauma that the victim has endured as a result of the criminal's actions. These statements are also taken into account when considering sentencing. But we don't have that in Hong Kong. No. With a simple guilty plea the criminal is spared all that and, with a mute prosecutor, his counsel can get away with any old bullshit.

At the end of the hearing, sentencing was deferred pending probation reports. It was at the sentencing hearing that the only piece of truth that came out in court was heard by the magistrate. The probation officer described him as 'a recidivist'. Sleazebag was up again. 'I feel this is a very, very harsh term to describe my client. He is an artiste, he works with children... ' etc. etc. The magistrate pronounced sentence. He made a long speech about how these were very serious charges, how he had betrayed the trust of his closest friend, how he deserved a custodial sentence for his crimes and so on, but, in the light of the mitigating submissions, he was going to hand down a suspended sentence. I couldn't listen to any more. I got up to leave the court. I had been sitting on a bench in the public gallery. These are hard wooden benches. When I got up, my right leg, the one without the stent, had gone numb. I couldn't walk properly and hobbled out dragging my right leg behind me. I was told later that it was gleefully reported in the pub that night that I had stormed out of the court in high dudgeon.

He got six months suspended for three years. I felt totally let down by the criminal justice system. With all the litigation I've been involved in over the years, I have a lot of contacts. I know people who have influence. I could have used those contacts to intervene in the process and make sure the case went up to the District Court instead of being handled by a magistrate. I could have made sure that the pertinent facts got entered into evidence. But I didn't do that. I simply put my faith in the system to do its work and deliver justice. I didn't play any dirty pool. And now, just like the civil justice system, the criminal system had failed me.

Her Majesty Queen Elizabeth II used the term *annus horribilis* to describe the year when the deck dealt her all black cards. Personally I used a more Anglo Saxon term that I wouldn't normally voice in the presence of ladies. I felt totally isolated and alone. I had helped people whenever they needed it. I had given them my friendship, my counsel and my support and, in return, they had deserted me and left me by the roadside when I needed them most. And now I seriously questioned my own judgment. There seemed to be no one left that I could trust, least of all myself. I had put my faith and trust in someone who I thought was my friend, my ally, my confidant and my de facto son. But he had proved to be just a liar, a thief and a coward.

4

Renaissance

'There was a wandering Chinese named Cheng Huan living in Limehouse, and a girl named Shirley.'
Denys Finch Hatton
Baroness Karen von Blixen-Finecke, *Out of Africa*

Saturday, 9 July 2011. Ten years to the day since I was fired. My partner had told me three weeks earlier that she was moving out. She hadn't taken her stuff yet but was away on holiday with her youngest son. I was sitting at home alone with the black dog. The gin bottle was calling to me from the fridge. I'd been here before back in 2004 but this time there were no friends around me. No one to watch over me and help me climb back out of the pit. I could either sit here and just let the darkness swallow me up or I could do something about it. Fight back. Fucking hell Warham. You've done this before and you know exactly where it leads. Don't go there again. Get some fucking spine. You're better than this. You know you are. You beat it last time. You can do it again. Get some balls for fuck's sake. I had to get out of the house and find someone, anyone, to help me put the black dog back in its kennel.

Klaske Kragt is a slender, statuesque, Nordic blonde. She is a farmer's daughter from Friesland in northwest Holland and she is absolutely gorgeous. I'd first met her more than 20 years ago and was immediately struck by her. But I was married and she was involved with someone. We became friends and sometimes we went out together socially, but always with the proviso from her that there'd be no 'funny business'. On such occasions I'd always behaved as the perfect gentlemen. That was the thing about Klaske. You don't mess around with her. She's a strong, well travelled woman with her own opinions and views on life. You only get one chance with her and you'd better not cock it up.

I've always preferred the company of women to men, especially when I'm in trouble. Blokes are useless when it comes to sorting things out. You go down to the pub, get pissed, chew the fat and come away none the wiser, especially if you're trying to resolve problems. Slap her on the arse and tell her to shut up is not much of a solution. Women, on the other hand, look at things differently. They point out things that a bloke would never think of. They give you perspective from a completely different point of view. In my experience, if you need help and advice in such situations, turn to a woman; if you can find one that will speak to you that is.

I went to The Duke. It was safe to go in there because LTC was staying away during the period of his de facto sentence, so I didn't have to worry about Simpson coming out of his box. Simpson is my middle name. It was my paternal great grandmother's maiden name. It is also the name I use for my alter-ego when the red mist descends. He's not a very nice person. Klaske was sitting at a table outside with her best friend, Ailsa, a South African lady who reminds me of Chrissie Hynde. I joined the two rock chicks at their table. I'd already told Klaske what had happened early on in the piece. She, like most people when they first heard, was incredulous. But, unlike many, she was firmly in my camp. She was just the person I needed to help me with the dog. We drank some beer and some gin and talked. And then we went back to my house for a smoke and watched Pink Floyd's 1994 *Pulse* gig at Earl's Court on the DVD. She stayed the night and slept on the sofa in the lounge whilst I repaired to my bedroom on the top floor. When I surfaced around midday the next day she was still there. I gave her a lift home to her place and, before she got out of the car, she gave me a bollocking.

'Now listen, we got a lot closer last night at your place than we've done before. Don't do that again if you don't want to ruin our relationship.'

'OK, sorry, I won't,' I replied, suitably admonished.

That evening I was sitting at home on my own again. I wanted to see Klaske but I daren't phone her. She'd already warned me off. But faint hearts and all that. I went out hunting for her. It didn't take long to find her. She was sitting outside The Duke again. Was she looking for me as well? I didn't know but I could live in hope. We drank and talked and went back to my place again and she stayed the night again but this time she didn't sleep on the sofa. And that was the start of my rebirth. The beginning of a new life. But she didn't make it easy for me. She wasn't looking for someone on the rebound; someone like me. She made that clear and, at one point, told me that the party was over.

'That sounds like you're asking for commitment Warham. Forget it.'

One night I called her and asked if I could come over to her place. She said no and told me to stop calling her. I told her I'd come round and stand outside her house and sing love songs to her until she let me in. So I did. She lived on the second floor. After a few minutes, she slid open the door to her balcony, looked down and said, 'You're a persistent bastard aren't you? You'd better come up.'

And that's when our relationship metamorphosed into its imago stage. At our ages we both came with baggage. She had a couple of suitcases but I'd got a container load. She set some ground rules. We'd known each other for so long it was relatively easy.

'Now listen Warham, if we're going to do this we'd better get a couple of things straight. You can be a complete arsehole sometimes and I can be a real bitch. So we need to know that from the start.'

Couldn't argue with that. She also told me she'd prefer not to see Simpson very often, if at all.

Klaske and I have one thing in common. Neither of us are morning people. Unless I'm forced to, like when I was working, I don't start functioning until at least 11 o'clock. Friends know not to call me before midday if they want anything. If my phone goes in the morning I know it won't be a friend so I don't bother answering it. I have a theory about this. We, all of us, have an internal body clock. That's why we get jet lag. I think it's set when we are born. I was born at a quarter to midnight and that doomed me to be a night-time person. Well, I say doomed. I like the night, especially the early hours when the rest of the world is asleep and the silence is complete, except for the sound of nocturnal animals and insects going about their business. It has a serene, ethereal quality about it. This was a problem when I was a child. My mother's idea of a lie-in on Sunday morning was 9 o'clock. Then the bedroom door would open and the light snapped on. We had those clear 200 watt light bulbs. It was like being illuminated by a searchlight climbing over the fence of Stalag

Luft III. No slow crawl up the gentle ramp from sleep to wakefulness in that house. Instead of dimmer switches and gentle candlelight throwing soft, base-3, curved penumbrae, we had arc-lights casting stark, angular, base-10, black shadows.

To start with, we both kept our own places. We are both very independent and we needed our own insurance policies in case things didn't work out. But they did and, after a while, Klaske brought her stuff over to my place and moved in. Despite the fact that we'd known each other for many years, there was much we didn't know about each other. We spent the evenings sitting in the garden sharing a beer together, watching the sun go down and exchanging stories. During the 20s and 30s in East Africa, before the days of commercial radio and television, people had to make their own entertainment. Often they lived miles apart, working on their farms and plantations. Visitors were a welcome relief from day-to-day life, especially those who were good storytellers. They were in great demand. On those evenings in the garden exchanging stories, I felt transported back to those times as Klaske held me mesmerised by her tales of travel and adventure.

She told me how, after studying horticulture and environmental science at college, one day in her late twenties, she resigned from her job, sold her house, packed up, bought a one-way ticket and set out to see the world. When she was leaving, her mother asked her when she would be back. Her father knew his daughter well. He had the wanderlust in him as well but it had never been fulfilled. 'What, you think she's coming back any time soon?' he replied. She told me stories of riding her motorbike across India. Of being arrested and imprisoned by the police for riding into a restricted area. Of having her ankle badly broken after being forced off the road by a passing truck during another motorbike trip through Greece, and being told by the local doctor to bathe it in seawater to fix it. Of leading trekking parties in the Himalayas and having to make life-or-death decisions when one member of a particular party could go no further. Should she stay with him and try to weather the night or leave him and make a perilous night-time descent alone to fetch help? She chose the latter and she chose correctly. She saved the man's life. She told me all this and much, much more besides. I thought I'd done a lot in my life and seen much of the world but Klaske puts me to shame. She is really one amazing woman. I asked her how it was that she had never been married and had been alone since her break-up from her ex. She told me that many men find her intimidating, especially men who've spent a lot of time in the Far East. They want a woman who is subservient and subordinate to their needs and requirements. Me, that's the last thing I want. I want a woman who thinks for herself, who has opinions, who questions and challenges. And I found one in Klaske.

The first love of my life was Jill Robinson. We were together for more than 20 years. I first met Jill when I was working for Monarch. On 21 July 1983, I was the first officer on a B757 flight from Gatwick to Faro. One of the cabin crew came onto the flight deck and told us there was a passenger down the back who was afraid of flying and getting really agitated. I always felt sorry for people who have a fear of flying because, in my experience, it's the most efficient way of getting from one party to the next. The cabin of an aircraft can seem claustrophobic, mainly because you can't see out of the front. Often if you let people like this have a look out of the front windows, it calms them down. This was, of course, pre-9/11, before locked cockpit doors and everyone having to creep around in fear whilst the politicians use national security as an excuse to strip away our civil liberties.

'Bring her up the front and I'll show her my knobs and switches,' I said to the hostie. In these situations you never know what to expect. Often, when you get told that a young boy wants to come for a look, it's not the boy – it's his dad. Then he stands there and tries to ask intelligent questions. You try to humour them and be polite but, sometimes, I couldn't resist having a bit of fun.

'Gosh there's a lot of switches aren't there?'

'Yes, 597 to be precise.'

'Do you know what they're all for?'

'Not a clue but don't worry, they've all got labels on them. Look at this one. ESS AC BUS. Remind me again, skipper, what does that stand for?'

Or 'Do you always fly this plane on this route?'

'Tell me, do you have a car?'

'Yes.'

'Do you always drive it or does your wife drive it sometimes?'

'No, sometimes the wife drives it.'

'When you do drive it, do you always drive it to the same place?'

'No, of course not.'

'Well then, why should I always drive this plane on this route?'
Cue puzzled look trying to work out whether or not he's having the
piss taken out of him.

The flight deck door opened and there stood Jill Robinson. She
was beautiful and, just at that moment, the sunlight angled in through
the cabin windows and shone through the thin summer dress she was
wearing showing me the outline of her body in silhouette. I invited
her to take a seat and we chatted. I was right. Being able to look out
of the front windows calmed her down and, before she returned to the
cabin, I elicited the flight number she was returning on at the end of
her holiday. By a happy coincidence, it happened that I was also
operating that flight and I invited her onto the flight deck for most of
the trip back. By the end of it I had her phone number. Needless to
say, it wasn't a coincidence. I'd been into crew control and talked a
friendly rostering clerk into putting me on the flight.

I didn't call her straight away. In fact I didn't call her for a year.
My dance card was pretty much full at the time and there wasn't the
opportunity to pursue new leads. That was the situation up until the
time when a woman I was dating relatively frequently told me that
she was going up to London for a night out with the girls and would
be staying over. However, her plans changed and she thought it
would be a nice surprise to come round to my place unannounced at
two o'clock in the morning. It might have been, had it not been for
the fact that I was actually in my bedroom entertaining another lady
when she arrived. This led to a most unseemly confrontation between
the two parties concerned, with the result that they both informed me
somewhat vociferously that they would prefer not to spend time in
my company in the future. So it was that, a year after first meeting
Jill, my dance card suddenly became vacant and I gave her a call. She
worked for Thames Television in London and I went to Euston to
meet her for lunch. That was the start of some of the happiest years of
my life so far. When I got the job with Cathay, she packed in her job
and came to live in Hong Kong with me. It was during the golden
years of Cathay, before the bean counters got control. We travelled
the world together and did amazing things. We took the Orient
Express from London to Istanbul, waking up one morning in our state
cabin on the ship to the sight of our transit through the Corinth Canal.
We flew on Concorde from London to New York to do our Christmas
shopping in Manhattan. We saw Guns 'n' Roses at Madison Square
Garden. We went on safari in Kenya and then learned to scuba-dive

in the Seychelles on our way home. But our favourite place was Mauritius and Le Touessrok Hotel became almost a second home. Jill was the love of my life. She was my friend, my lover, my confidante and my soul mate. When I first took her to introduce her to my mother, I asked what she thought of her.

'Well, for some reason, she seems to understand you,' came the reply. As always with mothers, she hit the nail squarely on the head. She did understand me. She knew what makes me tick. We had some wonderful years together, but then we made a terrible mistake. She got very involved in the Animals Asia Foundation that we had set up together and, at the same time, I got very involved in my work for the HKAOA. The mistake we made was that we did not reserve enough time for each other, to nurture our love. We got so wound up in what we were doing that we started to drift apart. And by the time I realised what was happening it was too late. Words were said between us that could never be taken back and, in 2004, we split up. Between us, we had broken it.

I often rationalised afterwards that many (or maybe most) men never get to have a true love in their lives. They leave school, go to work at some mundane job, marry someone who is convenient, start a family, spend two weeks each year in Majorca during works stop-fortnight and devote the rest of their lives to trying to pay off the mortgage, the school fees and the bills before retiring on a meagre state pension if the government hasn't already stolen it by then. I had had a brilliant job. Before it was taken from me, I got paid to do something that I truly enjoyed. I travelled the world. I'd seen and done things that most people never even get the chance to see or do. My mother always told me I was lucky. I disagreed. I am a firm believer that you make your own luck in life. If you're born with a talent, exploit it to the full. If an opportunity arises, grab it with both hands and make the most of it. So, I rationalised, I've had a good life, I've experienced things that most men can only dream of and, if that's over now, then I'd have to live with my memories and be grateful for the times that I'd had. It was a very hard road to travel to get to that state of mind but that's what I managed to do.

After Jill, I had another relationship. Like all these things, it began with high hopes and optimism but, ultimately, it too failed. It started when SKiNC was in its heyday. I suppose my apparent rock 'n' roll lifestyle at the time was attractive to someone who had spent a relatively sheltered life up until then. But the novelty wore off and, after a while, she stopped coming to the gigs because the music we played was 'too noisy'. It didn't help that I was going through a very difficult time personally with all the problems I had to deal with and it didn't make me the easiest of people to live with. After that, it wasn't a long stretch from parties and late nights to pipe and slippers in front of the telly. That was never going to work for me. When it came to an end it was no one's fault really. It just didn't work out. We both tried but we both failed. I guess I couldn't give her the sort of life that she wanted.

And then Klaske and I got together. I cannot believe my luck. Yes Mother, if you're listening from your new home in the stars, this time I really am lucky. Most men don't even get one bite of the cherry and I've been given two. I have found the second great love of my life. I have found another woman who truly understands me, who knows what's hidden deep down inside me and what makes me tick. I have found another true friend, lover, confidante and soul mate. And, this time around, I'm going to do everything in my power to make sure that I don't fuck it up again.

Early in 2012, Klaske and I went to The Duke one afternoon for a beer. We sat down at an outside table. I didn't notice that Hagon was sitting at the next table in the corner. Klaske turned and said to me, 'Oh dear, I suppose it had to happen. Look who's inside.'
I turned round and saw Jimmy Lau and his father, Jimmy Senior, sitting at the bar.
'Who? Jimmy?'
'No. He's just gone to the toilet. It's LTC.'
'What? What the fuck's he doing here?'
Then I noticed Hagon and the penny dropped. This was the day that he would have got out of prison had the magistrate done his job properly and here he was with the whole team to give him moral support. Just then the waitress came out with our beers.
'I didn't know you were serving fucking thieves and liars in here now.'
She scampered back inside and Hagon shrank into his corner.
'Let's get the fuck out of here before I do something I'll regret later.'
I went inside to pay the bill. He was still in the toilet. Jimmy Senior and I went back a long way. When the original founder of The Duke, Sandy Nichols died intestate with an estranged wife and two sons in

the UK and a partner in Hong Kong, we both worked with the two families involved to help sort out the mess. He was sitting there at the bar right in front of me but I didn't know what to say to him. So I said nothing. And he did the same. Jimmy told me later that his father felt exactly the same way as me. He just didn't know what to say. When Jimmy first told him what his son had done to me, his first words were, 'Why does it have to be John of all people?' I paid the bill and we left.

A few days later, we were sitting at home in the early evening and my phone went. It was a friend calling to tell me that LTC was in The Duke drinking. My mind was raging again. After 20 minutes or so, I turned to Klaske and said, 'I'm sorry babe but I'm going to have to go down there and sort this out.'

'All right, if you have to, but try not to do anything stupid,' was her reply. I didn't know what I was going to do. I wanted to see him inside where he belonged. I'd thought about provoking him until he took a swing at me. That would put him in the slammer while he was still on a suspended sentence. I'd thought all sorts of things but, when I walked into the bar, I had no plan. But Simpson was well and truly out of his box by the time I got there. I went to the far end of the bar and spoke to Ricky Hie, the owner. I told him he had a choice to make. Either he served me and barred him, or he was losing my custom. Given that I spent a lot more in there than LTC did (unlike him I actually paid my bar bills), I thought it a good argument. But it was completely unfair of me of course. It wasn't Ricky's problem and he pointed that out when he said we were both his customers and he shouldn't have to choose. Simpson walked over to the bastard and knocked the beer out of his hand. It smashed on the floor and he started screaming like a girl.

'What are you doing? What are you doing?'
The biggest of his mates grabbed Simpson by the jacket and pulled him away. Ricky came over and we went outside.

'I'm telling you Ricky, it's him or me. Either you bar that cunt or I'm not coming in here again.'

'I can't do that John.'

'OK, well you've just lost my custom.'

'Well, will you pay your bar tab before you go?'

'No I won't. Tell that fucker to pay it.'

And with that I left. I went home to Klaske and told her what had happened. I told her that, despite her best advice, I had gone and done something completely stupid. In short, I'd behaved like a complete arsehole. We sat and talked for a long time. She pointed out that all we had to do was wait. That he couldn't help himself. That, in time, he'd do the same thing again to someone else and then people would see the truth. That it didn't matter what other people think. It's our life to live it as we choose and nothing else matters. She was right. It was a turning point in my life. I resolved there and then that, from now on, things were going to be different. If people didn't like the way I lived, tough shit. If people didn't like the things I said, tough shit. If people didn't like my attitude, tough shit. If people disapproved of me and Klaske, tough shit. In fact the lot of them could all go fuck themselves. From now on we're living life our way.

Klaske also told me something else. She said that when Ricky asked me to pay my bar tab, I should have given him an unsigned cheque and told him to get LTC to sign it. That's what I mean about women's advice. Completely different perspective. It was a loose end though and it wasn't Ricky's fault. A few weeks later, he got married. For a wedding present I sent him what I owed him together with a generous tip.

5

Cost Benefit Analysis

'If automobiles had followed the same development cycle as the computer, a Rolls Royce would today cost $100, get a million miles per gallon, and explode once a year killing everyone inside.'

Robert Cringely

On 2 September 2006, a Royal Air Force Nimrod XV230 exploded in mid-air and crashed 25 miles west-north-west of Kandahar Airfield in Afghanistan killing all 14 military personnel on board. The pilot had reported a fire in his bomb-bay. He tried to reach Kandahar Airfield, making an emergency descent from 23,000 feet to 3,000 feet. An RAF Harrier followed the Nimrod down and its pilot reported seeing a wing explode, followed a few seconds later by the rest of the aircraft. [1]

The report of the initial board of enquiry published on 7 December 2007 concluded that the most probable cause of the crash was leaking fuel having come into contact with a supplementary cooling pack air pipe at 400 degrees Celsius in the No. 7 tank dry bay after entering a gap between two types of insulation. The aircraft caught fire and 14 people lost their lives because of a fuel leak that should never have happened. As a result of public pressure, coupled with the findings of the coroner who led the inquest into the deaths of the crew members, who stated that the entire Nimrod fleet had 'never been airworthy from the first time it was released to service' and urged that it should be grounded, the Secretary of State ordered a Nimrod Review board to be convened and set out its terms of reference on 13 December 2007. It was chaired by Hon. Sir Charles Haddon-Cave QC.

Born on 20 March 1956, Haddon-Cave was educated at King's School Canterbury and read law at Pembroke College, Cambridge where he gained his MA. He was called to the bar at Gray's Inn in 1978 and Hong Kong in 1980. He practiced at the commercial bar from 1980–2011 and was appointed Queen's Counsel in 1999. He had previously appeared in many major aviation and marine disaster cases such as the Manchester air disaster (1985), *Herald of Free Enterprise* (1987), Kegworth air crash (1989), *Marchioness* disaster (1989), *Braer* disaster (1993), BP Trent tragedy (1993) and the Knight Air crash (1995).

On 28 October 2009, Haddon-Cave presented his report. It was summarised by the statement, 'Its production is a story of incompetence, complacency and cynicism. The best opportunity to prevent the accident to XV230 was tragically lost.'

The report accused the Ministry of Defence (MoD) of 'deep organisational trauma' resulting from the strategic defence review of 1998; of sacrificing safety to cut costs, resulting in a 'systemic breach' of the military covenant and branded a safety review of the Nimrod MR2 carried out by the MoD, BAE Systems and QinetiQ as a 'lamentable job'. It also condemned the change of organisational culture within the MoD between 1998 and 2006, when financial targets came to distract from safety, quoting a former senior RAF officer who told the inquiry, 'There was no doubt that the culture of the time had switched. In the days of the RAF chief engineer in the 1990s, you had to be on top of airworthiness. By 2004 you had to be on top of your budget if you wanted to get ahead.'

The damning report singled out ten people for criticism. Five were from the MoD, including two very senior military officers of four-star rank, three from BAE Systems, and two from QinetiQ, a private company specialising in defence technology.

General Sir Sam Cowan was promoted to four-star general in September 1998 and appointed the first Chief of Defence Logistics in April 1999. In this role he was responsible for carrying out the government's plan to unite the separate logistics support agencies for the Royal Navy, Army and RAF into a single Defence Logistics Organisation. In 2000 he announced a target of reducing costs by 20 per cent by 2005. Mr Haddon-Cave was scathing about this money-saving edict. He wrote: 'The strong impression one gets from the witnesses and the evidence is that the "strategic goal" of 20 per cent and other required financial savings were implemented across the board with a ruthless, if not "Stalinistic", efficiency.' Mr Haddon-Cave criticised General Cowan for not giving enough thought to the impact of imposing his cost-cutting target. He should have realised it could come at the expense of safety and airworthiness, the report said. Cowan left the post in August 2002.

Air Chief Marshal Sir Malcolm Pledger succeeded Cowan as Chief of Defence Logistics in September 2002 despite later admitting to Mr Haddon-Cave's review he did not believe he was fully qualified for the job. The report noted he was to some extent 'handed a poisoned chalice' but it went on to criticise him. It suggested he was torn between delivering the target of 20 per cent cost savings and supporting the conflicts in Afghanistan and Iraq that were then underway. Mr Haddon-Cave said he should have questioned whether it was 'feasible, realistic and sensible' to press on with the 20 per cent goal at the same pace and within the same timescale. 'There should, at least, have been pause for thought,' the report said.

Group Captain George Baber was the leader of the MoD integrated project team (IPT) responsible for a safety review of the RAF's Nimrods that took place between 2001 and 2005. Mr Haddon-Cave accused Group Capt. Baber of a 'fundamental failure of leadership' in drawing up the 'safety case' into potential dangers in the fleet. He allowed himself to be distracted by other matters, failed to follow processes he himself introduced and did not take reasonable care in signing off the project, the report said. Mr Haddon-Cave noted he appeared to have been more interested in 'trumpeting' the fact that it was the first safety review of an old aircraft than ensuring its contents were correct. He wrote, 'He failed to give the Nimrod safety case the priority it deserved. In doing so, he failed, in truth, to make safety his first priority.'

Wing Commander Michael Eagles, as head of air vehicle for the Nimrod, was supposed to be in charge of managing production of the safety review. But the report found that he delegated the project 'wholesale' to an MoD civilian worker called Frank Walsh, who was too inexperienced and not competent enough to manage it. Mr

Haddon-Cave wrote, 'Michael Eagles failed to give adequate priority, care and personal attention to the NSC task. He failed properly to utilise the resources available to him within the Nimrod IPT to ensure the airworthiness of the Nimrod fleet.'

Frank Walsh was safety manager for the Nimrod review and primary point of contact with the BAE Systems team carrying out the work. The report noted that he should never have been placed in the position of having to manage the project with little or no supervision or guidance. But it said he assessed hazards himself in a 'slapdash' manner and failed to alert his superiors when he realised he had overlooked important issues. Mr Haddon-Cave wrote: 'Frank Walsh's failure to put his hand up and admit to his superiors that he had overlooked matters, and then effectively to cover over his mistakes, is his most serious failing. In doing so, he failed to act honourably. In matters of safety, there can be no compromise on openness and honesty.'

Chris Lowe, as chief airworthiness engineer for BAE Systems, was heavily involved in preparing the main documents in the Nimrod safety review. The report said he bore the heaviest responsibility for the 'poor planning, poor management and poor execution' of the project. Mr Haddon-Cave rejected his claim that he was only keeping a 'top level' eye on the review and said he was 'clearly very much hands-on'. Mr Lowe was ambitious for himself and his company, and hoped the Nimrod project would enhance his standing and open up new commercial avenues for BAE Systems, the report said. But he 'underestimated the nature of the task and overestimated his own abilities', ignoring the fact that the review was flawed and not finished, Mr Haddon-Cave found. The report said: 'What really mattered was producing an impressive-looking set of reports on time which could be trumpeted by his department as a success. He was ultimately prepared to draw a veil over the incomplete nature of the work. The actual content, quality and completeness of the work was not [of] paramount importance because he, like most others, assumed the Nimrod to be "safe anyway" because of its service history.'

Richard Oldfield was the leader of the Nimrod review for BAE Systems. The report found he did not come clean about large gaps in the analysis of possible risks and failed to manage the project properly.

Eric Prince as BAE's flight systems and avionics manager, played a key role in the Nimrod safety project. Mr Haddon-Cave said: 'He too was prepared to see the customer be given a deliberately misleading impression as to the completeness of the work.'

Martyn Mahy was Nimrod review task manager for defence technology firm QinetiQ, which was the independent adviser for the project. Mr Haddon-Cave criticised him for failing to do his job properly in certain key areas and failing to give any real independent assurance. The report noted that he either signed off or approved the signing off of BAE Systems reports without reading them.

Colin Blagrove was employed as technical assurance manager for the Nimrod safety review. It was his ultimate responsibility to ensure QinetiQ did not sign off anything unless it was appropriate to do so. The report found that he failed in this 'critical' task.[2]

The strategic defence review of 1998 that was the prime cause of the catastrophic change in ethos in the armed services was initiated and condoned by the government of the warmonger Anthony Charles Lynton Bliar a year after he came into power. As the prime minister at the time, he is, therefore, directly responsible for the deaths of 14 personnel who were serving their country. They put their faith and their trust in a chain of command, which had a duty of care and a responsibility to protect them. Those people, from the highest level all the way down to the junior managers, betrayed their trust and let them down miserably. Why? And in pursuit of what? Arrogance, incompetence, money and self-aggrandisement are words that spring to mind. The question may be asked, where was the cost benefit analysis when the cuts were decided upon? The obvious answer is there was none. The costs were clearly considered but there the analysis, if it can be called that, ends. A 20 per cent costs cut across the board is not an analysis. It was a politically expedient, arbitrary figure selected without any consideration of the probable consequences. And its implementation was ruthless. Even when the strategic situation had changed markedly by 2002, the same misguided policies continued to be pursued by the successors to the original architects. The original in-house Nimrod safety review, which came about in part because of repeated reports and complaints by the operational crews, was a cover-up and a whitewash. And the chain of command was characterised by unqualified, inexperienced and incompetent managers.

Now, where have we heard a similar story before? Arbitrary targets, such as chopping RTKs (revenue tonne kilometres), imposed by bean-counter mentality senior management. Refusal to acknowledge and/or address flight safety concerns being voiced repeatedly by operational crews. Rigged and pre-determined in-house reviews of safety issues such as roster instability. Appointment of inexperienced and unqualified managers such as a DFO with no relevant qualifications or operational experience whatsoever. Oh yes, I remember now. Cathay Pacific Airways, Operation Better Shape.

Charles Haddon-Cave's father, Sir Philip Haddon-Cave KBE CMG, had a life-long connection with Hong Kong. He served as its Financial Secretary from 1971 to 1981 and as Chief Secretary from 1981 to 1985. His son, similarly, has a long connection with the territory. During the time when Tony Tyler was chief executive of Cathay Pacific, he approached the airline with a view to undertaking an in-depth safety review of its operations. His offer was declined. On 13 April 2010, Cathay flight CX780 from Surabaya to Hong Kong, a twin-engine A330 aircraft, suffered a double engine failure and made an emergency landing on arrival. The final report of the accident investigation by the Hong Kong CAD was not published until July 2013. However, in the interim period, in March 2011, John Slosar replaced Tyler as chief executive; coincident with which Charles Haddon-Cave undertook a month-long audit of the company at a cultural, organisational and governance level. This was initially trumpeted to be a full, open and frank review, the results of which would be passed on to all concerned within the airline. The story soon changed. The report rapidly became an 'eyes-only' document for senior management and only selected excerpts were published to the employees in general in what was dubbed by one wag as 'the SCMP (*South China Morning Post*) version' of the report. During his review, Haddon-Cave attended a monthly flight operations safety meeting. The room was packed. It was standing room only and there was a lively Q&A with lots of debate. Afterwards, he was standing in the Dakota Bar talking to one of the members of the flight safety committee. The conversation was reported to have gone along the following lines.

'Well, that was an interesting meeting.'

'Yes, it was.'

'Is it usually that well attended?'

'No.'

'Are there usually so many questions and so much debate?'

'No.'

'Are you suggesting that it was a put-up job for my benefit?'

'Yes.'

His report was particularly scathing about Cathay's industrial relations policy towards its pilots and, in particular, its handling of *The 49ers* issue. It recommend that, unless and until the company came out into the open and admitted responsibility for the fiasco, the stigma would remain and there would continue to be little trust between the pilots and management. A number of people were singled out for criticism.

Barley, who was DFO when *The 49ers* were fired, had retired in 2002 but retained the position of chairman of the Board Safety Review Committee which meets every six months in Hong Kong. It's a nice little sinecure with a stipend and travel perks. After the report came out his post was terminated. He was last heard of in July 2014 taking up the position of general manager operations at Fiji Airways. Let us hope that the pilots there have done their homework and give him an appropriate welcome.

One might ask, in the light of the Haddon-Cave report, has the corporate ethos now changed? In May 2010, Cathay was fined the equivalent of HK$26 million by the Korean Fair Trade Commission for its air cargo pricing practices. In November of the same year the European Union announced the imposition of a fine of EUR57 million on Cathay for price-fixing on air cargo charges. In April 2013 a New Zealand court imposed a fine of NZ$4.3 million for anti-trust law violations. In June 2013 it was fined CA$1.5 million by the Canadian Competition Bureau. In February 2014 the airline agreed to pay US$65 million to settle an anti-trust class action in the USA accusing it, similarly, of taking part in a conspiracy to fix air freight shipping prices. In November 2014, Cathay was fined AU$11.75 million by the Australian Competition and Consumer Commission also for air cargo price-fixing. Many other airlines that were also involved in these price-fixing cartels have had similar swingeing fines imposed on them, but the 'everyone else was doing it as well' defence is no excuse. These repeated offences speak to the underlying ethos of the airline's corporate culture. Of course, whilst these fines were imposed relatively recently, some of them relate to offences committed ten or more years earlier when the likes of Turnbull, Tyler and Chen had their hands on the tiller; not to mention the zoologist DFO Rhodes who became director cargo after his removal from that post in August 2010.

Notwithstanding matters of ethics, how do these massive financial penalties stand up to a cost benefit analysis? Let us forget for a moment concepts such as net and future present value and just do some simple arithmetic that even a zoologist should understand. At current exchange rates (November 2014), these fines come to a total of US$153.8 million. Let us assume that these offences took place over an eight-year period from 2002 to 2010 and look at the annual report for 2006, in the middle of that period. Cargo ATKs (actual tonne kilometres) are reported as 10,391 with a load factor of 68.3 per cent. This generated a turnover of US$1,536 million, which equates to 21.76 per cent of the airline's total turnover. After tax profit attributable to Cathay Pacific shareholders is reported as US$524 million. Taking 21.76 per cent of that figure as a realistic estimation gives profit for cargo services of US$114 million. If we take one eighth of the total fines levied for the eight-year period, this gives a figure of US$19.2 million which equates to 16.86 per cent of profit for the year. Simplistic though the arithmetic is, we're in the right ballpark. Around 17 per cent of the profit generated on cargo operations was lost because senior managers broke the law. So, the questions must be asked, has this behaviour really been in the best interests of the shareholders and, if not, who should be held responsible?

Turnbull was ousted from the position of chairman of Swire Pacific in January 2006 after less than a year in the post. His departure came hot on the heels of the House of Lords judgment in favour of *The 49ers* in the UK, although whether or not the two incidents were related is a matter for conjecture. After leaving Cathay he was involved in the disastrous Allco Finance Group collapse in 2008 and has held various non-executive directorships in a variety of companies such as Green Dragon Gas Ltd., Greka Drilling Ltd., Sands China Ltd. and The Wharf (Holdings) Ltd.[3] He is occasionally to be found hanging around like a bad smell in the Captain's Bar of the Mandarin Oriental Hotel.

On 19 April 2010, Cathay announced that Philip Chen Nan-lok was severing his ties with the Swire Group after a career spanning 33 years. Again, coincidentally, this came on the heels of the Hong Kong High Court ruling in favour of *The 49ers*. Whether or not his dismal performance as a witness for the defendants (or brilliant performance for the plaintiffs) during the trial had anything to do with his departure is also a matter for conjecture.

Later that same year, it was announced that Rhodes, also a main witness for the defendants at the High Court trial, would be moving from the position of DFO to director cargo; a definite move down in the pecking order. If these other 'moves' were a result of their failure to produce the goods against *The 49ers*, how come Rhodes survived the chop? There is a story that did the rounds at the time, possibly apocryphal, that when he was called in to receive his marching orders, he went in lawyered up. He has a reputation as a hoarder. He keeps documents and records going back a long time; perhaps as an insurance policy? When he went into the meeting, so the story goes, he threatened to spill the beans on what really took place during *The 49ers* fiasco; which revelations might open up a number of people at least to severe embarrassment if not possible criminal charges. Of course, this is only scuttlebutt. Whatever the reasons, he kept his job albeit in a diminished role. In September 2013 he was demoted further to the post of director people. Or perhaps he got out of cargo just before the shit hit the fan. In any event, of the five main protagonists directly responsible for the mismanagement of industrial relations with Cathay's pilots, he is the only one to have survived.

The same cannot be said of Tyler. His departure from the post of chief executive was announced in December 2010, ostensibly due to his approaching retirement age. Unlike the others though, he did not go quietly. He did the rounds of the media giving statements and interviews, some of which were almost MacArthuresque in nature with promises of 'I shall return'. These culminated in a luncheon speech on 17 March 2011 at the Foreign Correspondents Club (FCC) in Hong Kong. The speech itself was more of the same but, during the Q&A, a question was asked from the floor that showed he had finally learned something.

'Tony, there's a book coming out about *The 49ers*, what do you think about that?'

'I'm sure it'll be a best seller,' came the reply; and no more. Finally he had learned to keep his trap shut where we were concerned. In July 2011, he took up the position of director general and CEO of the International Air Transport Association (IATA), which is the trade association of the world's airlines. Some aviation pundits are of the view that IATA is one of the biggest price-fixing cartels in the industry. If that is true, then, given past experience, he should fit in well.

The next time I saw Tyler was on the BBC being interviewed about Malaysian Airlines flight MH370 which went missing on 8 March 2014. Later that month, during an interview on CNN, Chris McLaughlin, senior vice-president of external affairs for Inmarsat, whose engineers were able to plot probable position lines from data received from the missing aircraft, had questioned why, even after the loss of Air France flight AF447 in the South Atlantic in 2009, there was still no global legislation to make aircraft direction and distance reporting compulsory. He went on to say, 'On ships, you have long range identification and tracking and they have to log in every six hours... well obviously on aircraft they need to log in at 500 [to] 600 knots every 15 minutes. That could be done tomorrow with the existing technology that we have [already] but the mandate is not there globally.'

His statement is quite true of course. Third-generation glass cockpit aircraft onwards had the option to have this type of equipment fitted. When Cathay took delivery of its first Boeing 747-400 in 1989, it came as standard fit, as did further deliveries of Airbus A330 & 340 aircraft. At first it was seen as a great novelty and the operations staff in FOCC (flight operations control centre) took great delight in being able to continuously monitor the positions of all the aircraft on their watch. I remember on one occasion during a flight from Australia to Hong Kong, whilst transiting Indonesian airspace, being called up by an FOCC bod to be informed that I was 70 miles off my flight planned track. I thanked him very much for the information and advised him that if he'd like to pop up to the flight deck and have a look out of the windows at the massive line squall of Cbs (cumulonimbus clouds) that I was trying to circumnavigate whilst crossing the ITCZ (inter-tropical convergence zone), he was more than welcome. The novelty soon wore off when the first bills for services from the satellite operators started coming in. The equipment was rapidly downgraded to transmit what was considered to be 'essential' information only, such as engine performance monitoring telemetry. It did not include position reporting.

But who would be resistant to a globally mandated position reporting system for aircraft? Or, perhaps a better question might be, who would have input into drafting such legislation? An obvious answer would be the airlines and their global representative, IATA. At the IATA annual operations conference held in Kuala Lumpur on 1 April 2014, Tyler stated that, 'It is difficult to believe that an aircraft can disappear under the current technology.' Well, not if the technology is disabled to save money it's not. He announced that IATA would convene an expert task force that will include ICAO (International Civil Aviation Organization). 'This group will examine all of the options available for tracking commercial aircraft against the parameters of implementation, investment, time and complexity to achieve the desired coverage,' he stated. He also said that live streaming of data is an issue that should be 'looked at quite carefully', but questioned the technical practicality of having 100,000 flights daily streaming all data. Presumably his degree in jurisprudence qualifies him to pose such a question. Bit of a difference from Chris McLaughlin's statement that it, 'could be done tomorrow'. In the interview I saw later on the BBC he crystallised the waffle when he said words to the effect that, 'We'd have to consider the cost.' My immediate thought when I heard him say this was, 'Try telling that to the families and loved ones of the passengers that were lost on that flight. I wonder what the result of their cost benefit analysis might be.' It took me straight back to that union/management meeting in the 90s when Turnbull sat across the table and said, 'We've done the CBA on accidents and we can afford a hull loss every three years.'

But, true to Tyler's word, IATA announced the formation of its Aircraft Tracking Task Force (ATTF). Two months later, in June, this new group issued a 'Frequently Asked Questions' newsletter. One of the questions posed in this document is:

> *Didn't the industry face the same issues after AF447 and do nothing?*

The response given, in part, is:

> The AF447 Final Report recommendations related to locator beacons, deployable flight recorders and other accident-specific

location capabilities, *not specifically flight tracking* [emphasis added].

It is correct to say that the BEA report did make recommendations relating to locator beacons and flight recorders. However, in addition to those recommendations, in paragraph 4.1.1 of the report, the BEA also recommended that EASA and ICAO:

> Study the possibility of making it mandatory for aeroplanes performing public transport flights to regularly transmit basic flight parameters (for example position, altitude, speed, heading).

So, at best, the ATTF Q&A statement is misleading and, at worst, it is untrue.

In addition to this, following on from Chris McLaughlin's interview, on 11 May 2014, little more than a month after the formation of the ATTF and immediately prior to the conference on aircraft tracking hosted by ICAO in Montreal on 12 May, Inmarsat made the following announcement:

> Inmarsat has confirmed it has proposed to ICAO a free global airline tracking service over the Inmarsat network, as part of the anticipated adoption of further aviation safety service measures by the world's airlines following the loss of MH370.

> This service is being offered to all 11,000 commercial passenger aircraft, which are already equipped with an Inmarsat satellite connection, virtually 100 per cent of the world's long haul commercial fleet.

> In addition... Inmarsat will also offer both an enhanced position reporting facility... and a 'black box in the cloud' service under which... historic and real-time flight data recorder and cockpit voice recorder information can be streamed off an aircraft...

> Rupert Pearce, CEO of Inmarsat, said: '... we are confident that the proposals we have presented to ICAO and IATA represent a major contribution to enhancing aviation services on a global

basis. In the wake of the loss of MH370, we believe this is simply the right thing to do.'

So, from this, it appears that we have a ready-made, off-the-shelf solution that, in the words of Chris McLaughlin, could be implemented 'tomorrow'. And it's free. Surely ICAO, IATA and the world's airlines should jump at this opportunity to improve flight safety in a quantum leap? But they haven't and the ATTF Q&A paper doesn't even mention the Inmarsat offer. Why not?

On Monday, 9 March 2015, almost a year later, Tyler gave a lunchtime speech at the FCC in Hong Kong. The title of his presentation was, 'The Airline Industry's Challenges and Opportunities'. Coincidentally I happened to be in Hong Kong and went along to listen to what he had to say. It turned out that the whole thing was an unashamed lobbying opportunity on behalf of the airlines, and in particular Cathay Pacific who had five senior board members in attendance, on who should pay for the new proposed third runway at CLK, Hong Kong Chek Lap Kok airport. (Needless to say, according to him, it should be the government, i.e. the taxpayer, and not the airlines.) He did, however, make some reference to aircraft tracking in the early part of his speech. The gist of his remarks was that the technology is not yet in place to implement a global aircraft tracking service. Again, this seems to be totally at odds with Inmarsat's view; so who is right? The Q&A session after the speech was revealing.

Keith Bradsher, *New York Times*:
Q. You talked about how on the tracking issue it's a question not simply of cost but of technology. But that said it seems to move *so* slowly ah… and we get these episodic interest, expressions of interest such as after the difficulty, initial difficulty in finding AirAsia. Would it be helpful for IATA to set some kind of a very clear deadline for picking a tracking technology or will this debate over the different space-based technologies and so forth go on for several years?

A. Um… I, I don't think it *is* moving that, that slowly I mean really you know er… er… twelve months after the erm… after the disappearance of MH370, or within twelve months, ICAO had convened a conference they, they had um… various task forces had, had met, discussed the issue reported and so on and a clear direction was set... only these things, these things don't happen overnight erm... but nevertheless it's important to get it right rather than to, to rush for one particular technology. For example you know if, if, if erm... you know there's a debate going on. It's not quite the same issue, but there's a debate going on about what's called deployable erm... flight data recorders. So in other words should, should aircraft have some sort of flight data recorder that will, you know, if, if it does go into the ocean will separate itself from the aircraft and float on the surface. That debate's going on and at the same time the debate's going on about streaming flight data recorders. Now if you're going to *stream* flight data you certainly don't need a deployable flight data recorder so let's, let's, let's look at, you know, in a... clear light of day, let's take our time to make sure we're backing the right horse and then... make sure that that really delivers and I think that's the important, the important way. That's the way the industry's always developed. It's been successful in the past, let's make sure we don't um... you know, because of the pressures and the clamour to er... to produce an instant solution, let's make sure we don't get it wrong.

Tara Joseph, FCC President:
Q. So you don't think we need a deadline?

A. The industry is working fast there is, there's a deadline in terms of the, the new 15 minute tracking is, is designed to be in place by November next year so that's very clear. That's what we're working to at the moment erm... and, as I say, I personally believe that when the space-based ADSB starts to be um... a reality we, we may see um... we may see other ways of doing this and they may give us, point us in a different direction but let's wait and see.

The Author:
Q. Tony I'd like to just um... follow up on this business about aircraft tracking. Now you've given us er... reasons why there's the amount of delay there is and complexity of different systems. How do you reconcile all that to the statement made by representatives of Inmarsat in May last year prior to the ICAO

conference, that with current technology they have in place *now*, um… they could implement it *tomorrow* and that they would be able to cover 95 per cent of the aircraft erm… of the airline um… mainstream airlines. So you're telling us though that the technology isn't there. Inmarsat are saying though they can implement it tomorrow. So there's a bit of a dichotomy there – could you explain that to us please?

A. Erm… yes and again I'm not a, I'm not a technical expert John. You probably know a lot more about the technical side than I do but erm… Inmarsat as you, as you say it doesn't offer global coverage and some of the areas where it doesn't offer coverage are, are areas where, where… er… are really the areas that you're concerned about, because they offer coverage largely, you know, where there are other um… technologies that, that currently work as well. There may well be that they're covering some, some blank spaces which, which are not covered by anybody else but I believe that, that it's important with new, other new technologies emerging and a competitor of Inmarsat is, is erm… Ariane is planning to launch a lot of satellites which will, which will give full global coverage. I do think it's important that we, as I said earlier, that we back the right horse erm… and that erm… we, we, we make sure that it's something that *is* sustainable financially for, for airlines because this is, you know, this is, it is, it's a consideration you *cannot* ignore and one that will long-term do the job as well as it can and, and, and others who are much better qualified than I to assess the technical erm… advantages and disadvantages of various schemes are, are suggesting we're not yet at the, at the point where we know for sure the right way to go.

Of course, I didn't say that Inmarsat doesn't offer global coverage. What I said was that they could cover 95 per cent of the *aircraft* currently in use. In fact, Inmarsat's website states that:

We currently operate 11 satellites in geosynchronous orbit. We position our satellites to transmit radio beams in two global configurations, covering the oceans and the major landmasses. Their combined footprints provide seamless worldwide communications coverage, except in the extreme polar regions.

So it seems that coverage is not an issue. (They certainly cover the area in which MH370 was lost. It was only because of Inmarsat's technology that the search and rescue effort had any idea where to focus their resources.)

The drawback to Q&A sessions at presentations like Tyler's is that you only get one bite at the microphone, so to speak. There is no opportunity to pose follow-up questions such as, 'In your reply you mentioned financial considerations Tony, but Inmarsat is offering this for *free*. Where is the cost in that?' Or, 'Have you actually spoken to Inmarsat and analysed their offer and, if so, what are the *specific* reasons for your refusal to accept it?' But, because of the forum rules, those questions went unasked and, therefore, unanswered.

So, despite all the hot air that has been released into the atmosphere over the last 12 months, the question still remains, why haven't the airlines and regulators taken up Inmarsat's offer, if only as an interim measure at least until such time as a permanent solution can be implemented? A cynic might be tempted to conclude that there are other forces at work here; such as whoever finally gets the contract for global aircraft tracking will be in for a multi-billion dollar contract. We've seen repeated scandals in the aerospace industry during the years that I've been involved, starting with the Lockheed bribery scandal dating back to the 1970s, not to mention the accusations levelled against BAe in 2007, amongst others. Could it be that similar commercial considerations are in play?

A journalist I met at the FCC lunch asked me afterwards to provide him with some more information on the Inmarsat question. I did this and he forwarded it to a colleague who was tracking the issue. The reply came that his colleague had heard Tyler make similar remarks at a lengthy IATA media event in December and did not think his remarks at the FCC really advanced the ball. He also commented that, 'Arguably, IATA is sitting on the ball and not letting anyone advance it'.

There are many questions raised on this issue to which, at the present time, we do not have answers. I guess time will reveal the truth.

There is one issue on which Tyler and I are agreed though; and that is his standard of technical knowledge. This was demonstrated by another question from the floor at the same luncheon.

Q. Jet engines over the years have become more fuel-efficient but haven't got any faster. Is there any reason for this?

A. Erm... I'm not, I'm not a physicist or an engineer but um... friends who are tell me that making aircraft fly supersonically, which is really the next boundary if you like, is enormously expensive erm... enor... enormously difficult technically and therefore enormously expensive and to generate the sort of forces you need to do that you've got to burn a lot of fuel and you've got to erm... have big heavy engines which then burn more fuel so erm... if you look at what the market wants the market seems to say, you know what, flying along at about 550 miles an hour erm... to get, to get round the world and getting, you know, a 16 hour flight from Hong Kong to New York or whatever is probably, is probably far enough and long enough that enough people will pay enough money to make that work. If you start to make it much faster it costs so much more that people aren't prepared to make it work so I expect we'll stay with current speeds for the foreseeable future.

If only we'd been told that when we were studying aerodynamics in the 1970s, we could have advanced aircraft design by leaps and bounds. All you need to fly faster is big, heavy engines.

6

Training

'What is chiefly needed is skill rather than machinery.'
Wilbur Wright – letter to Octave Chanut, 13 May 1900

On 1 June 2009, Air France flight AF447, an Airbus A330-203, departed Rio de Janeiro Galeão airport bound for Paris Charles de Gaulle carrying 228 crew and passengers. At 2 hr 14 min and 28 sec into the flight, the aircraft crashed into the South Atlantic Ocean killing all on board. The aircraft was not in radar coverage at the time of the accident, making location of the crash site very difficult. It was not until 2 April 2011, almost two years later, that the wreckage was finally located on the ocean floor at a depth of 3,900 metres. An accident investigation was conducted led by the French Bureau d'Enquêtes et d'Analyses (BEA). The English version of the final report of the investigation was published on 27 July 2012.

One of the prime purposes of aircraft accident investigations is to determine the probable cause(s) of the accident with a view to learning from experience and putting in place solutions to ensure that similar events do not happen again in the future. So, before we examine the causes of the accident, what have we learned so far? We have learned that, because of the remote location of the crash site, finding the wreckage was extremely difficult, time consuming and expensive. Of course, had the aircraft had an independent automatic satellite position reporting system enabled, such as that provided by Inmarsat, that task would have been made considerably faster, easier and far less expensive. At the time of the crash, the aircraft was still in Brazilian airspace in the ATLANTICO FIR under the control of Dakar Oceanic ACC. A system called Eurocat, which facilitates automatic satellite position and altitude reporting to ATC, had recently been installed in Senegal on an experimental basis. However, the controllers on duty had neither been trained in its use nor even issued with user guidelines. It was, therefore, useless. Due to atmospheric conditions prevailing at the time, the crew could not establish communication with Dakar ACC on the only other means available to them, HF radio; a notoriously unreliable and antiquated system dating back to the 1940s. So, the aircraft was flying in a remote location, outside of radar coverage, with no operational satellite facilities and no voice communication. In short, other than the crew, no one else really knew where the aircraft was for certain. Does this all seem familiar? Of course it does. Almost five years later, Malaysian Airlines flight MH370 was in exactly the same situation and has yet to be located despite an extremely difficult, time consuming and costly search exercise having been mounted. As mentioned earlier (and despite IATA's assertion to the contrary), one of the 41 safety recommendations made by the BEA in its report was to, 'study the possibility to make it mandatory for aeroplanes conducting public transport flights to regularly transmit basic flight parameters (for example position, altitude, speed, heading).' Good idea, one might think. In fact, a very good idea. But, to repeat the words of Chris McLaughlin almost five years later, 'the mandate is not there globally.'

In this respect then, what have we learned? Seemingly nothing. Well, that's not quite true. We have learned something. As well as learning that locating the wreckage of aircraft which crash in remote areas is very difficult, we have also learned perhaps that aircraft operators are reluctant to spend money on technology that might only be used in anger once in a blue moon. Perhaps their risk management analysis models do not justify the expenditure. If so, there is an obvious solution to their reticence. If aviation regulators mandated the use of such technology, they'd have no choice. Either you have this stuff fitted and operational or you can't fly through our airspace, simple as that. There is precedent for such an approach. When mode C altitude reporting secondary surveillance radar transponders were first introduced back in the 70s, aircraft operators were given a limited time in which to upgrade their equipment or face an airspace ban. It worked. But why have the regulators been so reluctant to impose such legislation this time around? It couldn't be due to political lobbying by self-interest groups such as the airlines could it?

Looking at the way Flight Time Limitations legislation in Europe was watered down to the lowest common denominator by the EU Parliament in October 2013 on the 'advice' of such self-interest groups and so-called 'experts' who have little practical knowledge or experience of professional aviation, and despite strong opposition from the affected pilots' representative associations and against the advice of the EU's own transport committee, a cynic might conclude that this is, indeed, the case. Whatever the reasons, in my opinion, the regulators have been derelict in their duty to protect the travelling public from foreseeable risk.

So much for wreckage location, but what actually caused the crash of a modern, four-year-old, state-of-the-art, fly-by-wire aircraft? The BEA report stated that the accident resulted from the following succession of events:

> Temporary inconsistency between the measured airspeeds, likely following the obstruction of the pitot probes by ice crystals that led in particular to autopilot disconnection and a reconfiguration to Alternate Law;
> Inappropriate control inputs that destabilised the flight path;
> The crew not making the connection between the loss of indicated airspeeds and the appropriate procedure;
> The PNF (pilot not flying)'s late identification of the deviation in the flight path and insufficient correction by the PF (pilot flying);
> The crew not identifying the approach to stall, the lack of an immediate reaction on its part and exit from the flight envelope;
> The crew's failure to diagnose the stall situation and, consequently, the lack of any actions that would have made recovery possible.

So now we know the how. The pilots allowed the aircraft to get into a stall and, having done that, failed to take the correct recovery action to return to stable flight. A clear case of pilot error surely? Case closed. No. Fortunately, accident investigation has come a long way from its early days of finger pointing and blame apportionment. Now we need to look at the why. Why did a crew of three apparently fully qualified and experienced airline pilots get into a stall in the first place and, more to the point, being able to recognise their error, why did they not take the correct recovery action? Let us look at the first question. How and why and did they get into the stall?

Lesson three in *ab initio* basic flying training, after completing instruction in primary and secondary effects of flying controls, is recognition of, and recovery from, low speed stalls. There is a good reason for this. If the airflow over the wing becomes disturbed instead of smooth, it becomes aerodynamically stalled. In this condition the wing does not produce any lift and, unless the situation is corrected, the aircraft will descend until something stops it, such as the ground. Or the ocean. Each aircraft has a set of specific airspeeds at which it stalls in different configurations in 1G flight. These speeds vary as the square of the load factor so that, if we are pulling 2G, the stall speed doubles. Stalls are characterised by low airspeed and airframe buffet. So, the airspeed indicator (ASI) is your best friend. It is the first visual indication that you are approaching the stall. To recover from this, all you have to do is increase the airspeed by lowering the nose of the aircraft and/or increasing power, and all will be well. It is a straightforward manoeuvre and routinely practised during training.

However, there can be further complications. If one wing stalls before the other one, the stalled wing will drop producing a roll, which can develop into a spin. In this condition, the aircraft rotates about its vertical axis and, depending upon aircraft characteristics, this may also be accompanied by pitch and roll oscillations. Both the rate of rotation and oscillations in pitch and roll can vary in intensity from mild to severe. It is a very disorientating manoeuvre, especially if it happens when you are not expecting it, which is usually the case unless you deliberately spin the aircraft, for example during training and aerobatic manoeuvres. Like the simple low speed stall, there is a spin recovery procedure but, unlike the low speed stall, it is not so straightforward. Having recognised that you are in a spin, you must now determine in which direction the aircraft is spinning; to the left or the right. This might seem to be obvious – but it is not. With all the noise, the buffet, the G forces and the world spinning around you it is easy to become disorientated and difficult to determine immediately. But in this situation we have another best friend. It is called the turn indicator (TI). The TI does not get disorientated. It always points faithfully towards the direction in which the aircraft is turning. So now we have recognised that we are in spin, we have determined the direction in which we are spinning and now we can take recovery action. The standard actions consist of four steps:

Power off
Full opposite rudder
Pause
Stick centrally forward

We now need to hold the controls in these positions until the spin stops whereupon we centralise the rudder to maintain balanced flight and recover from the ensuing dive. But there are a couple of wrinkles here. On some aircraft, when you take recovery action, the rate of the spin actually increases before recovery. This is a trap for the unwary. It may lead you to believe that you have applied the wrong rudder and exacerbated the situation. This is exactly what the spin gremlins want you to think in their attempts to get you to reverse your rudder input. Do not be fooled by them. Always trust your TI. And be careful with pitch control when recovering from the dive. We already know how the stall speed varies with load factor, so be careful not to pull too hard on the stick or you may induce another stall, which could flick into another spin. Spin recovery is a smooth co-ordinated manoeuvre. During my basic training, it was practised repeatedly until the level of skill necessary was achieved and the recovery actions became second nature. Having attained that initial skill level however, like many other manoeuvres, regular practice is required in order to maintain proficiency. There is one other point to note here. Spin recovery is not an instinctive manoeuvre. For example, if you are in level flight and a wing drops, it is instinctive to apply opposite aileron to level the wings. If you want to descend, it is instinctive to push the stick forward. And, given sufficient knowledge of its causes, i.e. too low an airspeed, recovery from a simple stall is instinctive. That is not the case with spin recovery. Unless you have been shown how to do this, it may take you a long time to discover for yourself the correct technique by trial and error, as many early aviation pioneers found out to their cost.

So, going back to our question of how and why the pilots of AF447 allowed their aircraft to get into a stall, and remembering that the primary indication of an impending stall is a low ASI reading, the first thing that happened in the sequence of events was that, at 2 hr 10 min 05 sec into the flight, they lost all airspeed indication. How could that possibly happen on a state-of-the-art aircraft? For the answer to that we need to look at where the ASIs get their information from. When an aircraft moves through the air it generates a pressure against that air. This is called dynamic pressure. The air itself also has inherent pressure in its free, undisturbed state. This is called static pressure. All we need to do is compare these two pressures and the difference between them will give us a measure of airspeed. The two pressures are sensed using a pitot probe mounted on the outside of the aircraft fuselage. The probe is named after the French engineer Henri Pitot who first invented it in the early eighteenth century. An outside air temperature (TAT) probe is also fitted as temperature information is needed to compute the correct airspeed from the pressure information. Output from the probes is fed to an air data computer (ADC) which does the necessary calculations and presents the result on the ASI as an indicated airspeed. The A330 has three independent pitot probes, three independent ADCs and three independent ASIs. How could all of these fail at the same time? The answer is ice. Clouds at high altitude are composed mainly of ice. If ice blocks a pitot probe, the airflow through it is reduced, or stopped altogether, and the pressure data output is useless. To stop this happening, the probes are electrically heated but, in the case of AF447, the heaters weren't up to the job. And this wasn't the first time it had happened on the A330. Both the A330 & 340 had a history of problems with probe icing from their introduction into service.

The BEA report goes into great detail about these problems, the type of meteorological conditions in which such problems might be expected and the various engineering fixes, such as redesigned probes, that have been tried over the years to remedy the situation. In this respect the investigators did a very creditable job. Under 'Causes of the Accident' their report stated, 'The obstruction of the pitot probes by ice crystals during cruise was a phenomenon that was known but misunderstood by the aviation community at the time of the accident.' Amongst its engineering recommendations were:

> ➤ Acceleration in the replacement of Thales 'AA' probes by 'BA' probes, initiated on 27 April 2009. By 11 June 2009, all the probes had been replaced;
> ➤ Following an Airworthiness Directive issued by EASA, replacement of Thales 'BA' probes by Goodrich probes in positions 1 and 3, from 4 to 7 August 2009;

➢ Air France internal decision: replacement of Thales 'BA' probes by Goodrich probes in position 2, from 18 January to 8 February 2010.

So, hopefully, the engineering aspects of the problem should now be remedied.

But we need to ask more questions. Surely, just the loss of airspeed information should not result in a hull loss? Indeed not. Loss of airspeed indication is not an insurmountable problem by any means. There are a number of other secondary indications that can be used to determine, or at least infer, airspeed. The first of these is the groundspeed (G/S) readout from the aircraft navigation systems, of which there are three. These use a combination of satellite positioning (GPS), inertial reference units (IRU) and ground based radio beacons to determine the aircraft position to a high degree of accuracy. By calculating the rate of change of aircraft position they compute the G/S which is displayed on the pilots' primary flight displays (PFD). This is completely independent of pressure information from the pitots. In still air, G/S is equal to true airspeed (TAS). If we have a 10 knot headwind component, if TAS is 250, then G/S will be 240. Similarly if we have a 10 knot tailwind then G/S will be 260. Therefore, knowing the wind, which can also be displayed by the navigation systems, with a bit of simple mental arithmetic we can estimate the airspeed quite accurately from the G/S display. This is exactly the technique Ken Carver used to recover his Cathay Pacific 747 B-HOX back to Hong Kong on 17 January 2000 after the TAECO engineers in Xiamen failed to follow correct procedures and left his pitots blocked with debris after a repaint job. There are other techniques that can be used which come under the heading of basic airmanship or 'know your aircraft'. In various configurations, such as different flap settings, altitudes and so on, there is a pitch attitude and power setting that will put you in the general ballpark of your target airspeed. For example, on the B747-200 on the approach with gear down and full flap, you needed $1.5°$ pitch attitude and a power setting of 69 per cent N_1. Obviously there are small variations to this depending on wind conditions, turbulence etc., but if you have no airspeed indication you can be confident that you're in the right ballpark and certain that you're not going to stall. Now, some ex-military pilots will dispute this and say that the only way to be certain is by looking at angle of attack (AoA); that is the angle of the airflow relative to the wing. This is true but, whilst civilian aircraft, including the A330, are fitted with AoA sensors, unlike fighters which are designed for ACM (air combat manoeuvring), the information derived from them is not displayed to the pilots. It is used instead by the flight control computers (FCC) to determine certain performance parameters and, amongst other things, generate an aural warning to the pilots on approach to the stall. We shall consider this later. So, when the pilots of AF447 lost all their airspeed information and if they knew their aircraft, why didn't they simply fly pitch attitude and power setting to maintain control until the information was recovered or, better yet, just leave the autopilot (AP) and autothrust (A/T) engaged to deal with the problem?

As usual, it's not quite that simple. Both the AP & A/T need input from the ADCs (and therefore pitot probes) to operate correctly. If they don't have this information they basically say, sorry mate, I've got no idea what's going on here, I'm disconnecting, over to you, time to do some of that pilot shit. So it was that, at 2 hr 10 min 05 sec, simultaneously with the loss of all airspeed information, the AP & A/T disconnected. There was an added complication. Also because of the loss of the ADCs, the FCCs downgraded the flight control laws from Normal to Alternate Law. In this mode, some flight envelope protections which normally prevent the pilots from exceeding certain limits are lost. In this case, pitch and roll limitations are lost as well as, significantly in this case, stall protection which, in Normal Law, prevents the pilot from stalling the aircraft by automatically pushing the nose down. That was degraded to a less protective mode which can be overridden by the pilot. Even so, despite all that, the aircraft was still perfectly flyable. All the pilot had to do was maintain pitch attitude and power setting until the ASIs were recovered. But he didn't do that. Instead, the BEA report states that at 2 hr 10 min 16 sec, 11 seconds after the onset of the problem, 'The PF made rapid and high amplitude roll control inputs, more or less from stop to stop. He also made a nose-up input that increased the aeroplane's pitch attitude up to 11° in ten seconds.' Why would he do that? The target pitch attitude in cruise flight is around 2°. Why would he pull the nose up instead of maintaining the status quo? To find out the answer to that, we need to look at some other factors, starting with the crew complement.

The captain was 58 years old. His total flying hours were 10,988 of which 6,258 were as captain and 1,747 on type. He was an experienced pilot. The last time he had practised a 'Flight with Unreliable IAS' exercise during simulator training was on 22 April 2009. The last time he had practised stall recovery in the simulator was during his A320 (not A330) type rating conversion in May 2001.

The co-pilot who was in the right hand seat operating as PF for the sector was aged 32. His total flying hours were 2,936 of which 807 were on type. The last time he had practised a 'Flight with Unreliable IAS' exercise during simulator training was on 2 November 2009. The last time he had practised stall recovery in the simulator was during his A320 (not A330) type rating conversion in September 2004.

The other co-pilot, who was in the left hand seat at the time the series of events commenced, was 37. His total flying hours were 6,547 with 4,479 on type. He was well experienced on the A330. The last time he had practised a 'Flight with Unreliable IAS' exercise during simulator training was on 6 December 2008. The last time he had practised stall recovery in the simulator was during his A320 (not A330) type rating conversion in November 1998.

So, the obvious question is, why had none of the pilots ever been trained in stall recovery on the A330, the aircraft they were operating? For the answer to this question, we need to look at the Cross Crew Qualification (CCQ) training criteria for the Airbus A320/330/340 series of aircraft. The aircraft are classified as 'similar' in characteristics and, under the training regulations in force at the time, if you had already completed a full type rating conversion on the A320, in order to become qualified on the A330 and/or A340, all that was required was to complete a 'differences' course in relation to the new type. The differences course did not include repetition of stall recovery training.

I will now express a personal opinion. When my flying career ended in 2001, I had a total of 14,600 flying hours. Of these, the majority were on various Boeing types, 707, 737, 757 & 747 but for the latter part of my career I operated the A330 & 340. I had a total of 2,453 hours on both types. I was initially checked out on the A330 and completed a CCQ course on the 340 later. In 2010 when I became a flight simulator instructor, I renewed my ratings on the A330 & 340 in separate simulator rides and later completed an A320 differences course qualifying me also to instruct on that type. I have accumulated around 1,000 hours of additional instructional time since I came back into the profession. The fact is that, in many respects, the aircraft are similar but, in other respects, they are quite different. In particular, the A330 & 340 are much heavier than the 320 and, therefore, have a lot more inertia which gives them different handling characteristics. Now, the control laws incorporated in the FCCs are programmed to mask these differences as much as possible but they are not perfect. Some differences still remain, such as cross-wind handling characteristics. Similarly, the A340 at high takeoff weights (TOW) and aft centre of gravity (CG) has very different rotation characteristics from the 320 & 330 in terms of the stick force required. This is neither anything new nor is it confined only to Airbus aircraft. The Boeing 747-200 exhibited similar characteristics depending on TOW and CG position. It is something that, as pilots, we were trained to deal with in the normal course of events. And of course, there is an obvious difference between the A340 and the 320 & 330 in terms of the number of engines. A four-engine aircraft has much different performance considerations from its twin-engine sisters in terms of the engine failure case. On the occasions when I was scheduled to fly both types on the same day, I always took a few moments to adjust my thinking from four-engine to two-engine mode (and vice versa) before takeoff. This is not to say that CCQ is in any way unsafe. It is quite manageable given proper initial and recurrent training. And of, course, it is a great sales pitch for Airbus because, if a pilot is cleared to operate both types concurrently, rather than being restricted to only one type as is usual, it saves a whole lot of money in terms of the pilot establishment required to operate the fleet. The accountants love it.

Back to AF447 and the question, why did the PF pull the nose up instead of maintaining level flight? At the time the aircraft lost its ASIs, the PF was the most inexperienced pilot on the crew and the captain was not on the flight deck. At 1 hr 35 min into the flight whilst cruising at FL350, the captain was in the left hand seat and PF was in the right hand seat. They saw weather ahead on the weather radar. Because of the relatively high ambient air temperature, they were unable to climb higher to get above it. Ten minutes later at 1 hr 45 min, the aircraft entered a cloud layer with associated slight turbulence. A few minutes later the turbulence increased slightly in strength. Shortly after, at 1 hr 52 min, the turbulence stopped. Again the PF discussed with the captain the possibility of climbing the aircraft to get above the weather but the temperature was still too high. A short time later the captain woke the other co-pilot to take his place and went for his in-flight rest. At around 2 hr 00 min the captain attended the handover briefing before leaving the flight deck. During the briefing, PF said to the other co-pilot, *'Well, the little bit of turbulence that you just saw – we should find the same ahead, we're in the cloud layer, unfortunately we can't climb much for the moment because the temperature is falling more slowly than forecast.'* At 2 hr 06 min, the pilots again discussed the possibility of climbing to a higher level and at 2 hr 08 min PF adjusted the aircraft heading 12° to the left to avoid the weather. At 2 hr 10 min 05 sec the AP and A/T disconnected and the ASIs were lost. It was shortly after this that PF made the high amplitude roll inputs 'more or less from stop to stop' and pulled the nose up. These inputs triggered momentary stall warnings. The aircraft was at high altitude around 2,500 feet below the recommended maximum ceiling for the weight and temperature. The last thing you should do in such conditions is make large and rapid control inputs. But he did make such roll inputs. Why? I have seen this many times in the simulator with low-time, inexperienced pilots under stress. There is a tendency for them to make almost involuntary 'twitch' inputs on the sidestick and grip it much too hard. The simple remedy is to ask them to take their hand off the stick, let the aircraft ride the turbulence, relax and try again. But there was another problem they had to contend with. With failure of the ADC inputs, the control laws reverted from Normal Law to Alternate 2 Law (ALT 2). In Normal Law, a roll input on the sidestick demands a roll rate. Thus, once the desired bank angle is reached, all you have to do is centralise the stick to neutral (thus demanding a zero roll rate) and the aircraft will maintain the desired bank angle with no further input from the pilot. In fact, all you have to do is release the sidestick as it is spring loaded to neutral in both pitch and roll. That's why the 'take your hand off the stick' solution works if a pilot is over-controlling. But only in Normal Law. In Alternate 2 Law, a roll input on the sidestick now demands an aileron deflection, not a roll rate. In order to stop the roll, the pilot has to make an opposite roll control input. Simply releasing the stick to neutral will not now stop the roll. In these circumstances, unless you have received proper initial and refresher training, it is relatively easy to get behind the aircraft and set up a pilot induced oscillation (PIO) where the rolling motion becomes increasingly divergent. The data readout from the FDR shows that was exactly what happened in the case of AF447. It also shows that the PF continued to have difficulty in maintaining roll control for the remainder of the flight until control was taken by the other first officer. But by then it was too late to recover the situation.

As for the pitch input, it could be postulated that the PF had expressed a desire repeatedly to get above the weather into clear air and that was his intent. This is discussed in the BEA report, as is the captain's decision to leave the flight deck in less experienced hands just when the aircraft was about to enter potentially adverse weather. Of course, increasing the pitch attitude was completely the wrong thing to do in the circumstances. Over the next nine seconds, PNF read out the electronic centralised aircraft monitoring system (ECAM) messages displayed on the main system screen associated with the various failures 'in a haphazard manner', according to the report. The crew co-ordination was failing. There is very precise standard operating procedure (SOP) to be used in failure cases associated with ECAM management. This is practised repeatedly during simulator training until proficiency is attained. It is designed to ensure that systems failures are dealt with in a logical and precise manner. PNF did not follow his SOP. Whilst this was happening, PNF also pointed out to PF that the aircraft was climbing and asked him several times to descend. In response, PF made several nose down inputs but the aircraft continued to climb and was soon passing 37,000 feet. It was now 2,000 feet above its cleared altitude and was nearing the maximum recommended altitude for the weight and temperature. It was flying into 'coffin corner' where there is no margin between the low speed stall and high speed buffet. At 2 hr 10 min 36 sec, the ASI information displayed on the left hand primary flight display (PFD) became valid again although the speed displayed on the standby ASI was still erroneous. (We do not know about the speed on the right hand PFD as that was not recorded on the FDR). The displayed speed on the left hand PFD had been erroneous for 29 seconds. It now indicated 223 kt and the aircraft had lost 50 kt from its original cruise speed. On seeing this, PNF should have taken control of the aircraft, since he was the only one with valid information, pushed the nose down and increased power. But he didn't. Perhaps he assumed that PF's display had also recovered like his own. At 2 hr 10 min 47 sec, thrust was reduced to 85 per cent N_1 and the pitch attitude was 6° with an AoA of 5°. At 2 hr 10 min 50 sec PNF called the captain several times to return to the flight deck and, one second later, the stall warning triggered in a continuous manner. At this point, power was increased to maximum but PF continued to make nose up control inputs, precisely the opposite of what was required. The AoA continued to increase and the trimming horizontal stabiliser (THS) began trimming nose up and moved from 3 to 13° over the next minute and stayed there, or thereabouts, for the remainder of the flight. Around 15 seconds later, both the left hand PFD and the standby ASI airspeed indications returned to normal and indicated 185 kt. PF continued to make nose up inputs. The aircraft eventually reached its maximum altitude of 38,000 ft with AoA and pitch attitude at 16°. At 2 hr 11 min 37 sec the PNF finally announced 'controls to the left' and took over control by pressing the button on his sidestick. Unfortunately PF then almost immediately retook control without any announcement or callout and continued to pilot the aircraft. The situation had now deteriorated to the point that the aircraft was in a full stall and there was confusion over who was actually flying the aircraft. PNF, as the more experienced pilot, should have taken control to recover the aircraft. He tried, but instead of pushing and holding the takeover button on his sidestick to lock out PF's incorrect inputs, he only pushed it momentarily which allowed PF to regain control. It was another mistake which has also been repeated in other jet upset incidents. At 2 hr 11 min 42 sec the captain re-entered the flight deck. During the following seconds, all recorded speeds became invalid again and the stall warning stopped after having sounded continuously for 54 seconds. The stall warning stopped, not because the aircraft had recovered from the stall, but because the data being received from the AoA sensor and ADCs was outside pre-programmed parameters and, therefore, considered to be invalid by the flight warning computers. The aircraft was now descending through 35,000 ft with a rate of descent of 10,000 ft/min and an AoA in excess of 40°. The aircraft was now subject to roll oscillations to the right which sometimes reached 40°. The PF made a roll input full left to counter this but still held full back-stick for the next 30 seconds. At 2 hr 12 min 17 sec the PF finally made nose down pitch inputs, the AoA decreased, the speeds became valid again and this caused the stall warning to be triggered again. At 2 hr 13 min 32 sec the aircraft passed through 10,000 ft with both pilots making control inputs simultaneously whereupon PF finally said, *'Go ahead you have the controls.'* At 2 hr 14 min 17 sec the ground proximity warning system (GPWS) 'sink rate' and 'pull up' warnings started and continued until the aircraft hit the water 11 seconds later with a descent rate of almost 11,000 ft/min (125 mph), a forward G/S of 107 kt and a pitch attitude of 16.2° nose up.

On the face of it, the whole episode was a litany of mistakes by the pilots. When the airspeed indications first became invalid caused by blockage of the pitot heads, they should have followed the 'Flight with Unreliable IAS' checklist. This is a paper checklist contained within the quick reference handbook (QRH) and contains some memory items concerning pitch attitudes and power settings to be set in various phases of flight. These memory items relate to airspeed failure at critical phases of flight such as takeoff and climb above and below 10,000 ft. But the pilots never even considered use of the checklist. Why not? As part of its investigation, BEA conducted a comparative analysis of reports and statements by crews involved in 17 other events that occurred in similar conditions to those of AF447. It concluded the following:

➢ The crews had difficulty analysing the situation;
➢ Use of the 'Unreliable Airspeed' checklist was rare;
➢ Because of the numerous warnings, some crews experienced difficulty in choosing an appropriate procedure to follow;
➢ Others did not see the purpose of applying this procedure given that, in the absence of certainty about the unreliability of the airspeed, their interpretation of the title of the 'Unreliable Airspeed' procedure did not lead them to apply it;
➢ Some gave priority to controlling the pitch attitude and thrust before doing anything else;
➢ The triggering of the STALL warning came as a surprise to many of the crews, which led them to consider it as spurious.

So, the crew of AF447 were not alone in having difficulty analysing and identifying the cause of the problem and, therefore, deciding on an appropriate response. What this tells us is that the procedure is not effective and needs to be redesigned and the training that crews receive in this aspect of abnormal operations is inadequate and needs to be substantially revised.

Next, why did PF over-control the aircraft at the onset of the problem? We have already discussed the 'inexperienced twitch' and roll PIOs, but there is another issue; that of high altitude aircraft handling. In the days before modern full-flight-regime autopilots, pilots routinely used to physically fly the aircraft at high altitude.

When I flew 707s, the only autopilot was basically a wing leveller, an altitude hold function and a pitch wheel that seemed to be connected to the elevators by a rubber band. It was much easier simply to fly the aircraft manually so we used to takeoff, fly to cruise altitude and then engage the autopilot, such as it was. At top of descent we would then disconnect the autopilot and fly the aircraft from cruise altitude to landing. We were used to routinely handling the aircraft at high altitude where more gentle control inputs and finesse are required than at lower levels where the air is much denser. The modern trend is now to engage the autopilot as soon as possible after takeoff (often at around 500 ft); one of the reasons for this being put forward that it reduces pilot workload enabling more attention to be directed towards management of the overall situation. That is as may be, but it also means that pilots now have much less experience of high altitude aircraft handling, which was the situation that the PF on AF447 found himself in.

But why did both pilots fail to recognise that their aircraft was stalled and take the correct recovery action? After all, the stall warning generated by the FWCs (flight warning computers) sounded continuously for 54 seconds. This is a very loud aural warning that sounds STALL, STALL, STALL, repeatedly through the cockpit speakers. How could they have possibly ignored that? It is a well known physiological fact that, under stress, the senses begin to shut down and one of the first to go is hearing. This phenomenon has been recognised in human factors studies for many years. There is a well known story of an F4 Phantom pilot being downed by a ground-to-air missile during the Vietnam War. He was rescued and the CVR (cockpit voice recorder) recovered from his aircraft. He swore blind that the aural missile radar warning system on his aircraft had failed which was why he did not take evasive action. When the recording was played back the aural warning could be heard loud and clear. It hadn't failed at all but the pilot never heard it because, under the stress of the situation, his hearing had shut down. So, perhaps, the pilots of AF447 never heard the stall warning and, even if they did, like some of the pilots in the other 17 incidents studied by the BEA, they thought it to be spurious. In any event, they failed to recognise the situation they were in and take the correct recovery action. With the exception of a very, very small number of extremely rare documented cases, pilots do not crash aircraft deliberately. Again, their training failed them. The PF had not practised stall recovery in the simulator for five years, let alone high altitude stall recovery. Despite the fact that I can easily recite the spin recovery actions all these years after my original basic training, the last time I actually deliberately span an aircraft is more than 15 years ago and I would not attempt to do so now without some additional refresher training and practise. How can we expect pilots to perform critical manoeuvres such as high altitude stall recognition and recovery as a matter of second nature unless they are given regular refresher training?

There is one final point on stall recovery from the position that AF447 found itself. As mentioned earlier, the THS had auto-trimmed almost to its maximum nose up setting and remained there, or thereabouts, for the rest of the flight. Because of this, even with full forward stick, there was not enough elevator effectiveness to get the nose down far enough to recover from the stall. I have replicated the flight conditions of AF447 in the A330 simulator. Now, admittedly, the simulator is not specifically calibrated to perform such manoeuvres outside of the 'normal' flight envelope, but it might give us a few pointers. In my experience, with an AoA in excess of 40°, the only way to get the nose down far enough to un-stall the wing is to manually trim the THS nose down using the trim wheel mounted on the side of the centre pedestal. Even then, it requires a pitch attitude of 12° nose down or greater to get out of the stall and then very gentle handling is needed to recover from the ensuing dive without inducing a secondary stall. In Normal Law, the maximum nose down pitch attitude that is permitted on the A330 is 15°. However, in routine operations, an A330 pilot would not see a pitch attitude greater than 5° nose down. Thus, there would be a tendency not to want to exceed what is 'normally' seen unless one had received specific training. Remember, I practised this in the simulator having thought about it first, with full knowledge of what was going to happen and having planned my recovery actions. For the pilots of AF447, it was dark, they were in turbulence and icing with multiple, seemingly conflicting, warnings going off accompanied by considerable airframe buffet and roll oscillations. On my best attempt it took almost 11,000 ft to complete the recovery and return to level controlled flight. At that time, there was nothing in any of the training material that referred to use of manual THS trim for stall recovery.

None of this is to excuse the pilots of AF447 from responsibility for the accident. They lost control of a serviceable aircraft as a result of which the lives of all on board were lost. But, clearly, their training did not prepare them adequately to deal with the situation in which they found themselves. It is not all bad news however. Partly as a result of this accident, the Airbus training procedures have been substantially revised. One of the main revisions is to place much greater emphasis on manual handling of the aircraft. In the days when cockpits became more and more automated, one of the rationales behind this was that many aircraft accidents were put down to 'pilot error'. The logic of the time went that, if we automate as much as possible of the routine piloting tasks, remove the pilot from the handling loop and place him in more of a monitoring role, then clearly the 'pilot error' accidents will reduce markedly. The emphasis in training then shifted away from manual handling skills to systems operation skills. This might seem to be logical, but the logic was flawed. Unfortunately, when things start to go wrong, some of the first systems to be lost are the AP and A/T, as happened with AF447. So now we have a pilot with reduced handling skills, even in the normal flight regime, suddenly being faced with a multiple failure case requiring a high degree of proficiency in manual skills for which he has had little training or practise. Again, the news is good here. On Airbus conversion courses now, after the first familiarisation trip in the full flight simulator (FFS), the next two sessions are spent with the automatics turned off banging around the circuit and doing upper air work gaining competence in manually flying the aircraft in Normal, Alternate and Direct Laws. It is a vast improvement and recognition that automation is not the be-all and end-all of improving flight safety. In fact, in some cases, it serves to exacerbate the situation. It is now recognised that there are times when we actually need to reduce the level of automation to deal with a given situation. It can be summarised by the advice that, if the automatics start doing something that you don't understand, resist the temptation to go head down and start fiddling with the flight management computer (FMC). Instead, drop a level of automation and revert to basic modes such as heading and vertical speed (V/S). And if that doesn't work, press the big red button on the stick, look out of the windows and do some pilot shit. Know the pitch attitudes and power settings for your aircraft in different flight regimes; set them and you can be confident that you will soon have the situation back under control. The quickest way to adjust the flight path of an aircraft is by manual manipulation of its flying controls – provided you have the appropriate training and experience, that is.

It would be nice to be able to report that, with the lessons learned, everything is now hunky-dory in the training world. Unfortunately that is not the case for one main reason. The usual one main reason. Money. The FFS phase of airline conversion training on the Airbus types that I conduct consists of 9 sessions of 4 hours each. This is a total of 36 hours, which is further divided into 18 hours in the PF role and 18 hours in the PNF role for each pilot. It is enough; but only just. Provided the candidates are of at least average ability, well briefed and motivated, then all the necessary manoeuvres can be completed to a basic level of competence. But that is all. Some airlines, most notably in my sphere of experience, Chinese airlines, specify 11 FFS sessions. These extra 8 hours of training make all the difference. There is more time available actually to repeat and to practise manoeuvres to get the candidates to a level of confidence in their own ability rather than mere competence. But, of course, with simulator time coming in at around US$600 per hour, the accountants generally don't want to spend the extra money. After all, if the pilots are competent, what more do you need? Why spend another five grand on them just to make them feel more confident?

And there is another problem. For years there has been talk of a pilot shortage. Pilots hang on this in the hope of seeing a recovery in remuneration and terms of employment that have been eroded year-on-year by the bean counters who now run the world's airlines. So far it has proved to be a forlorn hope as we have watched the proliferation of low-cost carriers epitomised by the likes of Ryanair, one of the most detested airlines in the business by its crews and passengers alike. Perhaps this time around it really is going to happen. In a report published by Boeing in August 2013, it was predicted that airlines will have to hire 498,000 pilots – about 25,000 each year – to support all the new aircraft they are expected to add to their fleets over the next two decades. The most pronounced shortage will be in the Asia Pacific region, where 192,300 pilots will be needed, according to Boeing's forecast. North America follows with a projected demand for 85,700 pilots and Latin America will be in need of 48,600. Analysts say the brunt of the shortage will be felt by regional carriers that operate half of the USA's scheduled flights. They simply won't be able to compete with the larger airlines. Add to this the fact that one traditional source, former military pilots, has now dried up. These days the military is short of pilots, not mustering them out, like in the post-Vietnam years through the 1980s. So what is to be done?

In the past, airlines planned ahead and ran training schools like Hamble that I attended in 1973. With cutbacks, these have become much less common. There are still training schools that offer *ab initio* to full airline qualification but these are expensive. Some cadets that I have trained on the A320 on courses like this have paid EUR220k for their training. They enter the profession with a huge debt already hanging around their necks and end up working for low-cost carriers on minimal wages. When I graduated from Hamble in 1975, we were required to repay part of our training costs to the tune of GB£6k. In net present value terms, this equates to GB£53k. So, in today's terms, the cost to the candidate has almost quadrupled whilst remuneration has been slashed to the bone, to the extent that some pilots have to take second jobs just to be able to pay the bills. So why do people still enter the profession? The answer is simple. If you have the flying bug, you will do anything to get into the air. Whatever it takes. If you want to fly, you will put up with being buggered around and work for next to nothing just to achieve your dream. Unfortunately the bean counters know this and exploit it to the full. But even that will not solve the problem. To fulfil the projected pilot shortage they have now come up with a new ruse. Currently it takes approximately two years to qualify from *ab initio* to line qualification with a basic CPL. They want to shorten this to fill the void, but how to do that? Simple. Cut back on the level of basic training. In collusion with the regulators, a new form of licence called the multi-crew pilot licence (MPL) has recently been introduced. The blurb sounds very impressive. Here is a typical advertising spin:

> The MPL is a new initiative from the International Civil
> Aviation Organisation (ICAO), which was adopted by the Joint
> Aviation Authority (JAA) and the European Aviation Safety
> Authority (EASA). The course was introduced after comments
> from the world's airlines that the traditional training path
> through CPL/IR to an airline could be improved utilising modern
> technologies and training methodologies. The MPL syllabus
> incorporates a large amount of simulator flying; specifically
> structured to develop the skills required of an airline pilot, in
> particular multi crew operations and threat and error

management. This is in contrast to the CPL/IR syllabus, which is single pilot focused and not specifically aimed at training as a pilot for the role of first officer in a modern generation jet airliner.[4]

Or another:

The modern airliner flight deck has changed significantly over the past decade whereas the route to training airline pilots has changed little from the traditional route outlined in Annex 1 of the Chicago Convention, 1948. An ICAO study, commissioned in 2004, reviewed the regulations, structure and methodology by which airline pilots were trained and a new philosophy for better training and preparing pilots for the modern Multi-Crew environment was born, in the form of the Multi-Crew Pilot Licence, in 2006. Our Multi-Crew Pilot Licence (MPL) Training course incorporates airline specific Standard Operating Procedures (SOPs) from an early stage in training and this requires an airline to mentor pre-selected cadets through a bespoke course and into type, base and line training on a specific aircraft; taking about 18 months to achieve licence issue, from where line training and employment with the mentoring airline commences.[5]

The most significant point is contained in the last sentence. It only takes 18 months instead of 2 years using the traditional route. Some MPL schemes offer qualification within 14 months. But there is something that is not mentioned in the blurb. At the end of the training, the pilot's licence is only valid whilst he or she is employed by the 'mentoring' airline. If, during the time it takes for the MPL holder to attain 1500 hours of flying experience, the pilot leaves the airline for any reason then the licence is no longer valid. It is a dream come true for the HR department. Should the pilot put a foot wrong, it's out-on-your-ear time and your licence isn't worth a dime. In such a situation, if you had operational or safety related concerns, would you dare to speak out and raise them? This is no more than indentured servitude. And, what is more, this MPL does not even give the pilot the qualifications to go along to the local aero club and hire a simple spam-can to bang around the circuit and get some stick time. The reason is simple. The training course for the MPL comprises of only

70 hours of actual flight time in an aircraft with no single pilot (solo) time and the remaining 180 hours of training are conducted in the simulator. Compare this with the qualification for a basic CPL, which requires 250 hours of actual flight time including at least 100 hours of solo time. The MPL is just a cheap way to fill the right hand seat of a transport jet with a pilot's assistant so that the accountants can get their return on investment and cover for the fact that they have failed to make adequate investment in training for the future. Ask yourself one question. If your wife and kids were on board an aircraft that got into a similar situation to AF447, who would you rather have on the flight deck; an MPL holder with absolute minimal qualifications and experience or a properly licenced and experienced CPL or ATPL (airline transport pilot licence) holder? The airlines are relying on pilots who have been properly trained in the traditional way to effectively conduct on-the-job training with fare paying passengers on board to bring these MPL holders to a level of experience where they can then take the flying tests required to obtain a proper CPL. And they are doing this in collusion with the regulatory authorities.

In my opinion, this is not about 'tailoring' the training product to suit the modern airlines' needs. It is about cost-cutting plain and simple. It is a retrograde step in flying training and one that we may have cause to regret in the future. When I was asked to take part in instruction in an MPL programme, I refused.

7

Navigation

I have always enjoyed mathematics. It is the logic and elegance of the solution that I find attractive. It is very definitive. There is only ever one answer, or number of answers, that can be correct. There are no grey areas. If only solutions to problems in life were that simple to determine. And, of course, mathematics is central to navigation. It was during my navigation lessons at Hamble that I was introduced to the concept of spherical geometry. The idea that you can have a triangle composed of three right angles captivated me. And, if you are standing on the North Pole and you want to go to London, what direction do you need to go? South obviously. But what if you want to go to Nairobi? South again. Ulan Bator? South. In fact, from the North Pole, everywhere is south. How do you solve that conundrum? I also particularly liked the concept of dead reckoning, which was the main means of long range navigation before the introduction of radio aids. It is, on the one hand, very precise because it is simply a series of geometric vector solutions but, on the other hand, it is completely imprecise because if the forecast winds are wrong, you can end up miles away from where you thought you were. And who can trust the met forecast? Meteorology is similar to medicine and cookery. It is an inexact science.

I also loved the charts we used for plotting. Man's attempts to describe a three dimensional body in a two dimensional plane. The

Mercator, first conceived by the Flemish cartographer Gerardus Mercator in 1569, the Lambert Conical Orthomorphic and the Polar Stereographic. What ingenuity. Imagine a hollow globe with a wire frame representing the lines of latitude and longitude. Put a lamp inside, wrap sheets of paper around it in various planes and trace the lines projected onto the paper. We were also taught 'old school' navigation techniques like astro. This is how the mariners and explorers of old used to find their way around our planet. I knew most of the constellations already because my father taught them to me as a young boy. He taught me that Cassiopeia was our constellation because it described a big W in the sky. He'd used astro himself when he was flying Catalinas on long range North Atlantic patrols. We used to watch Patrick Moore's programme *The Sky at Night* on TV together. He was one of the first pioneers of getting the general public involved in mass observations. In these days of the interweb it's common practice but, back then, it was a novel concept. In the early morning of 17 November 1966, when I was 14, the Earth was due for a spectacular display of the Leonid meteor shower. Patrick wanted as many people as possible to observe the phenomena and then send him details of their observations. We wrote in to his programme and they sent back a star chart to show us where we should be gazing. On the appointed night, my father and I bundled ourselves up in our warmest clothes, boiled up a Thermos flask of hot tea and drove to Hook Moor, 20 minutes away from where we lived in Garforth, West Yorkshire. Back then it was an isolated spot, high up and with no light pollution. The wind was blowing at around 20 kt with frequent strong gusts and it was freezing cold, but we persevered. There was one other problem; 8/8ths of stratus cover at 1,000 ft. We sat up there for two or three hours and didn't see a bloody thing. We weren't the only observers to have the same problem. On his next show, Patrick related some of the reports he'd received. One wag reported, 'Rockets observed: from the sky nil, from the wife, plenty.' My father fell around laughing. I laughed along with him but didn't really understand the joke because I had yet to discover the nuances of the fairer sex.

I found everything to do with navigation fascinating and still do. But, in these days of triple INS (inertial navigation system) & GPS, those traditional methods of navigation are a dying art. I remember sitting over the North Pacific one night in an A340. The time between en-route waypoints is an hour or more in that area so, to while away the time, I got out my chart and plotted a running fix from the long range NDB (non-directional beacon) on Shemya in the Aleutian Islands. After I had finished and produced a nice cocked hat that confirmed we were on time and track, my first officer asked me what I was doing. When I explained that I was just checking our position, he looked at me as though I was from a different planet.

'We've got triple GPS, why on earth are you doing that?' he enquired.

'Well, what are you going to do if we get a total GPS failure?'

'It's never going to happen.'

'How do you know?'

'It's never happened before and it's not going to happen now.'

'But you don't know that do you? Just because it's never happened before doesn't mean it won't happen. After that BA 747 had a four engine flame out in volcanic ash over Indonesia, they said it could never happen again, but it did didn't it?'

'John, you're living in the Stone Age. You're just a dinosaur.'

'Pterodactyl if you don't mind and for your information it's the Cretaceous period you cheeky little twat,' came my witty riposte.

But the old school nav techniques had saved me once. I was flying an Aztec back from Norway to Teesside one night and had a total electrics failure. One of the alternators was already unserviceable when I set off and, about one and a half hours out from destination, the other one went tits-up as well. So now I'm sitting over the North Sea with only battery power remaining for the rest of the flight and the battery would only last for 30 minutes at the most. If it was a clear night it wouldn't have been a problem but it wasn't. The cloud base was forecast to be around 500 ft so I'd need the ILS (instrument landing system) or at least an SRE (surveillance radar element) talk-down. But no electrics means no radios and no ILS. So, what to do? I couldn't make a radio call to advise ATC of my situation because I was out of VHF range and there were no other aircraft around to relay for me. But, Teesside knew I was coming because I'd filed a flight plan. So, I turned everything off to conserve the battery for arrival and flew the aircraft using my torch to see the instruments. Back then there was a Consol radio beacon in Stavanger in Norway. This is a long range navigation aid that was developed during WWII. The beacon transmits a signal consisting of dots and dashes over a period of 60 seconds. Depending on where you are in relation to the beacon, you will hear a variable number of dots and dashes during the transmission. So, you listen to the signal, count the dots and dashes and from that you can determine which radial you're on from the beacon. So, every ten minutes, I turned on the ADF (automatic direction finder), took a Consol count and then turned it off again and plotted the result on my chart. When I was ten minutes out of Teesside and certain I had enough battery power left for the landing, I turned on the ILS. The forecast wind was for landing on R/W 24 and I was aiming to put myself on finals about 25 miles out. The localiser needle was at about one third scale deflection. I was right on the money. Later on that night in the bar I was having a beer with one of the ATC guys and he said to me, 'We knew you were coming because we had your flight plan and we picked you up on radar about 70 miles out. But we couldn't work out how you managed to get yourself so close to the centreline and stay there. How did you do it with no ILS?' I explained to him about the Stavanger Consol beacon. He was ex-RAF, in his fifties and very old school. He was amazed. 'Consol? My god! We used to use that during the war. I didn't think they taught you young sprogs stuff like that anymore.' But they did, and that night it saved me. But, now they don't teach it anymore. Like my first officer said, we've got triple GPS, what's the point?

The point is this. In my experience in training, pilots are becoming over-reliant on the FMC. One of the prime considerations in good airmanship is positional awareness. You should always know where you are in relation to the nearest airfield, whether or not you're heading away from or towards it and your approximate distance out. Here's a typical scenario in training: aircraft at 4,000 ft on a downwind radar heading of 010, 10 nm northwest of the airfield for vectors to land on the R/W 18.

ATC: 'Say distance and bearing from the airfield.' [Cue immediate head-down fiddling with the FMC by at least one, if not both, pilots.]

'OK guys. What are we doing? You've both gone head down and no one's looking after the aircraft. What should we be doing now?'

'One of us should be flying the aircraft.'

'Right, so you're PF so you do that and let him work out the bearing and distance OK?'

'OK.'

'So, PNF, what's your bearing and distance from the airfield?' [Cue immediate return to fiddling with the FMC.]

'OK. Let's just freeze the sim for a moment and have a look at where we are. Have a look at your ND. What's that big white needle?'

'The VOR [VHF omni-range].'

'Yes, and where is the VOR located?'

'On the airfield.'

'Good. So the big white needle's pointing directly at the airfield isn't it?'

'Yes.'

'So what's your bearing from the airfield?' [Cue ten seconds of scribbling on a bit of paper trying to work out the reciprocal of the inbound bearing indicated by the VOR.]

'OK, if you can't work out the reciprocal quickly, put your ND in Rose Nav and read the tail of the needle. By the way, the quick way to calculate the reciprocal is to add 200 and subtract 20 or subtract 200 and add 20 depending on which quadrant you're in. Now, we've got the bearing so what's our distance?' [Cue slight hand movement towards the FMC then hesitation.]

'Woops. Almost. Where's the distance readout?'

'On the DME [distance measuring equipment].'

'Exactly, it's right there in front of you isn't it? So there's no need to go anywhere near the FMC is there?'

'No.'

'Exactly and look how much quicker it is to just read the raw data instead of diverting your attention away from the prime tasks of flying the aircraft and looking out for traffic, especially in the terminal area.'

But it's not really their fault. This is the Xbox generation and they've been brought up to trust the computer above all else. Before we had FMCs, we did all our nav from raw data. We tuned the VORs manually, set the course bar with the required radial, listened to the ident to check we had the right beacon and worked out our position from the indications on the RMI (radio magnetic indicator). It's an absolute basic skill but it's falling into disuse, only to be used in a so-called emergency if both FMCs fail. On that definition, before we had FMCs I guess we were flying in an emergency situation all the time. It's the same with descent profile. If you ask how the profile's going, again it's straight into the FMC to see what the box says. What's wrong with the 3x table? 3x the height in thousands plus 10 miles gives you the minimum distance you need to touchdown, give or take a bit for the wind and weight variations. So if you're at 30,000 ft you need 100 nm. It's really that simple but, again, it seems to be a dying art. It takes a couple of seconds to calculate instead of 20 seconds of head-down fiddling with the FMC. Perversely, despite the perceived safety problems in China, in my sphere of training I have found the Chinese pilots I've trained to be much better at raw data nav than their European counterparts. This is due in no small measure to the fact that they are still required to conduct raw data approaches with no assistance from the FMC, AP or A/T during their flight checks. It's not that they're better pilots; it's just a matter of training and practise.

Having said all that, despite my love for navigation and its mathematical intricacies, that doesn't mean to say that I've never been uncertain of my position. Far from it. When I was in basic training at Hamble, there were two local flying areas. The first was over the Isle of Wight. Navigation was simple. You took off, flew down the Solent to the Fawley Power Station chimney that stood out like a dog's dick irrespective of the visibility, and there was the island right in front of you. Couldn't miss it, and recovery was a simple reversal of the process. The island also had an added advantage that there was a nudist colony sheltered by a small cliff to the north. If you approached at about 2,500 ft, throttled back in a glide so they couldn't hear you, you could pop out over the cliff and do a couple of steep turns overhead and watch the ladies running for cover. The other area was a trapezium shaped box to the northeast of the airfield and the southwest corner of the box was delineated by a small market town called Wickham. It had a particularly unique road layout around the market square, which you couldn't mistake; that is if you could find the bloody town in the first place.

One evening I had completed a solo detail in the northeast area and it was time to go home. I'd left it a bit late because I'd been enjoying myself so much that I didn't properly keep track of the time and dusk was now falling. This was bad because I hadn't done any night flying training yet and was only in the early stages of instrument training. But I reckoned I'd still got enough time to get back and land before sunset, which was the cut-off point. But, in the gathering gloom, I couldn't find Wickham. As my ETA came and went, there was no sign of the bloody place. I pressed on with my calculated heading to recover to Hamble and then I heard another aircraft call up for a QDM. This is a magnetic bearing to the airfield which is generated when the pilot makes a VHF transmission. One of the squiggly amps boxes in the tower shows a position line on a cathode ray tube and the controller passes that to the aircraft. Good idea, I thought, and called for a QDM as well. 'No bearing' came the response. No bearing? No bloody bearing! I must be really lost!! What I didn't know at the time was that 'no bearing' means you're directly overhead the station in what is known as the 'cone of confusion'. But no one had told me that. Minor feelings of panicky discomfort began to set in. It was getting darker but what to do? In the distance I could see the Fawley dog's dick. I know, home overhead Fawley and from there I know my way home without fail. So that's what I did. I was the last aircraft to land and my instructor, Dally Purcell, was standing on the apron waiting to meet me when I shut down. To say that I received an almighty bollocking would be a gross understatement. He ripped into me with a vengeance. Fawley was in the Bournemouth Special Rules Zone (SRZ) and I had entered their airspace without calling up and obtaining ATC clearance so they'd filed a violation against me. I had not kept a check on my flight time, had put the aircraft at risk and, in fact, from what he said, I had done everything wrong, including getting out of bed that morning. Worse was to come. Each instructor had four cadets under his care so, for the next three days, we all had to undergo navigation exercises on recovery to the airfield from unknown positions. The other three cadets cursed me roundly for my incompetence and the ribbing I received from everyone in the bar for the next couple of weeks was merciless. The senior guys on courses ahead of ours were the worst. If I never again hear the chorus of, 'We're poor little lambs who've lost our way,' it'll be too soon.

Doctor Andrew L. Miller holds the position of Professor in the Division of Life Science at the Hong Kong University of Science & Technology. He was born in Tanzania but at the age of four his family relocated to the Shetland Islands where he attended Anderson High School in Lerwick from 1970 to 1976. From there he then went to Gordonstoun School in Morayshire from 1976 to 1978 where he earned a Duke of Edinburgh Gold Award in 1977. He gained his B.Sc. with first class honours in Botany at Dundee University in 1981, spent a year at the Royal Naval College, Dartmouth, entering with a graduate rank of sub-lieutenant, before returning to Dundee University where he was awarded his Ph.D. in 1986. He also holds the appointment of Adjunct Senior Scientist at the Marine Biological Laboratory, Woods Hole, Massachusetts and was awarded both a Senior Research Fellowship by the Croucher Foundation in 2004 and a Visiting Fellowship by New College, Oxford from 2005 to 2006. To date he has published more than 40 research papers relating to his particular speciality, which is something to do with Ca^{2+} ions signalling something or other during *in vivo* differentiation, cytokinesis and other suchlike shit. To his friends he is known as 'Windy', likes a cold beer on a warm day and plays bass guitar for SKiNC.

When he married his wife Minnie in 2003, I travelled over to Dundee for the ceremony and then around 30 of the guests joined the newlyweds on the best honeymoon I've ever had the pleasure to take part in. We were a mixed bunch from all different parts of the world and, apart from our mutual connection to Windy, we didn't know each other from Adam; at least to begin with. There was a boat skipper from Woods Hole whose contribution to the post-wedding speeches (of which there were many) was, 'Wife? Wife? If the Navy had wanted you to have a wife they'd have issued you with a fucking wife.' There was Chicago Frank who owned some speakeasies and a slot machine franchise in the Windy City and was rumoured to be 'connected'. There was Mike who ran The Duke in Sai Kung. He'd flown into Glasgow, the wrong side of Scotland, got into a cab intending to go to the railway station to catch a train but must have enquired how much it would cost to go straight to Dundee before falling asleep under the influence of the quantity of in-flight refreshments he'd imbibed en route. He woke up in Dundee with a bill for 250 quid. These three stand out particularly in my memory but the rest of the bunch were also what are euphemistically referred to as 'characters'.

After the wedding ceremonials were completed, our party boarded a bus driven by an Irishman called Enda, who was standing for some position or other in the upcoming EU elections. During our trip, he was intent on canvassing our opinions on various issues of the day. After I had ventured the view that all politicians, especially EU politicians, were a bunch of lying, thieving, bastards who were only in it to see how deep they could get their noses into the trough and couldn't be trusted to give you the right time of day, he refrained from soliciting my advice any further. Enda was a very good driver though and we travelled across Scotland to the west coast, caught a ferry to Northern Ireland and then carried on west across country ending up in Shannon where we eventually disbanded and all went our separate ways. The whole trip took around ten days. Apart from our connection to Windy though, there was one other thing the group had in common; a love of music. Everyone had a talent of some sort, whether it was singing, playing an instrument of one type or another, even if was just the spoons or the table drum, or a mixture of the two. And we had a riotous time. It only took a couple of days to get to know each other on that road trip and we all quickly fell into a routine. Each place we stopped at for the night, we took over the local bar, begged, stole or borrowed some instruments to complement those we carried with us, and entertained the locals with our wide-ranging talents long into the night. Morning muster was usually quite quiet as we boarded the bus all nursing our various hangovers and injuries from the night before but, come 11 o'clock or so, things would start to liven up. My morning routine for the quiet time was to pick up a copy of the day's *Times* and spend 45 minutes doing the crossword. It was on about day five that Minnie came and sat next to me and started chatting.

'Oh,' she said. 'That must be a difficult crossword. You've been doing it for five days now.'
I thought she was taking the piss but a quick glance at her face told me otherwise.

'Yes, bloody difficult actually Minnie. It's beyond me. Don't know why I bother really. I only do it to fill in the time 'til we start drinking again,' I replied, not wishing to disabuse her of her opinion of my limited mental capacities.

It was on this trip I met a Welshman by the name of David who was now living in Canada. We both had something else in common as well as Windy and the music. We both liked Guinness and, of course, were in the perfect location to pursue our mutual taste. We decided upon an experiment. We had both heard a theory that beer, especially Guinness, contains all the nutrients, vitamins and minerals that the body requires to maintain good health and fitness. So, for the last four days of the trip, we decided to put this to the test. We stopped eating altogether and simply drank Guinness for breakfast, lunch, afternoon tea, dinner, supper and, of course, bedtime snack to ward off night starvation. At the end of the trip when we were having a farewell breakfast of Guinness together in Shannon Airport, we both agreed that the experiment had been a complete success. Other than the fact that our faeces had turned black, we had suffered no ill-effects whatsoever. Well, there was actually one other slight side effect. People had been tending to avoid spending much time in our company for the last couple of days because the Guinness diet does make you fart a lot.

Minnie's home town is Paratong near Narvacan in the Philippines. It's located in Ilocos Sur in the northwest of the country. Windy and Minnie built a hotel and entertainment complex there called the Mango Trove Resort. It opened on 3 December 2011 and the whole of Sai Kung was invited to the grand opening, especially all the musos, because this was going to be three days of music and entertainment. But the question was, how to get there? The first option was to fly to Manila and then suffer a six-hour-long journey over roads that varied from averagely bad to downright crap. We didn't fancy that. But a bit of research revealed that there is an airfield called Vigan only 30 clicks from Narvacan. How to get there? There used to be scheduled flights there in the dim, distant past but no more. Then we hit upon the idea of chartering a plane to fly us in there. Further research found an air charter company called Navion Air Service based at Clark Airbase, the former USAF Airbase in Angeles City. It fitted the bill perfectly and, with five of us sharing the cost, was well within the budget so I went ahead and booked it. That's when things started to go wrong. One by one the other 'certains' for the trip dropped out until there was only Klaske and me left. Oh well, bugger the expense, let's do it anyway. We arrived at Clark on a scheduled flight from Hong Kong with Tiger Airways, two days before the planned grand opening, to be met by our pilot Jimmy L. Boyd. This guy was a retired USAF pilot with 28 years of military service under his belt and 4,000 hours flying single engine jet fighters including the F-102, F-104 & F-105. This was one experienced dude. He spoke with a laconic American drawl and had a very dry sense of humour. He was of indeterminate age (or rather I didn't dare enquire) but the lines on his face showed he had not lived a quiet life. He picked us up from the main terminal at Clark in a 60s Chevrolet Impala. On the windshield was a sticker proclaiming that he'd completed 100 Wild Weasel missions during the Vietnam War. In simple terms, the task of a Wild Weasel aircraft is to bait enemy SAM anti-aircraft defences into targeting it with their radars, whereupon the radar signal is traced back to its source allowing the Weasel or its team-mates to target it with air-to-ground munitions for destruction. Sounds simple enough but, in fact, it was one of the most, if not *the* most, dangerous of missions to undertake, which explains their motto, 'YGBSM'. You Gotta Be Shitting Me. Instead of avoiding SAM sites like the plague as everyone else did, these guys actually invited them to light them up with their radar and risk being taken out. And this guy driving us in his Chevy had done 100 missions. I couldn't resist the temptation to ask him about it.

'Jimmy, I'm looking at the Wild Weasel patch on the windshield. Have you really done 100 missions?'

'Yeah Jaahn, I did that.' I was in awe of this guy and thought it best to just shut the fuck up before I made a fool of myself. Then we arrived at the aircraft for our charter. It was a vintage low wing monoplane, a 1949 Ryan Navion-A. It was originally designed and built by North American Aviation along the general lines of their most famous wartime aircraft, the P-51 Mustang. Our example was finished in polished aluminium and she was absolutely beautiful. Also in his hangar there was a vintage Beech 18 undergoing restoration and parked outside was an old Cessna 337, a type I flew myself in my air taxi days. Jimmy told us the history of his Navion-A. He'd bought it in the US after he returned from Vietnam. A local aircraft museum had asked him if they could use it as part of their display. Three days before he was due to deliver it to them, there was a big fire that burned down the museum and all its exhibits. A close call. Like many vets, Jimmy found it hard to settle in the US so he went back to southeast Asia, had the aircraft shipped over and he'd been there ever since.

As we flew north to Vigan in the afternoon sunshine, the winds were light with unlimited visibility. Perfect flying weather. There's a scene in *Out of Africa* when Denys Finch Hatton first takes Karen Blixen up in his Tiger Moth. She is in the front seat and reaches out her hand over her shoulder to Denys. They hold hands together as she marvels at the spectacle unfolding below her. As we flew on, I was sitting in the right hand seat next to Jimmy and Klaske was sitting behind me. I reached my hand over my shoulder to her and we shared our *Out of Africa* moment. It was idyllic. I felt totally in love and at peace with the world.

When we landed at Vigan, as we taxied in I saw that Windy had sent an air conditioned eight-seat people mover and driver to collect us. He was standing there with a piece of cardboard with JOHN WARHAM written on it in large letters. Given that we were the only aircraft to have landed there in three weeks, it seemed a bit superfluous. In fact, we found out later, the only people to use the airport on anything like a regular basis were the local mayor and other government dignitaries. But I couldn't resist it. I walked up to him and said, 'Who are you looking for?' He waved his piece of cardboard at me. 'No. Not me mate. He must be coming in on the next plane.'

The drive up to the Mango Trove took about 45 minutes. We went through the old town of Vigan. There were houses there that were built of wood with intricate carvings that looked as though they dated back to the Spanish colonial period and there were horse drawn carriages similar in design to the type you see in films about the Amish. This was serious back country. But there was a worrying feature about some of the other buildings we saw en route. There seemed to be a lot of 'resorts'. Many of them consisted of just an unfinished concrete frame with some rubble thrown in for good measure. But some didn't even bother with the frame and rubble. It seemed to us that if you had a couple of old plastic chairs and a tin table, you just stuck them at the side of the road and put up a resort sign. This was worrying because the accommodation at the Mango Trove wasn't finished yet so Windy had booked us into another resort a ten minute walk down the road. We needn't have worried though. Windy did us proud and our resort even boasted a swimming pool. The room service breakfast wasn't up to much though. The fried eggs could have easily been used to re-sole a pair of miner's boots and the sausages looked as though one of the many street dogs hanging around the place had just shat on the plate. Other than that, and the fact that the plumbing had a habit of regurgitating our next door neighbour's deposits back up into our lavatory whenever they flushed theirs, it was five star all the way. And our next door neighbours were a couple called Pat and Mandy. They'd come over from Singapore for the celebrations. I'd met them before. Pat is a mean blues harp player and he'd jammed with SKiNC a few times when he was passing through Hong Kong. But, of all the people who'd been invited to the grand opening, we were the only four to actually make it from overseas. Well, no big deal. We'd just have to play louder.

After we'd settled in to our resort, we repaired off to the Mango for a few evening warm up beers. We didn't party too hard that night as we had an early start the next day with festivities scheduled to commence with a champagne breakfast at 10:30 and a full day and night of celebrations to follow. There was one disconcerting moment that evening though when Pat got up on the stage to sound check his harps and mics, during the course of which he rattled off a couple of blues classics.

'Ah good,' said Klaske. 'The real singer's arrived.'

'What d'you mean babe? Are you telling me I'm no good?'

'No, of course not. You're good, but he's better.' You can always trust the Dutch to tell you straight.

The next morning we duly reported for duty at 11:00; only half an hour late so not a bad start. As always in the Philippines, things did not go exactly according to plan and, as the day wore on, plans had to be continuously revised to cope with unforeseen contingencies. Given the two maxims that 'the key to air power is flexibility' and 'you can never iron out a fluid situation', and also given that I'd lived with these maxims for most of my professional career, I thought these inconveniences should pose no problems. The first major problem that arose was with the guests of honour; the local mayor and the chief of police. Rather rudely, neither of them actually turned up. Whether or not this was due to local politics, or they hadn't been bribed enough, was difficult to ascertain. Minnie seemed to be related, in one way or another, to just about everyone in the community and most of the town were at the Mango, either as guests or employed as staff, so I surmised that it couldn't be that they were attending any other party. The ribbon-cutting ceremony was due to be conducted by the mayor at 12:30, but was delayed pending his arrival. At around 14:00 I was summoned when, without warning, Minnie requested over the PA the presence of Captain John Warham on the stage. I found the use of my former rank somewhat embarrassing at first but was soon put at ease when I found that everyone else on the stage was a captain as well. There was the captain of the fire department, the captain of the electricity department, the captain of the local school, the captain of the sanitation department, the captain of the roads department; in fact there was captain Uncle Tom Cobley and all. Minnie thrust a pair of scissors into my hand and informed me that I was taking the place of the mayor and was to cut the ribbon. I took my new duty very seriously, cut the ribbon with all the dignity I could muster dressed in shorts and T-shirt and formally declared the Mango Trove Resort to be well and truly opened and may god bless her and all who sail in her. Unfortunately, shortly thereafter, a rather unseemly incident took place in which I was accidentally involved, although through no fault of my own.

The Catholic Church is very much in evidence in the Philippines, so next on the order of ceremonies was a blessing by the local priest. As I am not very keen on organised religion of any sort, I thought it best to vacate the stage and took up a position at the end of the bar intending to stay out of the way. Apart from anything else, I had already noticed that, sticking out from underneath his cassock, the priest was wearing a very expensive pair of hand-made Italian leather shoes. In a community where half the people go barefoot because they can't afford even basic sandals, I found this rather incongruous; but I held my tongue. I had often noticed when flying over the Philippines that every town and village has a big, expensive, white building. They stand out for miles. Churches. It has always seemed a contradiction to me that, in communities so poor that they struggle to put food on the table, the Catholic Church spends its money on flashy buildings instead of putting it where it's really needed; in amongst the poor. But perhaps my blasphemy is the reason for what happened next. The priest stood on the stage, chanted some mumbo jumbo and then descended and, using what looked like a silver salt cellar, began to process around the area sprinkling holy water, that he'd no doubt just got from the tap, over all and sundry. From my station at the end of the bar, by the time I realised what was about to happen, it was too late to get out of the way. I can now only relate third party observations as to my reaction when the holy shower hit me. My own recollection is that I gracefully stepped out of the way. However, some have described how I cowered with my hands scratching at my face screaming, 'It burns, it burns.' Still others have reported that my head turned through 360 degrees and I mouthed foul oaths and curses speaking backwards in ancient tongues. Whatever the truth of the matter, all I know for sure is that Klaske and Windy didn't stop laughing about it for three days and, even now when it gets mentioned, they still fall about in gales of glee.

The non-appearance of the chief of police caused another problem. As a present for the dignitary, Windy had obtained a one litre bottle of what he assured me was the most expensive and sought after whiskey in the local area. Since its intended recipient was a no-show, something had to be done about it. So Windy, Pat, me and a chap called Sonny, who was yet another of Minnie's cousins, sat down at a table. Windy uncapped the bottle and poured out four shots. We all took a sip.

'Och Johnny. Can ye taste the peat in that?' he enquired.

'No, actually I can't,' I replied less than tactfully. 'All I can taste is road dirt and methanol. This stuff is fucking rotgut and the best thing you can do with it is use it to strip those doors that need repainting.' With that I repaired to the bar for a cleansing ale. The consequences of this were dire. Pat and Sonny took it upon themselves to demonstrate that the offending liquor was perfectly serviceable and proceeded to polish off the bottle between them.

There was a band playing during the day. They went for a break around dinner time and returned at about 20:30 in the evening for the night-time celebrations. There was nothing too remarkable about that except that, for the daytime set, the lead singer came dressed as a man and for the night-time set he (or she) came dressed as a woman. Later on in the night, Windy, Pat and I got up on stage and did a couple of blues sets. Because of the effects of the rotgut, the next day Pat had no recollection whatsoever of ever being on stage and wouldn't believe he was until Mandy showed him the photographs she'd taken. Then there was the effect it had on Sonny. He was a bit of a karaoke fan and, when I was singing, kept climbing onto the stage and attempting to wrest the mic from me. When I was in my teens, I did three years of training in Shotokan Karate. One of the things you learn is good balance and how to adjust your stance to fend off blows by using your opponent's energy against him. You can make yourself almost immovable. It's a bit like facing a fast bowler. You don't have to hit the ball hard to score a boundary. All you have to do is use the energy that the bowler's already imparted to the ball and gently guide it on its way with the bat for four penn'orth. So, during one of Sonny's assaults, I simply positioned myself so that, when he ran into me, he bounced off. Unfortunately he then lost his balance and fell off the edge of the stage. Windy tells me that the story is still told in the bars and bazaars of Paratong about how the *banyaga* flew into Vigan in his private jet, body checked Sonny and threw him off the stage. Later that night, or actually in the early hours of the morning, he finally ended up spread-eagled on the dance floor where he slept the night. It turned out he was the village drunk and renowned for 'erratic' behaviour. But apparently he surpassed all previous efforts that night. Even his favourite granny wouldn't speak to him for days afterwards.

And the dance floor was the scene of some other entertainment as well. Not many people in the town had seen a six-foot Nordic blonde before so a lot of the young girls wanted to talk to Klaske and kept inviting her up to dance. And there was a table of young teenage boys who were eyeing her up as well. They sat there for a long time drinking copious amounts of beer, egging each other on and summoning up Dutch courage. Eventually, whilst Klaske was dancing with another young girl, one of the boys leapt from the table, charged onto the dance floor and gave it his all. He was showing all his best moves and giving the Travolta performance of his life. Afterwards, Klaske came and sat down at a table with me and I said, 'Well you've pulled there babe.'

'What d'you mean?'

'That young kid over there.'

'Which one?'

'The one in the blue shirt. Didn't you see him?'

'No. What happened?'

'Him and his mates have been gawking at you all night. He finally got up the courage and jumped on the dance floor and gave you his whole John Travolta routine. Didn't you see him?'

'No, never even noticed him, I was dancing with that young girl.'

The poor lad, he'd tried his best only to go completely un-noticed. Still, he'd pulled it off in front of his mates and they were none the wiser.

After the day and night of ceremonies at the Mango Trove, we got back to our resort at early o'clock to find the gates had been locked, presumably to repel invaders. They were about 15 ft high and un-scaleable. However, there was a tree a few yards down the road which grew over the fence and hung into the garden. I surmised that it would be a simple matter to climb the tree, drop agilely into the garden and open up the gates from the inside to allow the remainder of our party to enter. I commenced my ascent. On the way up, I did notice that the fence was topped with barbed wire and various sharp pieces of metal designed to remove the testicles of anyone foolish enough to attempt to straddle them. As I was thinking of reconsidering my plan, a loud voice rang out from below.

'John get down from there NOW!' It was Klaske employing a tone of instructional voice I'd never heard her use before. She teaches kindergarten children and I can only assume she has practised this oft

142

times before when controlling her charges. It is very effective. I got down immediately. She told me later that her main concern was that, should I get injured, there would be no medical treatment available because all of the hospital staff had been at the party and were now passed out drunk, or stoned, or both.

When it came time to leave Narvacan and head off home, there was one final problem. I'd agreed the price with Jimmy in Philippine pesos but arranged to pay him in US dollars that I'd bought in Hong Kong before I left. Once I got to Narvacan, I realised I'd used the wrong exchange rate and needed to get some more pesos to make up the difference. I went with Minnie to a local ATM but, as usual, things didn't go quite as expected; in fact I ended up having an argument with the machine. It was inside a small ante-room attached to the bank which was closed at the time. I put my card in the machine and a female voice started talking to me.

'The card you have inserted is invalid. Please try another card.'

'No it's not,' I replied. 'I used it a couple of days ago and it was fine.' I put it in again.

'The card you have inserted is invalid. Please try another card.'

'It isn't. I just told you. It worked fine two days ago.'

'The card you have inserted is invalid. Please try another card.'

'Aren't you listening to me? I've already told you my card is fine.'

'The card you have inserted is invalid. Please try another card.'

'Listen to me you stupid woman. My card is fine. Just give me some bloody money.'

'The card you have inserted… '

She eventually gave me my money on about the tenth attempt but by that time I was screaming at the woman and threatening violence. Minnie was looking at me quite strangely and another woman who was in there with a couple of small children was shielding them behind her skirts in case the mad, screaming *banyaga* tried to eat them. After we landed back at Clark, Jimmy drove us from his hangar to the main terminal to catch our flight back to Hong Kong. We were standing by his Chevy and I explained about my cock-up on the exchange rate and how I was paying him in a mixture of US dollars and pesos. I handed him a roll with a rubber band around it expecting him to count it. Instead, he just weighed it in his hand, said in his laconic drawl, 'Feels about right Jaahn' and stuffed it in his pocket.

There was one other thing that happened on the way up to Narvacan. I'd told Windy that, on our flight up from Clark, we'd fly overhead the Mango Trove, do a couple of orbits and wave to everyone. The Navion-A was equipped with a basic RNAV. There was a VOR to the north of Narvacan so I plotted a bearing and distance to the Mango Trove and plugged it in. We homed in on that, but I had also equipped myself with a half-mil topographical chart just in case a bit of Mark 1 eyeball nav was required. Unfortunately, there had been quite a bit of rain recently and the floodplain around the river delta in the area didn't look much like what the cartographer had drawn.

'Can you just orbit here a second Jimmy? It's got to be somewhere around here,' I requested.

After a couple of orbits, Jimmy said, 'All looks the same down there don't it Jaahn.'

Just then, a voice came from behind me, 'Give me the fucking map.' I did as I was bidden and Klaske directed Jimmy to the east a couple of miles. There was the whole of the Mango Trove crew jumping around and waving to us.

So, despite my lifelong fascination with the intricacies of navigation, I don't do it any more. I leave the navigating to Klaske now because she's better at it than me.

8

RTB

'Contract (n.) – *A voluntary, deliberate, and legally binding agreement between two or more competent parties.*'
www.businessdictionary.com

One of the perks of working for an airline is the cheap travel. It's called many things. Rebated travel, sub-load travel, concessionary travel and a number of other terms, but they all mean the same thing; cheap travel. You can buy discounted tickets at rates that are not available to the general public. The amount of the discount varies. An ID50 ticket means the price is discounted by 50 per cent and, similarly, an ID90 ticket means the price is discounted by 90 per cent. There are terms and conditions attached to these fares. Typically on an ID90, you are listed as sub-load which means that you only get on the flight if there are no full-fare paying passengers to fill that seat. The reality is that you only get on if the aircraft isn't full. Well, that's not so bad. Sure, it can be a pain in the arse if you want to go somewhere on a particular day and that route is busy. If there are several flights to your destination that day, it can mean hanging around the airport as each flight departs waiting to see if you can get on. But hell, at only 10 per cent of the normal price what do you expect? Usually, the lower the discount, the lower the number of restrictions so, under certain circumstances, an ID50 ticket virtually guarantees that you can get a seat. These discounts are available not only to the employee, but also to his or her spouse and children, so this is a very valuable perk financially. And it gets better. It doesn't just apply to flights on the airline you happen to work for. Airlines have interline agreements. In these they agree to give similar discounts to other airlines' employees in return for the same courtesy being extended to their own staff. The main international agreement is called the Zonal Employee Discount Agreement (ZED) and there are hundreds of airlines worldwide that are parties to this. It means you can travel anywhere in the world at a fraction of the normal cost. And it gets even better than that. Many airlines also extend the same perk to employees who have retired, albeit that there are restrictions on the number of tickets that you are allowed to purchase in any one year. Cathay Pacific has such a staff travel system and, when I joined the airline in 1985, its terms were specifically included as part of my contract of employment.

In the late 90s, as part of their corporate re-engineering exercise, Cathay introduced a new staff travel scheme. At first blush it appeared to include improvements on the old scheme. As an example, the old scheme only permitted dependant discount to a legally married spouse. The new scheme extended this to common law partners by permitting nomination of a specific person outside of marriage. There were other such carrots to tempt the palate and signing over to the new scheme was purely voluntary. But there was a downside to this new scheme. A large downside. Whereas the old scheme was contractual in nature, the new scheme was a company policy and contained the infamous words, 'As the same may be amended from time to time in the sole discretion of the company.' We had seen this all before in 1994 with the unilateral imposition of a new set of rostering practices and a new employment contract touted as being purely voluntary. It was, but those of us who chose not to volunteer were subsequently victimised and penalised. So when this new 'voluntary' opportunity came along, and in the light of my previous experience with the Swires, my instinct told me not to trust them as far as I could throw them and, along with many others, I chose to remain on the old staff travel scheme.

This time we did not get penalised; after all what could they really do? Then, in 1999, they tried another bite of the cherry. During the contract negotiations that year they tried to move everyone across to the new scheme. I was leading the AOA negotiating team and was having none of it. In the end they conceded the point and, in the agreed 1999 contract, there was an addendum which specifically preserved the contractual right to staff travel for those who wished to retain that right rather than sign over to the new policy. It also contained some other clauses unrelated to staff travel where they had tried to impose similar 'policies' in place of contractual entitlements which we did not accept. This addendum became known as the Green Pages because, surprisingly enough, it was printed on green paper. It was prefaced by the words: 'The following Salary Scale and Benefits Sections 1–12, outlined in these Green Pages, are applicable to all Expatriate Pilots and Flight Engineers employed prior to 1st April 1993 and form part of the Conditions of Service and are contractual rights.'

Pretty specific one would have thought. Not so to the Swires, as it turned out. When *The 49ers* were sacked on 9 July 2001, we all received a package of documents by courier. One of the clauses in the documents related to Retirement Travel Benefits (RTB). It stated that: 'You will not be eligible for retiree travel.'

Well, how can they do that, you might ask? At the time we were all asking bigger questions. How can they just fire us all with no justification, maliciously defame us in the international media, destroy our reputations and our careers and get away with it? They seemed much more important questions requiring immediate answers. And, in any case, I was not eligible for RTB right at that time. Under the terms of the contract, in order to qualify for RTB, you had to have reached what was known as the relevant age; 50 or older. I was 49 and still had a year to go. In the middle of everything else that was happening, it got pushed to the bottom of my action list. However, ten months later, when the dust had settled somewhat, it came back to the top. On 29 April 2002, having reached relevant age in March, I wrote to the man who had signed our dismissal letters, the DFO, Ken Barley, in the following terms:

> I refer to your letter of 9th July 2001 in which you attempted, unlawfully, to terminate my employment with Cathay Pacific Airways Limited ('the company').
>
> Pending resolution of the various legal actions outstanding against you and the company in respect of this and certain other matters, and as an interim measure only, since I recently attained my 50th birthday I now require the company to provide me with Retirement Travel Concessions in accordance with my Conditions of Service. You are required, therefore, to provide me with the relevant documentation by return.

Reply came there none. No big surprise there then. Since we'd filed court cases against the company in multiple jurisdictions, they'd long ago stopped replying to any letters from us, probably on legal advice and to stop them putting their size 9s in their mouths any further. So, what to do about it? File another court case against them in the midst of everything else that was happening? To be honest, we had neither the time nor the resources to pursue it right then. And there were other developments.

Chris Sweeney, one of *The 49ers*, was married to Judith, a flight purser with Cathay. She applied for staff travel tickets for Chris as part of her spousal entitlement. They were granted. Oh, so it seems we could be OK then. But wait, not so fast. The person in charge of staff travel was a man by the name of Bob Nipperess. He originally started out in airline work as a cabin attendant but had worked his way up into management. Judith received a letter from Nipperess dated 26 February 2003 in which he stated:

> It has been a longstanding principle of the Company that employees whose employment is terminated should not enjoy access to concessional travel under the Cathay Pacific Airways Staff Travel Scheme. As such Mr Sweeney is not entitled to, and should not have been granted access to the Cathay Pacific Airways Staff Travel Scheme.

> … we wish to advise that we will be withdrawing your husband's access to the scheme with effect from 14th March 2003.

The same thing happened to another of *The 49ers*, Quentin Heron. He was married to Elaine, also a flight purser with Cathay. She received a similar letter from Nipperess also dated 26 February 2003. The company's staff travel website contained a similar statement relating to dismissed employees and continued to do so over the ensuing years. And again, Elaine received another letter from Nipperess dated 5 March 2007 wherein he restated their position. It said in part:

> The Company's travel benefits are intended for current employees and retirees only. A former employee whose employment was terminated by the Company is, as previously stated, excluded from our Staff Travel Scheme.

… Your husband, Mr Heron, was lawfully dismissed by the
Company upon payment of wages in lieu of notice. On that
basis, he is excluded from the Company's Staff Travel Scheme,
whether in his own right or through his spouse.

So, there we had it. Pretty comprehensive. They held that we had no
contractual rights to RTB and that was that. But then something
happened to change all that.

Courtney Chong was the Vice President of the Flight
Attendants' Union (FAU) during the 1992 Cathay Pacific cabin crew
strike. After the strike was over, despite assurances to the contrary,
she was victimised by management and sacked on trumped up
charges of theft of company property. They also publicly defamed
her. She sued the company and her case was settled out of court in
1998. But they also did something else. They refused to honour her
RTB entitlement, so she sued them again. In December 2009 she won
her case and received judgment in her favour from the High Court.
Naturally, Cathay appealed. They lost the appeal and judgment was
again awarded in Courtney's favour by the Court of Appeal in
November 2010. This was a whole new development. Although
Courtney's contract was different from ours, in that her RTB was
contained within a staff handbook and much of her case revolved
around whether or not this formed part of the contract; in the event
the court ruled it did. She ultimately received her RTB and
compensation for the period over which it had been denied in the
form of money she would have saved on tickets she actually flew
during that period.

On the back of Courtney's victory, Doug Gage and I filed
similar actions early in 2011 in the High Court to enforce our RTB
entitlements. First mistake. We rapidly discovered that, because at
that time our individual claims were for less than HK$1 million, the
procedure dictates that we should have taken our case first to the
Labour Tribunal rather than going straight to the High Court. We'd
received bad advice from our lawyers. Needless to say, Cathay's
lawyers took great delight in pointing this out in their usual arrogant
fashion and we were forced to withdraw the action and start afresh.
So, in August 2011, we filed new actions in the Labour Tribunal.

The first hearing in the tribunal was highly entertaining. Doug
and I had come fully prepared and ready to do battle. They sent along

a trainee Swire prince minion. He applied for an adjournment stating that the person responsible for managing staff travel matters, Bob Nipperess, was not available because of prior commitments. The tribunal chairman was not amused. This minion was asking the bench to believe that, in a company the size of Cathay Pacific, there was only one person who could deal with the matter. Presumably if he is away on leave or otherwise unavailable, the whole edifice collapses around the Swires' ears. Minion received a severe roasting and costs were awarded in our favour for the inconvenience. We were both working for Oxford Aviation Academy (OAA) as simulator instructors at the time so we put in for our daily rate which was duly awarded and the chairman instructed it should be paid immediately; 'And I mean today' as he put it. Minion was sent packing with his tail between his legs to report back to his boss on how dextrously he'd handled the situation.

The next hearing was scheduled for three weeks later with a specific instruction that they'd better come prepared this time. These tribunal hearings are good fun. Although, obviously, everyone takes legal advice first, no lawyers are actually allowed into the hearing and so you get to speak for yourself. All remarks are generally directed through the bench but the rules are reasonably relaxed. If you ask the bench to address your opponent directly, permission is often granted and so it was the case at the subsequent hearing. In the light of the Courtney Chong judgment, our case had precedent on its side. On top of that, their defence was so full of holes and inconsistencies that no reasonable person would possibly believe it. But they pressed ahead anyway. Doug and I had great sport pointing these out to the chairman and he frequently shook his head, presumably in disbelief. It was also good fun to actually question Nipperess directly and then listen to him trying to talk his way out of the various holes they'd dug for him and themselves. But, that aside, one of the purposes of the Labour Tribunal is to try to get the parties to settle their differences at the preliminary hearings, thus saving the time and expense of a full trial. We had come fully prepared to do just that. But they had not. With all the usual arrogance and pomposity that we had come to know so well from these people, they simply behaved as if they were above the law and refused any form of reasonable compromise. At that point our claim for damages for the pair of us totalled HK$1.17 million. They offered 300k; the usual Swire derisory offer. The tribunal chairman suggested splitting the difference. Nipperess refused and the case was handed up to the High Court. Result! That's exactly where we wanted to be in the first place. I spoke to him outside after the hearing was over and lost my rag a bit.

'You know Bob we came in here ready to settle this and save the cost of yet another court case.'

'The law states clearly that… ' but I didn't let him finish.

'We'll see what the fucking law states in the High Court,' and with that we left.

So now the legal machine had to be geared up to grind into action once more. We instructed the same barristers that Courtney had used; Martin Lee and Frances Lok. Martin Lee, QC, SC, JP, is a Hong Kong political activist, lawyer and former legislator. He was also the founding chairman of the Democratic Party in Hong Kong. He came highly recommended, as likewise did Frances, and was relishing the thought of tearing Nipperess to pieces again on the stand as he had in Courtney's case. The whole laborious process of exchanging witness statements, affidavits, discovery motions and other necessary documents commenced. And this was when the futility of their defence was exposed. We had carefully considered our strategy. We had also done the same in predicting what their defence(s) might be. Always try to put yourself in your enemies' shoes. So we did not disclose all our evidence at the outset; rather we fed it to them piecemeal so that they had to respond in like fashion. In this way we led them into a trap.

Firstly, we just said that they had breached our contract by refusing to grant us access to RTB. They responded by saying that they had never done such a thing and it was all our own fault. If we had simply applied for our RTB access cards they would have been issued to us. We were ready for that. We produced the letters to Judith and Elaine and the website statements which demonstrated that this was patently untrue. It forced them to change tack.

Next they tried the, 'We didn't know how to get in touch with you,' approach. If we'd only applied once we had reached relevant age, they would have given us RTB cards but they didn't have our contact details and kept no records of such for past employees. Apart from this argument still being refuted by our previous disclosures, we had another card up our sleeve to counter this one. I had kept in touch with a colleague, Don Grange, who had served with me on the AOA General Committee. He had resigned from Cathay in disgust before he reached 50. One month before he attained the relevant age, he received a completely unsolicited letter from them at his home in the

UK enclosing his RTB card with full instructions on its use. He swore an affidavit to that effect which raised the question of how they managed to do this if Nipperess' assertion that they kept no database of past employees' contact details was true. He couldn't be telling lies could he? Surely not.

Then at the end of 2011, Doug and I received letters offering to issue us with RTB cards if we would fill in a simple application form. Success, you might think. We've rolled them! But wait, not so fast again. Read the small print. Included on the form was a clause that said: 'I understand that retiree travel concessions are for recreational travel only, and they must not be used for any business or commercial purposes.'

OK so far. I can live with that. Staff travel always had that proviso. Then it went on to say: 'Misuse of concessional travel for business/commercial purposes or any abuse of the privileges by me or my eligible dependants will result in suspension or withdrawal of all travel privileges for me and/or my dependants concerned.'

Hmm. Slight alarm bells ringing here. The business bit is OK but what other 'abuse' are they talking about? They could dream up anything they want if they just wanted to strip me of my RTB. Stop being so cynical John. Where's your faith and trust in these people to act honourably? But then the last paragraph was a cracker: 'I also understand that Cathay Pacific Airways Limited reserves the right to reject any of my applications for travel concessions if improper use of concessional travel by me or my eligible dependants is suspected.'

What? They've got to be joking. Firstly that would strip me of my contractual entitlement and, secondly, give them the ability to cancel my RTB completely on mere 'suspicion' of wrongdoing. Now where have I heard this before? Oh yes, I know. DGP. Police, judge and jury all rolled into one neat package. They must think I'm an idiot. Fuck that. I returned the form duly filled in but with the offending paragraph deleted. This prompted an exchange of letters in which Nipperess questioned why I found the paragraph offensive. I replied with words to the effect that I didn't trust them as far as I could throw them. But then, a couple of weeks later, I received another letter enclosing my RTB card. Result this time surely? No, far from it.

The letter also contained an 'administration procedure' for application for tickets. Under 'normal' circumstances, people with an RTB card have access to an online system called iJourney. With a username and password, you simply log in, book your tickets, pay for them, check schedules and availability and change dates and times if necessary all with a few keystrokes. Your tickets are then issued immediately and delivered electronically. It's a seamless system. Would we be afforded such access? Not on your life. For us, we were to be treated as a special case. We would have to fill in a paper form, which we must first apply for, and then deliver it either in person or via fax to the staff travel office. There good old Bob had put together a 'dedicated team' to deal with our applications which, with a deliberately cumbersome payment and refund system, could take anything up to three weeks to process. Effectively he was saying that, yes we'll give you RTB, but in order to get a ticket you have travel overland by camel to our office in Ouagadougou (bringing a short engine and a lead acid battery with you to power the generator), fill in a papyrus in Sanskrit (not forgetting to bring your own stylus and ink), pay up front in Polish zloty (at an exchange rate to be determined at the time) and then camp out for three weeks in the desert whereupon your tickets may or may not be issued. Martin Lee put it more succinctly. It's like being given an ATM card with no PIN. They were denying us specific performance. It was just another attempt to discriminate against us and make our lives as difficult as possible. They tried to say that, because we were insisting on our contractual entitlements rather than accepting their new policy, the iJourney system could not be programmed to deal with our ticket applications. This was more bullshit. There were other retirees who, like us, had stayed on the Green Pages. Their RTB entitlements were administered exclusively through iJourney. We got two of these, Nigel Demery and Malcolm Hunter, to swear witness statements and affidavits to that effect, together with screen shots from the iJourney system demonstrating the application process, and entered them into evidence. But Frances insisted that we should try out the 'administration procedure' so both Doug and I did at different times. Our applications were refused by Bob's dedicated team. Another nail in their coffin.

There was also another issue that was under dispute. The matter of compensation. Courtney had received compensation for all of her flown tickets from the time that she was denied RTB. Surely we should get the same? Oh no. Not according to them. They would only consider compensation from 2010, the date that we had decided to challenge them on the back of Courtney's ruling. Our position was that they had knowingly and repeatedly misrepresented the situation to us over the period of years from the time we were sacked and, with each such statement, this generated a new cause of action. The legal principle is known as negligent misstatement. The point of our taking this stance is that, in general, claims for damages must be initiated within six years of the initial breach. On this basis, we were out of time. But, in special circumstances, the court has the right to use its discretion and waive the six year rule. We held that this was such a case.

As part of the legal process, we were required to go through mediation. A meeting was arranged for 18 June 2012. We'd suggested a couple of mediators but they turned them down. They wanted one of their own choosing. That was fine by us. We didn't care who it was. Our case was so strong that even someone who was biased in their favour couldn't help but see the futility of their defence. Unlike our opponents, we went into the meeting without a lawyer, but fully briefed by Frances to be polite and businesslike. She had a good grasp of my opinion of the opposition from various remarks I'd made to her during our consultations and was concerned that I might expand on them during the mediation. She needn't have worried. I'd been facing these jokers across the table for years. The meeting turned out to be quite revealing. The notes I made at the time are reproduced below verbatim.

Present: John Warham (JW)
           Doug Gage (DG)
           Nipperess (RN)
           Fiona Chow (RN's Assistant)
           Hunsworth (TH) [Cathay's solicitor]
           Mediator (MS)
           MS' Secretary

Commenced 13:30, terminated 18:00. During that time we were only in the same room together for around one hour. The rest of the time they spent in breakout.

These notes aren't necessarily in chronological order. Rather they are a summary of the discussions on the various points.

Opening remarks by JW along the lines of, we are here in a spirit of co-operation. I think we can all agree that we've spent enough money on lawyers over the years, let's see if we can put this one

to bed without the need for more court proceedings. [Nods all
round and rictus grin from RN.] Let's start with what we are
agreed on. We are agreed that the Green Pages confer a
contractual right to RTB, there's no dispute over that any more.
[More nods all round.] As we see it, the differences between us
can be summarised very simply. First there is the matter of
specific performance in that, even though we have our RTB
cards, we still cannot obtain tickets because of the administration
procedures that have been put in place and, secondly, there is the
matter of damages for the time that our contractual rights were
denied to us plus our legal costs to date.

Debate ensues ref the admin procedures. RN describes how he
has put together a 'dedicated team' who are fully briefed to deal
with our special situation. Explains it is impossible to
programme the computer to deal with us so we have to be
handled manually.

JW responds that the system isn't working and we are still being
denied our contractual rights because we can't get tickets. Why
can't we be put in iJourney like other retirees who have retired
on Green Pages such as Nigel Demery?

RN says Demery has transferred to the new scheme on
retirement. [I believe this is a blatant lie. Will check with NJD.]

First breakout.

MS: Are your negotiations usually this cordial?
JW: As I told you in the briefing Mark, I may not particularly
like these people but this is business. I'm just trying to get to the
deal. This is not about personalities.
MS: Would you like to come and chair our partners' meetings?
[This just to assure Frances that, in accordance with instructions,
we were both polite *and* nice.]

Some shuttling to and fro by MS. Meeting resumes.

Discussion about issuing of the RTB cards. RN restates their
position that they would have issued the cards had we only

applied earlier. Says they have no admin procedure in place to issue cards when retirees reach relevant age. They all have to write in and apply.

JW: What about Don Grange? He retired back in '97 and you sent him a card two months before he reached relevant age without him applying or filling in a form.
RN: No that's never happened, not in the time that I've been in the department since '94.
JW: Yes it has, Bob. It happened to Don and there are others. I've got copies of the letters.
TH: [Looking very surprised] You say you've got letters?
JW: Yes.

Breakout.

MS: Have you got the letter here?
JW: No but I can get the lawyers to send it over.
MS: That's an ace. Why haven't you told them this before?
JW: I know it's an ace. We were holding it in reserve to play it at the right time. Every time we play a card they have to change their story. We were waiting for the right time to undermine their story.
MS: Now's the time to play it.
JW: OK, I'll get it sent over.

Don Grange letter arrives and MS asks permission to show it to the opposition. Agreed and he shuttles to their breakout room.

During further shuttling, the following discussions take place between MS, JW & DG.

MS: They say that you are out of time because you didn't file within six years of reaching relevant age.
JW: No. We say that the breach commenced with the letter of 9 July 2001 when they sacked us. It specifically denies us RTB and they misrepresented the position to us then and continued to do so over the years until the outcome of the Courtney Chong case. It was only then that they acknowledged our contractual rights. We have letters from RN consistently and continually

156

denying *The 49ers* and their spouses any form of travel benefits whatsoever throughout that period to 2010. We also say that they are still denying us specific performance because the admin system RN has put in place is deliberately designed to stop us gaining access.

MS: Oh I see what you mean. If I don't pay my secretary her wages in January, then she only has six years to claim them. But if I don't pay them in February as well then a new six year clock starts ticking and so on.

JW: Exactly and that's our position.

After more shuttling:

MS: They say those letters are irrelevant because they weren't written to you and that some of the people were on a different contract – not on Green Pages.

JW: Well of course they would, but we say it goes to show exactly how they've treated all of *The 49ers* all along and they show intent.

MS: Yes, a judge would look at the overall picture and the letters do shine brightly. What about the July 2001 letter? TH says he hasn't seen it.

DG: It's here in the bundle.

MS shuttles off to show it to them.

[This is very significant. Either RN has withheld the letter from TH or he hasn't read the bundle. Either way, TH got bushwhacked. What else has RN withheld?]

At some stage RN tried to bluff his way out of the Don Grange letter by saying it was probably in response to an application from Don. JW refuted this.

The first offer:

Meeting resumes and RN asks TH to present their offer.

TH: We're in the Court of Final Appeal in August where all the other issues will be decided and we'd like to see this one dealt with as well. [Why would he mention that?] We are prepared to offer you full access to iJourney and administer you in exactly the same way as all the other retirees and give you the same entitlements as them; that is, unlimited travel. Also, we are prepared to offer you HK$300k in compensation to divide as you see fit.

JW: Would that be a contractual right to RTB or would it be company policy?

RN: Company policy.

JW: Is that 300k each or in total?

TH: In total.

MS: [hurriedly] I suggest we take a break now to consider the offer.

I had already briefed MS that their standard negotiating strategy is to low ball. I asked him to convey to them not to do that to us because to do so in any negotiation is a sure fire way of pissing off your opponent.

Breakout.

MS: We're making progress here. They're offering you access to iJourney. That's a big concession.

JW: No it's not. What they're trying to do is strip away our contractual rights and make our RTB subject to company policy. We've seen this in contract negotiations all the way back to 1994. They offer a carrot to entice you to sign over to company policy and then strip you of your benefits.

MS: Well wouldn't you prefer the protection offered to the other 20,000 employees?

JW: No, they have no protection. I'd prefer to keep my contractual rights. In any case, the company policy doesn't give access to first class. The Green Pages give us first class.

MS: Oh I see.

JW: And as for the money, it's a joke. They haven't changed their position from the Labour Tribunal. They're still saying January 2010. In a negotiation, the parties are supposed to move towards each other. They're not moving at all. It's standard Cathay negotiating technique. I've seen this for years in my dealings with them. They take something from you then offer it back as a supposed concession and demand another concession in return. And they haven't even addressed the issue of legal costs.

MS: Your costs seem very high for such an early stage in the case.

JW: Here's the itemised bill.

MS: Well at the current rate of burn, the numbers don't work out. For a, call it, HK$1 million claim, you've already spent half of your damages.

JW: Yes that's why we've made a sanctioned offer to put them on indemnity costs. We'll get it back.

MS: [Shakes his head] No it doesn't work that way. And are you aware of the rules about funding other people's court cases?

JW: If you're talking about champerty, yes.

MS: I don't know where the money's coming from. Is it the union?

JW: I'm not telling you.

[Big alarm bell here. Why would he ask that? He's a big mate of TH or has at least known him for years. Despite all the stuff about confidentiality from MS in the pre-meeting briefing, something doesn't smell right.]

Counter offer.

We put in a counter offer of our sanctioned offer plus our legal costs. MS shuttled it to them.

MS returns with another offer of iJourney company policy plus HK$500k in total.

We reject it, thank him for his time and good offices and leave. We did not see RN again but saw TH in the corridor as we left. He didn't look happy.

Other exchanges.

At some point I mentioned the Courtney Chong precedent, RN got quite hot under the collar and tried to say it has nothing to do with our case.

JW: Yes Bob I know it was partly about whether or not the handbook was included expressly as part of her contract but the fact remains she was denied her contractual RTB by you and the court awarded her damages in compensation for the money she had spent. It is the same in that respect and it sets precedent. [He didn't like that much.]

RN tried to question my claim with respect to airports not served by CX such as LGW.

JW: I didn't want to go to LGW Bob, I wanted to go to LHR but Oasis was offering a cheap deal so I took it. Had you not denied me my contractual rights I would have travelled to LHR on Cathay. [I think we put that to bed as his attempted challenge was half-hearted and he gave up quickly.]

Regarding the January 2010 issue:

TH: It is my very strong advice to Cathay that your entitlement to damages only extends from then.

[I resisted the temptation to remark that it was presumably also his very strong advice that they could defeat our S21B and defamation claims. Frances would have been proud of me.]

During some of the shuttling;

MS: I feel like a man carrying a lighted candle in a fireworks factory waiting to see which side explodes first.

Summary.

The opposition were ill-prepared and in disarray as evidenced by the length of time spent in breakout. We bushwhacked RN with the Don Grange letter. A good time to play one of our aces. RN bushwhacked his own lawyer with the July 2001 letter. TH reports higher up the food chain than RN. Has RN been keeping information from his superiors as well? Perhaps now the lid might come off.

In the light of the revelations re. letters etc., surely TH must now advise them that their case is full of holes and they can't possibly go to court with it? Or will he keep on milking the cow?

Finally, why did MS ask where the money was coming from? I didn't like that little exchange.

Conclusion.

Nothing has changed in their camp. Same old attitude, same old negotiating techniques; arrogant and bullying. At least the mediation box has been ticked and we can get on with the proceedings themselves. And we had some fun!

We'd tried hard to negotiate a settlement but there was nothing for it but to apply for a court date. We got one; in December 2013. More waiting but, never mind, we're used to it.

9

Interlude

'Life is what happens to you while you're busy making other plans.'

John Lennon

In some ways the waiting is the worst part because you have no control over the timing. The preparation's complete. The game plan's in place and there's nothing you can do to hurry things along. But it's always there in the back of your mind nagging away. As Christmas approached at the end of 2011, we were halfway there. Soon be in the right year at least. Not long now. Only eight months to go. Well, nine months really. It's not until the end of August. But Mike Fitz-Costa's comment kept coming back, 'You've been telling me it's only n months to go for the last ten years John.' How to fill the time? I was going to turn 60 in 2012. I've had a myocardial infarction. I've got arteriosclerosis and an aortic aneurysm. You don't know how much time you've got left. Don't just sit there wishing your life away. Get off your arse and do something. So we did. We went travelling. Although by this time money was getting tight, I reasoned it didn't matter because I'd get my tickets refunded when we won the RTB claim.

For Christmas, we hired a villa in Tobago called the Pink House on Mahogany Ridge. Sandy Easton was operating a Monarch flight to there from Gatwick. His wife, Jan, had retired from Monarch by then, but she was going with him, so the four of us shared the place over the holiday. We had a great time, like old friends do. The house was owned by a lady called Sandra who lived in the villa next door. Despite being a woman of a certain age, she was still a rock chick at heart. She'd been around in London in the 60s and knew a lot of the musos who were on the scene back then; moderately significant

163

people like The Stones and The Beatles. She had a Trinidadian partner called Gerry. Like Sandra, he also was a gentleman of a certain age and, according to her at least, an inveterate womaniser. It didn't seem to bother her though. The pair of them still loved to party and we spent a couple of memorable evenings in their company. Unfortunately though, potential legal implications prevent me from expanding further on this particular story.

Initially, there was a slight problem. Klaske and I had travelled down to Tobago from Hong Kong via London. We spent a few hours there to drop off our cold weather clothes with my son Richard, who lives in Charlwood near Gatwick, before jumping on the Monarch flight to Tobago. By the time we got there, we'd been travelling almost non-stop for 28 hours. Hong Kong and Tobago are antipodal points meaning that the time change is 12 hours. By the time we arrived there, Klaske and my body clocks were totally out of sync with local time. The four of us went out for dinner on the first night and Sandy's first officer and his wife joined us. We'd never met this couple before and, by way of small talk, he started asking me intelligent questions about my job as a sim instructor. I was incapable of intelligent talk, small, medium or large, and so did not come across as a very approachable, or indeed likeable, sort of individual. Klaske was not quite as bad as me, but still was not her usual self. And then when we got back to the villa, Sandy and Jan were ready for some shuteye but we were now just waking up. So we continued to party until about eight o'clock in the morning and then retired to bed just when they were getting up. It took us a couple of days to get acclimatised before things ran more smoothly, but our jet lag did lead to one memorable exchange. It was late in the evening and the four of us were sitting on the balcony by the pool. Jan decided it was time for bed and started turning all the lights off. We weren't anywhere near ready for sleeping, so Klaske said words to the effect, 'Can we leave those on and we'll turn them off when we go up?' to which Jan replied, 'Well all right then, but no shagging on the balcony.' I guess our falling about laughing in response did not really assist much in ameliorating the situation. It was all a far cry from the days, in our late 20s and early 30s, when I was still working for Monarch, when Sandy and I used to meet up to go out for a drink in the pub in the evening and not manage to return home for three days. There'd often be someone we'd come across who was having a party and we'd tag along; just for a quick one you understand. But then one thing would lead to another and before we knew it, the sun was coming up and it was time to go for breakfast; which would develop into lunch, a hair of the dog and the next party venue. Apparently today, so I'm told, it has an official title. Binge drinking. If only we'd known. If only the health and safety nannies had been around back then to warn us of the folly of our ways. We just thought we were having a good time. But, fortunately, it doesn't seem to have done us any harm. No one got hurt and we've survived unscathed into our more mature years. As long as Keith's still rocking, there's hope for the rest of us and bugger the nannies.

On Christmas day we hosted a party for the whole of Sandy's crew. A couple of days earlier we'd gone out shopping for supplies and stopped at a local supermarket to pick up some groceries. They had some young lads at the checkout to pack our purchases into brown paper bags. As we approached the checkout, this young kid saw Klaske. I guess he hadn't seen many six-foot blondes before because his eyes popped out of his head and he started having trouble walking properly, due primarily, we surmised, to some stiffness in the groin area. After a couple of minutes, the manager sauntered over to him and said, 'Stop you behavin' like a stupid boy an' get on wit' yo' work.' Stupid boy. That became our catchphrase for the rest of the holiday. I also decided to adopt the Tobago driving style which involves hanging your right arm out of the window and waving languidly to other drivers and passers-by whilst using your left hand to do everything else such as steering, changing gear, indicating etc. This is obviously an acquired skill which requires some practice and, after a couple of near misses, I was instructed to revert to more orthodox techniques.

The party itself was a memorable day, made all the easier when the time came to tidy up the mess that more than 20 people make over a period of however long it was. Being mostly cabin crew in attendance, Jan simply called out, 'Clear in,' and the team went to work. Within minutes the whole place was tidied up and all the trash collected and stowed in gash bags ready for the garbage men to cart away. It was a miraculous transformation and saved us the necessity of getting off our, by then rather drunken, arses to do any form of manual labour.

Our Caribbean Christmas being over, we flew back to Gatwick and arrived on the 28th. I knew something was amiss because we couldn't get on stand for around 45 minutes and, instead, were held on the tarmac. When we finally disembarked the terminal was in chaos with people milling around everywhere. As we made our way through the crowds, I remarked to Klaske that I wondered what all the commotion was about. A woman passing by overheard me and with wide eyes said to me, 'There's a bomb scare!'

'Oh really,' I replied. 'Well I'm not scared, are you?' Clearly she was because she looked at me as if I was an escapee from a lunatic asylum and made her way as rapidly as the throng would allow in the opposite direction. Bomb scare. It's poor use of the language. Bomb threat, bomb warning; fair enough. I'd received enough of these during my career. A message would come through to say a threat had been made. These were coded with different levels of perceived risk depending upon how and when the information had been received. We had a laid down set of procedures to be followed in such events and we simply carried them out. There was no point in being scared. If it was your turn for real then, other than follow the procedures designed to minimise the damage in the event of an explosion, there wasn't much else you could do about it. Fortunately in my own experience, they all turned out to be false. Not that it's always the case obviously. But, overall, in the risk analysis, the chances of being on board an aircraft with a genuine bomb are pretty remote. You're much more at risk of being injured in your own home with all the dangerous equipment laying around in the kitchen. Especially Breville toasted sandwich makers. In male hands they're lethal. There's nothing more guaranteed to ruin your whole evening than second-degree burns to the lips and inner lining of the mouth received from a late night snack, prepared after returning from the pub, delivered by scalding hot tomato juice and molten Cheddar cheese, vintage, extra tangy or otherwise, erupting from a Vulcan product of one of those infernal devices.

When we arrived back at Gatwick, it wasn't the end of our holiday travels yet. We were going to spend New Year with my daughter, Nicola, who lives in Brighton (well Hove actually), but before that, we were travelling to Holland to visit Klaske's family. This was to be my introduction as the new boyfriend. Klaske was born in Delfstrahuizen, a small village in Lemsterland in the province of Friesland in the north of the country, and her father still lives in the local area. The nearest airport is Groningen. I'd checked out all the scheduled airlines that flew there from London but none of them fitted the bill for a day trip; morning arrival and evening departure.

After our Narvacan adventure, the solution was obvious. We chartered a Piper Navajo to take us there from Shoreham which was nice and handy to Brighton. Nicola, her husband Christian and Richard came along for the ride and spent the day exploring the town whilst we did the family thing. I couldn't have been made more welcome by Klaske's family despite the language problem as her father and brother don't speak English. Her two sisters and their various children do though, so all was not lost.

And I learned a new Dutch word while I was there. The weather for the flight out was excellent; a cold, clear morning with unlimited visibility. We could see halfway across Europe. The forecast for the late afternoon was not so good with low cloud and rain expected in the south of England. The pilots had requested that we make sure that we arrived punctually back at the airport for the late afternoon departure. Being an ex-air taxi man myself, I sympathised with them and ensured that we would arrive on the dot. There was a slight problem though. I couldn't find them when we got there. We were in the terminal when my phone rang. It was Nicola who informed me that they were waiting for us in the charter terminal next door. As we were making our way over there, I was mumbling to myself words to the effect of, 'Why didn't they say to meet in the bloody building next door instead of dicking us around. Now we're going to be late etc. etc.' That was when Klaske's older sister, Femmy, made a remark that I had *kapsones* and the two of them had a chuckle together. Klaske explained to me later that this translates colloquially into English as someone who 'walks beside his shoes'. As we would say where I come from, 'too big for his boots'. Oh dear! Not a good first impression but, as always, you can trust the Dutch to speak their minds. On the flight back, the weather behaved as forecast and the cloud cover started halfway across the North Sea. By the time we reached Shoreham it had clamped. We made an RNAV approach and broke cloud at around 400 ft with only a small sidestep manoeuvre required to line up with the runway. The pilots did a sterling job and I thanked them and remarked how the equipment had improved markedly since I was air taxiing. Just as well really. In my day we'd have ended up at Gatwick and the landing fees would have wiped out the entire profit on the trip.

After New Year, we travelled back to Hong Kong. Only seven months to go. It's said that time flies when you're having fun. Well we'd been having a lot of fun but time was doing anything but flying.

Quite the reverse it seemed to me. It was moving like the hour hand on a Salvador Dali clock. The longer the time available, the more time you have to create imaginary problems in your own mind and then spend time worrying about them. Have we got everything covered? Have we missed anything? Have they got any aces up their sleeves? Have we got enough money to last the course? What if? If you have enough time, these imaginary problems can become a self-fulfilling prophecy if you let them. And, if you're not careful, the black dog will then come sniffing at the door. You must maintain control to keep him at bay. Unfortunately, as my mother always told me, patience is not one of my strong suits. I was definitely standing at the back of the queue when they were handing out that particular virtue; and that made the waiting all the harder for me to bear. What next to do to while away the damned time?

In February, I was invited to give a lunchtime talk at the Foreign Correspondents' Club (FCC) in Lower Albert Road. The subject was, 'The Cathay Pacific 49ers – A Pilot's Point of View'. It was a good opportunity to re-emphasise to the assembled journalists and other interested parties the fact that our case was pivotal to the future job security of everyone working in Hong Kong. For the most part I met with a sympathetic audience, with only one Swire prince plant there to try to ask difficult questions. He was easily dispensed with. The journos were particularly receptive to my message as some of their number had recently been peremptorily fired by one of the local newspapers and treated in much the same way as us. A report of the talk was written by Jonathan Sharp and published in the FCC's monthly magazine, *The Correspondent*. Here are some excerpts:

> John Warham does not pull any punches when he
> excoriates the management of Hong Kong's leading airline.
> 'Malicious' and 'vindictive' were just some of the words
> Warham used in an address to a Club lunch. He charged
> that Cathay, not content with sacking the pilots in a row
> over terms and conditions, subsequently made life as
> miserable as possible for them by, for example,
> misrepresenting their income tax so that they faced
> swingeing tax bills and forcing them to leave Hong Kong.
> 'They then set about destroying our careers and
> reputations' by having the pilots effectively blacklisted by

major airlines. 'We were pariahs in a profession we had devoted our whole lives to.'

The fallout from the summary cull included the break-up of some marriages and families of sacked pilots. Warham went so far as to say that in his opinion the deaths of three of the 49ers, two men and a woman, after they were sacked were 'the direct result of what these people [at Cathay] did to us'.

He reserved particular venom for former Cathay chief executives Tony Tyler and Philip Chen, at times almost eliding their names into 'Tyler'n'Chen' – as if they were a single malign entity.

The many vicissitudes of the legal saga, which at one stage spread across four jurisdictions and caused a rift in the ranks of the pilots that led to many accepting management settlements, are recounted in a book by Warham.

One of the bitterest blows came on Christmas Eve 2010 when the Hong Kong Appeal Court reduced by two-thirds defamation damages of HK$3.5 million previously awarded to the pilots. 'That wasn't the best Christmas present I've ever received.'

But it's not just about the money or the pilots. The point that Warham stressed was that the 49ers case affects every man and woman employed in Hong Kong under the city's employer-friendly labour laws.

The pilots' stance should resonate with, among others, FCC journalists who in recent years have been shocked to see colleagues at local and international media outlets abruptly shown the door for breaking ill-defined rules on political correctness in the newsroom.

And those journalist unfortunates have not had recourse to the kind of financial resources that have enabled the 49ers to sustain their battle. Warham declined to say what the pilots' legal costs were, adding that Cathay managers had resorted to dirty tricks to find out where the money had come from.

Final legal closure to the saga of the 49ers comes on August 27 with a ruling by the Court of Final Appeal. Warham acknowledged that the 49ers' struggle has always been an uphill one, but asked if he was confident of winning at this final stage, he unhesitatingly replied: 'Yes, we are'.

Excellent article. Couldn't have put it better myself. But still six months to go. OK, we're getting there, but what next?

It was my sixtieth birthday on 25 March. For my fiftieth, I'd gone to New Orleans for ten days to listen to the blues in its home. Music. There was the answer. But how to combine it with something memorable? One of my favourite cities in the world is New York, particularly Manhattan. The first time I went there I was captivated. It's just like it's portrayed in films. Vibrant, noisy and in your face 24/7; and the New Yorkers take no prisoners with their wise-cracking, wry humour. Just my kind of place. It also has one of the greatest rock venues in the world. Madison Square Garden. I'd been there only once before; in 1991 when I went to see Guns 'n' Roses. I trawled the listings to see who was coming up soon and there was the answer. Bruce Springsteen. The Boss! I'd been a fan since the 70s but I'd never seen him live. He played three gigs at Wembley Stadium in July 1985. Tickets were like rocking horse shit but I managed to get four through a friend who was in the business. But then the job offer from Cathay came along. I had to leave the UK in March with no chance of getting back there for at least four months, so I gave my tickets away to people I thought would appreciate the show. They went, had a great time, bought me the T-shirt, concert programme and all sorts of other memorabilia but I wasn't there. Now here was an opportunity to put that right. Of course, the concert was sold out within hours of the tickets going on sale. There was nothing for it but to use the scalpers. I ended up paying US$750 for a pair of tickets with a face value around one third of that, but they were good tickets; centre stage and only four rows back from the front. So it was that, on Monday 9 April 2012, Klaske and I entered the mighty arena at the Garden and saw The Boss. It was his Wrecking Ball Tour and the show lasted well over three hours. It was sensational, phenomenal and every other superlative that you can think of. Another tick on the bucket list. We spent a few more days in Manhattan and did the tourist thing. Went through Central Park to the Dakota Building, walked over the Brooklyn Bridge, stood outside the Chelsea Hotel which was closed for renovation, bought some boots in my favourite boot store in Greenwich Village, cruised the many bars and clubs that the city has to offer and ate hot dogs and falafels with everything on in Times Square at midnight. And then we went home. Only five months to go.

On 3 June, Johnny Winter played a gig in Hong Kong and we went along. The last time I'd seen him was back in the 70s but he'd lost none of his skill since then. He stroked the fret board with his long, slender fingers and coaxed beautiful riffs from his axe. It was great to see so many young people there. I was quite surprised that they'd heard of Johnny Winter but it demonstrated to me that the blues is alive and well with the next generation and will be for generations yet to come. But he looked really ill. He only stood for the opening number. For the rest of the gig he sat down on a chair and, at the end, had to be helped off the stage by a couple of minders. He died just over two years later in a hotel room in Zurich. A great loss to the blues world but, like many other artists who went before him, he has left an enduring legacy to the world. Would that we could all say the same when our time comes.

Nearly there; just two months to go. At the beginning of July, we flew back to Holland and spent a couple of weeks there. First we had a few days in Amsterdam and stayed at the Hotel Americain. It's a beautiful old building on Leidsekade and has a great bar with the walls covered in photographs of the many famous musos and film stars who've stayed there over the years. The weather was cold though and I hadn't come properly prepared, but a visit to the Waterlooplein flea market soon fixed that. I bought a brand new second hand leather jacket for EUR70 to keep me warm.

We went to the Resistance Museum where I was struck by the many similarities between Dutch and British colonial history and its repercussions for the Dutch nationals living in the Far East during WWII. The Rijksmuseum had recently reopened following an extensive renovation and we spent a day wandering round it marvelling at the art and other exhibits it contains. While we were in the area, we drove over to see Klaske's family again and it gave me the opportunity to make a more favourable impression on Femmy than on my first visit. After Amsterdam we hopped on a ferry to Terschelling in the Frisian Islands off the north coast and spent a few days there. This was one of Klaske's old stamping grounds when she was younger and we caught up with some of her old friends from those days. It was there that I rediscovered my cycling skills, which had lain rusty for some years. I was amazed by the amount of drag that my new leather jacket was able to generate in the face of a strong wind blowing off the North Sea whilst cycling amongst the sand dunes. That was the sole reason why I had difficulty keeping up with Klaske, even when she had a flat tyre at one point. It certainly had nothing to do with a lack of fitness on my part. And of course, being close to the sea, I had to try a dip in the briny. The temperature hadn't improved any from my recollections of my mother booting me into that same North Sea off the rocky beach of Robin Hood's Bay in Yorkshire in my childhood. It had the same effect on my 'nads as my dip off the beach near Budgewoi. In Australia, though, they call it spanner water because it tightens the nuts.

After our Dutch sojourn, we flew to England where we spent a few days touring round the North Yorkshire Moors and the Cleveland Hills. We visited Robin Hood's Bay for old times' sake but on this occasion I didn't bother with the bathing formalities, I just had a couple of pints in a pub on the seafront instead. At one time, Klaske had led hiking tours around the area from Whitby across the hills and moors to the west coast so she was on familiar ground. We stayed for a night at The Lion Inn on Blakey Ridge near Kirbymoorside. The Lion is an old sixteenth century inn and, at an elevation of 1,325 ft, is located at one of the highest points in the North Yorkshire Moors National Park. I had fond memories of being snowed in there when I was flying air taxis out of Teesside back in the 70s. If you were lucky, it would take the local farmers a couple of days to clear the roads with their snow ploughs after a good dump, so there was nothing for it but to bed down in front of one of the roaring fires in the bar and await rescue.

We got back to Hong Kong at the end of July. Only a month to go. On 4 August we caught a gig by Snow Patrol and that was it. Only three weeks to go! We'd made it!! After all the doubts, the anxiety, the drudgery and the sheer exasperation of the last nine months, the waiting was finally over.

10

Court of Final Appeal

'This is the end, my only friend, the end
Of our elaborate plans, the end
Of everything that stands, the end
No safety or surprise, the end.'

The Doors, *The End*

The Court of Final Appeal in Hong Kong is located in the former French Mission Building located on Government Hill at 1 Battery Path in Central. After the experience of being in the House of Lords in the UK some six years earlier, one might expect it to be housed in a similarly imposing building like the Palace of Westminster. But it's nothing like that. Instead it is quite a small building constructed in neoclassical Edwardian style topped by a cupola; the original building dating back to 1842. The courtroom itself is quite small with limited capacity for spectators and relatively poor acoustics. This was where our fate was to be decided. I brought my children, Nicola and Richard, over for the trial. I wanted them to witness for themselves what it is like finally to reach the end of the road, go to the highest court in the land, have your future vested in the hands of five people whom you've never met, with no possibility of any further appeal, and hope to receive justice. You are effectively at their mercy and all you can do is hope that your counsel makes convincing arguments. It is nothing like the way things are depicted in films. To say that I was nervous would be akin to saying that having your testicles crushed in a vice is slightly discomfiting. Everything that we'd done for the last 12 years was riding on this; 17 other men, their wives, partners and their families' futures were to be disposed of here. The responsibility I felt was an almost unbearable burden to endure. What if I'd got it wrong? What if it goes against us and we're financially ruined? What if the sky should fall in? What if, what if anything you can imagine? I should have been happy finally to be there but, actually, I felt anything but happy.

It's a strange thing. People often ask pilots how they deal with the responsibility of having an aircraft full of people and their lives dependant upon you. They ask, 'Don't you worry about all the things that could go wrong?' The answer is no. The responsibility doesn't bother me at all. If I have 5 passengers or 500 passengers, or if I'm just on my own, it makes no difference to me at all. I know that my job is simply to get the aircraft safely from A to B and I know that I'm good at my job. When I get the aircraft to its destination, I've done my job and that's that. It's the same with technical failures. They don't concern me. I have been trained to deal with all likely contingencies and I know that I have the skill, experience and confidence to handle whatever might occur. Perhaps pilots lack imagination when it comes to flying. If you worried about everything that might happen, then you'd never get airborne. So we don't worry. If you do, then don't be a pilot. Be something else. Not everyone is suited temperamentally to the job.

If only I could have felt that confident and relaxed when I walked into the Court of Final Appeal. But I didn't. Rather the reverse. This was a new and completely unexpected sensation to me. I hadn't felt this way at any of the many other hearings and trials I'd attended throughout the years. I'd felt the responsibility yes, but I'd never felt the lack of confidence that I was experiencing now. And it didn't hit me until the actual morning of the trial itself. It was very unnerving. I didn't understand it at the time, and neither did Don who was with me that morning. He was gung-ho and ready for action and couldn't understand why I wasn't feeling the same way. I thought about it afterwards and tried to rationalise why I reacted in the way that I did. And I think I found the answer. After what had happened in the Court of Appeal and, subsequently, in the criminal courts, I had completely lost faith in the system. Rather than being something to be trusted to get to the truth and deliver at least a form of justice as I had previously believed, I now saw it as random and arbitrary; not to be relied upon at all. On the morning of 27 August 2012 we walked into that building and, as far as I was concerned, we might as well have been attending a lottery draw.

The bench comprised of five judges. Generally speaking, for important cases, there is always one overseas judge included on the panel. In our case it was Lord Neuberger of Abbotsbury [LN]. At the time of our trial he held the position of Master of the Rolls in the UK, to which he was appointed on 1 October 2009, and it had been announced earlier in the year that he was to be appointed President of the Supreme Court in the UK (previously the Appellate Committee of the House of Lords) with effect from 1 October 2012. This is the highest position in the UK legal system. The chairman of the bench was the Chief Justice of Hong Kong, Geoffrey Ma Tao-li [MA], assisted by two permanent and one non-permanent judge of the Court of Final Appeal; Justices Syed Kemal Shah Bokhary [KB], Patrick Chan Siu-oi [PC] and Robert Tang Ching [RT].

Each of these men came with differing reputations and histories. In particular, however, Bokhary was considered to be the most liberal, hard-working judge. He frequently wrote dissenting opinions which were considered by legal scholars to be 'intellectually superior' to opinions written by other judges. He was known as the 'conscience of the court'. We were glad to have him aboard.

Neuberger on the other hand, whilst having a reputation for a sharp intellectual mind, had recently given a couple of judgments, and made comments, in the UK which gave pause for thought. In May 2010, he gave a controversial, extempore dissenting judgment that the trade union Unite, representing British Airways cabin crew, had not complied with ballot rules under trade union legislation. Fortunately for the cabin crew, his view was in the minority. In July 2010 he also ruled that peace protesters in Parliament Square in London who had camped out in Democracy Village should be evicted. In May 2011, while commenting on super injunctions, he said that social media sites like Twitter were 'totally out of control' and society should consider ways to restrain them.

Notable in Geoffrey Ma's CV was the fact that he was a member of the Working Party on Civil Justice Reform in Hong Kong, which came into effect in April 2009. It was aimed at lowering legal costs and improving access to justice. He was critical of judges who were too lenient in civil proceedings with time-wasting parties. In a speech he gave that year he warned lawyers against devising new tactics to make civil proceedings unnecessarily lengthy and inefficient.

We went into bat with our usual team of Clive Grossman [CG] and Kam Cheung. The opposition fielded their usual team of Adrian

Huggins [AH] and Robin McLeish. We were appealing the judgment of the Court of Appeal in overturning the breach of contract leg of our case and its reduction of our defamation damages. They were cross-appealing the judgment on the Employment Ordinance (EO) S21B leg of our case. We thought they had no chance. Even the clowns in the Court of Appeal had upheld Judge Reyes' original judgment on that issue. It didn't stop them though. It just meant we'd have to endure, yet again, Huggins banging on remorselessly with the same old failed arguments. It would be interesting to see how Justice Ma reacted to this time-wasting tactic.

As the primary appellants, we went first. The first morning session was spent with Clive putting forward our position on how the Discipline & Grievance Procedure (DGP) *vs* the EO provisions and the Conditions of Service 35.3 'three months' notice without reasons' clause should be interpreted in various situations. The questioning by the judges was very searching and re-visited all of the avenues that had been explored previously in the lower courts. Obviously, our arguments were in support of our contention that Judge Reyes' original breach of contract judgment that was overturned by the Court of Appeal should be re-instated. We held that the Court of Appeal judges had got it wrong when they fell for Huggins' line about the reason(s) for dismissal only becoming crystallised *after* the fact of the actual dismissals themselves and, therefore, that the DGP did not apply. Clive summarised this nicely in the following exchange, which took place immediately after the lunch break.

[CG]   My Lord, I just want to deal with... one or two points from this morning...

[MA]   Mr Grossman, can I just trouble you to pull that microphone [closer], because the acoustics are so poor I can't hear you, although I've heard most of what you've said this morning.

[CG]   I'm sorry, I'm relieved to hear that.

[LN]   At least he thinks he did [laughter].

So they were having the same problem with the acoustics as the rest of us. A pretty unsatisfactory state of affairs one might think.

[CG]   The issue came this morning with a question... my Lord Mr Justice Tang asked, about the timing of the letters in regard to the timing of the statements by Mr Tyler and Mr Chen. I think the position was... letters [were] sent out by DHL so some of the letters would have been received perhaps on the 9th or the 10th and others a few days later. I'm not sure much turns on that, but perhaps what is more important is a matter I should have emphasised this morning and it's this. The decision and the reasons for the decision to terminate... were given really... around about the 7th July. That's when they crystallised because that's where the end of the review was taken so the review finishes on 7th July, decision is made then who to get rid of and why and then the letters are sent out. So the reasons, just so there's no misunderstanding, pre-dated the dismissal letters, whatever was said in those letters.

And that was exactly the point! All the obfuscation fielded by the opposition about when the letters were delivered, when the defamatory statements were made and when the reasons for dismissal were disclosed was just smoke and mirrors. The fact is that the *real* reasons for the dismissals were decided upon in the Star Chamber meeting *prior to* any of the letters or statements being disseminated. Those reasons were disciplinary in nature and should, therefore, have availed us of the right to a hearing under the terms of the DGP. They chose to ignore that procedure and breached our contract. QED. Of course, we couldn't expect the opposition to just leave it at that. During their right of reply, Huggins put on a brave show but, unlike the Court of Appeal judges, these chaps were having none of his bullshit as the following exchanges demonstrate.

[MA]   Now in fact at page nine of the note that you gave us yesterday, you mentioned [the] statements by Tyler and Chen came after the notice, after the dismissals, but what I want to understand from your submission is would it make any difference if they came... before the dismissal, and if so why?

[AH]   Well, first of all, let me say why it matters that it came afterwards, because once the dismissal has become effective, once the dismissal has taken place, their case which was pleaded which was when it is alleged that misconduct is the ground for dismissal, that triggers the DGP, now we say and I hope we're not being simplistic about this, once the dismissal has taken effect, any subsequent statement that may be made by the employer cannot trigger the DGP because the DGP is there to determine whether or not the man can be dismissed, but by then the dismissal has already taken effect, and that is… it seems to us fundamental that if this is something that's said afterwards, and obviously the longer afterwards that it is said the easier it is to see that point, your Lordship, I'll then have to come to deal with the issue that troubles you, the court as to the proximity in this case was so proximate that I'll have to deal with the point that was being raised as to whether or not this is essentially one single transaction and I'll come to deal with that in a moment, but I think it is important to get the fundamental position that anything that's said after the dismissal has taken place, cannot trigger the DGP as a matter of construction in this case because by then there has already been an effective dismissal, so it was important that, on the facts of this case that the pleaded case and the way in which everyone proceeded was that the allegations of misconduct which they rely on came after the dismissal had already been effected… and the questions that you started with yesterday about look, when were these received, when were they not received, and my learned friend tried to jump on the bandwagon yesterday afternoon by coming back after lunch and starting telling you about DHL and what the likelihood was of when these things were received, I respectfully submit and you may have seen me shaking my head at the time, this is not what this court can do.

[KB] But Mr Huggins, do you accept that other than the DGP, which is in Appendix 1, that if the employer wanted to dismiss for a misconduct reason then that employer must, prior to dismissing the employee, afford the employee the chance to make his points… in other words follow the procedures?

[AH] And the only way that it could actually happen in real life is not the employer having it in his mind any kind of suspicion or wish or consideration…

[MA] No but do you accept that… if the real reason for a dismissal is misconduct then under the DGP the employer… must afford the employee the opportunity to go through the procedures. Now, do you accept that as the effect of the procedures?

[AH]   Not if what your Lordship is putting to me is if the employer has some unexpressed suspicion that he may be guilty of misconduct…

[MA]   No I'm talking… if as a matter of evidence the real reason for the dismissal was misconduct then the employee is entitled to have the procedures adhered to. Do you accept that as the effect of this contractual bargain?

[AH]   The problem I have, and forgive me if I'm appearing to be evasive, is that the question is, has unresolved issues as to what is meant by if, the real reason, because what does that mean?

[MA]   Well it's simple enough isn't it? I dismiss you because I don't like your face, I give you three months' notice, I dismiss you because of your moustache, three months' notice, it's nothing personal Mr Huggins. [Cue laughter all round and startled look from Huggins as his carefully groomed pride and joy is put under the spotlight.]

[AH]   My Lord, I'm delighted that you give me the opportunity to deal with the specifics…

[MA]   But the contract seems to [be specific] with misconduct and has elaborate provisions dealing with misconduct and on reading of it, it seems if the reason for dismissal is misconduct then you've got to afford the employee the right to go through these procedures, is at the moment the way I read it.

And that's exactly how it was meant to be read. I can state that as a certainty because I drafted the contract. Despite all Huggins' bullshit, Judge Ma got to the point. Basically Huggins was saying that, despite the obvious intent of the contract, they could sack us without giving reasons and then, n time later, come out and say the real reasons were disciplinary but we'd have no redress to the DGP because the contract is already null and void. What was Judge Reyes' phrase when Huggins put a similar argument to him? Positing bad faith? Lord Neuberger jumped in.

[LN]   Although you would say even if the employer's actual reason is a disciplinary ground which he's quite confident he could prove, nonetheless you say that if he simply dismisses without giving any reason, that's all right even if locked in his mind he knows that there is a perfectly good disciplinary reason but he chooses not to rely on it.

[AH] Your Lordship is right and because it is unworkable otherwise, it...

[LN] The unstated reason, to whom must those reasons... be stated?

[AH] The reason, matter of, contractually, the parties to the contract are the employer and the employee, the employee is the one to whom the employer owes the obligation to give notice as to the grounds for his dismissal.

[LN] If the employer says 'I dismiss you, for no reason, I'm simply dismissing you, here's three months' notice', and the employee goes to his room, and the employer then follows him to his room after five minutes and says, 'I think you should know that I think you have behaved disgracefully in a number of respects, and I'm telling you that now, but that's of course five minutes after I've dismissed you, the dismissal is complete', what then?

[AH] Well, my Lord, after the dismissal, an observation of that kind would, could not then trigger the DGP, because by then the dismissal's already taken place...

[LN] So even if it's five minutes afterwards, even if the employer announces to the world, five minutes afterwards 'I've dismissed him for this reason'?

[AH] I need to come right to the crux of this... Cathay's, the problem that arose is because Tyler and Chen who were not involved in the review panel which was designated with the authority to make the determination as to whether or not they should be sacked, made statements which were, went way beyond and were quite out of tune with, and were not... did not mirror what actually happened, now...

[LN] Before we go there, what do you say if it had been the same person who'd announced to the employee five minutes after the employee's been dismissed, or even ten seconds after the employee's been dismissed, 'these were the reasons', or 'those were the reasons locked in my mind', you say 'well hard luck employee, you can't rely on the disciplinary procedures', do you?

[AH] It's our submission that, may I... I know your Lordship wants to progress it, but you see, it seems to me there are so many different permutations because if the employer said, which is nearer to home, 'look, if the reality were look, Huggins, quite apart from your moustache there are a number of aspects of your behaviour which frankly I don't like, and I suspect, although I can't begin to prove, that you may have been involved in the contract compliance campaign', let's say for the sake of argument, there's no way I'd want to dismiss him for that 'cause there's no way I'd want to tell the world and any prospective employer that that's the reason for your dismissal.

[LN] But if the employer were to say, give a notice of termination to the employee face to face and then as soon as the employee has read it, well to say to the employee 'by the way I'm going to give a press conference at five, where I'm going to tell the world that you were dismissed for misconduct', now would it make any difference to your case?

[AH] If that was said beforehand...

[LN] No, it will be said after the letter of termination had been handed over personally...

[MA] Mr Huggins, I think perhaps let's just break for lunch because the questions which are legal questions, before we get to the facts, really are how you see the operation of this clause. It seems at the moment you're arguing that the DGP, the procedures, only come into operation if the employer says to the employee 'I'm thinking of sacking you because of a misconduct'. The employee then says 'I want to go through these procedures', it seems that you are saying that's when it operates. Where nothing is said by the employer about the reason for dismissal, he simply says 'you've got to go, I give you notice', then the procedures do not apply at all even though the real reason for sacking him which he either keeps to himself or he says ten seconds later to the employee, one minute later to the employee, or at five o'clock to the whole world that the reason is misconduct, in those circumstances it doesn't apply. That's what's going through our mind... in other words [the] short question is how do you see this contractual term being operated in law?

[LN] If I might add, first of all it seems to me, the company is the company and you can't say 'well X said and did this as an employee of the company' and 'Y said these were the reasons'. I mean the fact that two different people say it, they both say it on behalf of the company. It's the company we're looking at, not the individuals. Secondly the disciplinary procedures are part of [the] employment contract and we have those provisions about them being fair and being given [a] common sense approach. And Mr Grossman's point that it does seem unfair that you can dismiss for no reason and then five minutes later tell the world that the real reason is bad behaviour and you can't challenge the bad behaviour through the disciplinary procedure. And finally a statement to the world is a statement to the employee because the employee is a member of the world.

[AH]   … very helpful.

Yes, very helpful indeed. Not to Huggins though. After lunch he came in for more in the same vein. It was obvious to everyone that he was clutching at straws when he misquoted Monty Python as his precedent.

[AH]   My Lord, may I attempt to address directly, head on and without evasion, the incisive questions that were put to me before lunch.

Oh good. This should be a first!

[AH]   It is our respectful submission that however unpalatable it might seem at first glance, as a matter of legal logic, if a notice is served offering to make a payment in lieu of notice without cause, without identifying any grounds for dismissal, that is an effective termination of the contract, once the contract is terminated, it ceases to exist, it is dead, it is no longer alive, the parrot as they said in the skit is dead, it is deceased… if, may I also add this, you've got it from me already I think, but I want to spell it out clearly, in this case, your Lordships should not trouble yourselves with the additional questions which might arise at some other point, as to whether or not the dismissal is effected, effective in terms of time from the precise moment that the letter is sent out, or whether it only becomes effective when it's received or anything of that kind, we're not concerned with that in this case because of the way in which the matter's been pleaded,

The Ryan Navion-A – Vigan International Airport, December 2011

L – R: Author, Klaske, Windy, Minnie, Mandy, Pat.

Author with Steve Dullard on bass.
SKiNC gig, *Chinatown*, Wanchai, December 2004.

New York – April 2012

Madison Square Garden with The Boss

Court of Final Appeal – Day 1

Above:
It might as well be a lottery draw.
Left:
That's enough for one day, let's go for a beer.

Hong Kong Court of Final Appeal – Day 2, 28 August 2011

Front row:
Matt Rogers, Doug Gage, Kelly Fraser, Steve Shaw, Mike Fitz-Costa,
Becky Kwan, Clive Grossman, Kam Cheung, Benedict Chiu, Nicola Smith.
Middle row:
Angela Carver, Ken Carver, Don Fraser, Author, Klaske Kragt.
Back row:
Andrew Carrick, Malcolm Hunter, Roger Wilkinson, Nigel Demery, Richard Warham.

Mauritius, December 2012

AFTER THE ACCIDENT OF ZS-SAS HELDERBERG, THIS MONUMENT HAS BEEN ERECTED IN FOND MEMORY OF PASSENGERS AND CREW WHO LOST THEIR LIVES.

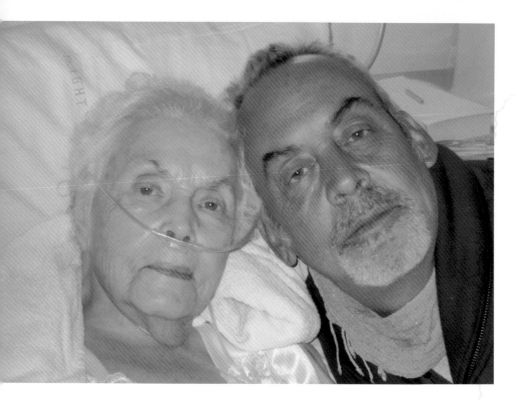

New York – April 2012

Bertha, January 2013

The Pineapple Beach Bar – Koh Samui

Above: Klaske and Daisy – the two ladies in my life.
Below: Sundowner time.

and I don't wish to complicate the matter any further with submissions on that issue, because it is accepted in this case and indeed they pleaded in paragraph 7 that we terminated the contract, and they were asked for particulars and they repeated that under paragraph 7, yes it was terminated, they were also asked for particulars as to the allegation they made that the DGP was triggered, would be triggered by one of two things, one allegations of misconduct, or a decision by the employer to dismiss on disciplinary grounds, that was their pleaded case... on that basis we respectfully submit that once the contract is terminated, it follows that it cannot, anything said thereafter cannot trigger an obligation to go through the DGP procedure, and that the employee if he is aggrieved by a statement in the subsequent publication to the effect that actually he was dismissed for misconduct, his remedy then is defamation, and if the employer then ceases, if the employer is then unable to establish that he was guilty of misconduct, then his remedy will be in damages, now we respectfully submit that that is the legal, correct legal analysis, it might then lead to the feeling that that's somehow unpalatable, we respectfully submit it's not, in *Gunton*, a different situation arose whereby the notice was void, was not an effective notice, it was void because on the face of it, it indicated that the dismissal was actually [on] disciplinary grounds.

Oh yes. Very direct, head on and without evasion I'm sure. Wouldn't want to hear what he'd have to say if he decided actually to be evasive. He continued with more waffle until Neuberger put a stop to him.

[AH]   Then, can I go back and just, if you'll forgive me doing it in stages, stage one is we submit that if somebody in the reviewing panel in this case, or any like case, has a particular suspicion that somebody might have been doing X, Y and Z which might have been described as misconduct, if that is not expressed to the employee in any notice, but instead there is simply a notice of dismissal without cause, again that existence of that suspicion cannot trigger the DGP... the plaintiffs' case was, and it's in paragraphs 15 and 16...

[LN]   Are you getting to the answer to the question I posed?

[AH]   I'm sorry my Lord?

[LN]   The question I posed is as a matter of law and the construction of this contract, how does the DGP become activated?

[AH]   If there is an allegation put to the employee prior to dismissal that he has committed some offence, misconduct within the terms of the DGP, and that it is the intention of the employer to dismiss him on that ground, then the DGP is undoubtedly triggered, without question.

[LN]   And only in that circumstance?

[AH]   Well, I think I have said that the expression, and expression, and express assignment of a re–, ground, a disciplinary ground for dismissal, triggers the DGP, so if at the same, if there were two notices, my Lord Mr Justice Tang I think put to my learned friend, suppose there were two notices go out on the same day, one say, at the same time, dismissal for cause, dismissal for, without cause… now if they both go out at the same time, that can't, I would have to concede that can't be right.

[LN]   Why? What's the logic when construing this contract that even conceding that, in your case you say, an employer can't serve a notice saying 'pursuant to clause 35.3, I am [terminating] your employment on three months' notice and… for your information I'm doing it because I think you have been behaving wrongly'. But why do you say he can't do that, as a matter of construction? Nothing to stop him, what stops him doing that on your case?

[AH]   Well, I understood from *Gunton*…

[LN]   But I'm asking about this contract, never mind *Gunton*. What is stopping the employer, if you're right, of doing something you say he can't do, which is serving a notice saying, 'well, clause 35.3 entitles me to terminate this contract on three months' notice, here's three months' notice'? Why is it invalidated on your case because he includes in the notice a reason which involves breach of discipline? What is it in the contract that stops him doing that, unless you have to imply a term and once you imply a term you're getting into difficulties?

[AH]   My Lord it seemed… it seems to me that the answer is this and I hope I'm getting it right, that the protection that Lord Justice Brightman was referring to in *Gunton*, and Mr Justice

Tang has asked me, well, what's the protection he was referring to, the protection intended by the disciplinary procedures was to ensure that the grounds given to the employee, if they are to be disciplinary grounds, he ought to have the opportunity of a DGP for this reason, that when he goes to an, for example, a new employer, which is as my learned friend was saying was jolly important, he can say to the new employer, 'look, here is the notice that I was given'.

[LN]   With respect, doesn't this completely sink your case? Because if that's the purpose then you walk straight into the point that the employer on your case can say 'here's your notice' without reasons and five minutes later can announce to the world, 'I'm serving this notice 'cause they've breached the disciplinary code'. But that's the very vice you say that this was designed to avoid.

[AH]   Well my Lord the, the, I have to be realistic that there has to be some intention of protection to the employee, that he should not be dismissed for, on a disciplinary ground, now in my respectful submission, that involves an expression in the notice of dismissal on a disciplinary ground...

[LN]   But why is it? If it's to have the commercial purpose you've described which is to protect an employee from being sacked for a reason which is publicised as being breach of discipline, if that is the purpose as you seem to accept it is, then it seems to me you walk straight into the [same] problem.

[AH]   Well my Lord, what they're saying in this case however though, is if it comes afterwards, the fact is the contract is, has already been terminated so it can't involve the triggering of a DGP, bear in mind in the facts of this case, Cathay actually offered to each of these employees to write a letter which they could show to any of their employees, future employers or anybody else saying 'look, this was without cause, never mind what may have been said by Tyler and Chen, we will confirm in writing to you... '

At this point Judge Bokhary jumped in with his four penn'orth.

[KB]   So this is where form of course trumps substance, 110 per cent because the letter simply says 'I dismiss you for no reason', but five minutes later or five o'clock you tell the whole world he's been dismissed for misconduct. The future employer knows that. What value then [is] the piece of paper that says 'I've been dismissed for no reason'? And the trouble with this, in another sense, is that it doesn't matter that the announcement came before the notice. If you are right, why should it matter that the press conference took place before the letters of termination, because it would not still have been an allegation to the employee on grounds given to the employee?

[AH] My Lord Neuberger was putting to me that a statement to the world would have included a statement to the employee, I was going to come back to that point and say before the dismissal that is right, after the dismissal, it would include publication to an ex-employee 'cause he's already been terminated, so before he is still an employee with the obligations attached to the DGP, once there has been an effective dismissal he is no longer an employee entitled to those obligations, they have gone, and we see that as…

[KB] But the way you postulate the legal effect of this is to render it almost nugatory, that, if the employer chooses to be benevolent and tells the employee 'I'm thinking of dismissing you, or taking action against you for a disciplinary offence that is misconduct, do you want to go through the procedures because you're entitled to', and then that's the only time when it operates? But if the employer… wants to get rid of the employee, then he can do that simply by writing a letter saying 'I dismiss you by giving you… three months' notice'. In the latter situation, the employee has no recourse at all to the DGP.

[AH] But my Lord, in that situation alone, uncomplicated by the fact that in this case Tyler and Chen went and said something else, but in the hypothesis that your Lordship put to me, in that event, the notice would simply indicate without cause and there would be no detriment to the employee at all, as far as any potential new employer's concerned…

[KB] Even though it's a complete lie because five minutes later the employer's telling the whole world, 'this person's been dismissed for misconduct', amounting to, they'll say, disloyalty to the employer, so your form, that is the letter which states you're dismissed without cause is paramount, it overrides any point of substance.

[AH] I can see how that can be said against it, but then consider this; is it to be said that in every case in which an employer feels that in his heart, that the employee has done something wrong and he says to him beforehand, 'look, I suspect you've done something wrong, but I can tell you now I'm quite sure I can't prove it and there's no way I've got evidence to pass muster at a DGP, I don't in any event think it would do you any good or me any good to go down that line, I am therefore going to choose to dismiss this without cause, here you are, goodbye,' now in my respectful submission, let us just take that case, because your Lordship is interested in the generalities not just the facts of this case, let us take that position, how is it helpful to an employer/ employee situation to say that in that event, the expression of that suspicion to the employee should trigger the DGP at which…

[KB] Well, then the analysis is that you're dismissing that employee not for the reason of misconduct because you've told him 'I can't prove it'. But on your analysis, if the employer tells the employee, 'I'm actually dismissing you for misconduct, but I'm not going to give you a chance to go through the DGP because my letter to you will simply say, I give you three months' notice,' on your analysis the employer can do that.

[AH] But my Lord, I thought I accepted at the start the, if the allegation be made prior to dismissal, so the dead parrot point doesn't come in, if the allegation be made prior to dismissal then one can see how the DGP…

[KB] So why do you make that concession? It must be, I would have thought, that you know according to this contract that after a disciplinary hearing you may not be able to dismiss him… for the reason of misconduct. And in any event, what's the difference between five minutes before giving the employee a letter, you say 'I'm going to dismiss you for misconduct', and saying it five minutes later, which was the position I think? It obviously makes the world of difference because you keep on talking about the dead parrot as if, I think it must have been on this basis, well the contract's dead then so nothing.

[AH]   Well, the… I keep coming back, I'm sorry, to the case we had to meet and we did meet which was that their case was after the effective termination had taken place, they, an allegation was made which triggered the obligations under the DGP, and we simply say, how can that be because it's too late, it's gone? I just don't see how one can put it any other way.

[KB]   I understand the point… well, that's only the way *you* put it.

[AH]   Can I now however come to nearer home because one of the questions put to me earlier, was well, let's actually look at this DGP and for example my learned friend took you to page 386 and to the provision which included such things as wilful misconduct or disobedience of lawful and reasonable orders, wilful neglect of the company's interests, conduct considered by the company to be prejudicial to its interests, now in our respectful submission, there, the learned judge has certainly not identified what misconduct in the statements of Tyler and Chen which were the, it was their case, it was where the allegations came from, they said the whole triggering came from the allegations of Tyler and Chen, nothing else, which comes afterwards, and with respect, we find it hard to see what the learned judge was saying, was finding was said in the statements of Tyler and Chen which came within any of those categories, I mean…

[KB]   What, accusing them of disloyalty? That's… what Tyler and Chen were saying. They were disloyal to the company's interests, acting against the company's interests. Doesn't that come within, I'm looking at the moment at clause 8.5, reasons for dismissal… wilful misconduct or disobedience of lawful and reasonable orders, that is not really working, conduct considered by the company to be prejudicial to its interests… wilful neglect of the company's interests? I'm surprised when you say you don't know what was being said.

[AH]   Well my Lord, because in the findings of the learned judge when he came to say partly for misconduct, he said the predominant reason, the effective reason was for participation in contract compliance…

[LN]   But no, he's looking at what was said.

[KB]   That's right. That's what you say. It doesn't mean you can substantiate it. You were dismissing these people for acting against the company's interests, that may or may not be true, it was found not to be true, but that was your position at the time, and the case made against you here, if that's what you're saying against me, I've got the right to go through the procedures.

[AH]   Because it was said after the dismissal.

[KB]   Well, right, yes it was said after the dismissal, but that was the reason why the 49 pilots were dismissed. That's what Tyler said, that's what Chen said.

[LN]   And why can't we look at the notice of termination, the press conference and Mr Chen's letter as one event? You said that Tyler and Chen went on to say something else, but I rather question that, because looking at the matter with common sense, it seems to me that it was inconceivable that... the three were not to be considered as one event. I can understand from the employers' point of view, that they had to explain themselves, because in the absence of explanation... it would be so natural for people to conclude that the 49 persons were dismissed because of their trade union activities. That may not have been good for the employer for various reasons. It would not be good so far as the public is concerned because a lot of people are sympathetic to trade unions. It would not be good for the PR of the company, especially with investors. They would have institutional investors, which would represent trade unions, and I can't imagine trade unions or pension fund investors would take kindly to a company which were out to bust a trade union. So looking at the matter with common sense, it seems to me that it was inevitable that Mr Chen and Mr Tyler would have to tell the public that their dismissal... was for cause and the cause was misconduct. And that is why I think it is necessary to look at the whole thing as one package.

Precisely put. Perish the thought that their reputation should be exposed to bad PR in an attempted union bust. Much better to just breach the contract, tell a pack of lies to the world's media and then employ a high-priced mouthpiece to try and bullshit their way out of it. Huggins banged on even longer flogging his dead parrot until the following exchange finally put a stop to him.

[AH]   Well my Lord, the passage which we rely on more than any other of Lord Justice Buckley is in the passage in which he says at page 470, 'in the present case in my view, the council could have determined the plaintiffs' contract of service without assigning any reason, or for any given reason other than a disciplinary reason, they did not however do so'. Now my Lord, the importance of that is that on the facts of this case it was clear that the, as far as the mind of the council was concerned, this was a disciplinary case.

[MA]   Yes, but it doesn't deal with the problems. Lord Justice Buckley clearly didn't consider that the question of what happens [when] subsequent to the notice which he contemplates, they give a reason. It doesn't deal with a case such as this. What it helps you on is, what is purely a hypothetical point in our case too, which is what happens if the employer has the disciplinary reason in mind but doesn't say anything about it at any time.

[AH]   It's for that reason, with respect, I was trying to give you the assistance you asked for on the generalities, and in relation to that we say mere suspicion is not enough, it has to be an allegation or expression…

[MA]   I feel that the difficulty comes if the suspicion is given air.

[AH]   Yes, my Lord, I can see that, we've seen that all along.

[MA]   If the answer to your submission is to again, to employ the language of Lord Justice Brightman, that is your submission [makes] complete nonsense of the protection that the DGP was supposed to [impart].

[AH]   Well my Lord, I can see how that would be so if you had two notices, so that the new employer wouldn't know which way to go, the facts of this case are most unfortunately, Tyler and Chen said what they did after the dismissals took place, and my learned friend used the words yesterday, 'we did nothing to seek to mitigate that', that's not true, Cathay did seek to mitigate that by making the offer which appeared in Barley's affidavit, which you'll, you had your attention drawn to in our submissions, I don't know whether you need me to take you to it now, I'm perfectly happy to, in which…

[MA]   Do you accept that for the purposes of the company, and in terms of the impact on the employees, they had in effect dismissed them and announced that they were doing it on

190

disciplinary grounds? The company obviously had to do it because it would cause tremendous confusion in the marketplace. People didn't know why the company all of a sudden had to lay off 49 pilots. What was happening to Cathay and so on and so forth…? Were they unsafe pilots? Had we been flying in planes piloted by them? So Cathay obviously had to speak to the public and obviously had to reassure other employees, if they'd meant to draw the line at 49. Do you accept that premise?

[AH]   I don't know whether this is going to [muddy] the waters in any way but let us suppose since we're talking about it, the general question, let's suppose that immediately after that statement had been made by Tyler and Chen…

[MA]   No let's not suppose anything, let's just deal with the facts. Did you say, 'no you may not take that view of the facts that Cathay needed to make it public and they needed to tell other employees'? I mean if you say 'no, you can't take that view of the facts', then in considering whether we take that view of the facts, we have to know that you argue against [that view].

[AH]   Forgive me if I didn't address the question, I apologise, may I take this opportunity my Lord, I was told after the case yesterday that your Lordship put a question to me which actually I couldn't hear and I didn't answer…

[MA]   Let's not worry about it, it may be not worth hearing. But anyway, now you've heard this question, what's the answer to it?

[AH]   Your Lordship could take that view.

[MA]   Yes, the one that I've just put now, we can take it that that is Cathay's purpose?

[AH]   No, I'm saying your Lordship could infer from the circumstances, I am not saying that is Cathay's purpose…

[MA]   We could infer that… so that would be for their purposes as if they had dismissed them on disciplinary grounds. After correct procedures, and as far as the impact on the employee is concerned, of course, now he's lost his employment, he's got a bit of money in his pocket, but I would have thought three months' salary is not all that important when you look at the whole of your career. And the world is told, and future employers are told, that he is dismissed on disciplinary grounds. And all of this without the protection of the procedures which may have exonerated him.

[AH]   I can only go back to the reality, my Lord, that as far as Cathay was concerned, what would they have done, what DGP, what should they have then done, what evidence should they then have advanced to a...

[MA]   But what about the point they should have kept quiet and say nothing, assign no reason, express no reason, and then they would...

[KB]   ... they should have kept quiet, if they kept quiet, then they would have dismissed for no reason. Cathay chose to tell the whole world these people were dismissed for disloyalty, misconduct essentially, acting against the company's interests. Now apart from the defamation part, it seems to me the DGP was there to cover exactly this sort of allegation against a person. You seem to be then saying well, well we've gone through what you said, you're saying 'well, bad luck, I terminated, I didn't give you a reason at the time, thereafter I can say what I want and the only fear I have is an action in defamation'.

[AH]   Well my Lord, that is not an insubstantial fear, but my Lord, may I...

[KB]   But that was Cathay's attitude.

[AH]   My Lord, Cathay as I said sought to mitigate to this extent, your Lordship may not think this is satisfactory, but they told each and every one of their employees through Barley, 'look we are prepared to give you a letter confirming to any employer or anyone else you like, it was without cause'.

[KB]   But what's the use of that when you've told the whole world that the real reason is actually they're disloyal?

[AH]   Your Lordship has put the point to me I clearly have been unable to give you a satisfactory answer, and my Lord may I respectfully say...

[KB]   I mean the only point of it is to give future employers a laugh. It's absurd to write such a letter after you've made such an announcement. You have a choice, you could try to go through disciplinary procedures. If you couldn't, your only other option was to keep quiet and they would know that, look here if you do things which they don't like they might give you three months' notice, but you have to take that on the chin, but you don't have to be branded as somebody guilty of [misconduct] 'cause they're not allowed to do that contractually. Never mind what the tort of defamation, not allowed to do that contractually, unless they go through the disciplinary procedures. Now [that's] why it's a bit difficult for employee and employer to understand the position very clearly, in that fashion.

[AH] My Lord, I have no more submissions to make, your Lordship has the written case, I have clearly been unable to improve that and I propose to, [with your] graces, I can sit down.

Yes, please feel free to do so, and the sooner the better. At the end of those exchanges, we were sure that we'd got our breach of contract appeal in the bag. Finally, they'd been faced with the difficult questions and they couldn't answer them. That's the trouble with lies; they're impossible to defend. All you can do is try to cover up one lie with another, then another but, in the end, you'll get found out and shown up for what you are.

Whilst our opponents, in reality, had no chance of succeeding with their appeal against the judgment in the Employment Ordinance (EO) S21B leg of our case, they pressed ahead anyway. To an extent, it was boring because, again, we had to sit through Huggins banging away with the same arguments he'd tried in the two lower courts without success. For a bit of variety, he had come up with some other precedents that he'd not tabled previously. I suppose you can't blame a man for trying, but he was at his obsequious best when apologising for his previous oversight.

[AH] I want to begin on the EO matter, with a personal apology because at the hearing before the learned judge, we submitted to him quite shortly that… if he, which we thought he would not but we were over-confident, if he came to the conclusion as in the event he did, that these people were dismissed for participating in the contract compliance… that we said there were two points, one that would not be activities of the trade union and, secondly, it would not be done at an appropriate time… The shock to us, that the judge rejected the evidence of Rhodes and Tyler and said 'look, they were not sacked for trade union activities… ', the court then found, as far as he was concerned and I've got to live with it, he found that the predominant and effective reason for their dismissal was the *perception* that they were participating in contract compliance. Now when we went to the Court of Appeal... we focused... the court's attention on, again, a point which we turned out to be over-confident about, namely that you couldn't possibly say that the carrying out of this form of action, work to rule, was protected... What we failed to do, and I take full responsibility as leader of Cathay's team, what we failed to do was the research which we have since done and which now forms the part two of our written case, referring to the English authorities, which we submit are highly relevant and I say quite openly that that is research which I wish with retrospect we had done before the Court of Appeal, so that your Lordship would have the benefit of the Court of Appeal's views on that.

[MA] I was wondering why [they don't] feature in the Court of Appeal's judgment references.

[AH] My Lord 'cause it was my fault, it should have done, and it didn't and I therefore quite openly say that that is why you've not heard the assistance of the Court of Appeal in relation to that, and why I'm a little uncomfortable in saying that the court erred in not appreciating that this was not activities protected... so I owe an apology to Mr Justice Stock, Madam Justice Kwan and Mr Justice Lam, for not having presented to them the material which we now present to you.

Rather a long winded way of saying 'I didn't do my job properly; basically I fucked up and now I'm going to try a different tack because I failed miserably at my first two attempts to wriggle my client out of being judged as union busters with no regard for the rights of their employees.'

The ensuing debate then covered a lot of ground we have been over before regarding what are protected, and what are not protected, union activities. But there were a couple of significant exchanges that, later, were to have a profound effect on the interpretation of the rights of workers in Hong Kong to undertake industrial action.

[MA] But Mr Huggins, if you are right, in Hong Kong in the absence of provisions which are similar to the UK provisions, then section 21B is a very limited protection, and may also lead to the absurd situation where, for example, a member who organised the strike or another action cannot be sacked. But if, as soon as he took part, he would be sacked as a member, as an employee. So I mean it doesn't make common sense, does it? I mean it can be an officer of the union and he instigated, he organised the strike, the action, and he simply cannot be sacked, whereas if he took part in the action as an employee, he could be sacked under 21B.

[AH]   Well my Lord, certainly I would query whether that's any more odd or absurd than the idea that protection should be given, should not be given to somebody who, his colleague next door who, for whatever reason hasn't got round to paying his member...

[MA]   No, not the colleague next door but the same person.

[AH]   Yes I know, what I'm saying to your Lordship, I don't think that's, I submit that it's not, no more...

[LN]   There's history in this when it comes to trade union immunities and things of this sort. It's not entirely logical.

[MA]   Mr Huggins, perhaps this is a suitable time to have a break here. It'll give you a chance to, that, I'm a bit worried about all those files on your lectern, they're going to collapse on you in a minute... perhaps we'll give you time, take a break.

After the break, the debate continued and the relevance of the new precedents Huggins had introduced came into question.

[MA]   I think Mr Huggins the problem is if one goes into very fine detail about precisely what the judges had in mind in the English cases so on and so forth, the game is not worth the candle. I mean we can't pronounce on that as if we were sitting on appeals for instance, or something of that sort. If we are shown authorities [from] New Zealand cases or Australian cases [for example]... you've dug up the English ones, and if it's covered with some doubt like this, one might say well, we'll just have to forego the pleasure of trying to find assistance in this case.

[AH]   It may be that your Lordships will come to the conclusion that the materials which I've apologised for not having referred to before are of no assistance.

[MA]   It's worth looking at but at the end of the day if it generates this kind of debate I don't think it's this court's business to say this is exactly what the English statutory scheme involves, this is exactly what the English court said and therefore doesn't help… we haven't read all the articles, all the academic commentary. It just may be too large an exercise to get into…

[KB]   I don't think they're of no use, it's just that on the problem which confronts us which is the meaning of trade union activities, does it include strikes, industrial action, because of the legislative setup, they haven't had the opportunity to focus on that question although undoubtedly they've had to look at what activities of a trade union means in terms of organising the strike or leading the strike, something like that, and to that extent they are useful.

[AH]   It might then come back to your Lordship saying 'well, look, we're going to have to look at it afresh in our… '

[KB]   But we understand, I mean I understand your two big points here apart from the assistance you get from the English authorities, the first is that the activities of a trade union don't include striking. I mean workers go on strike, workers at British Leyland go on strike, it's not Aslef or the Transport & General Workers Union that goes on strike. They may organise it, they may have called it and so on, but… the union doesn't itself go on strike. I think the point… is for something as fundamental as a strike, or industrial action it's strange that there's scarce, in fact not scarce, *no* mention of it in the context of activities.

And therein lay the problem. Whereas other more developed jurisdictions have legislation and precedent to define what are, and what are not, protected union activities, Hong Kong does not. The question was left hanging; would this court in its judgment seek to clarify such matters? We sincerely hoped it would. Their Lordships certainly couldn't water down any further the feeble legislation currently in force, so anything would be an improvement.

And finally the court dealt with our old friend; money. During the submissions on the quantum of the defamation damages there was a great deal of debate from both sides on precedent, level of injury caused, evidence of such, personal injury damages *vs* defamation damages and so on. We will not revisit all that was said in court here other than to mention two significant exchanges.

There was a ray of hope for us when Judge Bokhary opined on the matter of quantum during discussions on the precedents of two other cases of defamation in Hong Kong, *Chu* and *Yakoob*, which had been cited by Judge Reyes in his judgment.

[KB]   I wonder about that you see, I mean the Court of Appeal says in 186, in the circumstances of that case, three million dollars is an appropriate award, and he's not suggesting it was inappropriate, to award the same amount in the present case... Now I don't understand this kind of thing, all right Mr Yakoob was called a terrorist, a money launderer, a drug trafficker, and in terms of injuries to feelings and so forth and general reputation that certainly merits [a compensatory] award... but when it comes to the financial vindication, if Mr Yakoob was [in a] very small way of business, or was about to retire anyway, or was doing business at a loss in any event, so going out of business was a good thing for him financially, he may not get a very large award on that side of it, whereas the pilot who says 'well I'm a very high earner, every month I'm unemployed is a very great loss', you say the same thing about somebody who earns much more than a pilot, the loss is greater, you say something about, that sort of thing about somebody who earns much less than a pilot, the award is less, so if you render a pilot unemployable, the award is so much, if you render somebody who is a higher earner than a pilot unemployable the award is larger, for that component of it, and if you render somebody who earns less than a pilot unemployable that part of the component is smaller, one has to stick to the facts of the case.

Precisely. We were high earners and the damage to us financially was considerably more than someone in a lower paid occupation. The damages should reflect that. The 700k awarded by the Court of Appeal came nowhere near to compensating us for our financial losses, let alone the associated stress and anxiety.

But the far more significant point came during the debate on *how* the Court of Appeal came to the figure of 700k. In his judgment,

Judge Reyes set out very clearly how he had arrived at the figure of HK$3 million. The Court of Appeal did no such thing. There was nothing in their judgment to explain the logic and reasoning behind their decision. The significant point here is that, if there was no reasonable explanation, then we had a very good case that their decision should be set aside and the original award restored. And we know exactly where the figure of 700k came from, don't we? At one point Clive addressed the court on the subject in the following exchange.

[CG]   My Lord... the other point is... how the figure of 3 million
        came about and then how the figure of 700,000 came out. My
        Lord as far as the 700,000, I wasn't at the appeal as your
        Lordships may have seen, so this is what I'm told. It was a
        figure suggested by my learned friend, because... no, he says
        no, then I'll leave it... Mr Cheung who was there tells me, the
        court said to him 'well if it's not 3 million what is it?' and he
        said 700,000, but if he says no then it's no.

During this exchange, Huggins and McLeish sat there vigorously shaking their heads in denial of what Clive was saying. The same matter was brought up again later when Huggins was presenting his case.

[LN]   But I mean in the end if you say these two cases are unhelpful
        I can see that, but in the end there were aspects of this case
        that were worse. It went on for much longer, the
        dissemination was wider, and I quite see the argument that
        says that neither *Chu* nor *Yakoob* is very helpful, but the
        trouble with the Court of Appeal it can be said is that, in
        paragraph 190, they pluck 700,000 out of the air. Why is that
        the right figure?

[AH]   Well my Lord, your Lordship having mentioned *Gleaner* this
        morning will recall that in that case Lord Leicester made an
        attack upon the decision of the Court of Appeal in Jamaica in
        which it very substantially reduced the award of the jury, and
        Lord Leicester attacked that decision of the Court of Appeal
        to re-fix the amount, and said amongst other things, 'well,
        they haven't spelt out how they arrived at that particular
        figure,' and the Privy Council said 'well what do you expect

them to say,' you're complaining in effect to use the figures in our case that the court of appeal chose 700,000; why not 600,000? Why not 800,000? And the Privy Council said 'we're not going down this route'. For this reason, my Lord, and I think it's...

[KB]   But I think what my Lord is asking is just how did the 700,000... can you explain? Perhaps you can't, how the 700,000 figure was reached? Now Mr Grossman suggested that, that prompted you to shake your head together with your junior, when he said that was a figure which you had mentioned. But can you give us any idea as to where 700 might have come from?

[AH]   I'll do my, I'll do my best...

[KB]   Well?

[AH]   And my Lord I'll, I'll do my...

[KB]   Perhaps you can't.

Too damned right he couldn't. What Clive had described is exactly what happened. The 700,000 was a pluck by Huggins in response to a question from the Court of Appeal bench by Judge Lam. But, of course, as officers of the court, they couldn't possibly be lying could they? Clive had been questioned about the logic and methodology of the Court of Appeal in coming up with the reduced figure. He'd indicated where it came from. Now they'd put the same question to Huggins and all he had in response was a goldfish impersonation. The true answer was available for all to see in the transcript of the Court of Appeal hearing. It should have been staring them in the face; but it wasn't. The transcript hadn't been entered into evidence. It was a grave mistake and one that, ultimately, was to cost us dearly.

11

Judgment 2

'I ask you to judge me by the enemies I have made.'
Franklin Delano Roosevelt

We didn't have to wait long for their Lordships of the Court of Final Appeal to deliver their judgment; in fact, just less than a month. We were informed a couple of days beforehand that it would be handed down at ten o'clock on the morning of Wednesday 26 September. It was the same old procedure that we'd become used to. Report at the appointed hour, a clerk hands out copies of the written judgment and that's that. No pomp, no ceremony, nothing. Your future is given to you on a few pages of typewritten A4.

The night before, Klaske and I went for an early evening beer around five o'clock. We weren't going to stay out late as we had an early start in the morning because the traffic from Sai Kung to Central could be heavy in the mornings on weekdays. We got home around nine o'clock and, as I went to open the glass door that was the main entrance to the house, my foot stubbed against something heavy. The outside light was quite dim but, in the shadow, I found a heavy, single-ended open spanner, about 15 inches in length, with a lever bar on the other end. It was laying perpendicular to the door. 'What the fuck's that doing there?' I remarked to Klaske.

'I don't know, you must have left it there,' she replied.

'No I didn't. I've never seen it before, it's not ours,' came my response. It was then that I noticed the door handle. It was of the lever type but, instead of lying horizontal, it was tilted upwards at an angle of about 20 degrees. I put the key in the lock and opened the door, which led straight into the lounge. As I entered, I saw

201

immediately that something wasn't right. On the right hand wall of the lounge there was a cabinet. Its drawers and cupboard doors were all open. And, on the wall to my left, there was a window that had been broken.

'OK babe, I think we've been broken into,' I said. 'You stay here, I'm going upstairs to check the house.'

The house was on three floors with a door to the roof area. The ground floor was clear. I went up the stairs to the first floor. There were two rooms and a bathroom. One room was set up as my music room where we held band practises. It was clear. The other room was my study. It was clear, but my laptop was missing from my desk. The bathroom was clear as well, so I went up to the second floor. This floor comprised of two rooms; the master bedroom with en-suite bathroom and a small spare bedroom. Both were clear but our bedroom was in a mess and there were muddy boot prints on the carpet and duvet. Up another short flight of stairs, the door to the roof was still locked and the area was clear. Whoever had been in the house was long gone. I went back downstairs to tell Klaske we were safe and called our landlord, who lived close to us in the same village, to give him the bad news. He and his wife came round a few minutes later. We called the police and, whilst we were waiting for them to arrive, we started assessing the damage and checking on what was missing.

Fortunately there was no vandalism. You hear stories of burglars in the UK urinating and defecating in their victims' houses; for what reason, other than leaving their mark like animals do, it's difficult to fathom. There was none of that. Just the muddy boot prints all over the house. Klaske had recently received repayment of the rental deposit on her old place refunded by her previous landlord. Around HK\$20k. She'd put it in one of the drawers of the cabinet in the lounge. It was gone. My camera, which had been laying where I'd left it on the coffee table in the lounge, was gone as well. In our bedroom, some of Klaske's jewellery was gone, as were all my cufflinks and other bits and pieces. But the main thing I was concerned about was my laptop. There was a lot of very confidential stuff on it to do with our legal actions against Cathay over the years. A lot to do with our strategies, tactics, game plans, intel gathering and names of our confidential sources. And all our financial records relating to the cases were stored there; where we got the money from. There was also the original manuscript and research material from my first book along with all the files I'd put together personally for the Kindle version. It was a lot of work. But I'd backed all this stuff up on a stand-alone USB hard drive. The laptop was gone but the hard drive was still there. Relief! At least I hadn't lost the data. But what about the really confidential stuff relating to Cathay? If this was a corporate espionage job made to look like a routine break-in, well they'd got the laptop but it was password protected. Now that's probably easy to break, but surely they're too late? The Court of Final Appeal judgment was being handed down in the morning. There'd be no value to them, other than, perhaps, to identify who our moles were in their organisation. It might sound like paranoia, but we knew that, in the past, they'd used a contact in the police force to try to dig up dirt on the AOA general secretary. And I'd been warned a number of times over the years that I needed to watch my back. I had powerful enemies and, in a place like Hong Kong with its triad culture, individuals being physically attacked after they'd upset the wrong people was not unknown.

Anyway, no time to worry about that now. I've still got the data, that's the main thing. But it's the loss of personal things that are of little value to anyone else that hurts the most. I had a pair of gold cufflinks that belonged to my father. They were irreplaceable to me and now they were gone forever. There were the pictures I took when we went to see The Boss in New York. Being crap at admin like most pilots, I hadn't yet transferred those to the hard drive. They were gone too. But it's also the knowledge that someone has been in your home and gone through all your belongings. It's an awful feeling. It's a violation of your privacy, your sanctum; the place where you should feel safe.

Plod arrived and the fun began. The intruder had tried to jemmy the front door, failed, and then broke the small lounge window, opened the latch and got in through there. The fingerprint chap covered everything in black powder with his make-up brush. They wanted me to give a statement. I offered to write it myself but, no, the interviewing officer wanted to write it himself. That was going to slow things down I thought; and indeed it did. He asked me questions and wrote out my replies in longhand. I then had to go through each one to correct the grammar and spelling. His written English was good, but not good enough for a final draft that I was going to have to put my name to. And, towards the end of the interview, some of the questions started bordering on the bizarre. They started off fair enough.

'How much money your wife have in the drawer?'

'Around 20,000 bucks.'

'How much your camera worth?'

'I don't know. It's three or four years old. I can't remember what I paid for it. Around 4,000 bucks I suppose.'

'How much your laptop cost?'

'I think I paid around 15,000 dollars for it four years ago.'

'What's your job?'

'What? I'm a retired pilot, but I work part time as a simulator instructor.'

'You're pilot?'

'No. I used to be. I'm retired now. I teach people to fly on a flight simulator. You know, like those computer games you see in AsiaWorld.'

'How much you earn?' Now I'm thinking, what's that got to do with him?

'It varies. I work part time on a consultancy contract.'

'How much rent you pay?'

'What? Listen mate, what the fuck has that got to do with anything? What possible relevance can that have to do with being burgled?'

'My boss, he like to know everything.'

'Well I'm not telling you.'

'Do you have any enemies?' At that I just burst out laughing.

'Do I have enemies? Oh yes. I've got loads of them. You can start with the whole of the management of Cathay Pacific and the Swires.'

'What?'

'Cathay Pacific management. The people I used to work for.' Now he started laughing. 'No, I mean personal enemies,' he replied.

'So do I. I'm being serious. Check me out on the net and you'll see why I say that.'

The police didn't finish their work and leave until around two o'clock in the morning. There was no way we could sleep in the house that night. I telephoned the Mandarin Oriental and booked a room. We got there about three o'clock and went to bed. But we got very little sleep for what remained of the night. But at least it was only a five minute walk to the court house.

Don and Kelly met us in the foyer of the hotel that morning. We walked across the road to the Court of Final Appeal to pick up the judgment. There were press and media swarming all over the place. Becky Kwan was there as well. She'd come along to give us moral support but, by a quirk of fate, the court was also handing down the verdict on a long-standing dispute that the FAU had with Cathay over payment of holiday pay. She was retired now, and not on the best of terms with the new FAU executive, so she had no idea that their judgment was to be handed down on the same day. We went inside. At the duly appointed hour, the clerk came in and handed over the judgments. I could barely look. After all the years, this was it. What was contained in these pages would decide our fate. The general construction of judgments is that, after all the evidence and reasoning is explained in the main body, the last couple of pages summarise the findings. I turned to the back. It read as follows:

> 109. For these reasons (as well as the short additional reasons given by the Chief Justice, in his judgment which I have seen in draft), I would (a) dismiss Cathay's cross-appeal to set aside the Judge's award of $150,000 per plaintiff in respect of the Ordinance claim;

Yes! They've upheld Reyes ruling on S21B.

> (b) allow the plaintiffs' appeal to the extent of reinstating the Judge's award of a month's pay for each plaintiff in respect of the wrongful determination claim;

Result! They've overturned the Court of Appeal's judgment on breach of contract. We've got it back!

> (c) (i) dismiss the plaintiffs' appeal against the Court of Appeal's award of $700,000 per plaintiff for general damages for defamation, and (ii) dismiss the plaintiffs' appeal against the decision of the Court of Appeal to set aside the $300,000 aggravated damages for defamation awarded by the Judge.

Oh fuck. We've lost the money.

I was immediately torn between two conflicting emotions. Extreme elation because, on the one hand, we'd won all the legal points, and grave disappointment because, on the other, we were severely out of pocket. We were fully vindicated, but I was broke. Before going outside to face the media, I spent a few minutes scan reading the whole of the judgment. It had been written by Lord Neuberger with no dissenting views from the other judges. There was, however, an additional comment by Chief Justice Ma on the S21B issue. From a first reading it appeared to enshrine the right to strike as a protected union activity. I read it again. Yes, that's what it says. I turned to Don and said, 'Do you read this the same way as me? Does this give protection on the right to strike?'

'Yes, I think it does,' he replied. My god. This was huge. If we'd won this, it was a major change in the interpretation of the labour laws in Hong Kong. Prior to this, when workers went on strike in Hong Kong, the standard response was to sack them all and simply hire new people. But there'd never been a test case since the Basic Law came into force with the handover in 1997. This hadn't been one of our specific aims; rather it had come about as a spin-off from our claim that we'd been sacked simply because we were *members* of the union. We'd never undertaken any actual industrial action because, even if we intended to, we were sacked before we had an opportunity to do so. On the face of it, this was a major win for all employees in Hong Kong.

I spent a few minutes composing myself and then went outside to face the press. Becky was already out there giving interviews to camera. The FAU had won their case on holiday pay and it meant that Cathay was faced with a bill for hundreds of millions of dollars in unpaid wages. It was big news and she stole the limelight. I was so pleased for her. Even though she was no longer Chairman of the FAU, and representatives of the current executive committee from whom she was estranged were hanging around looking sulky, Becky had been the face and voice of the FAU for so many years that the press only wanted to speak to her. It felt so good to be able to share in her victory because it was hers. She'd initiated the original action even though the new guard had followed it through after she retired. I was also pleased in another way. I knew the press would focus on the money; they always do. And, given the deep disappointment I was experiencing in that respect, I wasn't sure if I could keep my cool if they pressed it and ignored the principles. When it came my turn to face the Q&A, it went straight to the point.

'How do you feel about losing the money?'

'Of course we're disappointed by that, but this was never about money in the first place, it was about the principles. We've been fully vindicated and Cathay have been shown up for what they are. And we've achieved what Lee Cheuk-yan and the Confederation of Trade Unions have been trying to do for years. We've won real protection for trade union members.'

I found the whole experience very difficult to deal with. I was trying to focus on the positives, of which there were many, but, at the same time, my concerns over the money were real. I knew some of my men were going to take this badly, but I personally now had a big financial problem. On top of that, the shock of the break-in at our house last night was beginning to set in. I felt sick inside. How could I possibly look after and protect my woman, Klaske, if I couldn't even guarantee her safety in our own home? My emotions were in complete turmoil.

After the photographs and the interviews were over, we retired to 'the office'; the Captain's Bar in the Mandarin Oriental. No sooner had we sat down to our first pint than I received an SMS from one of my BoBs.

'Pretty disappointing result after all this time.' No thanks. No nothing. I felt the anger rising.

'Yes, if you think that changing the employment law in Hong Kong is disappointing.' I responded.

'What was that?' Don enquired.

'It's from one of the BoBs. He's pissed off.'

'What did he say?' he asked. So I told him.

'What did you reply?' he again asked. So, again, I told him.

'Right. Turn off your phone, don't speak to anyone and don't reply to any more messages until you've had time to think about things. If you lose your rag now you'll just make things worse.'

As always, coming from Don, it was good advice. Knee-jerk reactions are invariably wrong and, given the stress I was under, it wasn't going to take much for me to blow my top. That's the last thing I needed to do right now. He was right. I needed time to think and work out how to deal with the new problems I was now facing. For the rest of that day and night, Don and Kelly did a great job of looking after Klaske and I. They were true friends to us. We ran up an appropriate bar bill in the office and then went out for dinner. There was no way that Klaske and I were ready to return to our house after all the turmoil of the last 24 hours, so the four of us decided to do a tour of the clubs and bars in Lan Kwai Fong. We ended up in Insomnia on D'Aguilar Street where we listened to some great live bands and then slept the night at Don's place in Robinson Road.

The next day, after breakfast, it was time to go back home and face the music. We went to the house to set about rehabilitating it. Two other good friends, Kevin and Teresa Hoban, came round and brought us some milk and groceries and offered their help in clearing up. It was a kind thought, and we were grateful for their support, but we had to do this on our own. Our landlord changed the locks for us and repaired the window. But we got his workman to seal it closed so it could never be opened again by someone trying to break in. Then we cleaned the house from top to bottom. As we did so, we discovered a few more things missing. Small personal items that were now lost to us forever like the other things we already knew we'd lost. It was a very difficult process for both of us but we just had to support each other and work our way through it. But I was still wrestling with the problem of how to look after and protect Klaske from risk and harm. I felt I'd let her down. It still irks me to this day that she might have been put in harm's way and I hadn't been able to stop that from happening. That night, when we went to bed, I double checked all the locks and windows and locked the bedroom door from the inside. It was about three months later that she said to me, 'Look, we've got to stop doing this. We've got to get back to normal somehow.' So I stopped locking the bedroom door; but I still check the locks and the windows.

And then it was time to read the judgment in full and analyse the judges' reasoning. In order to cover this here, it is necessary to quote quite extensively from the judgment itself. Some of this makes for heavy reading and for this I offer no apology. If we are to fully understand the implications of this judgment, which is now case law and sets precedent in Hong Kong, we need to analyse it in depth. If you would like to read the judgment in full, it is available for download on the Hong Kong judiciary website at http://www.judiciary.gov.hk/en/legal_ref/judgments.htm under case number FACV 13/2011.

Regarding the EO S21B issue, Lord Neuberger opined, in part, as follows:

32. The... issue before us resolves itself into a single question, albeit that the answer to that question is not straightforward.

That issue is whether Cathay terminated the contract of employment of each of the plaintiffs by reason of his exercising the right, at any appropriate time, to take part in the activities of the Union. The determination of this issue turns on (i) Cathay's reasons for dismissing the plaintiffs, and (ii) the meaning and effect of s 21B.

33. I turn, first, to consider Cathay's reasons for dismissing the plaintiffs. Having considered the judgment below carefully, the Court of Appeal summarized the reasons briefly in this way... namely,

> 'It seems clear that what the judge was saying was that the key reason for dismissal was Cathay's perception that the plaintiffs [and, I think, the other 49ers] were themselves the most active participants in the limited industrial action which had taken place (contract compliance) and the most likely adherents to the proposed and recently invoked MSS action.'

All parties accepted that that was an accurate analysis of the Judge's conclusion... I therefore proceed on the basis that the Court of Appeal's... summary is correct.

34. I turn then to the second question thrown up by this issue, which involves considering the effect of s 21B...

35. Subsections (1) and (2) of s 21B provide as follows:

'(1) Every employee shall as between himself and his employer have the following rights –
    (a) the right to be or to become a member or an officer of a [registered] trade union... ;
    (b) where he is a member or an officer of any such trade union, the right, at any appropriate time, to take part in the activities of the trade union.

(2) Any employer... who –
    (e) prevents or deters, or does any act calculated to prevent or deter, an employee from exercising any of

the rights conferred on him by subsection (1); or

(f) terminates the contract of employment of... an employee by reason of his exercising any such right, shall be guilty of an offence... '

36.   Section 21B(3) defines (i) 'appropriate time' as being either (a) 'outside the employee's working hours' or, (b), if 'within his working hours' is a time 'at which, in accordance with arrangements agreed with... his employer, it is permissible for him to take part' in 'any activities of the trade union', and (ii) 'working hours' as meaning any time when, 'according to his contract of employment, an employee is required to be at work'.

37.   Given that it is common ground that the Union is a 'registered trade union', the question of principle to which this case ultimately gives rise is the breadth of the expression 'activities of the trade union'... and, in particular, whether it extends to taking part in contract compliance (or, possibly, proposing to take part in MSS).

38.   On behalf of the plaintiffs, Mr Grossman SC contends that, given that it was conceived by the Union, initiated by the Union, voted on through the Union, organised by the Union, and enforced by the Union, contract compliance was, as a matter of common sense and language, an 'activity of the Union'. He reinforces that argument by contending that the expression 'activities of the trade union' should be interpreted generously, on the basis that, if it is not, the effect of s 21B(1)(b) and (2)(b) would conflict with common sense, and the outcome of claims based on allegations of breach of the section would turn on very fine distinctions.

39.   Mr Huggins SC, for Cathay, on the other hand, contends that industrial action, whether working to rule (which would include contract compliance and, arguably, MSS) or striking (i.e. withdrawal of labour), is not within the expression 'activities of the trade union'. That expression, he says, is apt only to cover actions which are performed by an employee for or on behalf of a union, as opposed to actions performed by an employee in his capacity of an employee, even where it is with

the support of, or at the behest of, the employee's union. In other words, the expression applies to acts such as attending meetings of, or on behalf of, the union, deciding on union policy, and implementing, organising or enforcing actions consequential on decisions of officials or members of the union, all of which are properly described as union activities. However, the expression does not, on this basis, apply to activities which are essentially those of an employee or of the employees generally, such as working to rule or striking.

40. This is... the most difficult (and quite possibly, the most important) question raised on this appeal. We have not been referred to any relevant decided cases on the issue in this jurisdiction, but there are a number of decisions of the United Kingdom Employment Appeal Tribunal ('EAT') which do provide some guidance... However... there are two difficulties about relying on the English cases. The first is that they are not entirely mutually consistent, and one potentially relevant decision is cogently criticised in one of the leading English employment law books – see *Harvey on Industrial Relations and Employment Law*, secondly, the UK 1992 Act contains many provisions which have no equivalent in the [Hong Kong] Ordinance...

41. As a matter of ordinary language, there is an obviously powerful case for saying that industrial action, such as working to rule or striking, is not one of the 'activities of the trade union'. Even where the union initiates, organises, and enforces, a work to rule or a strike, runs the argument, it is not the union which works to rule or strikes: it is the employees who do so. On this basis, therefore, the organising and enforcing of the strike or work to rule may be union activity, but the strike or work to rule themselves are not.

42. That argument is not without force. However, it seems to me that, once one takes into account common sense and practicality, there is an even stronger argument for saying that industrial action is within the expression 'activities of the trade union'. If a trade union has proposed, organised and proceeded to enforce industrial action (as in the present case, where... the

211

Union threatened to impose sanctions on members who did not participate in contract compliance), it seems to me that any employee participating in the action would think of himself... as taking part in an 'activity of the trade union'. So, I think, would any member of the public. Indeed, as mentioned above, in his letter of 27 June 2001 to all the pilots in connection with the threatened MSS, Cathay's director of flight operations actually referred to the pilots' potential involvement in that proposed industrial action as 'taking part in trade union activity'.

Oh. Nice of good old Ken Barley to give us a helping hand here!

43. Further, it would seem surprising if an employee who lobbied for, organised or policed such industrial action could rely on the protection afforded by s 21B, whereas an employee who merely took part in such action could not. The notion that, when organising a strike, an employee is participating in union activity, but when taking part in the same strike, he or she is not so participating, seems a somewhat capricious result in practical terms.

44. In practice, of course, it would scarcely be possible to describe striking as an activity in which an employee can take part, 'at any appropriate time', given the definition of 'appropriate time' in s 21B. But that does not mean that striking is not inherently capable of being one of the 'activities of the trade union' within s 21B: it merely means that an employee dismissed for taking part in industrial action consisting of a union-sponsored strike will rarely, if ever, be able to rely on s 21B. But it is wholly different where the industrial action consists of working to rule, such as contract compliance in this case, which... included measures that could only be carried out when the plaintiffs were not, by their contracts, required to be at work.

45. It might at first sight seem curious if some types of industrial action, or even some types of working to rule (possibly such as MSS, which the Court of Appeal said may well be different for these purposes from contract compliance), are outside the ambit of s 21B protection, when other types of

industrial action, such as most working to rule, are within its scope. However, I think that the answer is that (i) the scope to be given to the expression 'activities of the trade union' is broad, which produces a coherent and practical outcome involving relatively wide protection for employees, but (ii) such protection is circumscribed by the concomitant protection for employers, which is embodied in the 'appropriate time' limitation. Accordingly, most (possibly all) union-sponsored action is potentially protected by s 21B, but if the action is not carried out 'at an appropriate time', it is excluded from the provision.

46. That conclusion seems to me to satisfy the primary requirement of fidelity to the language of s 21B, as well as being a result which has the effect of being relatively easy to understand and apply, which is generally an important aim in the law, and particularly in the field of the law relating to labour relations.

He then quoted from the Hong Kong Trade Unions Ordinance to support his view.

51. I draw some support for the view that the expression 'activities of a trade union' extends to strikes and industrial action from certain provisions of the Trade Unions Ordinance (Cap 332), although it is right to record that neither counsel referred to it. Parts VI and VII of that Ordinance refer to the rights and liabilities of trade unions and employees in relation to industrial action. In very summary terms, ss 42, 43 and 43A of Cap 332 give 'a registered trade union' and any 'employee, or a member or officer of a registered trade union' immunity from civil liability in relation to any acts done 'in contemplation or furtherance of a trade dispute' to which the union (or the employee, member or officer) is party, and s 46 renders peaceful picketing lawful if carried on by persons whether 'acting on their own behalf or on behalf of a registered trade union... in contemplation or furtherance of a trade dispute'. These provisions all appear to me to be consistent with the notion that industrial action sponsored by a trade union is seen by the legislature, indeed as a matter of law, as being within the ambit of activities for which a trade union is potentially responsible,

and in which a trade union can fairly be treated as being engaged – ie that such industrial action is, as a matter of ordinary language, within the scope of 'activities of a trade union'.

He then went on to quote extensively from English case law and the United Nations International Labour Organization conventions to further support his view. He then concluded:

> 56. In these circumstances... I consider that the Judge was right, on the facts which he found, to conclude that the plaintiffs were entitled to compensation under... the Ordinance. So far as the measure of such compensation is concerned, there is no challenge by Cathay to the Court of Appeal's decision to uphold the Judge's award of $150,000 per plaintiff. Accordingly, Cathay's cross-appeal should be dismissed.

Crucially, in his addendum to the judgment, Chief Justice Ma added the following:

> 3. The conclusion reached by Lord Neuberger of Abbotsbury NPJ is that the industrial action which was said to be carried out by the plaintiffs in the form of contract compliance, came under the rubric of 'activities of the trade union' for the purposes of s 21B(1)(b) of the Employment Ordinance... As a matter of law, industrial action (including strikes) where such action has been proposed, organized and enforced by a trade union (as in the present case) will come under the statutory wording of 'activities of the trade union'.

He then went on to quote various extracts of the Basic Law, which governs Hong Kong since the handover, and the Bill of Rights which support his view. He further opined:

> (4) The right to form and join trade unions is to be given a purposive and generous interpretation, in common with the approach of the courts in respect of all fundamental rights and liberties. This approach percolates down to the relevant statutory provisions which deal with trade unions.

(5) It is quite clear that the constitutional framework militates towards a conclusion that in order to give proper effect to the right to join a trade union (the right to form a trade union does not arise in the present case), this will encompass not only the right to become a member of a trade union, but also the right to be able to join in the activities of that trade union.

(6) The function of a trade union is essentially to protect and advance the rights and welfare of employees, and one of a trade union's principal functions (indeed I would say the main one) is to deal with employers in this context. Conflicts and disagreements are bound to occur: from the employers' point of view, trade unions are seen to act as a brake on the employers' ability to maximize efficiency or profit as they see it; from the employees' point of view, trade unions help ensure that a level playing field can exist in which workers' interests are more fairly pitted against what is seen as the economic strength of the employer. Sometimes these conflicts or disagreements will lead to industrial action promoted or organized by trade unions.

(7) Hong Kong, in common with many jurisdictions worldwide, has adopted a policy of protecting trade union rights and activities. There are a number of references to international labour conventions in relevant constitutional and statutory provisions (I have already referred to the Basic Law and the Bill of Rights). Section 21B of the Employment Ordinance, which is the provision focused on under the first issue before us, is based on the International Labour Convention No. 98 (the Right to Organise and Collective Bargaining Convention 1949). That section, in specific terms, protects employees from being dismissed by employers by reason of membership of a trade union or participating in trade union activities. It is notable that becoming a member of a trade union and taking part in activities of a trade union, are described in s 21B(1) as rights.

(8)   I have earlier briefly alluded to industrial action which is promoted or organized by trade unions. Many people would think, and I agree, that this form of activity is precisely the classic form of trade union activity; crudely put, it is exactly the type of activity that will be undertaken by trade unions if driven to it. In situations where a trade union has 'proposed, organised and proceeded to enforce industrial action'… it is difficult to conclude that a worker who joins in such industrial action (whether willingly, as a matter of solidarity with co-workers or even under compulsion) is doing anything other than participating in trade union activity. Not to be lost sight of in the present context is also the immunity extended to trade unions and members of trade unions in relation to acts in contemplation or furtherance of a trade dispute… Industrial action will clearly fall within such acts.

(9)   This is not to say there are no limitations placed on the protection given to employees in relation to taking part in trade union activities: as s 21B(1)(b) of the Employment Ordinance makes clear, such activities must take place only at an 'appropriate time' (as defined in s 21B(3)) in order for the protection to exist.

(10) In summary, the view taken of the meaning of the 'activities of the trade union' by Lord Neuberger of Abbotsbury, with which I agree, is not only consistent with principle, common sense and the authorities, it is also consistent with the constitutional and statutory framework in Hong Kong.

So, in summary, the judgment defined what are 'activities of a trade union'. Specifically such activities *do* include 'industrial action (including strikes) where such action has been proposed, organized and enforced by a trade union'. This was a massive step forward for labour protection in Hong Kong. It had never been defined before because there had never been a test case since the Basic Law came into effect with the handover. But now we had achieved that. It is similar in nature to what we achieved in the UK where we established the legal precedent that the Employment Rights Act *does* apply to peripatetic employees. No doubt the Swires' mates would really be thanking them for what they had achieved, not only in the UK, but also, now, in Hong Kong as well. Not!

Unfortunately, there is still a hole in all this. Even though it is a criminal offence, the maximum penalty for breaching this section of the EO is only HK$150k. In the face of an unscrupulous employer who doesn't give a rat's arse for the law and doesn't care about committing a criminal offence in the worship of Mammon, the fine is no real deterrent. Fortunately, there are no companies like that in Hong Kong are there? So that's all right then. Otherwise we might have to lobby for the maximum penalty to be increased to say, HK$1 million, with an associated custodial sentence to give the law some dentition. Now there's a novel idea.

In the next part of the judgment, Lord Neuberger went on to discuss the breach of contract issue. The following extracts demonstrate his logic.

62. The interrelationship between clause 35.3 of the Conditions… and para 8.5 of the DGP is not entirely straightforward.

63. For Cathay, Mr Huggins SC eschews any suggestion that, even where Cathay informs an employee that he is being dismissed for gross misconduct, it can bypass the DGP simply by serving three months' notice or giving three months' pay in lieu. In my judgment he is right to do so. The DGP is… expressly incorporated into the Conditions. Accordingly, clause 35.3 cannot be construed in isolation, and must be read together with the DGP, and indeed in the context of the whole of the Conditions (which of course includes the DGP).

64. The Conditions also have to be interpreted bearing in mind their overall purpose, namely to provide a set of rules governing the employment of Cathay's employees, and this requires them, so far as possible, to be given an interpretation which is workable and clear, and which represents a reasonable balance between the interests of employer and employee.

65. If it was open to Cathay to determine an employee's contract for disciplinary reasons (to use a shorthand expression)

217

simply by invoking clause 35.3, it would mean that the procedures laid down in the DGP in a case where an employee is being dismissed for 'gross misconduct', within the meaning... of the DGP, could be circumvented, indeed rendered nugatory, by Cathay. It appears to me that, unless the wording of the Conditions ineluctably point to such a conclusion, it should be rejected.

66.   Once clause 35.3 is read together with the provisions of the DGP, it can be seen that it cannot be right to treat it as giving Cathay a right to determine on three months' notice (or with three months' pay), even where the determination is on the ground of gross misconduct, as such an interpretation would make a nonsense of the rights granted to an employee by the DGP, whom Cathay wishes to dismiss for 'gross misconduct'. In addition, there is the more specific point that such an interpretation would be hard to reconcile with para 8.5(b) of the DGP, which provides that, even if dismissal is warranted for a 'serious offence', it will normally be 'after the appropriate notice has been given or payment made in lieu of notice'.

67.   Accordingly, it seems to me clear that, dismissal for a disciplinary reason in accordance with clause 35.3 can only take place after the procedures laid down in... the DGP have been gone through.

68.   Mr Huggins takes his stand on this issue on behalf of Cathay on the fact that, in this case, the dismissal letter sent to each plaintiff was not expressed to be for disciplinary reasons, let alone for gross misconduct, and therefore, he says, the DGP had no relevance. On that basis, he submits that there was nothing to prevent Cathay from relying on its right to determine for no reason under clause 35.3. The fact that Mr Chen and Mr Tyler made their statements about the activities of the 49ers and the fact that those activities had led to their dismissal is irrelevant, according to this argument, because those statements were made after the dismissal of the 49ers: by the time those statements were made the 49ers were former employees.

69. On the facts of this case, I would reject that submission, forcefully though it was maintained. Once it is accepted (as Mr Huggins rightly does accept) that it is not open to Cathay to invoke clause 35.3 without going through the processes laid down by the DGP in a case where Cathay informs an employee that he is being dismissed for disciplinary reasons, it appears to me that it must follow that Cathay was obliged to go through those processes before it dismissed the plaintiffs on the facts of this case.

70. It is true that, in the dismissal letters, which formally communicated the determination of the plaintiffs' contracts, it appears that Cathay did not invoke or even refer to any aspect of their conduct... However, simply to focus on the dismissal letters, and to ignore what was being said by Cathay at around the same time, appears to me to be quite unrealistic – a triumph of form over substance, as the Chief Justice put it in argument. In my view, it would be thoroughly unrealistic not to treat the statements made by Mr Tyler and Mr Chen as part and parcel of a single exercise which included the dismissal of the plaintiffs from their employment with Cathay.

71. From the perspective of Cathay, it is quite clear that the dismissal of the plaintiffs and the publication of the statements were part of a single orchestrated exercise, no doubt carefully, hard-headedly, and (it is fair to add, subject to the other issues in this case) quite properly, conceived as a major initiative in a long-running and bitter dispute. From the perspective of the plaintiffs, they, together with the rest of the world, were being told by Mr Tyler and Mr Chen, within 24 hours of the dismissal letters having been posted, why they were being dismissed. So far as the precise timing was concerned, some of the plaintiffs may have received their dismissal letters before the statements were released, others may have received them afterwards. There was no suggestion of Cathay having ensured that the 49ers received their dismissal letters before the statements were published...

72. Particularly given that the issue arises in the field of employment law, where technicalities should be kept to a

minimum, it seems to me to be quite unrealistic to say that, in the present case, the plaintiffs were dismissed by Cathay for no reason. Strict contemporaneity cannot be the test: if it were, it would lead to the absurd result that, after dismissing an employee under clause 35.3 without giving reasons and telling him to clear his room, the employer could visit the employee, a minute later, while he was clearing his room, to tell him that he had been dismissed for disciplinary reasons. In my view, when considering the dismissal of the 49ers, it is not only unrealistic and highly artificial, but positively absurd, to treat (i) the dismissal letters themselves and (ii) Mr Tyler's statement and Mr Chen's letter and (although a day later) his statement as involving separate events, rather than individual aspects of a single overall exercise.

73. Furthermore, as Mr Grossman suggests, such an outcome would be wholly contrary to one of the main purposes of the DGP, particularly given their express emphasis on common sense and 'natural justice'. It would contrary to common and natural justice (in a colloquial and, quite possibly, in a technical legal sense) if an employee could be deprived of any opportunity to challenge allegations of gross misconduct through the procedures laid down by the DGP, while the employer was free to announce to the world that the employee is being, is about to be, or has just been, dismissed on the basis of those very allegations. As Mr Justice Tang pointed out in argument, Mr Huggins's case gets into real difficulties if one postulates a case where Cathay informs an employee that he is guilty of gross misconduct, and only thereafter dismisses him giving no reasons for the dismissal. If Cathay would thereby be able to avoid the DGP, it would be patently absurd; if it could not thereby avoid the DGP, it would appear fatally to undermine Cathay's case here, which seems to me to require strict contemporaneity of dismissal and reasons…

78. Mr Huggins raises three further points on this issue. The first is that the statements were not made by the individuals responsible for dismissing the plaintiffs. But the statements were purportedly made on behalf of Cathay, and both Mr Tyler and Mr Chen plainly had ostensible (and no doubt had actual)

authority to speak on behalf of Cathay. Mr Huggins also suggests that the statements did not reveal grounds for dismissal which fell within the ambit of the DGP. I cannot accept that point either: it seems to me plain that the allegations against the plaintiffs in the statements fell within... the DGP.

79.   Mr Huggins's remaining point is that it would be peculiar if the effect of reading clause 35.3 and the DGP together meant that an employee was better off if Cathay was intending to dismiss him for disciplinary reasons than if it was intending to dismiss him for reasons which involved no wrong-doing on his part. However, at least on the basis of the above analysis, there appears to me to be no capriciousness in the dismissal procedures. If the dismissal is not based on any wrong-doing by the employee, he is merely entitled to three months' notice, or three months' pay in lieu... However, if the employee is to have the 'stigma' of a disciplinary reason for his dismissal, then, as a matter of elementary justice, he is entitled to have the protection of the DGP procedure first, and the fact that this may give him a few extra weeks in his job, as against someone who is dismissed for reasons involving no wrong-doing on his part, is merely the consequence of that entitlement.

80.   For these reasons, I would allow the plaintiffs' appeal on the issue of whether Cathay was in breach of the Conditions, and restore the award of one month's pay made by the Judge to each plaintiff. It is only fair to the Court of Appeal, who took a different view on this issue, to record that they did not have the benefit of a number of the arguments canvassed before the Court of Final Appeal (many of which were raised by members of the Court).

No clarification needed here then, other than to add that, like Lord Neuberger, I too forcefully reject Huggins' rubbish arguments. The only question that the judgment raises is, perhaps, why didn't the Court of Appeal 'have the benefit of a number of arguments canvassed before the Court of Final Appeal?' Could it be because they hadn't taken the trouble to read the papers beforehand, came into court unprepared and, therefore, unable to challenge Huggins' preposterous proposals in any meaningful fashion?

But despite this ruling, there is still a loophole left open to an unscrupulous employer. All they have to do is simply sack the employee with no reason given, keep their traps shut and the employee has no recourse. Of course, if we had proper employment protection legislation, such as requiring the employer to give the employee written reason(s) for the dismissal, as is the case in more enlightened jurisdictions, then that loophole would be closed.

The final part of the judgment dealt with the defamation damages. He started by summarising the issues to be dealt with.

> 81. The Judge was of the view that, in the statements made by Mr Tyler on 9 July 2001 and by Mr Chen on 10 July 2001, the 49ers were being accused of 'being unprofessional, of being bad employees, and of not caring for Cathay's best interests or those of Hong Kong', and that this was defamatory of them. The Court of Appeal saw no reason to disturb the Judge's findings. There is no challenge by Cathay to the Court of Appeal's decision to uphold the Judge's conclusion that these statements were defamatory of the plaintiffs on the ground that they suggested that, to use the Court of Appeal's pithy description... [that] the plaintiffs were 'troublemakers upon whom Cathay could not rely', and... 'bad and disloyal employees'... What is under challenge by the plaintiffs is the Court of Appeal's decision to reduce the general damages awarded to the plaintiffs for this defamation from $3 million to $700,000.

So far so good. He then went on to describe the job in hand.

> 82. The function of an appellate court when considering an appeal against an award of general compensatory damages for defamation is normally to address two questions. The first is whether any of the trial judge's reasons for the award under challenge was erroneous. For instance, one of his reasons may have been based on a fact not borne out by the evidence, or may have been wrong in law or logic. If so, the appellate court must consider if the error vitiated the award.

Again, this makes sense. If the judge made an error in law, it may invalidate the judgment. He then continued:

The second, and broader, question which the appellate court must address is whether the figure awarded by the trial judge was too high or too low.

OK, this makes sense again. But the next point is important.

This does not involve the appellate court deciding what figure it would have awarded: it must limit itself to considering whether, in the light of all the facts and circumstances of the particular case, the trial judge went outside the generous range of general damages open to him.

So, the appellate court, including the Court of Appeal, should NOT assess damages itself, except in certain circumstances which he describes further.

Only if the appellate court decides that the trial judge adopted a wrong reason which vitiates his award, or that he went outside the permissible range, will it go on to consider for itself what damages to award.

So, since in our case, the judge did not make an error in law, the only ground for reassessing the damages is if he went outside the 'permissible range'. So, surely this is a subjective test? Let us see what else Neuberger had to say on this.

83. In the present case, I consider that the Court of Appeal were right to conclude that the award of $3 million to each plaintiff could not stand; I reach that conclusion on the basis of both of the two grounds upon which general damages for defamation can be challenged.

So, he considered that Judge Reyes went outside this 'permissible range' in his judgment. He went on to opine on his reasons for this.

84. First, it appears to me that the Judge wrongly equiparated the damage caused to each plaintiff in this case to the damage suffered by the plaintiff in *Chu Sik Kuk Yuen v Apple Daily Ltd and others*. In that case, Yuen J... awarded $3 million to a solicitor, who was wholly inaccurately reported as having

absconded with substantial amounts of her clients' funds, and who, as medical evidence established, consequently suffered from a significant bout of depression and prematurely gave birth to a baby who suffered from a life-threatening condition for some time.

85. I agree with the Court of Appeal that the libel in *Chu* were inherently far more serious than the libel in this case. It is hard to think of a more serious attack on a solicitor's professional reputation and on her feelings than the publication, in a newspaper with a large circulation, of a gratuitous and unqualified report that she has absconded with substantial client monies. By contrast, the statements in this case did not question the plaintiffs' character or their competence as pilots...

Oh really? So being called 'troublemakers' and 'bad and disloyal employees' doesn't question our characters, doesn't it? And being called 'unprofessional' doesn't relate to our competence as pilots, doesn't it? But the next part is a beauty.

Further, the great majority of the readers of the statements would have appreciated that the statements had been made by an employer in the context of a long-running and bitter dispute with its employees, where both sides were well entrenched, and engaging in megaphone diplomacy. As the Court of Appeal said in para 151 of their judgment,

'The statements were made in the context of a campaign on the part of the Union which could have resulted in serious disruption to the general public in terms of passengers as well as cargo transport by air.'

So the general public would realise that it was just rhetoric in the union dispute so it wasn't nearly so damaging. But, disregarding for a moment the disastrous effect that these statements had on our reputations and careers in the closed community of professional aviation, what has the fact that this could have caused 'serious disruption to the general public' have to do with it? Are they implying that it served us right for being such disloyal, troublemaking employees by refusing to accept changes that were impinging on the safety of the operation? Changes that, if they were permitted, really would have serious effects on the general public. Just like the Court of Appeal, it smacks of predisposition. He continued:

> 86. Equally, the damage suffered by the claimant in *Chu* was self-evidently far more serious than the damage suffered in this case.

Self-evident? Self-evident to whom? Self-evident to someone who has spent all his life in the legal profession and deeply sympathises with the lawyer's plight perhaps. Certainly not self-evident to someone who has spent 30 years building a career in professional aviation only to see it destroyed overnight by malicious statements deliberately designed to intimidate the rest of the employees into toeing the line. He went on:

> Quite apart from the self-evidently greater harm to reputation and feelings which must have been caused by the libel in *Chu*.

Feelings? Feelings? How the hell can he say this? Does he know how it feels to have your hard-won professional reputation totally destroyed? How can he? It's never happened to him. This is just subjective rubbish. He went on:

> It is true that the plaintiffs in this case claimed that their employment prospects had been severely affected by the defamatory statements, but they failed to establish any claim to special damages in this connection.

Well he's right here. And we've already discussed why that was. In today's litigious environment, it's impossible to get any prospective employer to say, 'I did not give you a job because of the things Cathay said about you,' for fear of a discrimination claim. They'll tell you that verbally in private but, get them to swear an affidavit to that effect? Not a chance. He went on to discuss this further:

> 87. The Judge plainly (and rightly) allowed each plaintiff something for loss of employment prospects. However, as just mentioned, there was no specific evidence which established that any plaintiff had been unemployed because of the defamatory

statements. There could have been all sorts of other reasons for any difficulty which a plaintiff had in getting re-employment. Those reasons would include, most obviously, the simple fact, harsh though it may seem, that some employers in the airline industry may have been disinclined to employ a pilot who had been dismissed as a result of a long-running, much publicised and bitter dispute with his previous employer, involving long term contract compliance and threatened MSS. In this connection, as Lord Hoffmann, giving the judgment of the Judicial Committee of the Privy Council in *The Gleaner Co Ltd v Abrahams*... said, 'it is usually difficult to prove a direct causal link between the libel and loss of any particular earnings', and such 'matters can be taken into account', on the basis that 'the strict requirements of proving causation are relaxed in return for moderation in the overall figure awarded'.

Good. So there is guidance here. Lord Hoffmann clearly recognised the problem. Of course, the problem now is to define the term 'moderation'. He went on to opine further with his comparison of damage in the *Chu* case.

90. The only aspect of the defamation in this case which could be said to be worse is that in *Chu* the defendant pretty quickly published a retraction and apology, albeit rather an anaemic one in all the circumstances. In this case, the statements were never retracted, and remained available through Cathay's website... for over eight years. However, no evidence was given to suggest that the retention of the statements on the website increased the damage to any plaintiff over and above the damage done by the original utterance.

Oh really? Well what about it being self-evident? You used it earlier, why not here? And what about them repeating their statements about George Crofts after the House of Lords judgment in his favour five years after their original defamatory statements? Their mouthpiece repeated in the international media that 'This decision in no way changes our opinion of Mr Crofts formed in 2001. We had genuinely lost confidence in his ability to work in the best interest of the airline and we will not be returning him to the flight deck of a Cathay Pacific aircraft'.

That's pretty bloody self-evident to me that they persisted with their malicious and vindictive campaign against us.

> Further, it was not suggested that the statements remained accessible for any malicious reason, and they were removed from the website as soon as the plaintiffs asked.

No, that's not true. They were removed when we entered the fact into evidence. They didn't remove them when we 'asked'. They were removed when they realised they could damage their defence.

> The notion that Cathay was not intending to be vindictive is supported by the fact, relayed to us by Mr Huggins... that Cathay had offered each of the 49ers a letter to be shown to prospective employers, confirming that he had not been dismissed for disciplinary reasons.

Oh please. Even his colleague, Judge Bokhary, made a mockery of this during the trial when he said, 'I mean the only point of it is to give future employers a laugh. It's absurd to write such a letter after you've made such an announcement'. But now you go and try to use this in mitigation. As for 'not intending to be vindictive', is that why they misreported our income to the IRD so we faced swingeing tax bills? Is that why they told the immigration people we were leaving Hong Kong? Is that why they tried to get us evicted from our houses? Give me strength. Next, one of the following paragraphs was an exercise in counter-intuitive reasoning.

> 92. For the reasons already discussed, the defamation was serious in that it involved significant criticisms of the plaintiffs as employees, implying, as the Court of Appeal said... that the 49ers were 'bad and disloyal employees meriting the termination of their services'. However, Cathay made no express, or even implied, suggestion that the plaintiffs' ability as pilots was in question or that their honesty was challenged.

Sorry? Then what do you interpret 'unprofessional' to mean?

> The 49ers were said expressly not to 'be relied upon to act in the best interests of the company in the future', and not 'showing the

227

total professionalism [Cathay] requires', and, arguably, of holding 'Hong Kong… to ransom'. Defamatory though these statements may have been, they constituted allegations of a very general nature, which would have been appreciated by the great majority of readers as having been made in the context of a bitter labour dispute.

Oh, so it's OK to say these things in the context of a bitter labour dispute, is it, and that makes them far less damaging? So if I'd told the world's media that the CEO had a $2,000-a-day cocaine habit with no evidence whatsoever to support such an allegation other than my suspicion, that would have been less damaging to his reputation if I'd said it in the context of an industrial dispute would it? What bollocks.

He went on to consider quantum.

93. It is true that an appellate court should be slow to interfere with the trial judge's award of general damages for defamation, simply on the ground that it is too high or too low.

Good. So why did they? Please enlighten us.

However, following the approach of the English Court of Appeal (admittedly in relation to damages awarded by a jury) in cases such as *Rantzen v Mirror Group Newspapers (1986) Ltd…* and *John v MGN Ltd…* it seems to me that, where damages are plainly too high (or plainly too low), an appellate court should set the award aside and substitute its own figure.

So, we're using UK precedent. OK, that's fair enough.

It is inevitable that many people will consider that there is a significant degree of inconsistency in the amount of general damages awarded in defamation cases, because (i) there is an inevitable degree of subjectivity in an area where there is so little logical or principled correlation between the damage suffered and money; (ii) opinions as to the seriousness of particular libels will legitimately vary; and (iii) the factual circumstances in which a defamatory statement is made, and the particular effect of a libel, will vary from plaintiff to plaintiff. However, given the importance of maintaining the reputation of the courts and of enabling parties in defamation disputes to compromise their differences, an appellate court should ensure that the inevitable inconsistency is kept within reasonable bounds. In this case $3 million was outside those bounds.

Yes, subjective like your opinion of the amount of damage caused to our careers by Cathay's vindictive and malicious lies about us.

94. Accordingly, given that the damages awarded by the Judge... were... plainly too high, this was a case where the Court of Appeal was plainly justified in stepping in and assessing damages themselves.

Oh I see. Plainly self-evident I suppose.

As to the quantum of those damages... it would have been appropriate in the normal way to award a sum which included significant amounts in respect of (i) consolation for distress, (ii) loss of reputation, and (iii) vindication. Further, item (ii) should have included something for loss of earnings.

Right. No arguments from me there.

However, general damages for libel have to be proportionate, as the English courts were reminded by the Court of Appeal in *Rantzen* and in *John*. And, in particular, bearing in mind the absence of any 'hard' evidence as to loss of job prospects, and what Lord Hoffmann said about the need for 'moderation', any sum included for loss of earning potential should not have been extravagant.

Here we go. Let's hear your definition of 'moderation'.

95. Bearing in mind these points, it seems to me that, in contrast with the $3 million awarded by the Judge, the $700,000 awarded by the Court of Appeal was plainly within permissible bounds.

So that's it, is it? It was in 'permissible bounds', so that's it?

I can understand why some of the plaintiffs may feel that this is on the low side, but, bearing in mind the factors discussed in the preceding paragraphs of this judgment, I am firmly of the view that it is not a figure with which an appellate court should interfere.

'On the low side'? Too damned right it's on the low side. Ignoring for the moment the principles you just enumerated, i.e. consolation for distress, loss of reputation, and vindication, just on loss of earnings alone $700k equates to less than three months' pay and allowances for me. Yes, I'd definitely classify that as 'on the low side'. I'd go further than that actually. It goes nowhere near compensating us for the damage caused to us. And it certainly doesn't satisfy the other principles that you yourself have quoted. It's fucking derisory.

It is true that the figure was not explained by the Court of Appeal.

No, it wasn't was it? How are you going to justify that after you used the methodology used by Judge Reyes to demolish his award?

However, in common with the majority of defamation cases, as Lord Hoffmann said in *The Gleaner...* once a court has identified all the relevant facts and circumstances relating to a defamatory statement, and has alighted on what it considers to be the appropriate figure for general damages, 'the matter is not capable of further analysis'.

Bollocks. I could use that argument back at you to justify Reyes' award. That's just a complete get-out. Why didn't you pursue it further to find out how the Court of Appeal came up with its figure? Why didn't you press Huggins to admit the true reason? Why don't you even mention Clive's submission that it was a pluck based on Huggins' answer to a question from the bench in the Court of Appeal? Why do you attach no weight to that? Or is it just too hard to consider that an officer of the court might have lied to you? Or is it that it completely undermines your reasoning?

96. It is argued on behalf of the plaintiffs that the Court of Appeal had wrongly failed to include in their award anything for the loss of employment prospects. If they had so failed, then I agree that they would have been in error.

Good. We're agreed on that then. They made an error.

However, it seems to me clear that there was no such error.

Oh really? I'm looking forward to hearing how you explain that.

Apart from the fact that any such error seems inherently unlikely…

Inherently unlikely? Is that the same as being self-evident? Subjective and arbitrary? I could say it was inherently unlikely that Judge Reyes made a mistake. But you didn't consider that when criticising his judgment did you?

… the Court of Appeal… as Mr Justice Bokhary PJ pointed out in argument, specifically quoted with approval a passage in *Gatley on Libel and Slander*… where it is stated that, while 'it may be virtually impossible to prove financial loss' ('such as loss of business or employment'), there will be cases where 'the damage is insidious and merits a substantial award'.

Yes, 'substantial' being the operative word.

The only reason for quoting that passage in a judgment, particularly after they had said that they agreed with the Judge that the plaintiffs had established no causal link between the statements and any employment difficulties they had had, was to explain that the Court of Appeal were including something for loss of employment prospects in the $700,000 they were awarding.

What bullshit. How do you know? They didn't specifically state that they were including an element for loss of employment prospects. You're just subjectively implying that in an attempt to justify your position. Let's list a few synonyms for 'substantial'. Considerable,

231

significant, notable, major, valuable. And you think any of those words apply to HK$700k, do you? Your salary is listed as GB£214,165 per annum. That's equivalent to HK$2.5 million at an exchange rate of 11.75; about what I was earning. So you think that GB£59.5k would adequately compensate you if you had your reputation impugned and your career destroyed, do you? Even the Employment Tribunal in the UK awarded George Crofts GB£70k just for breach of contract with NO element for defamation. Bloody outrageous.

And that was the judgment handed down on our defamation damages by the greatest legal minds that the UK and Hong Kong judicial systems have to offer. I am put in mind of the remark that Ian Hislop, the editor of *Private Eye*, made after hearing the verdict in a libel action that Sonia Sutcliffe, the wife of the Yorkshire Ripper, Peter Sutcliffe, brought against the magazine; 'If that's justice, I'm a banana'.

12

Bertha

'Said Red Molly to James, that's a fine motorbike,
A girl could feel special on any such like.
Said James to Red Molly, my hat's off to you,
That's a Vincent Black Lightning nineteen fifty-two.'

Richard Thompson – *1952 Vincent Black Lightning*

The first bike I ever had was a Vespa 150. So not a bike really; a scooter. It was 1968 and I was 16 years old. Back then you either had to be a mod or a rocker. Which to choose? The first consideration was that, when you got a provisional driving licence, you weren't allowed to have a bike over 250 cc until you'd passed your test. The range of 'proper' bikes available under 250 was a bit limited, whereas there was a whole range of Lambrettas and Vespas that looked pretty cool (or so I thought back then). The second consideration was the music, the clothes and the chicks. All things considered, I decided to be a mod.

I stripped the engine, bored it out and skimmed the head in pursuit of higher performance, then re-sprayed the frame, got the side panels chromed and put it all back together. We thought we were the bee's knees. However, after one particularly unfortunate incident when I got into a serious speed wobble, lost the thing and ended up with a broken collar bone and a very painful case of gravel rash (I was only wearing a light summer shirt and no crash helmet when I made contact with the tarmac), I decided it was time to switch to something with bigger wheels and, therefore, better stability. And anyway, by then, I had left school (so I could grow my hair longer now) and the music had changed markedly. So I switched to being a rocker.

The last bike I had, when I was living in Great Offley and working for Monarch, was a Suzuki GT380; a three pot two-stroke. But again, after another unfortunate incident when the bike ended up in a field after it failed to negotiate a bend and I had to walk two miles home and my mate Graeme Banks-Smith had to bring his flat-bed truck the next day to retrieve it, I decided it was time to stick to four wheels. (The fact that I couldn't quite remember which field it had ended up in also contributed to the decision-making process.)

Fast forward to November 2012. After we'd had the result from the Court of Final Appeal (even though it had not all gone our way), I decided it was time to buy a toy to celebrate so I started looking around for a bike. I wanted a classic old British bike; a Triumph Bonneville or a Norton Commando. In Hong Kong, they're few and far between, but a good friend of mine, Simon 'Bollix' Vallance, who owns a bike repair shop was keeping his ear to the ground for me. And then another friend who I'd known for years, Dave McKirdy, who as well as being a musician and a poet also rebuilds vintage British bikes, gave me some advice along the lines of, 'I don't know what fond memories you have of these old bikes John, but they are quite temperamental. They don't handle all that well, the brakes aren't all that good, the ride's pretty hard, they don't always start very easily and they require quite a lot of fettling.' When he put it that way it did bring back memories of pools of oil under crankcases, spark plugs in the oven on cold mornings and long walks home on wet nights. On top of that, some other biker mates were advising me to go for some Jap-crap, so we had a look at a couple of Yamahas. But they weren't what I wanted. And then, out of the blue, another friend, Douglas 'Trumpet' Waterston, told me he'd seen an advert from 'some French bloke' who was selling a Triumph Bonneville T100. But this wasn't an old classic. It was a 2004 model with a 790 cc twin engine made in the classic cafe racer style but with modern things like electric starter, disc brakes, good suspension and handling and oil seals that work. This was clearly what I was looking for.

That evening, I was sitting in Agua with Klaske having a beer and there was a French bloke I was sort of semi-acquainted with, by the name of Michael, sitting at the next table. I'd first got chatting to him one evening because he drinks pastis and that used to be my favourite breakfast accompaniment when I did a lot of skiing in Les

Trois Vallées. I asked him if he knew of some French bloke who was selling a Bonneville. Guess what? It turned out to be him. He was selling it because he'd recently had a bit of a hairy and his wife wasn't happy because they had a young daughter. We negotiated the price over a few glasses of anisette and I bought the bike sight unseen. I checked with Simon afterwards. He knew the bike and told me it was in decent nick so I transferred the money into Michael's account. We couldn't actually take delivery until after Christmas because he was going away to Finland to take his daughter to see the reindeer and we were going to Mauritius on holiday (we'd decided that we deserved a holiday as well and, even though money was tight, when I won the RTB that would take care of the air fares; so just do it). So, for her 2012 Christmas present, Klaske became the proud owner of a 2004 Triumph Bonneville T100. (Actually, since we couldn't get the bike until the New Year, on the day itself she got a copy of the T100 owner's manual that I printed out off the interweb with her name inserted on the front.)

It had been more than ten years since I'd last been to Mauritius. Because it had been 'our place' when I was with Jill, I'd stayed away but now I felt it was time to reclaim it. I had memories of Mauritius being a beautiful island with a truly multicultural society. Because it had been settled by many European nations during its history, including the British, Dutch, French and Portuguese, as well as various Asian visitors, the people are a true melange. And I wanted to show it to Klaske; I thought she would appreciate it. Unfortunately, as so often in life, the reality did not live up to the memory.

When I first visited the island, there were strict foreign property ownership laws. A foreigner could not own property unless they had a Mauritian partner. It seemed that these laws had been relaxed since my last visit. Previously you could drive round the island on the coastal road and enjoy beautiful views out across the Indian Ocean on all sides. We tried that on this visit but mostly what we saw were four-metre high concrete walls. Newly admitted foreign owners had bought up a lot of the beachfront property, built their villas and put up their castle walls to protect their privacy. It seemed such a shame and it was a great disappointment to me. But such is progress.

There was one place that was still the same though. The memorial to *Helderberg*, the South African Airways flight SA295, a Boeing 747-244B Combi, that crashed into the sea 125 miles northeast of Mauritius en route from Taipei on 28 November 1987. It was caused by a fire on the cargo deck and all 159 passengers and crew on board were killed. The source of the fire was determined to be from the front right hand pallet on the main deck cargo hold which had only class B fire suppression. The temperature of the fire was determined to have reached 600 degrees Celsius or more leading to speculation that an oxidant must have been present. The true source of the fire was never determined but conspiracy theories still abound.[6] One good thing did come about as a result of this accident. The restrictions on carrying dangerous goods on board passenger aircraft were tightened considerably and the Combis were eventually phased out. If you ever get the chance to visit the memorial, you should do so. It is a very poignant place (as is the memorial to Bomber Command in Green Park in London should you ever chance to visit there).

Despite the changes since my last visit, we still had a good time there; right up until the night of 4 January that is. We were sitting in a beach bar listening to some live music and getting ready to order dinner when my Nokia rang. It was my sister, June. She called to say that my mother had been taken to hospital with a suspected heart attack. Given that she was 93 years old, the prognosis was not good and I needed to get there ASAP. There were no flights available direct to London so I booked a flight on Air Mauritius to Paris Charles de Gaulle (CDG) departing the next afternoon. It was the start of one of the most miserable travel experiences I've ever had.

The flight time was 11 hours 25 minutes. So what, you might think. You're a long-haul pilot. You're used to 14 and 15 hour flight times. What are you complaining about? It was the woman sitting next to me. She had a cold. And she sniffed. Every 45 seconds for the whole of the bloody flight. That's 913 sniffs. By the end of the trip, I wanted to throttle her, stick my fingers up her nose, put duct tape over her face; anything to stop her infernal sniffing. I got virtually no sleep and arrived at CDG terminal 2E at midnight local time.

The first flight I could get out of CDG to LHR was a BA flight departing at 07:50. I had the best part of seven hours to wait. The BA flight went from terminal 2A. OK, I thought, get across to 2A, get something to eat and see if you can bed down in the terminal for a bit of shuteye. First problem; how to get across to the other terminal. The airport was effectively closed for the night. I could see the other terminal but all the walkways across to it were closed and locked. The only way to access it was via a shuttle bus. But the information desk was closed and there were no timetables so I needed to find out where it went from and at what time. I could see several bus stops outside with timetables posted in front of each of them. There was nothing for it; I had to go outside. Now you're thinking, so what? The 'so what' was that the temperature was almost sub-zero and all I had on was tropical gear that I'd taken to Mauritius. The only saving grace was that I'd taken my Waterlooplein jacket with me for some unknown reason. It did save me. I went outside and the timetable said the next bus was due in 25 minutes. OK, no biggie, I'll just go back in the terminal and keep warm until it arrives. Oh no you won't. The door I'd come out of was exit only and all the entrances were locked. I had to stand outside in the cold freezing my nuts off until the bus arrived. When I finally made it to terminal 2A, I thought my troubles were over. Dream on. Everything was closed. Restaurants, snack bars, coffee shops; the lot. But there were some vending machines. I got some Euros out of an ATM and set about finding some change. The place was deserted. Then I spied a couple of gendarmes strolling down the terminal towards me. Salvation! But when I proffered my notes for some change, all I was met with was a Gallic shrug and '*pas de pieces.*' When I finally boarded the BA flight for LHR I was dehydrated and knackered from the fitful sleep I'd managed to get in that godforsaken place. I slept for the whole hour and a quarter it took to get to London and went to pick up a hire car. If I never transit through CDG again, it will be too soon. Other than Lagos, if god wants to put an arsehole in the world, CDG is the ideal location.

I arrived in Leeds in the afternoon of Sunday 6th and went to the hospital to see my mother. The nurses had asked June earlier, 'Has she seen everyone?' to which June had replied, 'No, her son's on the way up from Mauritius.' The nurses had then said, 'Oh, she'll wait for him to arrive and then she'll go.'
When I got there June told me that Mum had more or less been in a coma for the last few hours. When I walked in she woke up.

'Ah, you're here then,' she said. We talked for a little and I told her about our new bike.

'Oh no. Not a motorbike, dangerous bloody things.' We talked some more for 20 minutes or so and then she went back to sleep. She returned to the stars later the next night without regaining consciousness.

When I got to June's place I thought that I'd be able finally to thaw myself out. No such luck. Her central heating boiler had failed. I slept the night in my clothes trying to keep warm and flew back to Hong Kong on the 10th.

And then I waited for June to let me know when the funeral was to be held. It seemed that that time of year is popular for dying so we had to wait in the queue to get a slot. I waited until the 16th and hadn't heard from June so I gave her a call.

'Any news?'

'What d'you mean any news? I sent you a text a few days ago.'

'What? I haven't received one, what's going on?'

It turned out the funeral was all arranged for the 22nd. This wasn't the first time that SMS messages from June hadn't got through to me. I booked tickets and Klaske and I flew over on the 19th. And knowing that I hate the cold, my dear old mum had arranged the weather perfectly for me. It had snowed quite heavily, thawed a bit and then re-frozen overnight. June wanted the funeral cortège to pull up in front of the house, but there was a problem. Because of budget cuts, lack of salt or the wrong kind of snow or whatever, the council hadn't gritted the roads and they were sheet ice. So I ended up with my brother-in-law Jim, my nephew James and various nephews-in-law out there with picks, shovels and snow-removing thingies clearing 40 yards of road so that the cars could get through. And give Klaske her due, she pitched in as well. There's nothing like a farm girl to help out in emergencies.

But there was one other thing that happened to add to the saga. By the time we got to the UK, everything had already been arranged for the funeral. I told June that I wanted to say something at the service, but she informed me that I couldn't. We were only allowed a limited time slot in the crematorium chapel and the speaking slots had already been allocated. That pissed me off a bit. But what happened at the service itself pissed me off a lot.

When I was doing research for my first book, I'd written to my mother and asked her to write something for me about how she met my father and their experiences together during the war. In return she sent me a letter. It seemed that June had given the sky-pilot who was conducting the service a copy of my letter. But that's not what pissed me off. What really pissed me off was that he used it in his address. He stood there talking about my mother and my father, using information that he'd got from my letter, *but he got the bloody details wrong*. I was sitting there fuming. I wanted to get up and shout at him, 'No. You didn't know my mother or my father, and now you're reading from my letter and you haven't even bothered to do the research properly. If you can't get it right just shut the fuck up.' But, of course, I had to just sit there and keep quiet. My mother wouldn't have liked it if I'd made a scene.

After the service, we went to a hotel for the wake. Klaske knew I was angry and told me to get up and say something. But I kept quiet because the god-botherer was there and I felt I might lose it and get stuck into him for being such a disrespectful, ignorant twat. But then Mavis, my mother's younger sister, came and spoke to me in the way that only my auntie can.

'Now listen to me sweetie. You only have one chance. If you don't get up and say something now you will regret it for the rest of your life so, if you want to say something, say it now.'

Mavis was right. I couldn't let this go by without saying something to my assembled family. After all, even though June is four years older than me, I'm the male head of the family. I did the usual glass-tapping thing to get the room's attention and got up to speak. This is what I said.

We've come here today to celebrate the life of my mother, Joan Bertha Warham.

Looking around the room, there are four generations of family and friends gathered here and I want to share some things with you all that you may not know about Joan.

But first, bereavement; how do we cope with it? For some here this is the first time that you've lost someone close and you are hurting. I remember the first time it happened to me. All I wanted to know was when does the pain stop? Well the answer to that question is that it doesn't. It is with you for the rest of your life. But it changes. Instead of being the sharp stabbing pain that you're feeling now, it changes with time into a dull ache that you learn to live with. It becomes part of your life, becomes a friend, and you learn to use it to remind you, to jog your memory and to remember and enjoy the memories of the good times that you shared together.

I'm going to share with you now some of my memories. When I was doing research for my book, I asked my mother about my father, about how they'd met and about his time in the Royal Air Force during the Second World War. She wrote me a letter and I'd like to read it to you now.

It's simply headed '*Facts leading up to my meeting your Dad*'.

I lived in Harrow, Middlesex when war broke out in September 1939. In 1940, things became very unsafe. Raids and bombing etc. My father worked for the BBC and was evacuated from Broadcasting House to a radio transmitter in Dorset so he was not with us.

In late 1940 my mother decided that we had to move to a safer place and she found a large terrace house to rent in Paignton, Devon. All arrangements were made over the phone. Mavis and Derek were only children. We also had three boys and cousins of my Dad's staying with us. They lived in the East End of London and had been bombed out. So early 1941, that's where we ended up.

Mother decided to take in paying guests as there were people coming down from London to get respite from the bombs. We were very busy.

By now it is Summer 1942. I opened the door one day to an RAF person who said he was stationed in Paignton for a few weeks and had we any accommodation free as his parents would like to spend a week with him before he moved on. He came in and all arrangements were made.

I learned that James Stanley Warham joined the RAF Volunteer Reserve early in 1939, spent most weekends training etc. War started on 3rd September 1939 and within weeks he was in uniform and stationed at Waddington, Lincolnshire.

It was a very cold Winter and they were housed in Nissen huts, no heat or hot water. He said they melted snow to wash and shave each morning. I don't know how long they were there. I think the next move was RAF Hendon in London when he joined Transport Command and spent some months escorting VIP personnel to secret meetings a lot of which were in Scotland. He grew to like Scotland and never missed those trips. His pals gave him the nickname of Jock.

I don't know where he was between 1941 – 1942. Incidentally, I was engaged to a chap in the army who I met at a dance straight after Dunkirk in 1940. I only saw him on short leaves and after meeting your Dad that Summer I knew the attraction was very strong on both sides. His mother warned him to toe the line as I was not free.

The night before he was to depart to Manchester en-route for Canada to learn to fly, he took me out to a local café where we talked and talked and ate sausage and mash. It was all over so quickly. I went to the station next day to see him off and he said he would write to me. The next episode will amuse you.

They arrived in Manchester and were there just over a week. A few nights before leaving they had a going away party. They were all out of their minds with drink. Your Dad wakes up the next morning to find himself engaged to a female called Sheila and so he departs these shores on the Queen Mary wondering how he had got into that mess. A few days later his mother got a phone call from this female who said, 'Hello my name is Sheila and I am engaged to your son'. Dear son was on the ocean sailing away and no way could she get her hands on him.

James Stanley knew that he had to get himself out of this stupid mess, which he did, but with mail taking so long to get from A – B some months were to pass. I also knew that my engagement had to end, which it did.

I was called up to go on munitions and in September 1942 departed from Paignton to go to Birmingham for a three month course in engineering. My life came down to basics. Eight of us lodged in a three bed house in a very rough area and more bombs. The three months soon passed and I learned to use a lathe and found my fingers were quite adaptable. From

241

*Birmingham I was sent to Worcester and worked in a factory
which had always been all male. Myself and another girl were
the first females. It was hilarious.*

*In the meantime I was waiting for mail from Canada which did
not arrive as his mother had given him orders not to dally with a
nice girl etc. He duly arrived in New Brunswick, Canada, and
was billeted with a nice family who spoilt him rotten. He did all
his ground training and then went on to Pensecola to do his
flying where he gained his wings. It was now 1943 and he
returned to the UK. After a short leave he was then posted to
Rhodesia in East Africa, also to Kenya, and was on Catalinas
with Coastal Command.*

*But now it had leaked through to him that I was free, the two
mothers had formed a friendship and passed on the news. I then
received the long awaited letter which said, and his actual words
were, 'Isn't it time you and I stopped working at cross purposes
and got together?'*

*He arrived back from East Africa in September 1944, was given
leave, loads of phone calls, I went to his home in Liverpool the
day before he arrived. We had a great leave getting to know
each other, his parents were delighted. The leave was almost
over when another bombshell. A telegram to say that his brother
had been killed flying over Norfolk. Stan's leave was extended
while we made funeral arrangements. Arthur's squadron leader
came to the funeral and advised us to discourage his mother
from wanting the coffin opening as there was only weighted
matter inside. The plane had crashed from such great height that
there was nothing to pick up. It was a very tragic time.*

*By now it was October. We had a quick trip to Southport to visit
relatives, managed to buy a ring in a shop in Southport and got
engaged on Southport station in the dark on October 11th and he
went back from leave. My father had now been sent to Droitwich
in Worcestershire. I was in digs near the factory so my mother
found us a cottage in Worcester and joined us.*

Stan had been posted to County Fermanagh in Ireland and I had a wedding to arrange which was very difficult. You had to beg, borrow and steal. A girlfriend was going out with a Yank and he turned out trumps and gave us food that we had not seen in years and so we were married on January 2nd 1945. After seven days leave he returned to Ireland. He was there 12 weeks, came home on leave and was then posted to Oban in Scotland. I went back with him. They were to do another course on Cats. There were four planes moored in the bay in Oban. The crews spent the days doing tests and exercises on the planes etc.

This was where I met David and Dolly. We had a very hectic three weeks, spent money that we hadn't got. We stayed in a hotel, the owner's husband was a prisoner of war in Germany and she made a great fuss of the Boys in Blue. Dug out bottles that had been put away for peacetime. All good things had to end, Stan departed for India and I back to Liverpool heartbroken.

I had been invited by Granddad to move to Liverpool to find a flat or somewhere to live as the war was just about over. I then had to go back to Worcester to pack up etc. My mother was not too pleased to lose me.

Stan arrived in India. His posting was RAF Station Kolar, South East Asia Air Force. He was now flying Liberators which he did not like. He said they were heavy, like flying tanks.

His eyes started playing up and he had a bad dose of conjunctivitis and was grounded. The war was now over, his demob number 26 was very low and he had to make his way to Bombay to await a ship home. He sailed on the Georgie early December 1945 and docked in Liverpool on Christmas morning. His Dad who worked in the Post Office had a permit to board the ship and so went aboard as soon as it landed.

Stan was allowed ashore at 5 AM Boxing Day morning and I heard his key in the lock at 6 AM. My feet took wings down the stairs.

What a story! May you live in interesting times. Depending on whom you believe, that's supposed to be either a Chinese curse or a Scottish compliment. Either way she certainly fulfilled that, curse or compliment. She lived a full and interesting life. And most importantly she found love. When she met my father she found the love of her life. She found her soul mate and she shared her life with him. Many people don't get to do that in their lives. But more than that, she had the love of her children, her grandchildren and her great grandchildren and we're all here now in this room. What more can we ask for or expect out of life? Remember that when you're hurting and remember it with joy.

One of the last conversations I had with my mother was about the advice she gave me as a child and as a young man and what I did with it. She always told me not to bother telling lies because I was crap at it and no one believed them anyway. She was right about that! She told me that I'd have to learn to control my temper otherwise it would get me in trouble. She was right about that as well!! But she often said to me at different times in my life, why can't you just do as you're told? Why do you always have to question things? Why can't you just toe the line and look for a quiet life? Well I couldn't and didn't and I recently said to her, well I must have got that from someone, from either her or my Dad. And when I said to her that some of the things I've done must have caused her pain and sleepless nights, her answer was simple. She said to me, 'Oh yes, but I always thought the best of you.'

'I always thought the best of you.' That is good advice for us all sitting here. Use it to live your life to the full and enjoy it as my Mum did hers.

For those of you who have a god, she has gone now to be with her maker and you can take comfort from that. For those of you who don't have a god, she has returned now, once again, to become part of the stardust that our world, our universe, was created from in the first place. What better way is there to renew the cycle of life that we see before us today, that we are all part of, right here in this room?

BERTHA

Let us celebrate the life of my Mum, Joan Bertha Warham.

We'd taken delivery of our new Triumph Bonneville T100 after we'd returned from Mauritius (me via Leeds). When we got back to Hong Kong again after the funeral, we decided to call her Bertha. My mother hated her middle name and she hated motorbikes as well (dangerous bloody things), so it seemed apposite.

There are a few anecdotes that I'll to relate to finish the story. There was only once that I can remember when I finally managed to get the last word in over my mother and render her speechless; at least for a few seconds. It was shortly after I got my command in Cathay on the 747. She was coming out to stay with me in Hong Kong for a couple of weeks and I was operating the flight into Kai Tak. On the approach, I sat her on the jump seat so she could watch. It was a bit blowy that day so there was the usual wrestling match as we came round the corner onto R/W 13 but the landing was nice and smooth, right on the target touchdown point. I pulled the reversers, brought the aircraft to a walking pace and turned off the runway to taxi to the terminal. As we were doing the after landing checks I turned to her and said, 'Well Mother, that's what I do for a living, now do you still want me to get a proper job?' She just sat there staring at me. After a few seconds she recovered herself and said to me, 'Your father would have been proud of you.' And then I couldn't speak for a few seconds.

The next story is about when I was sacked in July 2001. I didn't tell her at first. As well as everything else I was going through, I could just imagine what she'd say. 'I told you your mouth would get you in serious trouble one day. Why can't you just do as you're told?' etc. etc. I just couldn't face it. But, of course, I had to tell her at some point and so I went to see her in the UK in September. She was staying at Mavis' place in Chelmsford for a few days. It was a balmy autumn afternoon and Mavis was out playing golf. I bought a bottle of chilled Chablis to share and we had the garden to ourselves. I broached the subject.

'You know I've been telling you what's been happening with the union and stuff in Hong Kong?'

'Yes, what's happened now?'

'Well, things got worse and we got into a big industrial stand-off.'

'So what's happened?'

'Well, they've sacked 49 of the pilots and I'm one of them.'

'So you've been fired?'

'Yes.'

'When was this?'

'Ninth of July.' She was quiet for a moment and I awaited the inevitable storm of recriminations. And then she said to me, 'Do you think you've done the right thing?'

'Yes Mum I do,' I replied. And then she said the most incredible thing.

'Well that's all right then isn't it?' I was speechless. No matter how well you think you know your parents, you really don't until the crunch comes.

The other time when she said something to me that was completely unexpected was after I'd published my first book. I sent her the first copy with an inscription that said, 'Dear Mother. This is what your wayward son has been doing all these years whilst he's been away.' After a couple of weeks I phoned her to get the verdict.

'So what do you think, Mother?' I enquired.

'Oh, a lot of it's too complicated for me but finally you've achieved something.'

'What?'

'Well now you've finally achieved something.'

I was gob-smacked. So, everything else I'd done in my life so far counted for nothing on her scale of success. But I knew why she said it. It was because of my father. He'd met a lot of interesting and famous people both during his time in the RAF and on his travels. He always said he should write a book about it but he never got around to it. Well, I'd written a book. I'd achieved something that my father never did. That's why she said what she did.

Even though it's two years gone by now since she went back to the stars, sometimes, when something interesting happens, I still think, 'Oh, I'll have to give Mum a call and tell her about that.' And then I remember that I can't. I should have phoned her more often.

13

Money

'Money, it's a crime
Share it fairly but don't take a slice of my pie
Money, so they say
Is the root of all evil today
But if you ask for a raise it's no surprise
That they're giving none away'

Pink Floyd, *Money*

I had been budgeting on getting around HK$3.7 million in damages. As a result of the Court of Final Appeal's judgment, I only received 1.2 million. I was 2.5 million in the hole. This was bad. Very bad. My finances were already pretty stretched by this time and this did nothing to help the situation. And there was another problem as well. Legal costs. The Court of Final Appeal had made a costs order in their judgment. For the hearings both in their own court and that in the Court of Appeal, they made no order for costs. This meant that both parties had to wear their own legal costs for those two hearings. Their reasoning for this was that, in their own court we had won one leg of our appeal (breach of contract) but lost the second (damages). So the score was 1–1. Similarly, in the Court of Appeal, we had won one leg (S21B) and lost two legs (breach of contract and damages) but one of those was overturned so, again, the final score there was 1–1. So we couldn't recover our legal costs for the last two hearings. But they awarded us costs for the original High Court hearing. So that's in our favour one might think. But there was another problem. The dark side had made a payment into court which meant that, if the damages we received were not greater than the amount paid in, we

247

would only receive our own costs up to the date of the payment in and, thereafter, we would be liable for their costs. The original damages awarded by Judge Reyes were well in excess of the payments in. But, with the reduced damages, only 14 of us beat the payments in. Four of us did not. The three most senior and, therefore, the three highest paid; Doug Gage, John Dickie and me. Plus there was Greg England's estate. We had to make submissions to the court on the High Court costs because, up until now, it had not been revealed to the judges that there had been any payments in. This is standard procedure and is done for two reasons. Firstly, a party only usually makes a payment in if it thinks its case might be a bit iffy. It's a tactic used to put extra pressure on the opponent by putting him at increased financial risk. But, of course, you wouldn't want the court to know you have doubts about your case would you? The second reason that payments in are not disclosed prior to trial is that it might influence the judges in the quantum of damages they choose to award. Perish the thought.

Doug's damages fell short of his payment in by HK$115k, John's by HK$76k and mine by HK$6k. But, taken as a whole, the 18 of us together had exceeded the total payments in by HK$3.1 million. So, in our submissions, we made the case that the costs should be considered in the round. As usual, our opponents put forward two arguments. The first stated that, in consideration of their costs, the matter should be considered as a whole, but on the matter of our costs, the cases should be treated individually. The phrase 'cake and eat it' came to mind. We filed our submissions with the court in October and then it was back to the waiting game. Given the alacrity with which the judgment itself had been handed down after the trial, we were hopeful of an early result. But November came and went and we heard nothing. The courts were in recess over the Christmas break so we weren't likely to hear anything until the New Year. And now, because of the shortfall in the damages award, I reckoned I only had enough cash left to last another three months or so. After that, I'd be broke unless I sold my one remaining asset, my pub in the UK. But I didn't want to do that; it was my insurance policy. Basically I was now reliant on getting our legal costs back to sort out my finances. In the meantime I needed a loan to bridge me over the gap; so I went to the bank.

I'd had an account with HSBC since I arrived in Hong Kong in 1985. It had always been in good standing and, since 2001, I had a

Premier account. When you log in to their internet banking service, you're assailed with adverts for personal loans.

✓ Loan amount up to HK$3,000,000 or 10 times the monthly salary
✓ Income proof is not required
✓ Five-minute approval and instant disbursement

Good. Just what I needed to tide me over, so I applied online. No response. So I tried again. Still no response. So I went down to my local branch in Sai Kung and spoke to my Premier Relationship Manager.

'Hi, I've applied for a personal instalment loan but I've had no response. Can you tell me what's going on please?' I enquired politely. She logged into her computer and called up my account.

'You don't have job,' she responded.

'Yes I do. I work as a consultant.'

'No, only part time.'

'Yes, I know it's part time, but that's by choice.'

'But you have no regular income.'

'Yes I do. I get paid monthly.'

'But not paid into your account.'

'Yes it is. It's paid directly into my account.'

'No. No record here.'

'Well that's because you're looking at my HK dollar account. I get paid in US dollars. It's paid into my US dollar account.' She fiddled with the computer for a while.

'Not regular, not every month.'

'Yes it is. It gets paid in at the end of each month.'

'No. No income for September.'

'Well, that's because I went on holiday and didn't work that month.'

'So, not regular.'

'Well, because I'm a consultant, I only get paid when I work. I don't get holiday pay.'

'So, not regular.'

'Yes it is. How can you say it's not regular income when it gets paid in every month?'

'You need to show payslips.'

'I don't have payslips. I submit an invoice to the company each month for the hours I've worked and they settle my invoice by bank transfer.'

'Must have payslips.'

'But I've just told you, I don't have payslips.'

'Must have.' I was beginning to get a little frustrated so thought I'd try a different tack.

'OK, look this doesn't seem to be going anywhere. Here are copies of my income tax demands for the last two years. They clearly show my annual taxable income.'

'But not regular. Not in Hong Kong dollar.'

'No it's not in Hong Kong dollars. My employer converts the US dollars to HK dollars for income tax reporting purposes.'

'But Hong Kong dollar income not shown on bank statement.'

'No, of course it's not. I've just explained to you why that is. I get paid in US dollars.'

'Where Hong Kong dollar income get deposited?'

'What? What do you mean?'

'Hong Kong dollar income. Where it get deposited?'

'It doesn't. I get paid in US dollars. The income on my tax returns is my US dollars income converted to HK dollars.' At this point I can see the shutters coming down in her eyes. She can't tick the relevant boxes on her computer so it's just too hard for her.

'You need to print out bank statements to show HK dollar income.'

'What? You want me to go home, print out my bank statements in hard copy, the ones you're looking at right now on your computer screen, and bring them back in?'

'Yes, need to show regular Hong Kong dollar income.' Now I was getting somewhat exasperated. I resisted the temptation to blow my stack and instead, decided I'd better terminate the interview before I did something I might regret later.

'It seems to me that you're saying you can't help me. Despite the fact that I've got a regular income as evidenced by my bank statements and my tax returns, because it's not in HK dollars you won't give me a loan. Is that correct?'

'Yes.'

So much for no proof of income required, five-minute approval and disbursement and all the rest of the blurb. So much for a 25-year unblemished record. As I was leaving, the shutters came up again and she went into her standard PR guff.

'Anything else I can help you with Mr Warham?'

'Yes. You can stop staring at the bloody computer screen and find a way to give me a personal loan.' Clang, went the shutters again. There is a big lesson to be learned here. As you advance into your more mature years, do not EVER update your personal profile with the bank to tell them that you work part-time. And don't say that you're self-employed either. But the worst crime is actually to admit you're retired. If you do any of those things, don't ever expect to be given a loan. In the words of the *Little Britain* character, 'Computer says no.'

At this point, I had to borrow some money from a friend just to be able to survive until we could get the legal costs sorted out. I was now seriously thinking that I might have to sell the pub to survive. But, even with the position I was now in, it still went very much against the grain. Why should I have to lose that as well? It was also a source of income. It didn't make good financial sense.

I was planning some renovation work on the pub in the coming year and had budgeted the cost at around GB£25k. If I could borrow that from the bank instead of funding it from rental income, that would free up some equity to keep me going. So I tried to borrow the money using the asset for security, but came up against a new wall of resistance.

My company had held a business account with NatWest bank for more than 20 years. It had been in good standing for all of that time. The pub was fully paid off and the company had no debts or liabilities whatsoever, other than a personal debt to me for capital that I had originally put into the company when I first set it up. The accounts were filed each year on a going concern basis and I only repaid the loan to myself when there were sufficient funds available; the intention being that I would recover my capital when I eventually sold it. Also, since the government had set up a system of loan guarantees to assist small businesses and encourage banks to lend money to them in helping to bring the economy out of the recession, a loan should present no problem should it? Wrong. Very, very wrong. The experience I suffered at the hands of NatWest was characterised by poor communication, inefficiency, obfuscation and sheer cant.

Again, just like HSBC, their website promises easy application and loan arrangements. I filled in the application form online on 8

December 2013. The blurb on the website stated, 'For limited companies and for amounts over £25,000, we aim to give a decision within 5 days.' I waited five days. Nothing happened. So I sent a follow up email to their loan department. Nothing happened. So I telephoned my branch. I got through to a very helpful lady who sent me a loan quotation via email on 23 December. They wanted to charge interest at 7 per cent per annum. Hmm… a bit steep I thought considering the Bank of England base rate was fixed at 0.5 per cent. OK, well, press on regardless; I need the money. They wanted copies of the last two years' company accounts and a consent form to run a credit check on me. I sent them. By the 31st I'd heard nothing back so I sent them a follow up email. I got a reply on 3 January. They had offered two loan periods for a sum of GB£25k; three years and four years. The repayments would be GB£769.60 and 596.30 per month respectively. The email informed me that I had failed the Affordability Calculator on the three-year period. This seemed strange to me. In round figures, the company made GB£20k per annum after tax. How could an annual payment of £9,235.20 be unaffordable? They also spelt my name incorrectly in their reply. Lack of attention to detail. Their next email arrived on the 6th. It said:

> I am sorry to have to ask you for some further info.
> Could you tell me what your rental is for the property you live in in Hong Kong?
> Would you be able to send me your most recent months personal bank statement?
> Finally once approved a Personal Guarantee would be required from yourself and your wife. These do need to be signed on Bank premises.

They spelt my name wrongly again. I sent them the information they asked for but pointed out that it would be completely uneconomical for me to travel to the UK just to sign a personal guarantee form. I suggested that I could do this at their premises in Hong Kong or, failing that, sign the form, get it notarised and return it. By the 10th I'd heard nothing back so I sent them a follow up email. No reply, so I sent them another one on the 13th. I got the following reply:

> My apologies for the delay.

All our business loans have to pass an Affordability Calculator and this was today referred onto an Assurance Manager. This has now come back as declined.
I will call you first thing tomorrow morning to see if there is any information I have missed and one area I would like to clarify. My Area Director has been involved in the application as helping our customers is very important to us.

At least this time they got my name right. But now, apparently, I couldn't even afford the four-year loan repayments. Now I was getting a bit pissed off so I sent the following in reply:

Thank you for your reply.
I have to say that your Assurance Manager's assessment that a loan of 25k is not affordable is absolutely ludicrous. I have attached a spreadsheet to demonstrate the absurdity of his/her assessment.
The figures in the spreadsheet list the liabilities of the company from 2008 to 2012. These are taken directly from the audited company accounts. The ONLY liabilities that the company has are in the form of directors' loans, i.e. money that I personally have put into the company at various times. As I have said before, the accounts are compiled on a going concern basis. I trust that your Assurance Manager is familiar with the term and knows what it means. (Just to make it clear, the fact that the liabilities are listed as becoming due in less than 1 year doesn't mean that they have to be paid in that time period. It is an accounting exercise.) I only take out sufficient funds each year to repay these loans to minimise the company's tax bill. As you can see from the figures, in the last 4 years from 2008–12, the company's liabilities have reduced [by] GB£46,671.
On top of this, over the same period, the company has made a declared profit after tax of GB£61,005. (Just for your Assurance Manager's information, this means AFTER the reduction in liabilities has been taken into account.)
Therefore, to assess that a loan of 25k repaid over 4 years is not affordable is completely absurd.
After maintaining an account in good standing with NatWest for more than 20 years, I have to say that I find this treatment unacceptable. The application process itself is cumbersome and

inefficient. I originally completed a loan request online at the beginning of December and received no reply. I then booked a call from one of your 'managers' online and, again, received no reply. It was only after some persistence by me that, finally, I made contact with you and, I have to say, the standard of service provided by you has been the only bright spot in the whole process.

When I read in the press of small and medium companies in the UK being unable to obtain loans from the big banks to expand their businesses, despite the Bank of England flooding the banking system with currency through quantitative easing to stimulate the economy, since I live in Hong Kong, I tend not to take too much notice. Having now experienced this myself, I have complete sympathy for them. The big banks have the money but they will not lend it out. And, on top of that, given that the BoE MLR is 0.5%, the offer by NatWest of 7% interest is usurious. No wonder the UK economy is in such a mess.

In summary then, thank you very much for your time and effort. You can tell your Assurance Manager from me that he or she should try taking a course in basic arithmetic and, failing that, get a job as a consultant. They are very good at telling other people what to do whilst being unable competently to complete the task themselves.

Good. Well that's got that off my chest. Probably not much help in endearing myself to them but bugger it. I've had enough of being given the run-around. I got an email back the next day apologising and asking for copies of my HSBC personal bank statements for the last three months. I sent them and got another reply on the 15th. This was a beauty.

I am sorry about the constant emails however I unfortunately cannot get the loan passed by the Affordability Calculator.

The details that I am able to use for the affordability calculator are the Operating Profit figures for Years 2011, 2012 and 2013 as well as any evidenced additional monthly income you have. This has to be evidenced in monthly Bank Statements. For this reason I have taken the Consultancy figures of USD46527 less tax and converted to GBP which give me an annual figure of

£33600 (monthly being £2800). [Your additional] investment income cannot be proven as a monthly income.

Oh, here we go again. Just like HSBC. I had some investments that mature periodically but, because they're not regular monthly amounts, they can't be taken into account. She continued:

This then calculates that the annual Operating profit is £16182 (£7857, £28741 and £11948) and with the consultancy income of £2800 per month totaling £4148 per month. With the rental of £2165 this shows that this is almost 50% of your income and it is for this reason it has been declined.

So, just a minute. Despite the fact that the annual profit for the company alone is more than adequate to make the payments, it's still not affordable because the rent on my place in Hong Kong is too high. But I don't use the company's income to pay my rent. That comes from my earned income and my investment income. Oh, sorry, we can't count my investment income can we because it's not regular. Silly me. In closing she said:

If you have any other evidence of monthly income which I can see in your Bank Statements could you please forward these on to me.
I understand that your financial situation shows that this loan is more than affordable to you, however as responsible lenders we have certain criteria by which we are able to calculate these figures.

Ah yes. Responsible lenders. Like sub-prime mortgage lending. Like Royal Bank of Scotland and NatWest being fined GB£14.5 million by the Financial Conduct Authority for giving inappropriate advice to mortgage lenders. That kind of 'responsible' you mean? Perhaps that's why they're running scared. I sent another reply on the 16th.

Thank you for your email.
OK let's have one more try shall we?
Attached are copies of my foreign currency bank statements for 2011–13.
As you can see, I have income in GB£, US$ & EUR. This

income is a combination of earned income from my work as a flight simulator instructor, income from various investments that I have (including Jasper Leisure) and also income from royalties from a book that I published a couple of years ago.

I have listed the monthly income from these statements in the attached spreadsheet. I have converted the US$ & EUR income into GB£.

For your information, my GB£ income is not taxable neither is my investment income in Hong Kong. I only pay tax on income actually earned in Hong Kong and, with our generous tax system here, this only equates to around GB£3,000 per annum...

Anyway, in light of the above, surely this must now pass the affordability test? Here's hoping because, if it doesn't, then it seems to me there's no hope of anyone ever getting a loan from NatWest (unless you happen to be a big business that is).

The next day I got a reply.

Thank you so much for the additional information. The Affordability Calculator has now passed and the loan is with our Lending Team who will process the loan and advise me of the outcome. I expect to have an answer from them on Monday. As soon as I hear from them I will let you know what the next step will be.

Woo hoo! Result!! Persistence pays off. Should be plain sailing from now on. Not a chance. Ten days later I hadn't heard anything more so sent them another reminder. On 4 February I received the following from the Credit Department.

As per our conversation earlier today I write to advise you that your application for a business loan has been declined.

We aim to support small and medium-sized enterprises wherever possible by making credit and working capital facilities available to viable businesses. However, as lenders we must also act responsibly and assess all applications for credit carefully. Having considered the information you provided and completed our standard checks and assessments, I am unable to approve your application.

In order for the Bank to reconsider your request the Bank requires the additional information:

- Business account receives rental income – please clarify why VAT is being paid?
- The Bank is reliant on rental income to service the proposed borrowing and we therefore need to be comfortable with tenant quality with full details of the lease. Are financial accounts available from the tenant?
- Full details of the Red Lion – public house / restaurant / number of covers / location / competition / building condition (is there a recent professional valuation?).
- Details of your contribution to the proposition.

If you can provide the Bank with the above information to support your request, or show that your financial circumstances have changed, then I will be only too pleased to discuss it with you again.

What? No one has mentioned any of this before over the last two months that my application was being processed. So now I've finally jumped the affordability hurdle, the Credit Department sets up some new obstacles. I replied to her bullet points.

- The company leases the premises to a tenant. My accountant advised that VAT is payable on the rental income. Therefore, each rental invoice (and payment) levies VAT at the appropriate rate which is then paid, as required, to HMRC. Of course, any VAT incurred by the company in its other business transactions, e.g. for repairs etc., is offset against this. I do not understand why this question has been raised now at such a late stage in the application process. It has never been mentioned before.
- The current tenant has been in the premises continuously since September 2002, a period of more than 11 years. Throughout that time he has proved himself to be entirely reliable, honest and trustworthy. His current 5-year lease, a copy of which is attached herewith, was renewed in September 2012 and does not expire until August 2017. He has frequently expressed a desire to purchase the property from

me when I finally decide to dispose of it and, indeed, has invested his own capital in the premises when, at his own expense, he built a conservatory on the rear of the main building some 6 or 7 years ago. Having had various tenants since I first purchased the property in 1991, some more reliable than others, I can only describe him as the model tenant. In addition to this, he comes from the local area and is a family man. In answer to your last question, I will not trouble him to provide his own financial accounts in support of my application. I believe that his track record and longevity as a tenant speaks for itself and is more than satisfactory for the current purposes.

• The buildings are all well maintained and kept in good condition. The last valuation, a copy of which is attached herewith, was conducted in July 2006 by a local company, who put a valuation of GB£650,000 on the property.

• I do not intend to contribute anything of my personal funds to the project. That is the whole purpose of taking out a small business loan.

I got an email in response dated 14 February with an attachment headed 'Final Decline'. In it they listed two reasons for not allowing the loan.

• The lease term expires in 3.5 years. Any loan offered must be fully repaid within the 3.5 year timeframe.

• Expectations that some of the rental income would be set aside as provision… However… there is no customer contribution.

I made a revised proposal to reduce the loan to 22k so that it would be paid off within the 3.5 year lease period. They declined it again. I sent them one last letter on 21 February.

Thank you for your email of 20th inst. in which, yet again, my revised proposal for a small business loan of GB£22,000 has been declined; the reason being given this time that, 'Expectations would be that the customer contributes 50% to the overall cost and the Bank would look to lend 50% thus looking at a £12,500 loan'.

During the last 11 weeks that it has taken to process the loan application, at no time has any such expectation ever been mentioned. Rather the contrary. A great deal of time and effort has been expended in providing data and calculating the loan period to meet the affordability requirements for the full amount of GB£25k. If the bank's expectation from the outset was that it would only grant 50% of the requested amount, why waste all this time and effort? Surely it would have been far simpler and more efficient to have made this clear back in December at the time of the original loan application.

The logic of this '50% expectation' also escapes me. The only conclusion I can draw from this is that an applicant should first double the amount of the actual loan required in order to have any hope of obtaining the amount really required. Clearly this cannot be the case as it would involve negotiation in bad faith, hardly a precursor to a trustworthy business relationship.

So there we had it. Despite all the PR about being customer driven, caring and helping small businesses, it just turns out to be bullshit; just like the government's rubbish about helping SMEs to bring the economy out of recession. And as for being responsible and ethical lenders, I could mention the Libor scandal and the Serious Fraud Office's investigation into mis-pricing of interest rate options. But I just can't be bothered. We've heard it all before. There was one last avenue open. There is an appeals process. I lodged an appeal and on 21 March I received a reply offering to lend me 19k. Finally! And it only took four months. Most efficient I'm sure; but a bit short of the mark promising to give a decision within five days of the application. Well, I decided to take them up on their kind offer thinking that there couldn't possibly be any further problems. Wrong. During this time my divorce had been made absolute and I transferred 2 per cent of the shares in the company from Jill's name into Klaske's name. When I asked to draw down the loan I was told that, since she was a new shareholder, they would have to perform a full credit check on her first. Not again. During a subsequent telephone conversation, I received some helpful advice on how to get around this. It was suggested that I should remove her as a director, draw down the loan and then re-instate her once I'd got the money. I declined the advice, but in rather less polite terms than those I'm using here. Ethical indeed! And to quote their customer charter, 'Helpful Banking' – my arse.

Whilst all this was going on, I was bemoaning the problems I was having to a friend of mine. She runs a small business and recounted having exactly the same problems getting funding for her company. She told me she solved it by going away from the banks and using alternative finance. She gave me some website addresses to look at and I did some research. I got in touch with a group called Funding Empire. This is a peer-to-peer lending organisation. I filed a loan application for GB£30K on 18 March. The money was paid into my account on 14 May. The whole process was in stark contrast to the treatment I had received from NatWest. Afterwards, they asked me if I would write a testimonial for use on their website. I was more than happy to comply with their request. This is what I wrote.

What the owner says

NatWest bank failed me completely despite my having a long term business account with them and a proven track record with a viable business. At a time when their PR blurb says that they are there to help SMEs to grow their businesses to assist in the economic recovery, in my experience the truth is very far from the face they present. Their application process was slow, inefficient and cumbersome. Communications were erratic, emails went unanswered and phone calls not returned promptly. The rates they were offering were higher than their adverts say and the whole process seemed to be designed to put obstacles in the way rather than to encourage and assist me.
Funding Options, on the other hand, was a breath of fresh air. Their staff were helpful, courteous and efficient. They arranged a loan on beneficial terms and the money was in my bank account within 5 weeks of my initial application. (It might have been quicker but my own solicitor caused some delay.) I cannot recommend Funding Options' services highly enough.
Unless you're a big business with power and influence, forget the mainstream banks. They're so afraid of being caught yet again with dodgy dealing and bad loans, they've become hidebound and irrelevant to the general public. Private funding is the way of the future.

So this meant I had enough money to keep going for now. But life is full of surprises. Just when you think you're getting near your wits end and can't see a solution, sometimes it hits you with another problem just to make things worse. But sometimes it gives you an unexpected reward as well.

On 25 April, I received an email from my solicitor, Benedict Chiu. It seemed that the dark side had been doing their sums in relation to the interest charges that were accruing on the legal costs that had yet to be even ruled upon, let alone settled. They'd realised they were racking up at the rate of around HK$900k per annum. They sent us a cheque for HK$6 million as an interim payment on account to reduce the cumulative interest until we got to settlement. Four million had to go to paying off debts to some people who'd provided us with funding, but two million was mine. Result! I was solvent again!! If only they'd known how close they had come to fulfilling Turnbull's prophecy that they'd just run us out of money. But they didn't know. They will do now though!

The Court of Final Appeal eventually handed down its judgment on costs on 16 May 2013 after a seven-month wait. As usual, it makes interesting reading and demonstrates the sometimes arcane nature of legal proceedings. It stated:

32. We made an *order nisi* that:

   (a) The order made by the Judge as to the costs of both the trial of the preliminary issues and the trial itself, namely that Cathay should pay the plaintiffs' costs, should be reinstated, because the effect of my judgment is that the plaintiffs have largely won on each of the claims made against Cathay. It is true that the amount of damages they have recovered for defamation is significantly less than what the Judge awarded them, but their claim for any damages for defamation was resisted by Cathay, and they therefore had to come to court to get relief.

33. The respondents have applied to vary the order in relation to 4 of the appellants on the ground that each of them has

recovered less than the payment into court in respect of him. The fact that these plaintiffs individually have recovered less than the respective payment into court is not disputed.

34. In relation to 3 of these plaintiffs the respondents ask that the costs *order nisi* should be varied so that each such plaintiff pays the respondents' first instance costs... after the relevant payment in.

35. In relation to the seventh plaintiff, namely, the late Mr England, who died at an early stage of the proceedings although his claim had been continued by his personal representative, the respondents, presumably as a concession, ask there should be no order as to costs.

36. The respondents submit that a split order as to costs of this sort is the usual costs order consequent upon a failure by a plaintiff to beat a payment into court.

37. The appellants submit however that when looked at in the round this is a case where the respondents would have had to run the same defence and incur the same quantum of costs irrespective whether there were 17 or 14 appellants. Moreover, since collectively the appellants recovered more than was paid in, the appellants acting together were successful in beating the payments in.

38. The plaintiffs' claims were distinct claims. In such circumstance, insofar as these plaintiffs have failed to better the payment in, their position is analogous to co-plaintiffs who have failed. In *Viscount Gort and Others v Rowney and Another*, (1886)... 2 plaintiffs joined in one action, claiming separate and distinct causes of action, one plaintiff succeeded and the other failed. The English Court of Appeal held that the successful plaintiff was entitled to recover from the defendant the whole of his costs of the action and the defendant was only entitled to recover from the unsuccessful plaintiff the costs occasioned by joining such plaintiff.

39. The respondents also ask for a set off between the amounts due to them and the amounts due to the other plaintiffs under the split order because these actions have been pursued by the plaintiffs collectively. Such an order was made in *King v Sunday Pictorial Newspapers Ltd* (1924), where a mother and daughter sued a newspaper for defamation. The daughter withdrew her claim after the filing of the defence. The mother proceeded to trial and was awarded a farthing by the jury. Even so, she was awarded her costs by Lush J. When the learned judge came to deal with the daughter's costs he ordered that she should pay such extra costs as the defendants have incurred by reason of her having been joined but no more. He said:

'... I have no doubt that the plaintiff, Mrs King, would take care that the defendants received these extra costs from her daughter who withdrew, but as a matter of principle I think I ought to order, and I do order, that the defendants be allowed to set off these extra costs against those payable to Mrs King. For the purpose of set-off, I am, in my opinion, entitled to treat the plaintiffs as one. The view that I have expressed in stating that the defendants are only entitled to the extra costs occasioned by the joinder of the plaintiff, Miss Phyllis King, is supported by the judgment of Lord Justice Bowen in *Viscount Gort v Rowney*... and my order as to set-off is supported by the judgment of the Court of Appeal in the case of *Umfreville v Johnson*... '

40. In *Umfreville v Johnson* (1875) the English Court of Appeal ordered a set off but the basis upon which the order was made is not clear. In that case two holders of distinct properties joined as plaintiffs in a suit to restrain a nuisance. The plaintiff whose estate was farther away from the source of the alleged nuisance failed though the plaintiff whose property was nearer succeeded. Without elaboration, the Court of Appeal ordered a set off of such costs.

41. A set off would benefit the respondents if they are unable to obtain payment from any of these plaintiffs. In the present case, the joinder was entirely proper and probably saved costs.

We see no reason why the other plaintiffs should be burdened with the costs of any of these plaintiffs.

42. The order we make is that so far as these plaintiffs are concerned, each of them should pay to the respondents such extra costs as the respondents have incurred by reason of the joinder of each such plaintiff but no more. In the case of the deceased plaintiff we order that there be no orders as to costs. In relation to the other plaintiffs the costs *order nisi* in their favour will be made absolute.

So there it was. Clear as mud. Their decision was made on case law dating back to 1875, 1876 and 1924. On the one hand, this demonstrated how well read the judges (or their research assistants) are but, on the other, it left us with a problem. How do we define 'but no more'? Given that, between us over the last 13 years, the two parties had been unable to agree on anything, what chance was there that we'd come to an agreement on this issue?

We made a start on trying to find a methodology. We had previously employed the services of a law costs draughtsman to draft our bill of costs. It was a massive undertaking given the length of time the case had taken and the different lawyers and counsel that we had instructed over the years. Nevertheless the task had been completed so we were already well prepared to open negotiations. Unfortunately, our opponents were not. They hadn't even started drafting their bill. In one way, the longer the negotiations took, the more it was to our advantage because interest was accruing on the costs outstanding. The interest accrued from the date of judgment from the original High Court action, 11 November 2009, and the interest rate was set by the Chief Justice. For the last five years it had been set at 8 per cent per annum. Try getting that rate of return from bank deposits, or any other form of investment, in the current financial climate. But whilst that was all well and good, and made it very tempting to adopt the delaying tactics so favoured by our opponents, I just wanted to get the whole thing finished and get on with my life.

We put together a settlement proposal and sent it to their lawyers. We received a reply couched in their usual arrogant terms. We had constructed a mathematical methodology to calculate how to quantify the amount of their costs payable by Doug, John and I using the costs of joinder 'but no more' principle. It came to around HK$400k. They rejected it out of hand without proposing any alternative methodology. Instead they just said they wanted HK$2.5 million without any reasoned explanation as to how they arrived at that amount other than back-of-a-fag-packet estimation. We were miles apart. If we couldn't come to agreement we'd have to go before a taxation judge and that could take anything up to three years to get it finally settled. It looked like we were in for another long haul.

14

Justice

Since the LTC fiasco, I had not heard much from Pete Bissell. I tried to keep the lines of communication open with the occasional email but, with the rift that had opened up in the Sai Kung community, we didn't have much contact. But, in 2012, I heard through the grapevine that his wife, Deb, had been taken seriously ill. She'd suffered a spate of seizures which had left her with mobility and speech difficulties. I felt absolutely terrible. One of my oldest friends was in trouble and I couldn't, or wasn't being allowed to, come to his aid. I kept my ear to the ground though and heard that with physiotherapy and rehabilitation treatment, she was slowly getting better; but it would be a long road back to a full recovery.

Then, one evening in late November 2013, I was sitting with Klaske outside Agua having a cold one and Pete walked by.

'Hi Pedro, it's good to see you,' I called.

'Good to see you as well mate. Have I got a story to tell you. We need to meet up sometime soon,' he replied.

'Why not now? Come inside and we'll sit down and you can tell me now. Why wait?'

So we went inside, sat down together and he related his story to me. First he filled me in on Deb's illness and how her recovery was going. She'd virtually had to learn how to talk again but she was making rapid progress. I remarked that it didn't surprise me because, being Northern Irish, she always did have a gift for the gab. But what he told me next shook me to the core.

One of the problems that Deb was having in her rehab was dealing with numbers. It was difficult for her to grasp the difference between 500, 5,000 or 50,000. Similarly, she couldn't distinguish between 1234, 1324, 2134, 3214, 4321 and so on. This made it very difficult for her when using an ATM at the bank because she couldn't remember her PIN correctly. Fortunately Pete and Deb had an *amah*, Delores, who had been with them for years. She was part of the family and completely trustworthy. She would accompany Deb on shopping trips where she needed to use her credit card or to the bank to withdraw money and enter the PIN for her. Of course, if Pete was in town, he could do this himself but, with the Cathay rosters the way they are, he was often away from home.

Enter Martin Lau onto the scene. During Deb's illness he had been very supportive and helpful to them both, was in and out of the house on a regular basis, used the family car to run Deb around and seemed to be the model of propriety. A reformed character, in fact.

In early October 2013, he obligingly accompanied Deb and Delores to IKEA to buy some garden furniture. At the checkout, whilst Delores was entering Deb's PIN, he was in very close attendance. It wasn't until a few days later that Deb had occasion to look in her handbag, where she kept her card, and noticed that it was not in its usual place. It was actually there in her bag but in the wrong place. She thought it slightly odd but, with her various medical problems, she could also be a bit forgetful sometimes and dismissed it.

Then on 31 October, whilst Pete was away, Deb needed to go to the bank to get some money. She was getting ready to go with Delores and Martin happened along. The conversation went along the lines that she needn't go to all the trouble, he could just run down there in the car and get the money for her to save her the inconvenience. At this stage Delores was looking a bit quizzical, but he seemed genuine enough, so Deb gave him her ATM card and her PIN with instructions to withdraw HK$500. He came back an hour or so later and handed Deb her HK$500 and ATM card.

Almost a couple of weeks later, on 12 November, again whilst Pete was away, helpful Martin turned up at their house around 3 o'clock in the afternoon all dressed up ready to go to town. He proceeded to tell Deb a sob-story about how his family were in desperate financial trouble because, after his father's death, he needed to help them pay for the funeral. Things were tight and his mother's phone was going to be cut off if he didn't help out. He asked to borrow HK$30,000 from her. At this point Deb was very flustered by the whole thing but agreed to lend him the money. He then tells her that the *amah* needn't come with them to the bank, he'd drive Deb there himself and, with that, instead of using his own car, picks up the keys to Pete's pride and joy; his Jaguar. He knew where the keys were kept and, before Deb could say anything, he grabbed them and ushered her out of the door. On the way to the bank, he continues with his sob-story and now ups the loan request to HK$50,000. By this time Deb is very confused but she agrees to lend him the new amount and goes into the bank to withdraw it at the counter (she can't use her ATM card without Delores to enter the PIN) while he sits outside in Pete's Jag with the engine running. She gave him the money and he dropped her back at home and left in his own car.

When Pete got back the next day and found out what had happened he was astounded. He had a peer-to-peer talk with Martin who apologised to him. But Deb was still concerned. She was uneasy about her account and felt there should have been more money in there than there actually was but she couldn't be sure because of her problem with numbers. This prompted them to check the previous month's bank statements. On 23 & 24 October, there were two withdrawals each for HK$4,000. They had been made from the Bank of China branch in Sai Kung. Deb hadn't made any withdrawals on either of those days and, in any case, she always used Standard Chartered bank because that's where her account was held. And as for the withdrawal that he'd 'kindly' made for Deb on 31 October to save her the inconvenience of going to the bank herself, the statement showed that, instead of withdrawing HK$500 as instructed, he'd taken out HK$6,000 and kept the rest for himself.

Pete and Deb went to both banks to report the unauthorised withdrawals. They pulled the video tapes for the appropriate dates and times and there was the thieving bastard caught on camera three times stealing money from Deb's account. He'd gone to the house, taken Deb's ATM card from her handbag, used the PIN that he'd noted from the visit to IKEA, stolen money from her account and then returned the card. That was why it wasn't in the normal place in her handbag. And then he'd just helped himself to an extra HK$5,500 when doing his Good Samaritan act.

So, far from being a helpful, concerned friend, far from being a reformed character, he'd just been deliberately and calculatingly grooming two more people who'd given him their confidence and trust. But, worse than when he did the same thing to me, now he'd gone a step further. He'd taken advantage of Deb's condition and used it to steal from a disabled woman. It was just as I'd known all along. He is completely without compassion or empathy; he feels no genuine remorse and, in fact, shows all the characteristics of being a sociopath.

Shortly after I found out what had happened, I had lunch with Jimmy Lau's wife Isabella. I related the story to her and she was horrified. She told me that LTC's sob-story to Deb was a pack of lies. The funeral expenses had already been paid for by the family, so the fucker had just stolen the money for himself.

From my own experience I knew what was coming next, so I sent Pete an email.

> Pedro, I just want to give you a heads up on what's going to happen to you next so you can be prepared for it.
>
> There will still be some people who will take his side (very few but certain people come to mind). Next thing they'll be in touch with you and start trying to persuade you that he deserves yet another chance. They'll echo the sentiments about the effect *your* actions are having on his family (yours note, not his). Then the whispering campaign starts behind your back and before you know it, in the community, you are being cast as the bad guy in all this and him as the aggrieved party. I have been through this personally and, take it from me, it can be difficult to deal with. There will be many people (probably the overwhelming majority) who are on your side but they tend to remain silent. It's the vociferous minority you have to come to terms with. Best thing to do is ignore them completely, don't engage them, stick to your guns, know that their logic is fatally flawed and that you are doing the right thing.
>
> In my own case, I'd often read stories in the papers of victims of a crime having their world turned upside down and finding themselves cast in the role of the perpetrator. I never really believed it until it happened to me.
>
> Remember that, whatever happens, I've got your back.

As well as the effect on Pete, there was another spin-off to this. Many of the people that had given LTC their support when he stole from me now realised their mistake. Some of them just looked sheepish when they saw me, but some came to me to apologise personally. I had the same answer for all of them.

'You have nothing to apologise to me for. I hold you no malice whatsoever. You are, like me, a victim. That thieving cunt Martin Lau took you in and conned you just like he did to me. I'm just pleased that the truth has finally come out.'

There was one man in particular who I will not name here. I had always had great admiration and respect for him because of the way he had conducted himself during a very difficult time in his life when his wife left him alone with their two children. The way he looked after his family, nurtured his children, and still kept a sense of humour throughout all the tribulations that life threw at him, was a lesson to us all in my eyes. It was a huge surprise to me when he took LTC's side after he stole from me. When this man came to talk to me after it was revealed what had happened to Pete and Deb, he cried. My response to him was, again, 'You have nothing to apologise to me for. Like me, you were just taken in by that cunt's lies, deceit and treachery.' My words did little to staunch the tears. Another casualty.

Pete reported the thieving bastard to the police. There then followed a series of emails exactly as I'd predicted. LTC attempted to excuse his behaviour, made offer of recompense and attempted to transfer the blame for the consequences onto Pete. Exactly the same modus operandi that he'd used before. Pete copied me in on some of these emails and I could reproduce them here. But I'm not going to; the reason being that they are sickening to read. But in summary, they were the same emotional blackmail that he'd tried on me.

'I'm not sure if I could survive in prison. Think of what it'll do to my family, my mum, my brother, my sisters and the memory of my dad. My mother's just lost my father, think of the terrible additional stress it will put on her. I've been going through a really difficult time what with losing my father and all. And now I've been sacked from my job because of this. My life has been shit for a long time now but no matter what I do nothing goes right. I don't know why I do these things.' And on and on in the same vein. The 'poor me' tactic. He didn't think of the consequences to Pete and Deb or their families when he deliberately took advantage of, and stole from, a disabled woman did he? He didn't think about the terrible effect that his appalling breach of trust would have on Deb's recovery did he? And neither did he think of the consequences to his own family that now seemed so important to him. The only person he ever thought about was himself.

The police charged him with three counts of theft and his trial was set for 9 July 2014 (which was a strange coincidence). The magistrate sentenced him to two months in prison for each of the charges, the sentences to run concurrently. But the six months suspended for three years that he got for stealing from me was still in effect. Because two years had passed, the magistrate gave him a discount and sentenced him to an additional one month to run consecutively, making three months in all. As Lord Neuberger put it, 'on the low side' in my opinion, but at least he was finally going to pay for his actions. I was in court to watch as they put the metal bracelets on him and took him downstairs through the criminals' door.

I was reminded of Tony White's advice to me a couple of years earlier.

'Mucker, there's only one word to describe that facker. He's a facking thief. And there's a place for facking thieves. It's called the facking nick. And that's where that facker belongs.'

And that's what happened this time around. Finally the system put the lying, thieving coward where he belonged.

15

Negotiation

'Let us never negotiate out of fear. But let us never fear to negotiate.'

John Fitzgerald Kennedy

The court date for the RTB claim was set for December 2013. We'd been trying to come to an out-of-court settlement by written exchanges between our lawyers. It was getting us nowhere. We just kept getting responses in the same old vein. No real attempt to negotiate and close the gap between us. Just arrogance and repeatedly restating their original position on the date the damages should accrue from (in Hunsworth's very strong view). After the mediation meeting had failed to find a resolution, it just seemed that we were destined once again to meet in court. Not that we were afraid of that. Our case was so strong, and their defence so weak, that we were bound to succeed and they were bound to fail. But, to me, it just seemed a pointless exercise. A waste of time and money on both sides. And, in the meantime, our damages claim kept on escalating. Every time Doug or I travelled anywhere by air, we amended our claim to cover the cost of the tickets that would have been discounted if we had had access to RTB. The issue was going nowhere with lawyers' letters going back and forth, other than to rack up more legal fees. So we decided to try a different tack.

In September, I instructed our lawyers to contact the opposition's and propose that we have a party-to-party meeting, without lawyers present, to see if we could find some common ground and maybe close the gap between us. They agreed and asked us to contact Bob Nipperess directly to arrange a meeting. The first meeting was arranged for Monday 7 October at the United Services Recreation Club (USRC) on Gascoigne Road in Kowloon. Doug and I went there together and Bob came alone. The USRC was a neutral venue. I had suggested that we didn't mind going up to Cathay City but they declined my kind offer. Maybe they didn't want me to be seen in the building. We'd also thought about the Gotfried Room at the Aviation Club at the old Kai Tak airport; the scene of many of our meetings in the past. Maybe we could even arrange to get the pile-drivers to start up at 09:30 just for old times' sake. But that would just be childish wouldn't it? So we agreed on the USRC.

This first meeting was to sound them out to see if they really wanted to get it settled, or if it was just another delaying tactic that they could use to try to make themselves look good in front of the judge and show that they'd tried everything to settle before we came to court. We would see.

As far as we were concerned, there were six issues that needed resolving:

> They said that the fare structures under the Green Pages were no longer in force so they could not apply them in iJourney. That's why we had to be handled by the 'dedicated team';
> They were only offering access to carriers other than Cathay Pacific in accordance with interline agreements that were in place in 1999. (This was not acceptable to us because hundreds of other carriers had joined the system since then);
> Their offer of the Concessional Travel Policy (CTP) was only company policy. It was not contractual like the Green Pages;
> The terms of the CTP gave them too much latitude to withdraw the benefits on a whim without any recourse;
> Access to first class (FRCL) was much more restrictive under the CTP *vs* Green Pages;
> Damages.

Doug and I held a pre-meeting briefing. I had spent many hours across the table from these people and was used to it. Even though I may not like them personally, and the feeling's probably mutual, I put that aside. I was just there to do business. Doug, on the other hand, did not have my background. To him, it *was* personal. We made the perfect good-cop-bad-cop team. Here are my notes of the first meeting.

<u>NOTES OF MEETING 1 ON RTB</u>

Date: 7th October 2013
Time: 10:17 – 11:00
Venue: USRC
Present: Doug Gage (DG)
          Bob Nipperess (RN)
          John Warham (JW)

Fare Structures

RN explained the problem wrt Green Pages ID90/50 vs Zoned Fare structures and programming the IBS system and produced a table of examples of differences between the fares.

JW explained that Zoned/ZED fares were completely acceptable. It was only a problem with the contract language which had not been updated to reflect the introduction of Zoned Fares in ca 1993.

Agreed.

Access to other carriers

JW said the company's sanctioned offer as it stood only allowed access to carriers with whom CX had agreements in 1999.

RN said this is not a problem and access would be granted to all carriers iaw current agreements as per the CTP.

Agreed.

CTP vs contractual entitlements

Discussion on the principle that acceptance of the CTP and access to iJourney would not be taken to be acquiescence of contractual entitlements which will be preserved.

Agreed.

CTP 'rules'

RN explained the CTP rules wrt behaviour and abuse of the system.

JW explained that there is no problem with the dress and conduct codes. The problem is with the clause which allows withdrawal of RTB on mere suspicion of abuse.

RN gave an example of a recent incident and how the system gave the transgressor the right of reply.

JW explained why we are so concerned about this clause despite the right of reply assurance.

RN said that the words could be changed to allay our fears.

Words to be drafted.

Access to FRCL

Discussion took place on the meaning of a 'trip'. It used to be four sectors iaw the number of pages in a paper ticket. Now the current CTP definition is two sectors.

RN said that current Green Pages RTB retirees get only one ID90 FRCL trip (i.e. two sectors) per year.

JW stated that the intent of the RTB Green Pages as drafted during the 1999 negotiations was to grandfather access to FRCL in the same way that current employees on the Old Scheme have greater access to FRCL than the CTP.

RN noted that the actual words are silent and it had not been an issue up to now until JW had challenged it.

JW opined that this is an issue that we would ask the court to decide upon.

RN to consider the company's position prior to the next meeting.

Damages

General discussion on damages took place.

JW summarised the current position. Company offer is HK$350k total to JW & DG as per the mediation meeting. JW & DG positions are iaw their Sanctioned Offers currently before the court.

RN expressed the view that damages are open to negotiation.

To be discussed at the next meeting.

Other claimants

RN noted that the other Green Pages claimants (Messrs. Carver, Dickie & Sweeney) were quiet.

JW explained that we had asked them to wait to see if we could get to an agreement.

RN said that it would be best if any agreement could satisfy all claimants.

JW agreed to contact other claimants with this end in view.

Next meeting

The next 'without lawyers' meeting TBA.

John Warham
8th October 2013

I came out of the meeting with my objectives achieved. It was clear to me that they wanted to settle. This wasn't just a time-wasting exercise. We'd knocked off three of the issues straight away. Of course, they were the relatively easy ones, but it was a start. I knew that when we got down to the nitty-gritty, the money, it wasn't going be that easy. But I was optimistic. Doug didn't share my enthusiasm. He warned me, 'You can't trust these fuckers as far as you can throw them.' As if I needed reminding!

The next meeting was arranged for 18th October. Ken Carver happened to be in town and, since he was an interested party, he came along as well.

NOTES OF MEETING 2 ON RTB

Date: 18th October 2013
Time: 14:55 – 15:17
Venue: USRC
Present: Ken Carver (KC)
          Doug Gage (DG)
          Bob Nipperess (RN)
          John Warham (JW)

Access to FRCL

RN summarised the company's position wrt access to FRCL for retirees which remained as per the previous meeting and iaw documents supplied thereafter to support that position.

JW summarised the claimants' position that, since the Green Pages are silent, it might be interpreted either way. In court, CX would argue custom and practice, whereas the claimants would argue contractual right and intent of the 1999 negotiations to grandfather FRCL access in the same way as current GP employees.

However, in order to bring the matter to agreement, whilst the claimants do not concede the contractual point, they will not pursue it further at this time. Rather, they will accept the CTP Old Travel Scheme Retirees provisions as set out in the 15 Jul 1996 document supplied by RN subsequent to the meeting held on 7th October, with existing contractual protections preserved.

It was further clarified that those provisions allow for 6 ID90 trips per annum each for retiree and spouse, i.e. a total of 12 trips.

RN stated that iJourney now allows unlimited ID90 in business class.

Agreed.

Damages

JW summarised the claimants' views on damages. Their legal position is very strong given existing precedent in the Hong Kong courts and do not see why they should be out of pocket. Currently the total sum of all claims (including Messrs. Carver, Dickie & Sweeney) plus legal fees amounts to ca HK$2.45 million.

RN stated that the company would prefer to settle the claims with DG & JW in the first place and then deal with the other claimants afterwards.

RN confirmed in discussion that Messrs. Carver, Dickie & Sweeney's claims would be treated in the same way as DG & JW. The last remaining claimant represented in these discussions is Mike Fitz-Costa who will reach relevant age in ca 15 months.

JW stated that he did not speak for Quentin Heron as his claim was being dealt with separately.

RN said that the damages claims were being analysed and would be addressed at the next meeting. There are some issues about rebates available on other airlines to be dealt with. JW asked to be given details of these prior to the next meeting.

JW also undertook to supply, prior to the next meeting, updated claims for DG & JW reflecting tickets flown since the last Appendix II Revision 1 filed with the court.

Documents to be exchanged by JW & RN.

Access to iJourney

RN stated that access to iJourney would be granted once agreement 'as a whole' had been reached.

Next meeting

The next 'without lawyers' meeting to be held at 11:00 on 25th October at the USRC.

John Warham
18th October 2013

We were making progress. We still had a way to go but the general atmosphere was of compromise. We met again a week later. This time Doug wasn't available so I press-ganged Mike Fitz-Costa to come along and watch my back instead.

NOTES OF MEETING 3 ON RTB

Date: 25th October 2013
Time: 11:00 – 11:16
Venue: USRC
Present: Mike Fitz-Costa (MF)
          Bob Nipperess (RN)
          John Warham (JW)

Damages

RN summarised CX's position on damages.
They commence from the date of DG & JW's letters in 2010 and end upon the date of issue of their RTB cards. Letter to Malcolm Hunter on retirement was tabled to support the 'application date' point.

JW summarised the claimants' position.
The breach of contract commences on 9th July 2001 with the dismissal letters which specifically deny RTB.

The damages commence upon DG & JW reaching relevant age and are ongoing until such time as specific performance is granted.

CX repeatedly and continuously refused access to RTB throughout the period until admitting liability in January 2011. The paper trail is very clear. As the mediator said, 'The letters shine very brightly.' The 'We would have given you an RTB card if only you'd applied earlier' defence is refuted by the evidence.

The admin procedure does not work. No tickets have been issued so far. It's not just about ticketing. It's also about being able to check carriers, flight schedules, rebates etc. and obtaining tickets in a timely manner.

RN agreed that staff travel also finds the admin procedure to be onerous. It would be better for both parties to administer this through iJourney.

The legal cases concerning Courtney Chong and Chris Kelly were discussed.

JW stated that CX's advisors had been wrong on every legal point concerning *The 49ers* so far and opined that the court will rule that they are also wrong on this one.

Costs

JW updated the claimants' current legal costs. At the previous meeting an estimate of HK$650k had been given. An updated bill was tabled which showed costs to date of HK$949,250.95.

Both parties agreed that it would be far preferable to settle the matter now rather than go to court and incur more legal costs which would probably add another HK$1.5 million to the bill.

JW opined that, from the timing point of view, we would probably not get a court date for another year or so. Whilst the claimants are prepared to wait if necessary, it would be much better for all concerned if we could put the matter to bed and move on.

RN agreed that this is CX's preferred option as well.

Data

RN tabled some data analysis of DG & JW's claims.

There is no interline agreement for travel on Monarch (JW Item 57 LGW-TOB-vv). JW stated that, had he had access to RTB, he would have travelled on Virgin which flies the same route. Monarch was used because it was cheaper.

Similar argument for DG items 20-24 travelling on AirAsia. With RTB he would have travelled on Thai.

In any case, the totals were within HK$9 & 5k of each other respectively.

JW stated that, if we could agree the start and finish points, the numbers would fall out. We are not far from each other on the data itself.

RN asked if there is a mid-point to the claim.

JW replied that there is no mid-point. The claimants will not end up out of pocket.

Next meeting

The next 'without lawyers' meeting to be held early next week.

John Warham
26th October 2013

So, again we were making progress. They were at least looking at our claims although they were quibbling over some of the carriers we had used who were outside of the interline agreements. We might have some room to manoeuvre on those. But it was becoming clear that the main sticking point was the date at which the damages commenced. I'd told Bob that there was no mid-point. It was a negotiating position. In truth, the court might only award us damages going back over seven years rather than for the whole period. I talked it over with Doug and Don. Doug was adamant we should go for the lot. Don was more pragmatic. He thought if we could get a deal on the basis of seven years' damages, it might be doable. I went into the next meeting prepared to go either way. If they showed significant movement towards us, we could make a concession as well. However, if they did the usual Swire low-ball intransigent shit, they'd get the same back. This time there was no one available to come with me. It goes against all the standard negotiating training to go into battle alone, but I made a judgment call to keep things moving along and went in without a wing man. I talked it over first with Don and he counselled me to make a recording of the conversation. So I took a miniature recording device in with me. I was in two minds about that. Should I record it surreptitiously (as I had sometimes done in the past) or should I tell Bob I was recording the meeting and just put it on the table? There are advantages and disadvantages to both methods. Sometimes you have no choice but to use the sneaky way; like when you're trying to extract information off the record and you know for sure that the subject will clam up if he sees anything that might possibly be used to disclose the identity of the source at a later date. Also, in some jurisdictions, evidence obtained in such a manner is inadmissible in court. And, of course, there is always the risk of discovery, in which case all trust is blown. In the current situation, I decided to come clean. I just told Bob that, since I was on my own, I was recording the meeting, put the device on the table and switched it on. He didn't object. Don was quite surprised, both by my choice and Bob's reaction, when I told him about it later.

NOTES OF MEETING 4 ON RTB

Date: 31st October 2013
Time: 11:10 – 11:29
Venue: USRC
Present: Bob Nipperess (RN)
            John Warham (JW)

General

Legal aspects of both parties' cases were discussed.

Damages & Costs

RN tabled a revised offer for damages and legal costs totalling HK$800,000.

JW stated that the offer is a long way from meeting the required objectives.

JW tabled a revised offer with damages commencing at a mid-point of 01 August 2005 together with a reduction in legal costs iaw the following figures:

Damages	JW	814,776.40
	DG	350,897.76
Costs		766,567.95

Total		1,932,242.11

JW emphasised that this is a bottom line offer. Tabular data and ticket receipts were provided.

RN undertook to take the offer back to his superiors for consideration.

Next meeting

No further meetings are scheduled at present.

John Warham
31st October 2013

I came out of that meeting pretty angry. After everything I'd said to Bob about negotiating in good faith, it was the same old Swire bullshit. They come in with a ludicrous first offer of 350k, then they stonewall for a while and double their first low-ball and say, 'Look how far we've moved,' even though it goes nowhere near addressing the other party's objectives. And we're supposed to fall for it. Apart from anything else, it's just insulting. I told Doug about it and he wanted to tell them to fuck off there and then and see them in court. I was feeling a bit the same way too. But doing things in anger is not usually the right decision. Sometimes it's best to just sit and wait for a while, which is what we did. A week later I got an email from Bob requesting another meeting and attaching a table in which he wanted to 'establish some principles' for coming to settlement. But it was nothing new. The table just summarised four of the points that we were currently in disagreement over:

1. Start and finish dates of the damages accrual.
2. Administration procedure for issuing tickets.
3. Travel on carriers outside the interline agreement.
4. Reduction in damages claimed because, being sub-load tickets, we might not have got on the flight(s) we chose.

All they had done was to restate their previous position but, instead of presenting it textually, it was in tabular form. Another Swire tactic. Say the same thing that you did last time but present it in a different form so it looks new. We weren't falling for that one either.

NOTES OF MEETING 5 ON RTB

Date: 13th November 2013
Time: 10:15 – 10:40
Venue: USRC
Present: Doug Gage (DG)
Bob Nipperess (RN)
John Warham (JW)

Damages

RN opened the meeting by explaining that he wished to establish some principles for calculating the damages and provided a written table of 4 proposals. Each was discussed in turn.

JW stated that item 1 was not acceptable. It was not a new proposal, rather a restatement in words, instead of numbers, of the previously held position regarding time limitation.

JW stated that, similarly, item 2 was just a restatement of the previous position. The administrative procedure for the issue of tickets does not work.

RN said that the same procedure was used for some cabin crew and it worked.

JW replied that it has not worked for any of the claimants or their colleagues. Not a single ticket had been issued.

During discussion on item 3, JW pointed out that, had the claimants had access to iJourney, they would have picked carriers that had interline agreements with CX. Without such access they had no knowledge and, instead, picked the cheapest deal (which in all cases was cheaper than an equivalent ticket on CX).

RN requested that this point be reconsidered.

On item 4, JW explained that this defence was attempted in the Courtney Chong case and was dismissed by the court. The legal precedent had been set in the Hong Kong courts for calculation of damages in such cases.

RN stated that establishment of a framework of principles would be advantageous in calculating damages, not only for DG & JW, but also for Messrs. Carver, Dickie & Sweeney.

JW agreed but summarised by restating that items 1,2 & 4 were not acceptable. Item 3 would be taken under consideration.

RN then tabled some revised damages calculations for DG & JW compiled using actual ID fares, rather than taking a percentage of fare paid, and including the principle stated in item 3.

The calculations showed an issue regarding travel on SQ [Singapore Airlines] where only ID75 is available rather than ID90. Again, JW pointed out that, had access to RTB been granted, those trips would have been undertaken on CX or equivalent.

It was agreed to take the revised figures under consideration.

RN stated that he would come back with a revised offer at the next meeting.

Next meeting

Another meeting will be scheduled for next week.

John Warham
13th November 2013

We came out of that meeting with Doug getting very pissed off. Me too to be honest. They weren't moving at all on the date the damages started to accumulate or the cut-off date. I was now seriously beginning to think that Doug was right. I'd been wasting my time. But there was something in me that told me to keep trying. I'd been here before on the scope clause in 1999 when they stonewalled through all the weeks of negotiation until Barley rolled at the eleventh hour. We sent them a revised proposal, in response to their table of settlement principles, and held another meeting. Doug and I went in with the attitude that we weren't going to take any further bullshit on the issues. It was time to read Bob the news.

<u>NOTES OF MEETING 6 ON RTB</u>

Date: 20th November 2013
Time: 11:00 – 11:35
Venue: USRC
Present: Doug Gage (DG)
          Bob Nipperess (RN)
          John Warham (JW)

General

The principles for settlement were discussed.

RN stated that the company had difficulty with the use of the term iJourney in the latest document drafted by JW as iJourney was not introduced until 12 February 2013.

JW agreed that the term should be amended to read RTB.

Damages

JW confirmed that the settlement offer from the company made by email prior to the meeting was not acceptable to the claimants. Whilst general agreement on the calculation methodology had been reached, the discounts applied in the offer were unjustified and arbitrary.

RN pointed out the claimants' duty to mitigate the damages once the RTB cards had been issued.

JW responded that they had tried repeatedly to mitigate the damages but were met with a brick wall at every turn. Whilst it may work for other employee groups such as certain cabin crew and other retirees prior to the introduction of iJourney, the admin procedure has failed to issue a single ticket to the claimant group. The claimants feel that they have been singled out for special treatment, especially given the long history of relations between them and the company.

RN remarked that the offer reflects the principle that the claimants should bear some responsibility.

JW replied that the responsibility for the situation rests solely with the company. The contractual position had been negligently, if not maliciously, misstated to the claimants from the outset commencing with the dismissal letters of 2001. That position had been repeated continuously through correspondence and the company's website up until liability was admitted in February 2011. Even then the admin procedure has failed. The claimants have done nothing wrong and should not be out of pocket.

The issues of ID90 vs ID75 and travel on non-interline carriers were discussed.

RN restated the company's position on both issues.

JW repeated that, had access to RTB been given, the claimants would have selected CX iso travelling on SQ and, similarly, would have selected airlines that had interline agreements but, without access to RTB, they had no way of knowing.

After further discussion, JW stated that the SQ point could be conceded but the proposal contained in the revised offer from the claimants, supplied prior to the meeting, that 45% of the non-interline fares be refunded was a fair compromise and would stand.

Legal Fees

RN tabled a revised offer to pay the claimants' legal fees up to the date of the company's sanctioned offer.

JW agreed to check the figures and consider the offer.

Summary

General discussion took place on the progress of the negotiations and the manner in which they have been conducted.

RN remarked that he understood the passion that the claimants felt and that it would be a significant achievement if settlement could be reached.

JW agreed and undertook to supply a revised proposal based on the day's discussions.

Next meeting

Another meeting will be scheduled for later in the week.

John Warham

20th November 2013

Five days later, I got an email from Bob. It said:

Without Prejudice and subject to contract:

Dear John and Doug,

Further to the various discussions we have held in recent weeks, I write to advise the Company's offer in respect of the above matter.

Both parties have worked diligently to reach a settlement and in putting this offer together the Company has considered the various points you raised during our meetings.

We have sincerely tried to address these however there are some aspects which the Company cannot agree on. These aspects are:

a) Our legal advisers hold the view that if the matter proceeded to trial that it is unlikely any claim before January 2010 would be accepted by the Court.

b) If the matter proceeded to trial, regardless of the outcome, legal costs would be subject to 'taxation' and the sum claimed would be reduced in the region of 30-40%.

c) We are unable to accept any claim for travel on a carrier with whom we have no interline agreement.

Given the above, I am authorised to offer you a total sum of HK$1,300,000.00 (one million, three hundred thousand Hong Kong dollars) in full and final settlement. This is inclusive of legal costs, interest and claims relating to travel made by you in respect of this matter. I would also advise we are agreeable to the proportions which you indicated last week.

Further, our offer embodies the following principles:

1) full and final settlement in respect of all matters related to Retiree Travel Benefits (RTB) between you and Cathay Pacific Airways Limited.

2) includes the Company opening access to its iJourney retiree website and the travel policies and benefits contained therein.

3) you agree to be bound by the usage rules within the RTB policy which can be found in the retiree website.

If the above offer is acceptable, I will instruct our legal advisers to draw up a formal settlement document which will conclude the matter and arrange for the release of access to iJourney to you both.

I would like to thank you both for being prepared to amend your original claim and to meet informally in pursuit of reaching this settlement. I appreciate it is less than you claimed but hope that our final offer – which has been improved substantially – will illustrate our sincerity in reaching a resolution to this matter without the additional costs should the matter go to trial.

May I ask you to discuss the matter and revert by close of business today (25th November 2013)?

Kind regards

Bob

This, of course, was a beauty. All it did was restate their position without making any concessions at all and, to add insult to injury, he sends it in the morning asking for a decision by the end of the day. Standard technique. Time-line your opponent. And also note the comment about the offer being 'improved substantially'. Yes, improved over their low-ball starting point. Same old, same old. I sent him the following reply.

Dear Bob

Thank you for your email.

I write to confirm that your offer is not acceptable to us.
We will now proceed with the court case.
Thank you for your time and effort.

With best regards,

We thought that would be the end of it but, later that same day, he replied.

Dear John and Doug,

Thank you for your email. I'm disappointed that we appear to have been unable to resolve our differences.
Perhaps you could share your thoughts on what might be an acceptable alternative – I can but ask our senior team to further consider?

Also, I'm happy to meet later in the day if that would help.

With kind regards,

Bob

What might be an acceptable alternative? What the fuck did he think I'd been telling him over the last six meetings? Well, he'd asked for it, so I gave it to him.

Dear Bob

Thank you for your email.

I too am disappointed that we have been unable to resolve our differences through negotiation. However, there remain some fundamental differences between us where Cathay has refused repeatedly to change its position. We have covered these a number of times during our discussions but I will repeat them for ease of reference.

In your offer you state that:

a) Our legal advisers hold the view that if the matter proceeded to trial that it is unlikely any claim before January 2010 would be accepted by the Court.

Our own legal advice strongly contradicts this opinion. During our talks we tried to make some accommodation on this point by reducing our claim to commence at August 2005. In our last couple of meetings I had been under the impression that we had found a basis for agreement. However, in your latest offer, you simply restate your original position of 8 weeks ago. In fact there has been no acknowledgement at all of our concession; rather you have just restated an entrenched position. That is not negotiation. You go on to say:

b) If the matter proceeded to trial, regardless of the outcome, legal costs would be subject to 'taxation' and the sum claimed would be reduced in the region of 30-40%.

We have already offered you a discount of 24.82% on our legal costs to date as shown in our final offer dated 20 November. Your latest offer takes no account of this. In any case, in view of the manner in which Cathay has conducted itself throughout the proceedings thus far, at trial we will be asking the court to award indemnity costs. You say further that:

c) We are unable to accept any claim for travel on a carrier with whom we have no interline agreement.

We have explained repeatedly that, had we had access to RTB, we would have selected carriers that have interline agreements but, because we were denied access to RTB, we had no way of ascertaining such information. During our talks you have even acknowledged that the actual fares paid were lower than the CX equivalents for the same routes thus actually saving the company money on our claims. Even though this situation was none of our making, we offered you a 'split the difference' deal at 45% of the actual fare paid which you also acknowledged as being a fair and reasonable solution. We also conceded the SQ ID75 vs 90 issue to try to find accommodation. Your offer, however, takes no account of this. On this point, again, you do not negotiate but, rather, simply restate an entrenched position. Finally you say:

'I can but ask our senior team to further consider?
Also, I'm happy to meet later in the day if that would help.'

In view of the intransigent position that the company has chosen to take on these and other issues, I don't see how another meeting between us is likely to get us any closer to resolution, Bob, unless your principals are actually prepared to negotiate in good faith.

As you know, I am leaving Hong Kong for Europe on Wednesday and will be returning on 5th December for 5 days. In order to give you time to give the matter further consideration, and in one last attempt to find agreement without going to court, our offer of 20 November of HK$1,858,370.16 in full and final settlement of all our damages, legal costs and interest will remain open for acceptance until the close of business on Friday 6th December, failing which it will be withdrawn and we will proceed to court. In case you are not aware, a case management conference, at which we will apply to have the matter set down for trial, is scheduled for 12th December. The intervening time between the two dates should give us sufficient time to vacate the proceedings should the offer be accepted.

With best regards.

I'd had it with them. So had Doug. We were back to our 1996 AOA motto, 'Enough is enough'. As Doug had told me all along; they're never going to change their spots. Nipperess sent me a reply asking if I would be in email contact while I was away in Europe. I replied that I might be, but infrequently. I was going on holiday with Klaske and the last thing I wanted to do was spoil that by continuing negotiations. She'd already had to put up with all this (and very amenably I might add) for the last two months. We went to Amsterdam and I heard nothing from him.

We got back to Hong Kong on 5 December and I received an SMS on arrival from Bob asking if I could meet him first thing in the morning the next day. I replied that I'd just got back from AMS and was jet-lagged but could meet him in the afternoon. I also noted that

I'd just spent more money on my HKG-AMS-vv ticket and that would be added to my claim. He asked me to bring the ticket with me to the meeting so we could add it to the overall settlement and quoted me the ZED fare. Well that was promising. It looked like they were moving on their 'issue of the RTB card' cut-off date for the damages.

I went alone to the meeting the next afternoon with an admonition from my team not to compromise or take any more bullshit. Bob came in clutching two brown envelopes and a folder. The envelopes contained iJourney usernames, passwords and documentation on how to use the system for Doug and I. The file contained a settlement document agreeing to our final proposal. But there was one last wrinkle. I scan-read the document and there was a clause that said that each party would be liable for their own legal costs.

'Bob, it says here that we'll each be liable for our own costs. Is that a misprint?' I remarked slightly irritably.

'Oh, that's not what you said is it?' he replied looking a bit sheepish.

'No it's not,' I responded thinking from his reaction that this was one last try-on.

'OK, I can get that changed.'

'Thanks, then I think we have a deal.'

We shook hands, thanked each other and, as a parting shot, I remarked, 'Well Bob, we did it and now, hopefully, we won't have to see each other again.'

'Yes John, except perhaps in the staff travel check-in queue,' he replied amicably, and we both walked away.

It took a few days for the lawyers to vacate the court case, complete the legal formalities, and then it was settled.

The principles that we nutted out over those nine weeks of negotiations have subsequently been used to settle numerous other outstanding staff travel cases with both pilots and cabin crew. It's amazing what can be achieved given a willingness to negotiate in good faith and some persistence!

16

Settlement

'The biggest human temptation is to settle for too little.'
Thomas Merton

'You got to know when to hold 'em, know when to fold 'em.'
Kenny Rogers

We spent Christmas of 2013 in Koh Samui in Thailand. Having received the judgment on costs, the RTB settlement and looking at investments and income, I'd been doing some financial planning. We were renting our place in Sai Kung, but it wasn't sustainable in the long term; the rent was too high. And looking at the property market in Hong Kong, which was now running out of control, it was very obvious that there was nothing of the standard that I wanted that was anywhere near our budget. I wanted the things back that had been taken from me. I wanted a garden, a pool and to be near the beach. But, even if I sold the pub, I simply couldn't afford it on what I'd got available and be able to fund my retirement as well. To put it in perspective, when I sold my house in Hong Kong in 2006, I got HK$23 million for it; in round figures GB£2 million. To buy back the same place now would cost at least three, or even four times that amount. Out of the question. Of course, we could hang on and wait for the market to crash again, just as it did in 1997 during the Asian financial crisis and again during the SARS epidemic in 2003, when around 40 per cent was wiped off the property market each time. But I wasn't prepared to take that gamble, so we had been looking elsewhere.

Earlier in the year, around Easter, we were supposed to go to stay with Ken and Angela Carver in Phuket for three weeks. Unfortunately, Ken called a few days before we were due to arrive to tell me that he'd forgotten that they had the electricians coming in to re-wire the house, so the trip was off. Bummer. So Klaske and I decided to go away anyway and we plumped for Koh Samui. I'd been there before, but not for ten years or so, and she'd been to one of the neighbouring islands, Koh Pha Ngan, but, again, not for some time. We hired a self-catering, ground floor apartment on the beach in Mae Nam on the north coast of the island and spent a few days there. As we were coming to the end of our holiday, we had a conversation.

'You know babe, I really like it here,' I said.

'Yes, so do I,' she replied.

'You know something else? I think I could live here.'

'Yes, so could I.'

We talked some more when we got back to Hong Kong and decided that we'd return to Koh Samui and explore it properly later in the year. So, in July, we booked another self-catering apartment, more centrally located, slightly inland from Lamai, and went down there for three weeks. It wasn't on the beach but it had a swimming pool, came with a 4WD pickup and was owned by a retired English couple, Alan and Ann Woods, who lived in their house next door. Alan picked us up at the airport when we arrived and, on the drive home, we started chatting.

'Do you like quizzes?' he asked.

'Err… depends on what kind of questions they're asking,' I replied.

'Well there's a quiz night at our local pub on Wednesday night if you're interested,' he offered.

'Oh, well, maybe, thanks,' I responded. But his next question came as a surprise.

'Are you athletes?'

'What? Athletes?' came my response.

'Yes, because the local hash meets every Saturday afternoon if you're interested in that,' he replied.

'Oh, err… thanks, maybe.'

And that was how we got introduced to the local community. We went along to the quiz night, partnered Alan and Ann and a couple who lived next door to them, Wally and Adele, and we won! That led to some banter from some of the other locals who weren't that pleased to be defeated by a newbie.

'Bloody ringer. No wonder you won, you brought a bloody astronaut with you.' It was nice to be promoted to such dizzy heights, but it didn't last long. The next week we came last and I was rapidly demoted.

'Hah! Your bomber pilot crashed and burned this week didn't he?' came the jibes.

We went to the hash as well and met some more new people, which was fortuitous. (Unlike the quiz, I didn't win the hash. Rather, I met a Canadian guy named Bob Dickson whose claim to fame is that he always comes last. So I attached myself to him and walked the course, only going ahead in the last 100 metres to preserve his unbeaten record.) Klaske and I had spent the first few days driving all around the island in the pickup. We turned down every side road we could find, explored every back road and track and, in doing that, we'd decided on which part of the island we wanted to live. One of the advantages of Koh Samui is that it is a relatively small place. You can drive round the whole island in less than two hours. The big resorts and the nightlife are mainly in the north east around Bo Phut, Chaweng and further north. If that's what you want, it's easily accessible. In the south west it's quieter and there are very few big, resort-style hotels, mainly because the beaches do not shelve away as steeply as they do in the north. So, if it's peace and quiet you're looking for, that's the place to be; and that's the area that we had chosen. We'd approached a couple of estate agents but hadn't really been shown anything that made us sit up and take notice.

Then, on the hash, we met a couple called Dave and Claudia Wilkinson. Dave's hash name is Plays-Off-One because he's only got one leg. We were talking to them about our house hunting and Dave offered to introduce us to someone he knew, Matt Smith, who lived on the island. He isn't an estate agent as such, but he makes a living out of buying and selling land and property. We met up for a couple of beers at Dave's house and we chatted about what I thought at that time were the prime requirements. Has to be on the beach, has to have a garden, has to have a swimming pool etc. etc., in fact all the things that I'd had at my old place in Clearwater Bay in Hong Kong. Matt agreed to meet us the next day and show us some properties. We met in the morning at the Elephant Gate and he told us that, before looking at the beach front stuff, he wanted to show us something else.

We followed him north up the road a few hundred metres and then he turned right, heading east, going inland, away from the beach and into a coconut forest. Now I'm thinking, 'Where the hell is he taking us?' After a couple of clicks we pulled up outside a tall, grey, zigzag, ornamental concrete wall with a brown sliding gate. The gate opened and down the long garden in front of the house walked a couple, Keith and Janet Morriss, with their six-year old Alsatian bitch, Daisy. 'Welcome to our home,' was their greeting.

We didn't get into the house for the first hour. It is set in 5,500 square metres of land, just over 1.3 acres in UK terms or 3.4 *rai* in Thai measure. Keith worked as a horticulturalist. He had spent a lot of his life working in Northern Pakistan and Eastern Europe rehabilitating land, which had been cleared of landmines after various wars and conflicts, turning it back to agricultural use. And he had spent the last seven years living in this house landscaping the gardens and had planted a variety of exotic trees, flowers and shrubs. The garden in front of the house was given over to a large lawn, on which he'd made a badminton court. This was fringed by a water garden with lotus and water lilies shaded by a bougainvillea archway to the north, a sala ringed by broad leaved palms, orchids and tillandsia to the east and a kapok tree and shrubs to the west. The garden to the rear was similar in size but landscaped. It had a dam and a small stream running east-west through the centre with a covered bridge to give access to the upper half. The whole area was planted with all manner of trees including coconut palms, lime, avocado, araucaria, cannonball and jackfruit. There was also a pineapple grove alongside a covered nursery and potting area. In short, it was Eden.

Klaske, having studied environmental science at college, was in her element. Keith took us on a tour of his garden and described to us all the species growing there; where they came from, their flowering seasons, preferred habitats and all manner of other information. When we finally got around to looking at the house, it was a two bedroom single-storey house with two bathrooms, a kitchen, a verandah and a lounge big enough to hold a twenty-piece orchestra; or a five-piece rock band. There was also a two-car garage with a workshop and outside kitchen area. We sat down to talk.

My main concern was how much work it would take just to maintain the grounds, let alone start developing them some more. Obviously, he did a lot of the work himself. He told me that he employed a local lady, Keow, and her family to help him. She'd been working for him for more than six years and he'd trained her throughout that time, so she knew the place inside out. He said he did about three hours a day himself (personally I suspected more, in fact I suspected he spent most of his waking hours in the garden) but, that if we wanted someone to maintain it for us, they'd need to do about 17 hours per week; and that Keow would be the ideal person. We chatted some more and then we left. Matt took us to see four or five more places on the west coast with beach, garden, pool etc. That night, Klaske and I sat and talked.

'What do you think?' I asked.

'Well, what do you think?' she replied.

'No, I'm asking you what you think first.'

'And I'm asking you what you think first.' This was going nowhere quickly.

'Well, the first thing is that, other than the garden, that place doesn't tick any of the other boxes. It doesn't have a sea view and there's no pool,' I ventured cautiously. 'And it's not on the beach.'

'No, that's true, but it does have a good view of the hills behind it,' she replied equally cautiously.

'Yes, and we could always build a pool. There's plenty of land at the west end of the house that's not really being used for anything.'

'Yes, we could. And the beach is only a five or ten minute drive away,' she replied.

'I know. But what about those other places we looked at? They tick all the boxes,' I countered.

'Yes, they're on the beach, or overlooking it, and they've got pools, but they don't have as much space,' came the reply.

'I know. But what do you think?' I tried again.

'I'm not sure. What about you?'

'Me neither. Let's think about it for a couple of days.'

We were just fencing with each other. We flew back to Hong Kong and left it for a few days. In my own mind, I was trying to rationalise things. I really, really liked Keith and Janet's place. But it didn't meet the criteria I'd set myself. But then, were those the correct criteria? What was I trying to achieve? I knew that. I was trying to recover the things that had been taken from me. The just rewards for a lifetime of dedication to my profession. I deserved this. I'd worked for it and it was mine by right in return for what I'd done. But what is it that I wanted? I'd never liked the cold unless I was dressed for it when going skiing. Bit of a disadvantage for a Yorkshireman really. But after 30 years in the Far East, now I really hate the cold. I'd always imagined myself retiring somewhere warm, sitting on a tropical beach buying an early-morning-caught fish from a passing fisherman and putting it on the grill for breakfast. Sipping a cold beer and watching the sun go down in the late afternoon. But, of course, in my imagination, save for myself, a copper-skinned island girl and the passing fisherman, the beach was always deserted. But, unless you're Richard Branson and can afford to buy your own island, where can you find that? It's a nice dream, but that's all it is. Apart from which, I prefer Nordic blondes to copper-skinned girls, but that's just a personal thing; no offence intended to ladies of any other hues and colouring. But get back to the point Warham. OK, so you want all the things back that were taken from you, but does that mean they have to be exactly the same? Isn't it the style of life that you're looking for? Can't you achieve that using different tools? You used to want a Ferrari or an Aston Martin, but now you don't give a toss. Well, you're right. I don't want a Ferrari any more, but I still want to own an Aston Martin just once in my life. But not for keeps. Not for a day car. Just buy one, take it round the Nürburgring, frighten the shit out of myself and sell it on just so I can say I owned one. Yeah, right, very interesting. But this is about the rest of your life, not just a quick adrenaline rush. And you've got to provide a good life for Klaske. What does she want? More to the point, what does she *need* to give her the life she deserves? Oh fuck, I don't know, ask her. Oh yes Warham, take the easy way out. *You* should know by now. If you *don't* know by now, you better find out, and pronto. After a few days of arguing with myself, I sat down again to talk with Klaske.

'OK, I've had a think about things,' I started.

'Yes, me too.'

'You know all those boxes I wanted to tick?' I ventured. 'I think I might have got it wrong.'

'I've been thinking of that too,' she replied. That sounded promising so I pressed on.

'It's not about getting back the things I used to have. It's really about the style of life I want for us,' I said, holding my breath for the answer.

'Yes, I get that. Go on.'

'Well all that beach stuff, I don't think that's what's really important. What is important is having peace, tranquillity, space and privacy and I think Keith and Janet's place has got all that.' Now I was really holding my breath. I'd just turned everything that we'd talked about, and agreed between us before, on its head and scratched out all the boxes.

'I know what you mean and I think you're right,' came the answer. We talked about it some more over the next couple of days and decided to put in an offer. It was accepted. We paid the equivalent of HK$2 million for the place. For $2 million in Hong Kong, you'd be lucky to get a small shed with a rat in the corner; and only on condition that you promised to feed the rat three square meals a day for the next five years. We took possession of the house on 18 December 2013 and that's how Klaske and I ended up spending our third Christmas together in our own oasis of tropical paradise in Koh Samui.

But there was one other thing. Just before we completed the purchase, I got an email from Matt asking if we'd have Daisy as well. Keith and Janet were returning to the UK and couldn't take her with them. I had reservations. We weren't going to be spending much time in Thailand to begin with because we both still had commitments in Hong Kong and we'd still be spending the majority of our time there; at least to start with anyway. It wouldn't be fair to leave her alone for all that time. He assured me that it would be OK because Keow (who we'd already agreed to employ to look after the place while we were away) would come in every day to feed her and make sure she was properly cared for. So we agreed. And that's how Daisy got thrown into the deal with the house and became part of our family. And it's great to have a dog around the house once more.

We'd settled the RTB. That was a tick in the box. One less loose end to be tied off. But the successful result was much more significant than simply doing the deal because, as well as getting to agreement, we had a couple of other objectives in mind when we proposed party-to-party talks.

We knew that the Swires thought of me, if not as the Antichrist, then certainly as a very annoying long-term thorn in their side, the boxer who just won't lie down no matter how hard you hit him. Some years earlier one of my moles had told me that, at one point, before he was sent packing, Philip Chen headed up a small team that met once a month. Basically their brief was, 'What to do about Warham'. When I heard that, I fell about laughing. It had to be a piss-take. Maybe my mole was a double and he was feeding me misinformation, just as I used to do with one of their probes who came into my office to chat periodically when I was the AOA president. But, much later, shortly after Slosar was made chief executive, an emissary was dispatched to approach him with a message to the effect that, rather than just continue the war in the same way as his predecessor, it would make good business sense to engage me and try to negotiate a peace settlement. The response the emissary received was words to the effect that, 'But the company is under attack. We think it's just better to batten down the hatches and wait for the next tsunami to arrive.' Again, it made me laugh at the time to think that the mighty Swires were so afraid of me. Perhaps they didn't like my first book and were waiting for the sequel! But, unlike the previous intel, this came straight from the horse's mouth. So it had a serious side to consider. If this was true, which it seemed to be, then perhaps I was the block to reaching a negotiated settlement.

Consider this as an analysis. Since the early 90s, a number of Cathay's finest had taken on the pilots. Sutch never got his seat on the board in London because his attempt to bring the AOA to heel failed and he left behind him a company in the worst industrial situation it had experienced since the cabin crew strike, which also happened on his watch. Turnbull got the chop because he promised the people in the big house in London that he'd sort out the pilots once and for all. He failed when we beat them in the House of Lords, so he was given his P45. Same with Tyler. They crashed and burned in the High Court in Hong Kong on his watch so he was out on his ear as well. And there is a common thread though all three events; my own involvement either as union president, chief negotiator or, latterly, leader of *The 49ers*. Now, this all sounds pretty arrogant; that I was responsible for bringing down three of their top men in a row. The truth may be that there were other reasons for their departures but, if the perception amongst their peers was as I have just described it, given that the Swires are intolerant of failure, who in his right mind would want to take me on again and put his career at risk if it went wrong?

If this theory was correct, and I was indeed the blockage in the pipeline to settlement, perhaps the best way to finish this was for me to step down and let someone else take over the reins. I considered this – for about three milliseconds – and discarded the idea for two reasons. Firstly, my own sense of right and wrong, stubbornness, ego, call it what you will, but I was going to finish what I started and, secondly, if they really were that afraid of me, that gave me a lot of leverage at the negotiating table. Perhaps a better solution might be to try to change their perception of me.

Whether right or wrong, people have a self-image. My own is that I am a reasonable man. Hard-headed yes. Stubborn sometimes and ill-tempered sometimes as well. But not unreasonable. If you deal with me fairly, you will receive the same treatment in return. But, similarly, if you do me down, I will fight back. And the worse you treat me, the more I will fight you back. I do not think that is an unreasonable philosophy. But in counterpoint to that, I also believe that I am quick to praise success, to give thanks for a job well done and to forgive mistakes, provided that they are not the result of laziness or lack of effort. It is true that, in negotiation, I drive a hard bargain but, whilst I may be hard, I am also open to reason. I do not expect to come out of every negotiation with everything that I set out to achieve. That *would* be unreasonable. (In fact the only time I have ever achieved that was during the interim rostering practices talks under Labour Department mediation in 2000, and the 176-0 score line was their own fault. They didn't take the deal when it was offered to them three months earlier and, instead, tried to deadline us. But it backfired on them. They ended up deadlining themselves and got to a point where they had to settle or ground the airline. First rule of negotiation: know when to do the deal.) Negotiation is about compromise and finding common ground so that both parties can come away with most, or at least some, of their objectives realised and do a deal they can live with. Anything else is counterproductive and doomed to failure. If either side in a negotiation thinks they've been legged over, the deal won't last very long because the 'loser' will always come back for a rematch. Of course, there are always some show-stoppers; some issues that are on one of the party's 'must have' list rather than its 'nice to have' list. (Like commanders' discretion during the 2000/1 rostering negotiations which, ultimately, led to the sacking of *The 49ers*). If both sides' show-stoppers cannot be satisfied then there is no deal to be done at that point and it is time to walk away from the table. But this is all just basic negotiating strategy that any trained negotiator should know and understand as a matter of course.

So, when we proposed party-to-party talks on RTB, the first question to be answered was, would they engage? That answer came relatively quickly. Yes they would. So far so good. The next question was, who would they send in against me? The answer, Bob Nipperess, was revealing. When Bob was in his heyday, he did not have a particularly good reputation amongst the staff. He was known as being very much a company man, dogmatic and not much open to reasoning. Do as you're told or you're out. As we saw it, typical Swire mentality. However, he was no longer in his heyday. We didn't know when but, given his longevity, he must be coming up for retirement quite soon. He actually confirmed that to me early on in the RTB negotiations, but he also revealed something else. He was no longer head of the staff travel department. That job had been taken over by someone else and he had been moved to another department but, and this is significant, he had been detailed to sort out the RTB problem with the pilots. Now, this could be a poisoned chalice job. The new boss said, yes, I'll take the job but I'm not going to be held responsible for sorting out the mess he's left behind. He can clear the sick up off the floor before I enter the room. And the other point is that they were sending in someone against me who was now expendable. His career orbit was heading towards its perigee so, if he failed, he was going soon anyway, so nothing lost.

It was obvious from the outset of the talks that he was not in the decision-making chair. He openly admitted that himself. HK$2 million, which was the ballpark figure for settlement, was well outside his pay grade. He was just the minion reporting back to his grown-ups. I didn't have a problem with that. There is an old saw in negotiating tactics that says you need to deal directly with the person who actually signs the cheques. Speak to the organ grinder not the monkey. I, personally, don't subscribe universally to that saw. It depends on the circumstances. In the RTB case, if the puppet-master wanted to put an extra set of strings between him and me so as to be able to deflect the blame away from himself in case of failure, then that was fine by me. In fact, it was to our advantage. It was an opportunity to change their perception of me and, if it worked, perhaps we could get them to engage on the major issue as well; the legal costs. There we were talking in the ballpark of HK$12 million, at least two or three pay grades further up the ladder; not to mention the loss-of-face issues.

The successful result of the RTB negotiations, at least as I saw it and, hopefully, in their perception as well, showed that, even after all the time that had passed and the acrimony that had existed between us, I was still prepared to put all that aside, sit down at the table and objectively talk business. Even after the unpleasant exchange between Bob and I in the original Labour Tribunal hearing (which was more my fault than his because, inexcusably, I lost my temper a bit, even though he made his own contribution by refusing even the slightest compromise), ultimately we were still able to reach an agreement which both sides could live with.

So, we had successfully negotiated that first hurdle. Now, if we were to use the same tactics to deal with the question of legal costs, there was a timing issue to consider. We knew that the Swire spring manoeuvres game of musical chairs was due shortly and there were rumours that there was to be a change at the very top. Perhaps, if the rumours were true, it might lead to a new set of players to deal with who might take a different view from their predecessors. It turned out that they were true.

Early in the year, it was announced that Christopher Pratt, chairman since 2006, had resigned effective from 14 March 2014. The PR blurb said that it was due to retirement and that, he was '… not aware of any disagreement with the board of the company.' Hmm… so what's going on there then? No seat on the board with Swires in London for him; the usual progression for the Taipan in Hong Kong. But Sutch didn't get one either when he left in 1999, perhaps for the reasons we've already postulated. And the old 'retirement age' thing is always iffy given that some Swire board members continue well after 'normal' retirement age. Same excuse that Tyler cited when he left. Well, whatever the reasons, he'd gone. The last of the old guard was cleaned out. (Well in Hong Kong at least. Let's not consider the Swire board in London. Let's just keep this as a local issue. That's probably how they want to deal with it. Let the Hong Kong boys sort out their own mess and not dirty our hands.)

As per normal practice, the current chief executive, John Slosar, moved up to the chairman's position. Nothing unusual there then. But the next appointment might be significant. Ivan Chu was appointed to be chief executive. Aged 52, he'd been with the company since 1984 and was appointed chief operating officer in March 2011. Now he was getting the top seat and, at the same time, being appointed to the board of the parent companies, John Swire & Sons (Hong Kong) and Swire Pacific. This might be significant because this was the first time that an ethnic Chinese had been appointed to such a high position. In the bygone, colonial days of 'No dogs and no Chinese' on the club lawn, Chinese might occupy influential positions, such as comprador, but never a position of true authority. Even in more modern times there still had been a 'Chinese ceiling' in upper management. Was Ivan Chu's appointment a sign of the times? Could this be a new broom, a change in philosophy, or was it just the Swires finally dragging themselves into the twenty-first century? Time would tell.

OK, so what are we going to do about the legal costs? Just like the RTB issue, we'd been exchanging lawyers' letters and getting nowhere. So let's try to bypass them again and see if they'll re-engage. As we saw it, we had two options. Option one was to wait until the actual takeover in March, wait for Ivan to get his chairs under the table and survey the mess that had been left behind by the previous lot before deciding what to do to start fixing things. It had merit. He might not want to start wielding the big stick and making policy changes before the previous incumbents had cleared their desks. On the other hand, only an idiot would agree to take over a position unless he had examined the glassware first to make sure there were no poisoned chalices hiding at the back of the drinks cabinet. So, option two was to assume that he already had a good handle on the outstanding issues between us and strike while the RTB iron was still hot. It was a question of timing. Being an impatient bugger, I decided on option two and instructed our lawyers to contact the opposition's to suggest a party-to-party, without lawyers, meeting. We received a reply on 6 March agreeing to our proposal. They wanted to re-engage! They gave us a direct contact in Cathay by the name of Scott McEwan.

Mr McEwan was a new name to us. We did our research on him but didn't come up with much, other than that his official title was manager flight crew employee relations. No one in our circle had had any dealings with him so he was something of an unknown quantity. Now, this was good and bad. Bad because it's always preferable to know your opponent, background, experience etc., but also good because it looked as though he might be one of Ivan's new boys, perhaps with a different outlook on things. We made contact, but he wasn't available to meet before the end of March. We exchanged several emails trying to arrange the first meeting but he was spending a lot of time away in Australia, Canada and other places. This was interesting.

In recent years, various sub-branches of the main Hong Kong Cathay pilots' union, the AOA, had been set up in other countries and registered there locally. This meant that they could represent the interests of the pilots based there and so take advantage of the local labour legislation which offered greater employee protection than that of Hong Kong. We knew this had caused Cathay some problems. In the same way that they fell foul of the US IRS for not deducting withholding tax on earnings when they originally set up Veta Ltd in the early 90s as a vehicle for employing the pilots based there, they were in trouble again for not complying with local employment laws in other countries. A case in point was France where, in response to investigation by the local authorities, they decided to just close the Paris base. But that didn't solve it though because there were pilots based there who were more than happy to continue to assist the authorities; one of these being Ian Rodwell who had actually been a member of the Star Chamber. A case of poacher turned gamekeeper perhaps? Also, in Australia, the pilots based there were taking advantage of the enterprise bargaining legislation to increase their leverage. So, if Scott was spending so much time away trying to sort out the various messes left behind by the outgoing lot, that might be an indicator of the way they were going.

We continued to exchange emails and, eventually, our first meeting was fixed for 24 April at 15:00. We discussed a neutral venue. I'd told him that the venue didn't concern me and offered to go to Cathay City but was again turned down. They still didn't want me in their building it seemed. We eventually agreed on a conference room in their lawyers' office provided no lawyers were present. It had the advantage of being only a three-minute walk from the Captain's Bar for post-meeting de-briefings. Don had volunteered to be my wing man on these missions so it was going to be just like old times!

There were only four points on which we needed to reach agreement to settle everything and put it to bed.

> ➤ Quantum of CSC's predecessor's (Haldanes') costs;
> ➤ Quantum of CSC's costs;
> ➤ Quantum of JSM's costs in relation to the 3Ps;
> ➤ Interest calculation.

By way of clarification, the first point related to costs incurred by Haldanes prior to us sacking them and appointing Chiu Seto &

Cheng (CSC). Originally, Haldanes represented all of the Hong Kong based *49ers* but, in the end, only eight of them stayed the course. So, we simply took the total taxation bill for all of the plaintiffs and factored it for the eight remaining. It came to HK$1.385 million.

The second point related to CSC's total costs incurred for 14 of the plaintiffs for the High Court trial, costs up to the payment in dates for Doug Gage, John Dickie and me (the 3Ps) and no claim for Greg England's estate as there was no costs order made. In preparation for the negotiation, I had painstakingly constructed a spreadsheet to analyse the specific costs that could be assigned to each of the individual plaintiffs with dates, actions etc. This was not as easy as it may sound. The problem was that there were actually four different actions which had been amalgamated into one. For each of these four actions, there were some costs that could be identified to specific plaintiffs but some that were for the action in general. These general costs had to be apportioned across each of the plaintiffs for that particular action. Similarly there were other general costs that could not be attributed to each specific action so these had to be apportioned over the whole case. I could go into more detail but I don't wish to bore you any further. Suffice it to say that my methodology was designed to be mathematically based. If you have the data and it is analysed correctly, the only arguments available to your opponent in response are to challenge the validity of the data, dispute the methodology of the analysis or look for errors in the calculations. It was my guess that they had done neither anywhere near as much work as we had on verifying the data nor on coming up with an alternative methodology. There was some debate amongst our team as to whether or not we should supply them with such a detailed analysis because, should the negotiation fail, then they could use it against us in subsequent taxation proceedings. My gut feeling was that they wanted to settle and avoid taxation (as indeed did we), so our best chance was to give them the lot and, in that way, make them argue from our figures rather than something they'd scrabbled together at the last minute. It is always an advantage in negotiation to have your opponents working from your draft documents and data. In that way they have to negotiate you down rather than you having to negotiate them up. It gives you much greater control. So, on the basis of my gut feeling, we sent them everything prior to the first meeting. It came to around HK$9.8 million.

The third point was JSM's costs in relation to the 3Ps. Unlike us, they had not produced any detailed taxation bill for their costs. All we had received from them was a back-of-a-fag-packet estimate of HK$12.5 million overall. We didn't believe that for a moment. Not a chance. Because they believed in our cause, our lawyers and barristers had been working for us at discounted rates and our total costs came to HK$13 million in round figures. There was no way that JSM, Huggins and McLeish had been working for anything near what our guys were charging. We reckoned their bill would be at least twice, if not three times, as large as ours; especially given that Hunsworth, for JSM, had tried to drown us in paperwork repeatedly throughout the case; 200 page documents every three or four months produced by one of the highest-charging lawyers in town do not come cheap. But why would they not want to reveal their true costs? Could it be that the shareholders might not be very pleased if they found out exactly how much money had been spent over the years pursuing a losing case against their employees as part of their union bust? Perhaps we will never know. The last time I posed a similar question as a shareholder at the company AGM, they refused to answer my enquiries either verbally or in writing. In any case, we were happy to use their 12.5 million figure. Their lawyer's proposal on their counterclaim for the 3P's costs had been simply to factor the total amount by 3/18. This was, of course, rubbish. It took account neither of the payment in date nor of the 'cost of joinder but no more' limitation. They proposed HK$2.5 million. Again, we took a mathematical approach. I went through the court transcripts and analysed how much time Huggins had spent cross-examining each plaintiff. Having ascertained the total time spent on each of the 3Ps *vs* the total time, I came up with a factor for each. I then analysed each of the 3P's time and divided it into time spent on questions in relation to the general issues and time spent on questions specific to the 3Ps' personal circumstances. I then factored each of the 3P's costs again using the ratios derived from there. It was the best model I could come up with to deal with the 'but no more' proviso and, in any case, it was better than anything else they had come up with which so far was zilch. The figure came out at HK$385k; bit of a difference from HK$2.5 million.

The fourth item was calculation of interest. I thought it should be the simplest item but it turned out to be the most contentious in the end. We were using the generally accepted simple interest formula that, if there is a sum outstanding of *a* comprising of *b* principal + *c* interest, then if a payment of *x* is made in partial settlement, it should be apportioned to *b* & *c* in the ratio of *x*/*a* and further interest at settlement is then calculated on the outstanding principal balance of *b*-(*b* x *x*/*a*). They were using a different formula in which all of the payment *x* is deducted from the principal *b* so that interest at settlement only accrues on (*b*-*x*). We had not heard of this method before so I did some research. There is, indeed, such a method and it is called the Merchant's Rule. It was in common use in the late 1800s but was generally abandoned in the early part of the twentieth century, although there is still reference to it in mathematical textbooks. Why was I not surprised to find them still relying on such archaic methods? The important point is, perhaps, that the interest calculation using the two methods on the quantum of numbers we were discussing resulted in a difference of around HK$300k.

So we met Scott for the first time on 24 April. Unlike the RTB negotiations, I am not going to describe in detail what took place. I have already described the methodology we adopted and, suffice it to say, it stood us in good stead. Scott came in at a disadvantage as he had not been made privy to all of the previous correspondence on the matters between the lawyers. We provided him with copies of the same. He had also not been made privy to any of the previous offers and counter-offers. We provided him with the documents he lacked. There were other matters where he had not been fully briefed or advised prior to our meetings. Again we gave him what he needed. It became very clear to us that he had been tasked with getting to a settlement that we could both live with and, perhaps because he knew of my reputation, or perhaps because of what happened during the RTB talks, there was none of the usual Swire low-ball tactics. Our job came down to convincing Scott of the validity of our data and our arguments and then, having achieved that, to give him sufficient data and information for him to go back and do the same to his grown-ups.

In all my dealings with Cathay management, negotiating with Scott was a breath of fresh air, unlike anything I had experienced before. He came in with an open mind and a readiness to seek compromise. If only just one or two of my previous experiences could have been as pleasant. I am certain of one thing. Had they adopted a similar approach at the outset back in 1994 when changes needed to be made, we would not have ended up where we were now.

There is one anecdote that happened during our talks that is worth relating. We experienced quite a lot of difficulty arranging meetings because of the extensive amount of travelling that Scott was doing. And because of the destinations he was going to, and knowing the troubles that Cathay was having with the local employment laws in these places, I surmised that he had been tasked with sorting out all the mess that had been left behind by the previous clowns. (If he is successful that will be a huge feather in his cap and he will go far. Of course, if he fails, he will be thrown to the wolves. This isn't just a poisoned chalice; it's a whole case of strychnine. It's an ambitious project to take on and I admire his courage, even if it is a very high-risk strategy.) At one of our meetings I voiced this when I said to him, 'It seems to me Scott that you've taken on the job of sorting out all the industrial cock-ups that your predecessors have made.'
You need to adopt an Edinburgh Morningside accent when reading his response.

'I wouldn't quite use the words that you've selected John, but you're no' far wrong.'

After 24 April, we only held another three meetings until, on 13 October, he sent me an email making a settlement offer. I could live with the principal sums that were on offer but they were still trying to chisel me on the interest rate calculation. By this time I was getting very tired and I almost just threw my hands up and accepted it. But I spoke to Klaske about it. She said words to the effect of, 'You've come this far Warham, don't let them dip you now at the finishing line,' so I replied with a counter offer proposing to split the difference on the interest numbers. They accepted, so we saved ourselves HK$150k by one last email. Never sell yourself too cheap!

The settlement money went into our bank account on 6 November 2014 and that was it. After 13 years, 3 months and 6 days it was finally over.

And, so now, we have come full circle back to our table, sipping sundowners, at the Pineapple Beach Bar. Where shall we go from here to finish the tale? I have an idea. Let's embark on a little journey into the unknown.

.

17

Lessons

'No, no, no, that's not what we want you to think at all.'
Nicholas Peter Rhodes *ca* 1998

'What's my ambition? I want to try everything, live life to the full and, when I die, do it with a smile on my face. And I want them to put me in a fast hearse.'
Graeme Banks-Smith *ca* 1982

On 7 November 2014 I was in Hong Kong. I'd arranged to meet Don in our 'office', the Captain's Bar, in the afternoon for a few celebratory libations. After more than 13 years working together on our project we deserved it. The traffic from Sai Kung wasn't as bad as it usually is on a Friday so I'd arrived half-an-hour early. I sat down at our usual table, the barman brought over a pint of Carlsberg in my personal tankard, which is kept there on the shelves behind the bar, and handed me a copy of the *SCMP* to browse whilst waiting for Don to arrive. I opened the paper and the first thing I saw was this headline.

Cathay pilots set for Christmas work-to-rule protest as pay row rumbles on

The article was written by Phila Siu. I read on.

Cathay Pacific passengers could face a frustrating Christmas after pilots, unhappy with a pay offer, voted overwhelmingly in favour of industrial action.

315

Some 93 per cent of Hong Kong Aircrew Officers Association members voted 'yes' in an online poll asking them whether they wanted to press ahead with their first work-to-rule protest since 2001, a letter sent to members yesterday shows.

The letter did not state when the work-to-rule, or contract compliance campaign, would take place. But in an earlier letter, the union told members action 'must' start within 42 days of a vote result being announced.

Pilots said the action would see staff refuse to work on rostered days off, and would have a 'significant' impact, causing delays and cancellations.

Cathay is no stranger to threats of industrial action over the holidays; last year, members of the pilots' union voted to take action but agreed in December to hold talks. Cabin crew had also threatened action in 2012.

Some 2,100 of Cathay's 2,900 pilots are members of the union. About 90 per cent of members voted in the latest poll.

Pilots' union general secretary Chris Beebe said yesterday that industrial action was 'likely' but that the union wanted more talks with Cathay. A decision to scrap the protest would be 'contingent upon a better pay offer'.

In September, the airline offered Hong Kong-based crew increases of 4 per cent this year, 3 per cent next year and 3 per cent in 2016. For those based in Europe, the rises would be a percentage point lower this year and next. Those in New Zealand would get 1 per cent each year.

A 'disappointed' Cathay spokesman said further talks were planned.

'We have been in regular communication with the negotiating committee... and look forward to further discussions later this month,' he said. The nature of the airline business meant the company had to prepare resources to cover any eventuality.

'We will do our best to make sure that we continue to operate our flight services as scheduled.'

One Cathay pilot said the looming industrial action would have a bigger impact than the last such campaign in 2001, because the airline's staffing was significantly more stretched. Junior pilots were typically called in on their days off two or three times a month, cutting into their social lives, the pilot added.

'We will not be answering phone calls, unless of course we are on standby,' the pilot said, nor would crew arrive early to do preparatory work, as was usual.

The 2001 industrial action ended in the sacking of 51 pilots, 49 of them on one day. The 49ers, as the sacked pilots became known, engaged in a lengthy legal battle with the company.

I could not believe what I was reading. Talk about déjà vu. Management and union alike; had these people learned absolutely nothing from the last 13 years? The strategy, the tactics, they're exactly the same as before. Management engage in a sham negotiation and offer a derisory three-year pay deal. What next? Break off negotiations and approach the pilots directly with a new contract? Label those who refuse to sign as disloyal? Accuse them of holding Hong Kong to ransom? And the union come back with exactly the same tactics as we used in 2001. Contract compliance! Contract compliance for fuck's sake!! Have they not even got the imagination to come up with a new handle? It's like lining the troops up for a set-piece battle. Each side knows exactly what the other is going to do. No surprise attack. No ambush. No guerrilla tactics. Just give the order to advance and send the troops in to be mown down. Well, perhaps there is one difference from 2001. They can't just sack 49 pilots for working to rule because that would be against the law wouldn't it? We'd established that. Surely they've learned that at least? They wouldn't dare do that again would they? Well, actually they might. The thing they will also have learned if they have done their homework (which on current evidence I seriously doubt), is that all they'd have to do afterwards is keep their mouths shut and say nothing. However, just like last time, that's probably too difficult for them. But it explained one thing that had been puzzling me over the last couple of months. Sales of the Kindle version of my first book had dwindled to 3 or 4 copies a month; but recently it had surged to around 20 copies per month. They must be buying it to use as a reference manual. Both sides probably. I was flabbergasted.

When I was planning this book, I had intended to start this final chapter with the question, what have we learned? If I stick to that plan, on the evidence above, the answer is simple. Nothing.

THE END

But that doesn't make for very interesting reading. So let's modify the question. Other than the idiots referred to above, what have the rest of us learned? Before we try to answer that question, it may help our analysis if I first relate an incident that happened to me early on in my flying career.

All pilots have, at one time or another in their careers, made a serious error of judgment. Any pilot who tells you otherwise is lying either to you, to himself, or both. Sometimes the error will be the pilot's last but, thankfully, more often fate affords the miscreant a second chance. And I am not talking about slight inconveniences such as becoming temporarily uncertain of one's position. I am talking about serious mistakes with potentially fatal consequences. The lessons taught by such mistakes, once learned, will never be forgotten. They come under the general heading of, 'I Learned About Flying From That.'

When I was flying Piper Aztecs for Casair based at Teesside (MME), I learned such a lesson. We had two Aztecs, G-BBGE and G-BBPZ. GE was a truck. It never flew quite right. There seemed to be a twist somewhere in the airframe which meant that it would never trim out properly. It always seemed to be going ever so slightly sideways whatever you did. And the props wouldn't stay in sync for more than three or four minutes at a time. You were forever having to make small adjustments, little corrections to keep it going where it was supposed to be; and it made rumbling sounds as if in protest at being in the air. PZ, on the other hand, was a beauty. She trimmed out perfectly, the props once synchronised stayed there, the airframe sang with the joy of flight and all this made her three knots quicker than GE. Of the two aircraft, PZ was my favourite and I thought I knew her inside out.

But I was at a danger point in my career. I had been working for Casair for coming up to 18 months and now had 750 hours in my logbook; a far cry from the 225 hours I had when I first came out of training at Hamble (or so I thought). I knew the aircraft, I knew the routes and I had survived two winters of operations over the North Sea. In short, I considered that I knew the job and was good at it. And therein lay my fault. Overconfidence. I certainly had now acquired the skills and the knowledge, of that there was no doubt. But, at the ripe old age of 24, I lacked the circumspection that is part of good judgment. That can only be gained through hard-won experience and that was where I was lacking. But fate was about to teach me a lesson.

Casair had an engineering facility at Teesside for routine checks and minor repairs, but it was not equipped for heavy maintenance. For that we used Northair Aviation at Leeds-Bradford airport (LBA). As the junior pilot, it was my job to ferry the aircraft down from Teesside. I would leave them there, pick up an Avis hire car and drive back home. A few days later, once the maintenance was complete, I'd reverse the process. The flights were good fun. Wheels-up to wheels-down it was only a 12-minute trip through the Vale of York and it was an opportunity to enjoy some solo handling practice and perform a few manoeuvres not normally permitted with passengers on board.

So I had no complaints at all when I was detailed to do these trips; right up until one Friday afternoon in December 1976 that is. It was 16:30 when Jack Cassidy told me the maintenance on PZ had been completed earlier than scheduled and that I was to go down to LBA and pick her up. I was not happy. The reason for this was a young lady I was hoping to meet that evening. British Midland Airways (BMA) had some Viscount crews based at Teesside operating the MME-LHR-vv daily shuttles. One of the BMA cabin crew looked like Veronica Hamel from *Hill Street Blues* and I had the serious hots for her. I'd chatted to her a couple of times in the bar of the Cleveland Flying Club, the favoured watering hole of the aircrew in general, and it seemed that the attraction was mutual. The signals were all showing green. That night, the BMA crew were hosting a Christmas party in the club and Veronica was going to be there. It had been my intention to get in early and try to take things further. But being attractive as she was, I wasn't the only dog sniffing around and Jack had now put a spanner firmly in the works. I picked up an Avis car, hit the A19, the quickest way onto the A1 and Leeds, and put the pedal to the metal. At the time I owned a 1969 Mk I Ford Capri which had been fitted with a 3.0L Essex V6 engine. Had I been in my own car I could have made it quicker; but not by much.

When I got to Northair's hangar, it was all locked up and everyone had gone home for the night. PZ was sitting on the pan outside the hangar. I did a rapid pre-flight check. When I turned on the master switch to check the fuel contents, the outboard tanks indicated near empty. I switched tanks to the inboards. They didn't show much more either. But the fuel gauges on the Aztec were notoriously inaccurate, especially on battery power alone. It was much better to take the bungs out of the filler points mounted on top of the wing and have a look inside to see how much fuel was in there. I checked the outboards visually with my torch. There wasn't much in there but I thought it would be enough. I did a check of the inboards. It was more difficult to check these visually because there was a stepped well on the inboard end of the tank which couldn't be viewed from the filler cap. The standard practice was to give the wing a push and listen to the amount of 'sloshing' sound the fuel made in response to give an indication of contents. It may sound rather agricultural but, with experience, it was quite effective. The slosh I heard was less than I would have liked. I was now faced with a dilemma. If I wanted to refuel the aircraft, I would have to start up, taxi across to the north side of the airfield where the refuelling facility was situated, shut down, refuel and then start up again for departure. All this would take a minimum of 35 minutes; if I could get a fuel bowser to come out straight away that is. On a Friday night they only kept a skeleton crew on standby for unscheduled refuelling. In any case, I had brought PZ in for maintenance three days earlier and when I left her there she had a least two hours of fuel still on board. I knew that because I personally had filled her up in Aberdeen that day, flown her to MME and then on to LBA. No one else had flown her in the meantime and they surely couldn't have used all that much fuel in the maintenance checks could they? And the other dogs would already be sniffing around Veronica while I stood there prevaricating. I decided to go as is. I finished a somewhat hurried pre-flight check, fired her up, taxied out and got airborne.

Now, we could pause here and list all of the mistakes that I had made so far and construct the causal chain. But, if you have got this far into the book, you are quite capable of doing that for yourself without my assistance. Suffice it to say that my next mistake was an absolute *ab initio* novice blunder. At about 1,100 ft after takeoff, the left engine failed. I switched tanks from the outboard to the inboard and it came back to life. The outboard tank was empty. Right then and there I should have turned around and landed back at LBA. But I didn't. I carried on. About five minutes later, just over halfway to MME, the right engine failed. Again, I switched tanks to the inboard and it fired up. I was now five minutes out of MME. I had the mixtures leaned back as far as possible with the cylinder head temperatures peaked. My situation was now very, very serious. Teesside were using R/W 24 and I was approaching from the southwest. I called them up and asked for a straight-in approach to R/W 06 which would shorten my track miles to touchdown. The conversation with ATC went as follows:

'PZ request straight-in approach R/W 06.'

'Negative PZ. R/W in use is 24. Expect holding due to scheduled inbound traffic.' (It was standard practice back then to afford scheduled traffic priority over charter and light aircraft.)

'PZ, I say again, request straight-in approach R/W 06.' There was then a slight pause before the controller called me back.

'PZ do you have a problem?'

'PZ, I say again, request immediate landing R/W 06,' was my response. I should have declared a Mayday right then but I didn't. It would have meant an investigation by the CAA and my licence would have been on the line. Thank god that, being a small airfield, the pilots and the controllers all socialised together in the flying club after work. We all knew each other well and they got the urgency in my voice. The next transmission was what I needed to hear.

'PZ you are cleared to land R/W 06.' I was lined up on finals 3 miles out at 1,100 ft; 200 ft high on the glideslope. My training had kicked in. All the glide approaches I'd practiced at Hamble were paying off. Conserve altitude and trade it for airspeed if it goes quiet. Wait until you're certain you can dead stick it onto the runway before you descend. Remember to feather the props while you've still got oil pressure if they both quit. Just then the left engine ran down again. I turned on the cross-feed and it fired up again. I was now down to one tank feeding both engines running on fumes. I knew I could make the runway now and closed the throttles to glide it in but, with the distraction of the run-down, now I'd got too high. OK, so sideslip the extra height off just like Dally Purcell taught you in the Chipmunk. Be careful not to overdo it in case it uncovers the fuel lines and stops the engines. It doesn't matter if they stop now; it's a glide approach. OK, good, so we're well placed then. Concentrate. You're still a bit high. Bit more sideslip. Relax on the controls, be gentle, aim for smoothness, co-ordinate, let the aircraft do the work for you, she's your friend. Remember what Dally taught you.

In one way the last two minutes of that approach were the longest of my life but, in another, they went past in a flash as my brain raced to remember everything I'd been taught and make my hands and feet put that training into practice. I landed about halfway down the runway and taxied into the parking area without further incident; apart from the shaking of my hands as the adrenaline pump shut down that is.

The chief pilot, Alan Turley, was standing there waiting for me with a fuel bowser. ATC had contacted him on the squawk box in the flying club (he was attending the same party) and told him I had a problem. The flight manual of the Piper Aztec D states that the fuel tank capacity of the aircraft is 120 imperial gallons. We filled the aircraft tanks up. The bowser registered 117 gallons delivered. Ignoring extra fuel in the piping between the tanks and the engines (perhaps two or three gallons at best), I had only three gallons remaining on board after shutdown. At long range cruise, the flight manual listed the fuel consumption at 23 GPH. I had seven minutes of fuel remaining to dry tanks.

Alan took me into the office and sat me down. I was expecting the almightiest bollocking of my life. Perhaps it was because of his military experience flying Lightnings on minimum fuel as a matter of course, or perhaps it was because he'd been there himself at some point in his career or perhaps it was because of just that one word; experience. All he said to me was, 'John, I want you to promise me something.' I couldn't even look him in the face as I replied, 'What is it Alan?'

'I want you to promise me that you'll never do that again.'

'I promise you Alan with my hand on my heart, I swear to you that I will never, ever do that again,' I replied.

'OK then,' he said. 'When you've calmed down a bit and sorted yourself out I'll see you over at the club for a beer,' and with that he left.

I was absolutely gutted. The realisation of what I had done made me feel physically sick. I had betrayed every single one of the dedicated instructors who had spent their time and effort teaching me to fly. I couldn't even begin to count all of the rules I had broken. And I had let Alan and Jack down as well. They had put their trust in me when they gave me a job when no one else would. And look what I had done to them in return.

It was a very chastened John Warham that walked into the Cleveland Flying Club about an hour later. I bought a few beers for Alan and also for the controller who had given me landing clearance when I needed it. There was no report to the CAA and no further repercussions; just a very serious lesson learned and never to be forgotten.

People sometimes ask, you must have had some scary moments in your career and want to hear the gory details. I usually just laugh it off with some flippant remark about how nothing really happened that I wasn't trained to deal with. But, in truth, my Papa Zulu moment was the scariest; not because of any technical failure, but because of my realisation of my own propensity to make such a potentially catastrophic series of ill-judged errors.

Oh, and as for Veronica, she was otherwise engaged when I got to the party and we never did get together.

So, returning to the question of what have we learned, what we really need to know is, in all of what has happened over the last 13 years, have we had our Papa Zulu moment? Has a lesson been learned that will never be forgotten? To answer that question, we need to look for evidence, not simply of people paying lip-service to lessons learned, but for empirical evidence of a real change in ethos. To start our search, let us look at the report on the accident that occurred on 13 April 2010 to Cathay flight CX780; an Airbus A330.

To refresh our memories, this is the flight that took off from Surabaya and, at the top of climb, number two engine started to suffer power fluctuations with associated ECAM fault indications. The decision was made to continue the flight to Hong Kong during which the malfunctions persisted until, on descent, the number one engine malfunctioned as well. The crew put out a Mayday distress call on the approach to Hong Kong and the aircraft landed at a ground speed of 230 kt; almost double the normal landing speed. During the landing and rollout, the number one engine pod struck the runway, five of the main wheel tyres deflated and there were brake fires. The crew managed to bring the aircraft to a halt within the available runway length and evacuate the passengers, during which 57 of them were injured.

In the accident report 2/2013, published three years later by the Hong Kong Civil Aviation Department (CAD), it was found that the cause of the engine malfunctions was contaminated fuel containing super absorbent polymer (SAP) spheres uplifted from Surabaya. The cause of the contamination was the use of incorrect and inadequate safety procedures during maintenance of the fuel hydrant system. At the time, there was considerable debate as to whether or not the decision to continue the flight to Hong Kong, as opposed to turning around and landing back at Surabaya, was the correct one or not. As a direct result of that accident, Airbus issued a revised QRH checklist procedure entitled:

SUSPECTED ENG <u>FUEL</u> SYS CONTAMINATION

The procedure lists a number of actions to take to determine whether or not the cause of the engine malfunction(s) is due to fuel contamination. If it is determined that this is indeed the case, then it leads into a further checklist entitled:

<u>ENG</u> FUEL SYS CONTAMINATION

One item on the checklist states:

<u>WHEN FUEL CONTAMINATION IS CONFIRMED</u>

LAND ASAP

Now let us consider the implications of what this means. In the case of CX780, the problems *were* due to fuel contamination and, therefore, the decision to continue the flight was incorrect. But it's not that simple, because, at that time, these procedures were not in the book. They have only been introduced as a result of what happened.

SAP contamination is a phenomenon that had never been experienced before. A typical case of learning from experience, which has been a common thread throughout the history of aviation. So, putting aside what we know now for the moment, how did the crew, at the time, arrive at the decision to continue the flight? After all, general airmanship dictates that, on a two-engined aircraft, if one engine fails, you are now down to single-engine operation, an emergency situation, and the correct course of action is LAND ASAP. But, again, it's not that simple because the engine hadn't actually failed completely, it was still producing some power. So this is where the judgment call comes in. This is where the captain is responsible for deciding what to do in the best interests of protecting the safety of his aircraft and its occupants.

But who should be taking part in that decision-making process? The first officer? Most certainly because he is part of the operational crew. Amongst other duties, he is there to assist the captain in such circumstances with advice and formulation of possible solutions.

What about the engineering department? It depends on the situation. If the engine has failed catastrophically then there's no question. LAND ASAP and engineering has nothing to contribute at that point. But in the case of CX780, where the crew weren't sure what was causing the problem, engineering might be of considerable assistance in evaluating the situation. After all, they know a great deal more about the workings of the engine and the fuel system than the pilots do. They might be able to offer some advice and assistance in problem solving. So, using the maxim, aviate, navigate, communicate, get the aircraft stabilised, complete the ECAM and/or checklist items, get the aircraft pointing where you want it to go and then get on the radio to seek advice. So far so good.

What about the logistics section of integrated operations control (IOC)? Should they be involved? Now we start getting into the grey areas. That section has little technical expertise. Their only real interest should be where the aircraft is going to end up, if it goes somewhere other than its originally intended destination, so that they can deal with the logistical consequences of the diversion. Note that I say 'should be'. There is one factor that we haven't considered yet, and that is commercial pressure.

In today's world, everything has a price on it and the commercial pressure to save costs on all accounts is enormous. Airlines often trumpet their mission statement that, 'Safety is our first priority'. If only it were so. But the practical reality is often far different from that goal. All departments are under pressure, including Flight Ops, Engineering and other departments involved in IOC. The attitude is, get the aircraft home because if it diverts somewhere else it costs money that we don't want to spend because it will impact on the bottom line. In my personal experience, that is the reality of the situation. So when the pilots of CX780 called engineering and asked a question along the lines of, 'Do you think it's safe to carry on?' we have to ask the complementary question, was the reply they were given tainted by commercial considerations?

As a training exercise, I sometimes give my candidates the following scenario. You takeoff from R/W 25L at CLK. The wind is from 330 at 20 kt. Once airborne, you have a double hydraulic failure. Once you have secured the aircraft, completed the checklists and got everything under control, what will you do next? The answer that I invariably receive is, 'Call the company.' The conversation usually goes along the following lines:

'OK so why are you calling the company?'

'To let them know what's happened.'

'Well ATC has probably already advised them that you're in an emergency LAND ASAP situation so what more assistance can they give you?'

'They can tell us where they want the aircraft.'

'Yes, you can let them tell you. And let me tell you what their answer will be. They'll want it back at CLK because that's where all their engineering and logistics backup is. And would you be happy with that decision?' That usually causes some head scratching so we take the scenario further.

'OK, consider this. You are now in a situation where you have degraded flight controls, "slightly sluggish" response as the checklist puts it, with reduced pitch and roll capability because you've lost an elevator and some of your spoilers. And now you're going to attempt an approach in a 20 kt crosswind. Does that sound like the ideal option to you?'

'Not when you put it that way, no.'

'No, and it's not because 20 miles west of CLK there is Macau with a long strip of concrete pointing directly into wind which is going to significantly reduce your control problems; so if I'm ever in that situation, that's where I'm going because it's the much safer option and I won't be called upon to demonstrate my superior flying skills. And let me give you some more advice. If you *do* pull off a landing in CLK you'll be hailed as the conquering hero, but if you fuck it up and go off the side of the runway, the Monday morning quarterbacks will be the first to ask you why the hell you didn't go to Macau just before they hand you your P45. So, in this situation, you don't let IOC tell *you* what to do, you tell *them* what you're going to do, and only if you've got time to fit in the radio call in amongst all the other crap you've got to sort out. And when you get called into the office afterwards to explain why you just cost the company all that money by diverting, always remember the phrase, "I made my decision for sound operational reasons," and then ask if it's OK to go now and enjoy the rest of your day off with your family.'

The point of this is that, in the days when I grew up in aviation, the captain was given not only the authority and responsibility but also allowed to exercise that authority without interference from people who had no business being part of the decision-making process. Now, I'm neither saying that that is the ideal nor that it was without disadvantages. It led to the Transatlantic Baron syndrome and was a key causal factor in the British Airways Papa India Trident accident at Staines. We have come a long way since then with human factors and cockpit resource management training and we are much the better for it. But it can be taken too far and I believe we reached that point some time ago. The captain's authority has been so degraded by successive management edicts that some of the current generation of captains, who have no experience of the 'old days', for want of a better term, think this is the norm. They are afraid to make decisions without having them endorsed by a 'higher' authority. It is time for a reassessment.

Of course, one of the requirements to bring the scales back into equilibrium is strong leadership in the Flight Ops management, in particular the director flight operations (DFO). Like Jack Burridge back in my days in Monarch or later, Mike Hardy, in Cathay, the DFO must be prepared to protect his pilots from interference by administrators. If you do something wrong, if you cock up, then you're in for the high jump and fair enough. But that should be coming from the DFO or one of his uniformed deputies, not from some suit with no operational experience. Unfortunately in Cathay, with the advent of Barley et al, like the captain's authority, the DFO's position has been undermined to such an extent that most of his power has been usurped in thrall to the commercial department.

If the airlines truly adhered to the mission statement quoted earlier, we would not have a problem. Commercial considerations would have no part in operational decisions of the type we are discussing. But they do. We see evidence of it all over the profession. One of the worst examples of this is Ryanair in the UK. The culture of fear and the punitive fuel policy operated under the fiefdom of Michael O'Leary is, in my opinion, a disgrace to commercial aviation and a direct threat to flight safety. And the regulators are complicit in permitting such a situation, not only to develop, but also to continue unchecked. They have failed in their duty to protect the travelling public from such excesses. Space precludes me from expanding on my opinion but the *Mayday! Mayday!* documentary produced by the Dutch television company KRO, whom O'Leary sued for defamation and lost, is widely available on the internet. I invite you to watch this eye-opening documentary and form your own opinion. It encapsulates many of the topics that I have written about, both in this book and my previous one; the continual deterioration in safety standards from which civil aviation is suffering at the hands of the bean counters and ineffectual regulators.

But, returning to summarise what happened on CX780, one of my fears, which I voiced in my previous book, was that the crew were going to be hung out to dry like Peter Burkill, the commander of British Airways flight BA038, the B777 that landed short of the runway at Heathrow on 17 January 2008 after a double engine failure (also due to fuel problems, but in this case fuel icing). He was initially lauded in public by the BA CEO, Willie Walsh, but later, as a result of misinformation and repeated management failures to protect him, his career was ruined.

In relation to CX780, in 2011 I wrote:

Perhaps a better question to be asked is, with the benefit of hindsight, knowing what we know now, if faced with a similar situation and circumstances, would we make the same decision again? If the investigation concludes that the answer to this question is no and that the safest course would have been to land back at Surabaya, or another *en route* alternate airfield, who will carry the can? In this event, it is essential that the motivation and role of everyone in the decision-making chain, especially where commercial considerations were involved, be fully considered by the investigators in making their recommendations.

In fact, the accident report makes very little comment on the decision-making process itself other than to say that, 'the decision of the flight crew to continue the flight was considered reasonable.' So, it doesn't actually address the decision-making process itself directly, but at least the pilots weren't made scapegoats. Overall then, this accident report is a vast improvement on the CAD's hatchet job on, and their shameful treatment of, Captain Gerardo Lettich after the accident to China Airlines flight CI642 on 22 August 1999 at CLK. It seems that some lessons have been learned in that department at least.

So, with the benefit of hindsight, even though we know now that it was the wrong decision, the crew did their best with the information and knowledge available at the time and we have all learned from their experience; just as it should be. In fact the crew did more than their best. When the situation deteriorated and became critical, they were faced with a situation for which they had little previous training and, in the face of that, they used their basic flying skills and airmanship to save the aircraft and the lives of all 322 passengers and crew on board. Given the situation that, ultimately, they found themselves in, they did an outstanding job and, at the IFALPA Annual Conference in Panama City in March 2014, Captain Malcolm Waters and First Officer David Hayhoe were both the recipients of the Polaris Award. This award is the highest honour associated with civil aviation awarded by IFALPA. It is presented to airline crews in recognition for acts of exceptional airmanship, heroic action, or a combination of these two attributes.

But we still haven't answered the question, has the ethos in Cathay Pacific changed as a result of all this? What we really need to know to answer this question is, if get-home-itis caused by commercial pressure figured in the decision-making process, did all the senior managers from the relevant departments, including commercial, get together and say;

'OK we almost lost an aircraft there. We came so close to killing 322 people, we've got to sit down here and seriously reassess our priorities. Point one. No more commercial pressure on operational decisions. When Flight Ops says the aircraft's diverting, the aircraft's diverting and that's that. No cost apportionment, no budget analysis, no finger pointing at the weekly meeting. We make shed loads of profit anyway and the occasional diversion should be factored into the budget in the first place. If it's not, it should be and that's your failing, not ours, so go away and fix it. So, just to reiterate, no more commercial pressure on operational decisions. Got that?'

Did that happen? Did they have their Papa Zulu moment? Or was it just considered from the point of view of cost benefit analysis? One hull every three years? Perhaps we'll never know. We may find out next time a serious incident or accident happens. The Haddon-Cave report came out a year after the CX780 accident. I'm sure he must have made some recommendations in his report. If there truly has been a change of ethos, why not make that public to the flight crew in general to give them the confidence that their Flight Ops management has their backs? Why only publish the *SCMP* version? Of course, again, it would take strong leadership from the DFO.

And what of the travelling public? What do they think? I guess you can spin it two ways. 1. 'Didn't our pilots do a great job? Fly with us we're really safe.' That might fool some of the people, but it doesn't really explain things. Credit your passengers with some intelligence. Or, 2. 'OK, that was a really close one there, but we've analysed the whole thing and changed our procedures to make sure it can never happen again. So now we've made it even safer than before so come and fly with us. Oh, and by the way, our pilots did a great job as well.' The problem with option 2 is that you'd have to trust your PR department to get the words right and not make some completely numpty statements like they and Tyler did in the immediate aftermath of the accident. Bit of a stretch that one maybe. But, as a member, albeit a well informed one, of the travelling public, I'd much prefer the open approach of option 2 rather than the closed approach of option 1, which smells to me of cover-up. After all, the accident report is in the public domain for all to read if they so wish, so what is there to hide?

So, in summary, with the dearth of positive evidence available to us at this point, we can only speculate and hope against hope that lessons have been learned and that the corporate ethos truly has changed for the better. I, personally, would be very pleased if it has because I would feel that I had some hand in making that happen.

I started writing this chapter on 20 January 2015. Two days later on 22nd, I received a copy of a message from the current DFO, Richard Hall, to the flight crew. In it, he announced that, upon his retirement in April, his post would be taken over by Anna Thompson.

In his letter, Hall stated that, '[Anna] joined us in Flight Operations almost two years ago from an operational environment at Air Hong Kong [AHK] where she was Chief Operating Officer. She has extensive experience in the many facets of Cathay Pacific both operationally and commercially.' Further research reveals that she joined AHK in September 2011 having previously held a number of roles at Cathay. She has previously worked with [the] Swire Group/Cathay Pacific for over 21 years, with her most recent positions including General Manager, South East Asia (based in Singapore), and General Manager Airports (based in Hong Kong). She joined [the] Swire Group in 1990 having graduated from Trinity College, Oxford, with a BA (Hons) in Philosophy, Politics and Economics.[7]

So, they're putting another suit in the top job. Let us hope that her degree in philosophy stands her in better stead for the job than the last suit's degree in zoology.

Let us just consider one more point about corporate ethos within my ex-employer before we move on to more general matters. When Don sat down with me in the Captain's Bar that day, I berated him about what the hell the idiots (from both sides) are doing now, are they just destined to repeat history? In response he made a very valid point. Around 75 per cent of the current aircrew were not even in Cathay Pacific back in 2001 when *The 49ers* were created. The current batch of second officers hadn't even started their basic training. Similarly the managers. It's a new generation on both sides of the table and they need to educate themselves. When I was working my way up though the ranks, certain books were required reading. *Fate Is The Hunter* by Ernest K. Gann was one of them. It teaches us of the early days of commercial aviation and many of the lessons contained therein are as valid today as they were back then. *Flying The Line* written by George Hopkins and published by ALPA was another. It explains the development of unionisation, and the need for it, in our profession. When I got involved in the AOA, I had to educate myself in other matters such as economic theory and decoding balance sheets. *The Wealth of Nations* by Adam Smith (particularly his theories on the mobility of labour) and *Accounting for Growth* by Terry Smith were invaluable reference books, as was *Confessions of a Union Buster* by Martin J. Levitt on industrial issues. Let us hope that this new generation are as equally prepared to educate themselves before management precipitates, and the union plunges headlong into, another industrial confrontation; otherwise both sides may truly be destined to repeat history. There is another book that would also make a good reference manual for everyone in the current situation. It's called, *The 49ers – The True Story*! (As I mentioned earlier, I think some people have already realised that so perhaps all is not lost.)

So, to return to the questions posed at the outset and conclude this section; what have we learned and has the corporate ethos changed? Have they had their Papa Zulu moment? I have presented the evidence that I have at my disposal, you decide for yourself.

Now let us turn our attention to our old friend, money. All businesses are in the market to make a profit. That is an obvious statement, and a given, but now let's take it a step further. How much profit? As much as possible perhaps. All right, if we accept that as a premise, are there any constraints on how we make that profit? Surely there must be. We must remain within the law wherever our business operates, otherwise we are simply a criminal enterprise. And what about who we sell our products or services to? Are we prepared to sell to anyone who asks because it will increase our profits? If our business is to manufacture armaments, are we prepared to sell those arms to any and all extremist groups in pursuit of profit? Well, we can't can we because we've already said we must remain within the law and there are export controls on such things. Yes, but if there weren't, would we go ahead and sell them in that case? And what about if we sell them to a legitimate customer knowing full well that they are going to sell them on to a proscribed third party? Are we prepared to do that because, after all, it will increase our profits and that's our prime goal, to make as much profit as possible, isn't it? And what about our suppliers? Are we prepared to buy in supplies from anyone who offers what we need at the lowest cost? That will increase our profits. But what if we know these suppliers are using child labour or slave labour? Are we still prepared to do business with them in pursuit of profit?

What about finance? If we want to borrow some working capital, do we care where it comes from? If it comes from the profits of an illegal enterprise, such as a drug cartel, do we care so long as it's been laundered through the banks? After all, if we don't take it someone else will, so why should we care? And if we don't take it and one of our competitors does, that will give them a commercial advantage and that will certainly affect our profits.

And what about the people who work for us in our business? How much shall we pay them? The absolute minimum wages that we can get away with because that will increase our profits? Or do we need to pay them a bit more to encourage them to stay with us after we've trained them to do the job? Well, maybe it depends how much it costs to train them. We want to get a return on our investment because that will increase our profits. Might have to do a bit of number crunching on that one. And what about duty of care; do we have a duty of care towards our employees? Do we have a responsibility to keep them safe from harm in the workplace? Well, that could impact on our profits because providing them with safety equipment and training costs money. If it's legislated we'll have to do it anyway. But if it's not, why should we? Maybe we could move our business offshore to somewhere where we don't have to do that. That would increase our profits. But do we want to make our employees' lives happy? Do we want them to enjoy working for us? Do we want them to feel as though they're valued? Well, what the hell has that got to do with increasing profits? Ah, well some studies show that happy workers are far more productive than unhappy ones, so we might have to think about that as well. More productive means more profit, so we might need to crunch some numbers on that as well. Maybe do a cost benefit analysis.

And who are we making all these profits for? We'll have to put some of them back into the business, obviously, because that means we can grow our business and make more profits. But once we've done that who is it for? Is it all for us, the owners? Don't see why not, it's our business after all. And the shareholders of course, if we have any. Yes, the profit's there for us and our shareholders. That's why we're in business, to make ourselves richer. But what about sharing our good fortune with others less fortunate than ourselves? Do we want to try to make the world a better place for other people as well as ourselves? Why should we? We're the ones who've taken the risk and done all the hard work, why shouldn't we keep the rewards? We're not a charity after all are we?

What we are discussing here, of course, is ethics and morals in business. We cannot simply state that we are in business to make as much profit as possible without putting some constraints, some qualifications, on how we go about making those profits. But, perhaps the first question we need to ask in our analysis is, are there such things as ethics and morals in business any more, or are these now just simply outmoded concepts? There is certainly plenty of empirical evidence to support the latter precept. Just look at what's happened to the banks in the last five years. When I was growing up, your local bank manager was a man to be trusted and respected. Now you'll be lucky to find a local bank manager, they've been replaced by clerks and ATMs, and the whole of the senior management system is rotten to the core.

The Co-operative Bank is a case in point. When Jill and I first set up AAF, we looked around for an ethical banker; one that did not invest in oil companies, rain forest deforestation, money laundering and other shady dealing. The Co-op seemed to fit the bill. What do we find now? The supposed Methodist minister, Paul Flowers, the former chairman of the Co-op, turned out to be a Class A drug addict (using crystal meth, cocaine and ketamine to name but three) and regularly consorted with rent boys. It has also emerged that Flowers had two previous criminal convictions; one for gross indecency after he was caught performing a sex act with a man in a public toilet in 1981, and another for drink driving. If that wasn't enough, he'd had to resign from Bradford council in September 2011 when pornography, described as 'inappropriate but not illegal', was found on his work laptop.[8] Very ethical I'm sure.

And if it's not drugs and sex, it's other forms of criminal behaviour. The various scandals that have been uncovered recently, starting with the Libor rate fixing, are too numerous to list. And it's not just a few rogue traders (although some would like us to believe that), it goes all the way to the top. If it wasn't the senior managers themselves actually doing these things, they had knowledge that such practices were taking place on their watch (or if they didn't they certainly should have) and, if they didn't actually tacitly endorse them, they certainly did nothing to stop them; until they got found out and caught with their hands in the cookie jar that is.

To my mind, one of the worst offenders that epitomises all that is wrong with the banking system is the former chief executive of Barclays, Robert 'Bob' Edward Diamond. In June 2012, Barclays was fined a total of GB£290 million by the UK Financial Services Authority (FSA) for 'serious, widespread breaches of City rules relating to the Libor and Euribor rates' as well as facing other accusations of money laundering and tax avoidance. All this on good old Bob's watch while he was being paid GB£6.3 million per annum excluding bonuses.[9] He was finally forced to resign in July 2012 under pressure from the Bank of England governor, Mervyn King. So, what should we expect of him now? An admission of responsibility, a statement of contrition, an expression of remorse and an apology to all the people who suffered damage because of what happened on his watch? Not a chance. Following on from his statements in front of the Treasury Select Committee in January 2011 that the time for bankers to show any remorse for the failings that dragged Britain into the worst recession since the Wall Street crash is 'over',[10] in an interview published in the *New York Times* in May 2013, he stated, 'Do you want the truth? Up until all of this, I didn't even know the mechanics of how Libor was set. If you asked me who at Barclays submitted the rate every day, I wouldn't be able to tell you. I bet you if you asked any chief executive of any bank on the street, they would give you the same answer.'[11]

So that's it then. The, 'I didn't know what was going on, it's not my fault,' defence; a modern day variation on the Nuremberg defence. So, if I'm the captain of the aircraft and, whilst I am off the flight deck, one of my crew does something to put the safety of the passengers in jeopardy, it's not my fault because I wasn't there. What crap. Unless there are some extremely unusual and totally unforeseeable circumstances, as the captain, you are responsible come what may. It just doesn't wash. With responsibility comes accountability.

But what of the government and the regulators that allowed all this to happen in the first place? What responsibility do they carry? My vote goes to the one-eyed Scottish idiot as Jeremy Clarkson described him. (Now I know this will generate furious letters of complaint to my publisher from partially blind people, Scottish people and idiots [not to mention the PC brigade], complaining about my choice of words. The fact is, however, that the person we are referring to has only one eye [the result of an unfortunate rugby injury], and he is Scottish [as is one of my best friends], but I must admit that I may be doing idiots a disservice and for that I apologise in advance.) It was under Gordon Brown's 'light touch' regulation of the City that the worst excesses had their nascence and, according to the FSA report on the subject, it also contributed to the collapse of the Royal Bank of Scotland and allowed its bosses, including Sir Fred Goodwin, to walk away from the whole sorry mess without being disciplined.[12] Where is the accountability?

It is also Brown's use of off-balance sheet financing in the pursuit of the sell-off of the UK's national assets, including the National Health Service and the water distribution network (to name but two), into private and foreign ownership that has saddled future generations with a level of debt that is impossible ever to pay off. In my opinion, the man is a disgrace to public office. But his boss is even worse. The warmonger Bliar led the UK into involvement in a war that had nothing whatsoever to do with WMDs (for which the evidence was fabricated and none were ever found) but all to do with control of the world's oil supply. And now we have to sit and listen to him pontificating in his latest role as the Middle East Quartet's special envoy. It is sickening to watch him with his carefully choreographed hand gestures and body language lecturing us as if we are supposed to fall for the self-congratulatory rubbish he espouses. One of my colleagues at Hamble was the captain of a British Airways 747 on which Bliar was travelling one day when he was prime minister. His PA approached my colleague prior to departure with the message that, 'Mr Bliar requires that, should you or any of the crew encounter him during the flight, you should not speak to him unless he speaks to you first.' What a total dickhead. Who does he think he is, the Queen? The arrogance of the prick. It was the people who voted him in and now he puts himself above them and does not deign to talk to them. True characteristics of a megalomaniac.

When Bliar came into power it was towards the end of the Cool Britannia period of the 90s and he latched onto it (which is probably why it faded and died soon afterwards). Now Cameron spouts about multiculturalism and the inclusive society. The UK is neither of these things. Our society is divided. Go to any major city and, instead of the ideal he espouses, each ethnic group has claimed a piece of turf and set up its own ghetto with no intention of integration. Rather the reverse. Many of them are hell-bent on attempting to impose their own radical values on the rest of UK society, using violence if necessary.

Expansionist philosophies, whether religious or political, have been one of the major causes of conflict and war throughout human history. Currently the excesses of various factions of Islamic extremists are a major cause for concern worldwide. Just consider the logic of their philosophy for a moment. If you do not believe in the same god as me, you are an infidel, a non-believer, and I will kill you because my interpretation of the Koran says that I am justified in doing so. What is this supposed to achieve? Is this supposed to frighten everyone else into believing in the same things as you? Do you really think you can change people's beliefs by violence? You may change their behaviour but you will not change what they think. You will only impose your will on them until such time as your violence is met with superior violence and then they will exact their retribution on you. This does not convert others to your beliefs. Rather the reverse. It alienates others against those beliefs. But radical Islam didn't invent this latest barbaric behaviour. That great bastion of the Western religious establishment, the Catholic Church, did exactly the same thing, but in a much more organised fashion. They had the Inquisition which operated throughout the Catholic empire from its formation in the twelfth century up until its final abolition in the early nineteenth. It was responsible for torturing and murdering people in their tens of thousands for not believing in their supposed one true god. Infidel or heretic. Beheading or burning at the stake. What is the difference?

But who can we look to for solutions to turn around the malaise from which the UK suffers? I can think of no one who displays the qualities of honesty, leadership and integrity that are needed. The whole system is wracked by repeated scandals like MPs' false expenses claims and other forms of criminal behaviour. And as for the revolving door that operates between a position in government and a job in the banking sector or with one of the Big Four audit companies, that is influence peddling in pursuit of personal gain pure and simple. The system is corrupt. So, who amongst the current crop of politicians can we trust? Not a one as far as I can see. But this isn't just a problem in the UK; it's worldwide.

During the recent pro-democracy demonstrations, it was reported that the chief executive (as he is called) of Hong Kong, C.Y. Leung, received a payment of AU$7 million from Australian engineering firm UGL when the company was acquiring another firm, DTZ Holdings, of which Leung was a director. The payment, made in three instalments, was in return for an agreement that Leung would not compete with them or poach from his old company.[13] Leung did not disclose this payment prior to standing for public office and, when it was revealed, offered no plausible explanation for what was widely seen as a bribe. Instead, his defence was that it happened back in 2011, six months before he took over as chief executive, even though he received the third and final instalment whilst he was actually in office. So that's all right then.

But the most crass statement that he made during the demonstrations was that, if the government met student demands and allowed candidates to be nominated by the public, the population that earns less than the median monthly salary of US$1.8k could dominate the process. His actual words were, 'If it's entirely a numbers game and numeric representation, then obviously you'd be talking to the half of the people in Hong Kong who earn less than US$1,800 a month.'[14] Are those the words of a megalomaniac or what? And then he sent in the police using pepper spray and tear gas against completely peaceful demonstrators. When that didn't work, they tried to use criminal triad gangs to infiltrate the protestors and cause violence. The streets were eventually cleared of demonstrators after almost three months of occupation, but if C.Y. and his Beijing cronies think it's over they're dreaming.

The only person in the UK government I have heard speak out about the appalling betrayal by the Beijing government of the provisions of the Basic Law on self-determination for Hong Kong, which led to the pro-democracy protests, is Chris Patten; the last governor of Hong Kong. David Cameron hasn't got the balls to challenge the Chinese in case it upsets the UK's trading relationship which is so critical to his economic recovery plans. Money again. Cameron and his government's betrayal of the people of Hong Kong is on a par with that of the Chinese government; despicable.

We all have first-hand experience of many of the problems that I have been describing, but who's responsibility is it? Who should be held accountable? Well, our elected political leaders presumably. They're the ones we voted in to manage the country, or did we? During the last UK general election held on 6 May 2010, there was a total of 45,597,461 registered voters. Of these, only 65 per cent bothered to cast their ballot. And of this 65 per cent, the Conservative Party received 36.1 per cent of the votes cast.[15] So the Tories received a total of 10,699,444 votes or 23.47 per cent of the total electorate. Democracy anyone?

So who can blame the electorate for being so apathetic when all we see are repeated scandals, politicians who line their own pockets at the expense of those they are supposed to serve and protect and successive governments in thrall to big businesses that are allowed to get away with the most outrageous tax avoidance schemes, whilst the average tax payer is automatically fined GB£100 if they fail to file their tax returns on time?

We see the supermarkets operating monopolies, driving down the prices paid to small growers and suppliers putting them out of business. They are being allowed to take over the food supply chain and government does nothing about it. The large pharmaceutical companies charge exorbitant prices and use their patents to prevent others from manufacturing generic drugs that would benefit the health of people in Third World countries. And then we have Monsanto. As one commentator likes to describe them; 'evil, psychopathic, bloodsucking, agent-orange, polychlorinated biphenyl (PCB), saccharin, nutrasweet/aspartame, BST, rBGH, Roundup pesticide, genetically-mutant terminator seed producing, food-patenting bunch of modern-day nazi scumbags.'[16] A touch on the extreme side perhaps but he gets the point across.

But the individual who takes the biscuit for me is the Nestlé chairman, Peter Brabeck, who, in a 2005 video, made a statement suggesting that declaring water a right is 'extreme' and asserting that water is a foodstuff best valued and distributed by the free market. Now, in fairness, he has since issued clarifications and stated that his remarks were taken out of context but the question remains, what kind of person would make such remarks in the first place, out of context or not?

As an interesting aside, the website www.healthline.com defines psychosis as, 'A serious mental disorder characterized by thinking and emotions that are so impaired, that they indicate that the person experiencing them has lost contact with reality.' It goes on to advise that, 'It is important to see a doctor right away if you or someone you know is experiencing symptoms of psychosis.' On the basis of this advice, judge for yourself how many of the people we have discussed in the preceding paragraphs ought to make an appointment with their medical practitioner as a matter of some urgency.

But if you want to hear a real story of duplicity, deceit and double dealing in the modern aviation industry, here's one about Monarch Airlines, the company I worked for from 1979 to 1985 before I left to join Cathay Pacific in Hong Kong.

Since its formation on 5 June 1967, Monarch has been owned by the secretive Swiss-Italian billionaire Mantegazza family. The family's patriarch, Sergio Mantegazza, was recently rated at number 317 on the Forbes World's Billionaires List with a net worth of

US$2.4 billion. Up until recently, one of his sons, Fabio, was the chief executive of Monarch.[17]

In 2009, Iain Rawlinson was appointed to the post of executive chairman of the Monarch Group. Rawlinson has a background in banking and investment with Lazard and Flemings. He attended Cambridge University and spent a significant part of his career in South Africa. This was followed by leadership of the Fleming Family & Partners business in London. He is also an independent director of a number of companies and is a non-executive director of Parkmead Group PLC. Upon his arrival at Monarch, he initiated a reorganisation of the company. His approach to dealing with competitive pressures in the European market was reported to be via consolidation of carriers and creating alliances which would result in efficiencies. As Wikipedia puts it, 'Rawlinson built up and communicated a distinct investment case and track record for each of the Monarch Group's three businesses in order to allow the underlying value of each to be demonstrated.'[18]

Now that all sounds fine and dandy and reasonable doesn't it? After all it's a competitive industry and the owners brought in an outside expert to look over the organisation to see where it could be improved. Nothing wrong with that, it makes good business sense. But what was going on behind the scenes reveals a very different picture from the one that was being painted, not only to the world at large but, more significantly, to the employees.

In 2012 and 2013 the company posted a small profit and announced their intention to purchase 60 Boeing 737 MAXs. All seemed fine but, apparently, so it transpired later, behind the scenes all of the company's assets were being sold off. Aircraft, buildings, vehicles, office furniture; the lot. They were then leased back and, to the employees, outwardly everything seemed normal. Well, if that is true, it certainly demonstrated the 'underlying value' of the business.

And there was something else. The pilots all contributed to a defined benefit pension scheme. The Mantegazzas had taken a pension holiday during the 90s and built up a deficit of GB£158 million in the fund which, to date, had not been repaid.

And then, out of the blue, in June 2014, the company announced that it had made a loss of GB£100 million from January to April. (Of course that could happen if there was capital flight by the owners leaving the company facing crippling lease-back fees couldn't it?) Rawlinson stepped down in July 2014, reportedly after a vote of no confidence was taken at board level (and presumably trousering his nice fat bonus on the way out of the door). He was replaced by the group's managing director, Andrew Swaffield, coming in as chief executive who then announced that the airline was on the verge of bankruptcy and that, in order to survive, all employees' contracts had to be renegotiated and set a timeline of two months to reach agreement.

In the background, the services of the Seabury Group, a consultancy company founded in 1995 and based in New York, had been engaged. They presented a 'turnaround plan' involving swingeing pay cuts and massive layoffs. All of their recommendations had, of course, to be achieved before any takeover by new investors could possibly be achieved.

Now where have we heard this before? Standard bully-boy negotiating technique. Swaffield then pretends to negotiate with the pilots' union, but guess what else he does? He makes it a condition that the union sign a non-disclosure agreement (NDA) before he'll enter into the sham. Oh please. More déjà vu. Forget new aircraft orders. He cuts the fleet from 42 to 30 aircraft with the loss of 205 pilots' jobs. He now has the employees in such a state of panic that they'll agree to just about anything to save their jobs and he brings in those swingeing pay cuts of up to 34 per cent. But the worst is yet to come.

The Mantegazzas have announced they are pulling out taking all their cash with them and the company is now up for sale. Don't worry though, Swaffield has found a white knight investor to come to the rescue. There's only one drawback though. This new investor does not find the current pension fund 'acceptable' so the UK government-run Pension Protection Fund (PPF) has been approached to find a solution (all still under the cover of the NDA of course).

The PPF was established in 2004 to pay compensation to members of defined benefit pension schemes, when there is a qualifying insolvency event in relation to the employer and where there are insufficient assets in the pension scheme to cover PPF levels of compensation.[19] Well that's not too bad then is it? At least your pension's going to be protected by the statutory scheme. There's only one drawback to this though. The maximum compensation from the PPF is capped at GB£32.5k per annum and all index linking to contributions and related pensions before 1997 is lost. There were around 2,400 pensions (both aircrew and ground staff) affected by this together with thousands of other past employees. Ultimately the deal went through and, in some cases, the pilots' nest eggs were cut in half by the PPF cap, with the average loss at £145,000.[20]

Monarch was taken over by Greybull Capital LLP, owned by Marc and Nathaniel Meyohas, taking a 90 per cent stake with the other 10 per cent being held by the PPF. Little is known about these two French brothers who operate from a small office in Knightsbridge.[21] The takeover is now being trumpeted as a great commercial success with Monarch having been converted into a low-cost carrier à la Ryanair and easyJet. Never mind that around 1,000 people lost their jobs and the pensioners were shafted. And we really need another Ryanair don't we?

I relate this story out of personal interest as a colleague of mine from my Monarch days who retired after more than 35 years of loyal service has had a large portion of his pension stolen from him in this disgraceful episode. Let's hear his opinion on the subject.

> All this has been stage managed and directed by at least one (and possibly two) clever but despicable men for a ruthless family. The new investors, as well as being venture capitalists, have the reputation of being a vulture fund. They have bought in cheaply and will have the option to sell on as a neatly stripped and lean outfit to the highest bidder in a year or three despite their assertion that they are 'in it for the long term'. Only time will tell.
>
> We have been royally fucked. We watch and marvel at how easily we have been squashed like bugs. The whole case stinks to high heaven of nefarious scheming and heinously clever manoeuvring.

I couldn't agree more. Like that other great pension pilferer before him, Robert Maxwell, who defrauded his Mirror Group pension fund of hundreds of millions of pounds, Sergio Mantegazza is reported to have a penchant for owning expensive toys. At least the fat fraudster had the decency to fall off his luxury yacht, the *Lady Ghislaine*, into the Atlantic Ocean off the Canary Islands and drown. It might be considered uncharitable if one was to wish Sergio the same fate whilst on board his own vessel, the *Lady Marina*; so perhaps we'd best not.

I could rant on for many more pages about the inequalities and injustices in the world (we haven't even touched on global warming, pollution, waste disposal, overpopulation and child abuse [but if we get into the latter two I'll have to mention the Catholic Church again so best steer clear for now]) and I am sure that many readers could add to my personal 'grumpy old man' list, but it is time to change tack. So much for the problems, what about solutions?

When I was a child growing up in Leeds, there was a place called Quarry Hill Flats. It was an oval construction that resembled a fortress, situated at the end of Eastgate, the main thoroughfare through the centre of the city, and right opposite Millgarth police station. It was completed in 1938 and built on the Mopin system, using a light steel frame and pre-cast concrete supposedly thereby reducing material and skilled labour costs (money again). It was intended to replace the old back-to-back houses that were prevalent in the area and re-house the workers who occupied them. The original plans included a community hall, two swimming pools, gardens and play areas and a nursery. But because of cost overruns, caused in part by structural defects and corrosion in the steelwork, the community facilities were never built. It was eventually bulldozed in 1978. From grandiose plans it was an abject failure and turned into the worst slum in Leeds.[22] The people who lived there were seen as part of a subculture; an underclass. That's where the city council sent all the troublesome families and bad lads to live.

We have another form of subculture in UK society today, but it's not the Quarry Hill Flats type of underclass (although those still do exist); it's what used to be called the middle class. It's composed of professional people who were brought up in the Thatcherite era (and I won't even get started on the damage her monetarist policies did to our economy and to our society). They are now in their 30s and 40s, and many of them own their own companies. They feel so disenfranchised by successive governments' failures to keep their election promises, to listen to their needs and to do what they were elected for, to protect and further the best interests of our society as a whole, that they have now opted out of what might be called the mainstream economy. Firstly, they don't bother voting. What's the point when all you get is more of the same whichever way you cast your ballot? But, more importantly, they have learned how to use the system to their best advantage. If the government doesn't make the multi-nationals pay their fair share of tax, why should we? There are many ways to go about avoiding (and evading) tax and these are intelligent people. They exploit the loopholes to the maximum. And if people running the government have their noses in the trough and help themselves to the taxpayers' money to refurbish their second homes and employ family members in fictitious sinecures, not to mention the cost of having one's moat cleared out, why shouldn't we? So let's milk everything we can from the state. There are ways and means of doing that as well so that's what they do and feel no compunction about it at all. And as for your new laws and regulations designed to further restrict our rights and freedoms, you can forget those as well. Laws only work if people agree to abide by them. You can't police us all, despite your surveillance society, so we'll only comply with the ones that we deem appropriate.

This is true democracy in action. As the divide between the haves and have-nots gets greater instead of being narrowed, people have had enough and are taking the decision making out of the hands of corrupt politicians and taking control of their own lives. This is not just a local phenomenon. It is happening around the world and the internet provides a great tool for monitoring government and bringing its worst excesses under the public spotlight; which is why some governments are proposing legislation to restrict such freedoms further. They're doomed to fail because it's not a lumpen mass that they're trying to repress; these are intelligent, educated people who've simply had enough and have the knowledge, skill and expertise to bypass whatever protocols might be put in place. As an individual, I might have little effect, other than giving rein to my own sense of justice and fair play. But when many people come together as a group, they can make significant and lasting change to our society and government policies. It has happened before and it can happen again.

Personally, I don't mind if my bananas have spots on their skin and do not conform to the supermarkets' radius of curvature specifications. I'm not bothered if my tomatoes aren't exactly the right colour or a bit misshapen. And as for my carrots and potatoes, they can come in any shape or size you like. I don't even mind having to wash dirt off them before I cook them. I also don't mind if some fruit and vegetables are out of season and I have to wait for them to come back in. It makes for a nice change to my diet and gives me something to look forward to. What I do mind, however, is if they're full of chemicals, preservatives and colouring designed to increase their shelf life and make them look pretty. And what I really mind is if they're just tasteless and bland and have their nutritional value compromised by the processing to which they've been subjected. And what I really, really mind is that, if I buy something, my money goes towards aiding the supermarket giants' attempts to control the food supply. So we don't shop in supermarkets. Instead, we buy our produce from local markets and growers. Now, there are some things that you can only get from retail outlets. Important staple items such as McVitie's Chocolate Homewheat Digestives. In this case your choice is more restricted, but you still have the option to go to a small local retailer rather than one of the big chains. You might have to pay a few cents more but it's worth it to keep your money out of the hands of the conglomerates.

Of course, some of this means changing your shopping habits. Because fresh produce doesn't keep as long as the supermarkets' chemically 'enhanced' food, you might have to drop in at the market two or three times a week instead of joining the sheep in the checkout queue for the Friday night 'big shop'. Oh dear, what an inconvenience. And, instead of just boiling some water and adding it to the bag of chemicals that is purported to make mashed potato, you might have to rediscover the art of peeling said vegetable, putting it on to boil for 20 minutes and then mashing it up with a knob of butter (adding salt and pepper to taste). You might also rediscover that there are many other vegetables that, in their original form, don't actually come in a plastic bag out of the freezer. The thing you really will discover though is what food is supposed to taste like. Just recently, one of our neighbours swapped us a couple of avocados from their tree for some pineapples out of our garden (our avocado tree isn't old enough to be producing fruit just yet). The flesh was a deep yellow, similar in colour to the yolk of a free-range hen's egg that hasn't been fed on fish meal. The texture was creamy, almost custard-like, and the taste was nothing like anything I have ever experienced from a supermarket supplied item. (But please don't tell Monsanto because we grow our pineapples from the heads of our own plants. Even with all my legal experience, I wouldn't want to face a law suit for infringing one of their fruit patents.)

And, just like civil disobedience, if we act in concert we can make a difference. Recently, Tesco and Morrisons have both been reported as losing significant market share; in Tesco's case to its lowest level in almost a decade.[23] Now, admittedly, some of this is due to customers switching to discount chains such as Aldi and Lidl to save money, but there is also an underlying trend away from the food giants. If those of us who are of a like mind continue to be selective where we spend our money, as a group we can make changes to our society. Boycott is the word (and I'm not referring to one of the greatest opening Test batsmen that Yorkshire has ever produced, even if he could be a bit boring to watch sometimes and had to be deliberately run out on the odd occasion). It is relatively simple to incorporate into your life and it doesn't take a lot of effort. Just don't buy their stuff. It even has the poetic beauty of using their own weapon against them; money.

But what can we do about business ethics (or lack thereof) in general? It was reported to me that a senior Swire manager, after reading my first book, remarked, 'Yes, quite good but pretty one-sided.' Fair comment. He couldn't criticise the facts because they are all true (otherwise they wouldn't be facts), but anyone is free to hold their own opinion of my personal interpretation. But it was not written purely from the perspective of the disgruntled employee. I have personal experience of being on the management side of the table. The Animals Asia Foundation has grown from being a small, spare-bedroom operation to an international charity with an annual turnover of around US$10 million and I am the chairman of its executive committee. In the third quarter of 2014 we realised that our income for the year was not going to meet our forecasts and we were going to end the year in deficit. There are two reasons for this. One is that charity donations in general have taken a hit as a result of the global recession. But the second is due to a business decision that we took at the start of the year. The prime objective of AAF is to end bear bile farming in China. To date our modus operandi has been to build sanctuaries to house the animals we have rescued from the appalling conditions that they suffer on the bile farms in China. This is very capital intensive and costly to maintain. But an opportunity came our way to change our MO. A farmer approached us with a view to selling his farm along with all of the bears he had housed there. We did a feasibility study on converting the existing premises from farm to sanctuary and the results were promising. It would be far less capital intensive and, if we were able to find outside funding for its maintenance, it could provide a model for the government on how to actually close the remaining bear farms in China and meet our shared goal of ending bear bile farming forever in that country. It was an opportunity that we could not afford to pass up and so the decision was made to go ahead with the project. However, we encountered some problems that were not anticipated, which I won't go into here, and these have resulted in an unavoidable overspend against budget. This, coupled with the less-than-forecast income, has meant we have had to make some quite far-reaching changes in our organisation this year. They have involved cutting back on some of our non-core projects and the loss of some jobs.

These are not 'human resources adjustments'. They are not 'reductions in head count'. They are not 'letting people go'. They are none of the euphemisms that are used by the corporate re-engineers. These are decisions that affect peoples' lives, their hopes, their dreams and their ability to provide for themselves and their families. As one who has spent a lot of time fighting against corporate cutbacks in pursuit of ever greater profits, to find myself on the other side of the table making these hard decisions has been one of the most difficult situations I have faced in my life. But, unlike corporate big business, I have not done this in pursuit of profit. I have had to do this for the survival of the organisation and the ultimate attainment of our core goal.

To use an aviation analogy, the business of an airline is to operate aircraft. Many airlines diversify into reservation systems, hotels, car hire and the like. They then find themselves in trouble and have to divest themselves of their non-core businesses. At AAF, we have had to get rid of, or at least scale back, the equivalent of the hotel and car hire sides of our operation.

Jill and I originally set up AAF with a certain ethos and ethical values in mind; to be a caring employer and to treat others as we would wish to be treated ourselves. We are both determined that we will maintain those values. I have found the responsibility for making these changes hard to bear. I relate this story purely to demonstrate that I have experience from both sides of the table and so, to meet that Swire manager's criticism, my views are not entirely one-sided. However, my views on business ethics perhaps conflict with his and for that I make no apology.

It is the people in an organisation that count. They are not human resources; simply numbers on a spreadsheet to be sorted and manipulated. Some organisations are now purportedly coming to realise this, or so they would have us believe. But it is not enough simply to change the title of the head of department from HR director or personnel manager, or whatever, to manager people. There must be an accompanying genuine change of ethos. If the pyramid still exists with P/E ratios and shareholder returns sitting at the top and the people at the bottom, there will be no change in corporate culture. We need to stand the pyramid on its head and put the people at the top because, if you look after your people first, the P/E ratios and shareholder returns will follow. Perhaps this is a novel concept that goes against the theory taught on the MBA courses. But it is time for a new approach because the current model is not working. Once you have driven down employee costs to the lowest base level, where do you go from there? What if everyone works for nothing? Now where are you going to find an edge over your competitors? Drive down your suppliers as the supermarkets have done? OK, now where? No, the answer is that you need to supply a service or product that is better than your competitors' and to do that, you need people who are dedicated to your vision and who share your goals; and you will not achieve that if you continually attack your employees. After all, how much profit do you really need? Is it just so you can have the biggest boat in the harbour or the flashiest car in the car park or the biggest mansion? Or do you have a responsibility to your employees and to society in general to leave this world in a better state than you found it?

In the face of all these problems that we have been discussing, I believe that there is great hope for mankind in general and I am optimistic for the future; provided that is that we address the climate change, pollution, overpopulation and waste disposal issues as well, but, as I said earlier, I'm not going there because I've probably bored you enough already and it's almost time to pop down to the pub and continue the debate over a well-earned pint.

I believe that one of man's greatest achievements in the twentieth century was the *Apollo* missions to land men on the moon. (Conspiracy theorists need read no further and don't bother writing to me either. I'm not interested.) On 6 August 2012, *Curiosity*, a vehicle the size of a small car, landed on the surface of Mars. It was originally launched from Cape Canaveral on 26 November 2011. After a voyage of 8 months covering 563,000,000 km, it landed within 2.4 km of its touchdown target. The navigation feat itself is outstanding, but the re-entry programme is even more startling. With the *Apollo* landings, there were a couple of astronauts on board who could deal with any last minute hitches or unforeseen problems. Not so with *Curiosity*. The time delay between receiving a signal, computing a course correction, sending a signal back and its receipt and action precluded any last minute changes. Everything had to go exactly as planned; and it did. An amazing feat of navigation and engineering which, to my mind, trumps the *Apollo* landings. *Curiosity* forms part of NASA's long-term Mars exploration project and is a tribute to human ingenuity.

But, on 2 March 2004, more than seven years before the launch of *Curiosity*, the European Space Agency (ESA) launched a vehicle called *Rosetta*. It's objective was to rendezvous with Comet 67P/Churyumov-Gerasimenko more than ten years after its launch and release the *Philae* vehicle it carried on board to land on the surface of the comet. This it achieved on 12 November 2014. The numbers are staggering. Truly astronomical. The mission was some 11 years in the planning prior to its launch and involved the collaboration of 14 countries. It could not carry sufficient fuel to propel it for the whole journey so it used gravity assist manoeuvres through the inner solar system to accelerate to the required speed, flying by Mars once and the Earth three times, completing a total flight distance of 6.4 billion kilometers (6.4 BILLION). At its maximum velocity, P67 travels at 135,000 kph and *Philae* had to exactly match its speed to achieve a landing. The navigation feat of this mission to perform such an intercept outweighs that of *Curiosity* by several quanta, as does the engineering feat of the landing itself. Of course, as we all know, *Philae* bounced on landing prompting some members of the press to immediately try to portray it as a failure. I loved the ESA spokesman's response. 'Not at all. Not only have we landed once on the comet, we have landed three times.'

But apart from the technological achievement, think of what has taken place in the world since the mission's original inception in 1993. Wars have been fought, governments toppled, extremists of every hue have tried to return civilisation to the Stone Age, economic collapses, banking crises, massacres, mayhem, catastrophes and all manner of natural disasters. And through all of this, a group of human beings from many diverse backgrounds, nationalities and creeds have kept the faith. Some of the original members of the team have long since died or retired, and yet, their successors picked up the reins and continued to pursue their dream to a successful conclusion. Am I optimistic for the future? In the face of such magnificent human achievements to overcome adversity, who could not be?

And, finally, in answer my own question posed at the start, what have we learned, I will say this. Always look for good in others and believe in yourself. As you go through life, there will always be some megalomaniac, some bully boy or, (perhaps) even worse, some zoologist trying to tell you what to think and do. Just ignore them or, better still, refuse even to acknowledge them. That's what they hate the most. It pricks the bubble of their puffed-up, self-important egos. But be prepared to listen to genuine advice; heed the good and discard the bad. Never fight battles that you have no hope of winning. Sometimes delay is the preferred option to win the war. Consider the possible consequences of what you undertake and be sure that you are prepared to accept them. If you cannot afford to lose, do not sit down at the poker table; find another game. You are responsible, and accountable, for your own actions. No amount of apology or regret can change that. Once committed, you can't take it back. Always give help to others when circumstances permit. But, in the end, trust your own instincts, make your own decisions and walk your own path. It may be difficult sometimes. Some problems you encounter may seem insurmountable at first sight; but persevere. It is definitely well worth the effort. In return, win or lose, you will be rewarded with the peace of mind that you tried your best, you protected those weaker than you and those you hold dear. You did the right thing. And then you will be able to die smiling before they put you in the fast hearse.

REALLY THE END

Epilogue

As the manuscript for this book went to my publisher for editing, the industrial situation between the pilots and management of Cathay Pacific continued to deteriorate. The pilots were engaged in a contract compliance campaign which was having the expected result and flights were being delayed and cancelled. As the Chinese New Year holiday approached on February 19th, the soon-to-be-replaced DFO, Richard Hall, put out a missive to the pilots. It is worth quoting parts of this verbatim to see what we can glean from his words.

> Ladies and gentlemen,
>
> Next week sees the start of celebrations to mark the Year of the Goat – which triggers what is said to be the biggest annual human migration taking place across the boundary in China. Looking closer to home, contract compliance was introduced just before the Christmas and New Year celebrations, so it is perhaps timely as we approach the Lunar New Year to see where we have got to since then.

So much for the introductory preamble. Let us ignore the questionable grammar as that might be viewed as cheap point scoring and we wouldn't want to go there.

> Last weekend presented what to be frank, was a slightly worrying picture. High levels of sickness suggested that contract compliance was morphing into something else ahead of the Chinese New Year celebrations. Yes, our colleagues in ICM have recently been finding it increasingly difficult to contact crew and maintain overall roster stability. Tactical sickness – which is of course not claimed to be a part of legitimate contract compliance, further undermines our ability to maintain normal reliability of our schedule of flights.

I'm sorry. What was that? Tactical sickness? Is someone suggesting that the pilots are operating a sick-out campaign? I do hope they have the evidence to back this up because the last person who made similar statements without any evidence to support said allegations lost, not just one, but two defamation cases for the company. This is very uncertain ground. Let us see what else he has to say on the subject.

> There is always sickness and particularly so during the northern winter flu season. At this time it is noticeable that current sickness rates are higher than those of past years. Questions are inevitably asked when, as happened recently, a large number of those scheduled to work on a particular day in a particular category phoned in sick on the day.

Oh, I see. So the suggestion is that a group of pilots in a particular category conspired together to disrupt the company's operations. Now that's exactly what Philip Chen suggested under oath in court in *The 49ers* case and he didn't do very well out of that did he? Not a very good career move unless, that is, you're already headed towards the exit door.

> Normal levels of reserve are simply not intended to cope with such an eventuality. Indeed, questions would be asked if we did have such levels of reserve. To do so would be unsustainable for the business and, I venture, would be deeply unpopular with pilots who do not generally relish the prospect of reserve.

Ah yes. Now we come to the nub of it. So the implied threat seems to be that, if the pilots don't pull their socks up, they're going to be subjected to punitive rostering with maximum reserve and minimum days off. Now where have we heard that one before? Unfortunately, if the rosters are already somewhat punitive in the normal course of events because of a shortage of pilots, it's not really much of a threat now is it?

> Of course it would be quite unpalatable to think that professionals would declare themselves to be sick if in fact they were not.

Whoa. Stop right there. Be careful of accusing pilots of being unprofessional unless the company wants to see itself back in court yet again. You'd better have some damned good evidence to back up such an allegation.

Our customers, whose travel needs are disrupted as a
consequence, would have every right to question the professional
ethics of anyone who did so.

Ah yes, very clever. It's not the company that's calling them
unprofessional. It's the customers; pesky blighters.

To be clear, I believe that most of our pilot body, including the
GC of the HKAOA, would never countenance such activity.

Of course. The majority of you are thoroughly good chaps. It's just a
small minority of troublemakers and ne'er-do-wells who are causing
all this trouble.

It is well understood that the intent of contract compliance is to
make the point that good will is a two-way street. It has also
been claimed that there is absolutely no desire to upset our
customers or to harm their travel plans. Working as professionals
in a service industry as we all ultimately do, it is clear that our
customers' needs are second only to the safety of our operation.

Yes, good one that. Get the 'safety of the operation' message in while
you can. At least they've realised now that contract compliance is a
protected union activity thanks to *The 49ers*, so they have to be a
little more circumspect this time around don't they?

For most it will not need saying, but turning a blind eye to our
customers' needs will ultimately only cause damage to career
prospects and aspirations, by damaging the reputation of our
airline and all who work there.

Ah yes, the veiled threat again. Be mindful of your career aspirations
because we're keeping secret files on who the culprits are and
compiling another Hit List as we speak. Not having the best interests
of the company at heart. Unreliable. Can't be trusted. Loss of
confidence. All good *raisons d'être* in preparing the ground for
making 'painful decisions', taking 'prompt and resolute action' and
preventing Hong Kong 'being held to ransom', as one A.N. Tyler
once put it.

We've heard quite a bit of noise over the occasional unplanned three man crew operations. It is perhaps interesting to recall that when the RPs were originally formulated, the question of the occasional three-man operation was discussed. The view of the union negotiating team at that time was that in the event of sickness in a planned four man crew, if a flight could be legally operated with a three man crew, the aircraft and our customers would never be abandoned.

Now that's really a bit naughty. When the RPs were 'originally formulated' back in 1999, when I was leading the union negotiating team, no such concession was ever made. It is true that the idea was discussed but rejected except for consideration on certain north-south rotations where trans-meridian time change and associated cumulative fatigue was not seen to be so critical. So that's a bit of a porkie but, of course, who is around any more from those times to challenge the statement?

To put the issue in perspective, since contract compliance commenced, there have been six occasions when a flight has been preserved by operating with three pilots rather than the planned four.

So in the last two months, six flights have been operated without the contractually-mandated minimum crewing levels. The question might be asked, where does that fit in with 'safety being our first priority'?

There is no clandestine plot to slide in three-man crew through the back door. Quite the contrary, it has been on the agenda for RP discussions all along. Despite the inference in a recent association update that the subject is all about reducing recruitment needs, it is actually all about the ability to compete where we are sensibly able to, on a level playing field in a very competitive world.

Oh please. They've been trying to push through 3 man ULR for the last 14 years. It's only the pilots' union that's stopped them. They were trying to push it through back in my time on the union committee. If they thought they could get away with it they'd do it tomorrow. But it is quite right to say that it's been on the RP agenda 'all along'. **It's been on the agenda since 1999 and it still hasn't been sorted**. And the main reason for that is that they still don't know when to do the deal. They're still reaching for the unobtainable sweets on the top shelf.

> On another issue, it is surprising and disappointing to note that the HKAOA GC is now suggesting to its members that they not accept promotion opportunities that are being offered to some pilots. As pilots we all look forward to command and the rewards that come with being a Captain. For many the further opportunity of being a Training Captain or Senior Training Captain is also a reward and recognition of hard work and professional achievement. HKAOA members are being asked to delay their acceptance of C & T promotion opportunities.

Well there's a simple answer to keeping the training sausage machine churning out more low-time, blue-pyjama-clad automatons to fill the pointed-end seats and keep the customers satisfied. Treat the employees with respect. Make them feel that they are valued members of the company. Listen to their concerns and help to solve their problems instead of creating yet more with a dictatorial and over-bearing management style. Be a caring… Oh why bother. I'm wasting my breath. They're just going to carry on down the same old path.

> The HKAOA's recommendation to its members to turn down these opportunities can be viewed as intimidatory and divisive. It is surely unreasonable to ask pilots to forego professional advancement to positions that recognize and rewards their abilities and progresses their professional careers.

'Intimidatory and divisive?' The AOA? What the hell do you think your management style is? It is management that precipitated all of this when it was decided to embark upon a course of hacking away at the employees' remuneration and benefits. What are the multiple Conditions of Service the pilots now operate under if not divisive? That policy was deliberately designed to divide the pilot force. It is the Swire management style that attempts to intimidate the employees, not the AOA.

As we approach the Year of the Goat, there clearly remains much that needs to be done if we are to enjoy a more harmonious and progressive year than that of the Year of the Horse.

Yes, there is much to be done. There has been throughout your tenure as DFO and, in fact, way before that. But, guess what, it's still the same old issues that successive managements have failed even to address, let alone achieve positive change. All they've done is continue to serve up to the pilots more of the same. And, as a result, the company is now back in exactly the same situation in which it found itself 14 years ago.

> Ratcheting up contract compliance, or whatever it has now morphed into, is not the way to achieve this.

We're agreed on that. The way to achieve this is to negotiate in good faith, listen to your employees and address their concerns. Oh, sorry, I've already said that, but thought it worth repeating in case someone might be listening.

> Cool rational heads, sharing the problems and genuinely seeking mutually beneficial outcomes is what will ultimately succeed in ensuring that we maintain the reliable services that our customers value and provide all of us with career opportunities that are fulfilling and rewarding.

Easy to say if you are about to trouser your retirement cheque and head for the exit. It is a good quotation from the management gobble-speak manual though.

On top of all this, the results of an employee engagement survey conducted by Insync Surveys, an Australian company incorporated in 2006, and released in February 2015 are absolutely damning of the current state of employer/employee relations. They indicate a company in severe organisational distress with, on average, only 13.5 per cent of the employee group responding positively to key engagement performance indicators. Given that only 57 per cent of the employees even took the trouble to respond, god knows how bad the figures would be if the really disgruntled employees could be bothered to vent their frustrations. In a message to the crew dated, appropriately enough, Friday 13 February, the DFO designate herself described the results as 'pretty awful'. A gross understatement if ever there was one. The results are a damning indictment of the current management of what was once one of the market-leading companies in commercial aviation.

There was some good news though. In response to the question, 'Operations manuals made available to me are up to date', an average of 52 per cent of the pilots surveyed responded positively. So at least the clerks are doing a good job then.

But there has been one further development. On 28 February 2015, the DFO designate sent a letter to the chairman of the AOA regarding the ongoing RP negotiations. In it she stated:

> ...the Company is unable to accept the 'Final Offer' on Rostering Practices presented by the HKAOA on 13th February 2015...

> Having started RP discussions in early 2014... I therefore believe that the "Bargaining Process" for Rostering Practices has now been completed...

> I am writing to give three months notice to terminate the Rostering Practices 2007 Policy Agreement (RP07)...

> I very much hope that during the next three months we may still be able to come to an agreement... however if this is not possible... RP07 will be introduced as a Company Policy with effect from 1st June 2015.

So, in a carbon copy of events leading up to the sacking of *The 49ers* in July 2001, the RP negotiations have failed to reach agreement and, exactly as before, since they can't get what they want, they're cancelling the current agreement and unilaterally imposing a new set of RPs. But, no problem surely? After all, the letter simply says they're going to stick with the old agreement for the time being. Yes, but with one very significant difference. It will be a company policy and, therefore, subject to amendment at their sole discretion. And we all know what that means. Despite Hall's protestations to the contrary nine days earlier, this gives them a free hand to impose 3 man ULR and all that the pilots will have left to protect them against cumulative fatigue are the bottom-of-the-barrel, last resort, safety net of the provisions of CAD 371 – the absolute minimum legal requirements.

If that is permitted to happen, it will be a significant degradation of operational flight safety within Cathay Pacific Airways. And that is not just my opinion. It is a fact. But it can be prevented. All it would take is leadership. If all the captains stood together as one man and point blank refused to operate 3 man ULR, what could they do in response? Sack the first man to refuse? Sack the next one as well, and the next? Maybe they could sack 49. Now there's an idea.

When we looked back earlier over everything that has happened throughout *The 49ers* saga since 2001, I posed a question; what have we learned? I asked if they had had their Papa Zulu moment. I was optimistic but lacked empirical evidence to support my outlook. Unfortunately, in the light of current developments, I now have to modify my view.

History is repeating itself and the new choir is singing from a virtually identical hymn sheet. It goes to the highest level of management. Just as when they replaced Barley with Rhodes, they are kicking out a puppet, but at least operational, uniformed DFO and replacing him with a suit. Let us hope that this one will at least be able to recognise when she's on the backside of the drag curve, avoid the crash and, in the aftermath, not have to ask what caused it.

I am not optimistic. Rather the reverse. From my personal experience I am sad to have to report that, on the available evidence, there has been no change in ethos at all. Not one iota. After 14 long years, it's just more of the same.

THEY HAVE LEARNED NOTHING

Afterword

On 24 March 2015, my editor, Imogen Palmer, sent me the following email:

> Please take all the time you need to look through everything as I'm away for a couple of days, aptly going to look at aeroplanes at Duxford. I have a 10-year old boy who is completely obsessed with aeroplanes of all kinds, particularly 747s. I was quite keen on the idea of him becoming a pilot but I've rather gone off it since reading your book.

This set me thinking. If Imogen had gained this impression from reading my book, perhaps others would as well. This was never my intent. Quite the contrary. As well as setting down the facts for the record, the other main motivation for writing both of my books was to educate those who come after me in my chosen profession – to make them aware of some of the problems that they may face and, hopefully, assist them in avoiding some of the mistakes that we made when dealing with similar difficulties.

The underlying failures and malaise in modern corporate governance and ethos that I have described in these pages, mismanagement, greed, corruption, ignorance, or just plain incompetence, are present in all walks of life. No matter what trade, industry or profession a new entrant into the workforce chooses, at some point in time he or she is likely to face similar challenges to those that *The 49ers* faced. The lessons that we learned are still applicable irrespective of the field of endeavour.

In response to Imogen's message I wrote:

> I've been thinking about your comment above and it made me realise that, perhaps, other readers might have a similar reaction. It is not my intention. My career has been difficult, yes, but I wouldn't change my choice to become a pilot for the world. I have had a great life out of aviation and, if you have the flying bug, there's nothing you won't do to achieve your ambition. If your son wants to fly, let him. My intention in telling this story

is to forewarn others of the possible hurdles they may face and how to deal with them (so they don't make the same mistakes as we did.) I wouldn't want to turn any budding pilot away from aviation (except maybe from Cathay Pacific!) The bean counters won't always be in control. One day we will wrest our profession back from them. It might be your son who plays a part in doing that.

Glossary of Terms

Abbrev.	Full Form	Explanation
A/T	Autothrust	
AAF	Animals Asia Foundation	
ACC	area control centre	
ACM	air combat manoeuvring	
ADC	air data computer	
ADF	automatic direction finder	a radio navigation aid
AGM	annual general meeting	
ALPA	US Airline Pilots Association	
AoA	angle of attack	
AOA/ HKAOA	(Hong Kong) Aircrew Officers Association	
AP	autopilot	
ASI	airspeed indicator	
ATC	air traffic control	
ATK	actual tonne kilometres	a measure of cost efficiency used in airline operations
ATPL	airline transport pilot licence	
BA	British Airways	
BAE	British Aerospace	
BIA	British Island Airways	
BMA	British Midland Airways	
BoB's	Band of Brothers	the 18 of *The 49ers* who stayed the course to the end
CAD	(Hong Kong) Civil Aviation Department	
Cb	Cumulonimbus	
CBA	cost benefit analysis	
CCQ	cross crew qualification	
CDG	Paris Charles de Gaulle airport	
CG	centre of gravity	
CLK	Hong Kong Chek Lap Kok airport	
CPA	Cathay Pacific Airways	
CPL/IR	commercial pilot	

Abbrev.	Full Form	Explanation
	licence/instrument rating	
CTP	concessional travel policy	
(D)FDR	(digital) flight data recorder	
DFO	director (of) flight operations	
DGP	discipline and grievance procedure	
DME	distance measuring equipment	a radio navigation aid
EASA	European Aviation Safety Agency	
EAT	Employment Appeal Tribunal	
ECAM	electronic central aircraft monitoring system	
EO	(Hong Kong) Employment Ordinance	
ESA	European Space Agency	
ETA	estimated time of arrival	
FAU	(Cathay Pacific) Flight Attendants' Union	
FCC	flight control computer	
FCC	Foreign Correspondents Club	
FFS	full flight simulator	
FIR	flight information region	
FMC	flight management computer	
FOCC	flight operations control centre	
FRCL	first class	
FSA	Financial Standards Authority	
FWC	flight warning computer	
G/S	groundspeed	
GPH	gallons per hour	
GPS	global positioning system	a satellite based navigation system
GPWS	ground proximity warning system	
HF	high frequency	
IATA	International Air Transport Association	

Abbrev.	Full Form	Explanation
ICAO	International Civil Aviation Organisation	
IFALPA	International Federation of Airline Pilots Associations	
ILS	instrument landing system	a navigation aid
INS	inertial navigation system	a navigation system
IOC(C)	integrated operations control (centre)	
IRU	inertial reference unit	a part of the INS
ITCZ	inter-tropical convergence zone	a weather front between the northern and southern hemispheres
JAA	Joint Airworthiness Authority	
LBA	Leeds-Bradford airport	
LGW	London Gatwick airport	
LHR	London Heathrow airport	
MCG	Melbourne Cricket Ground	
MME	Teesside airport	
MPL	multi-crew pilot licence	
MSS	maximum safety strategy	
N_1		a measure of engine power
ND	navigation display	
NDA	non-disclosure agreement	
NDB	non-directional beacon	a radio navigation aid
OAA	Oxford Aviation Academy	
PF	pilot flying	
PFD	primary flight display	
PIO	pilot induced oscillation	
PNF	pilot not flying	
PPF	pension protection fund	
QDM		magnetic bearing to a station
QRH	quick reference handbook	a printed aircraft checklist
RMI	radio magnetic indicator	a navigation instrument
RNAV	area navigation	a navigation aid
RP	rostering practices	
RTB	retirement travel benefit	
RTK	revenue tonne kilometres	a measure of cost efficiency used in airline operations

Abbrev.	Full Form	Explanation
S21B		a section of the EO relating to anti-union discrimination
SAM	surface-to-air missile	
SAP	super absorbent polymer	
SCMP	*South China Morning Post*	an English language newspaper in Hong Kong
SOP	standard operating procedure	
SRE	surveillance radar element	a precision approach aid
SRZ	special rules zone	
TAECO	Taikoo (Xiamen) Aircraft Engineering Company Ltd.	
TAS	true airspeed	
TAT	total air temperature	the temperature of the skin of the aircraft
THS	trimming horizontal stabiliser	
TI	turn indicator	
TOW	takeoff weight	
ULR	ultra long range	
USAB	USA Basing	a wholly owned subsidiary of CPA
USRC	United Services Recreation Club	
V/S	vertical speed	
VHF	very high frequency	
VOR	VHF omni-range	a radio navigation aid
VSI	vertical speed indicator	
WMD	weapons of mass destruction	

Index

Anderson, James, 49

Baber, George, 89

Banks-Smith, Graeme, 234, 315

Barley, Kenneth Roland, 19, 93, 147, 190, 192, 212, 287, 327, 358

Beebe, Chris, 316

Bird, Lawrence, x

Biss, Carol, x

Bissell, Peter, 68, 267

Blagrove, Colin, 91

Blair, Anthony Charles Lynton, 91, 336

Bokhary, Syed Kemal Shah, 175, 185, 197, 227, 231

Boycott, Geoffrey, 346

Boyd, Jimmy L., 136, 143

Brabeck-Letmathe, Peter, 339

Bradsher, Keith, 99

Branson, Richard, 302

Brown, James Gordon, 335, 336

Burkill, Peter, 328

Burridge, Jack, 327

Cameron, David William Donald, 336, 338

Carver, Ken, 111, 277, 278, 279, 286, 298

Cassidy, Jack, 319

Chan, Siu-oi Patrick, 175

Chaston, Sally, 65, 71

Chen, Nan-lok Philip, 13, 15, 20, 21, 22, 23, 24, 27, 37, 94, 95, 169, 176, 177, 180, 185, 186, 188, 189, 190, 191, 218, 219, 220, 222, 303, 352

Cheung, Kam-Chuen, 5, 8, 16, 17, 18, 20, 22, 24, 32, 34, 35, 37, 39, 40, 41, 42, 175

Chiu, Benedict, 50, 52, 261

Chong, Courtney, 149, 150, 151, 153, 156, 159, 281, 286

Chu, Ivan, 307, 308

Clapson, Dave, 19

Clarkson, Jeremy, 335

Cook, Alastair, 49

Cowan, Samuel, 88, 89

Crofts, George, 55, 232

Dalton, Barry, x

Demery, Nigel, 153, 155

Diamond, Robert Edward, 334

Dickie, John, 248, 277, 279, 286, 310

Dickson, Bob, 299

Dullard, Steve, 47

Dullard, Sue, 47

Eagles, Michael, 89

Easton, Jan, 163

Easton, Sandy, 163, 164, 165

England, Greg, 34, 248, 310

Fitz-Costa, Mike, 163, 279, 280

Flintoff, Freddie, 48

Flowers, Paul, 334

Fraser, Don, v, 2, 50, 51, 52, 56, 174, 205, 206, 207, 283, 309, 315, 331

Fraser, Kelly, 50, 205

Gage, Doug, 34, 43, 149, 150, 152, 153, 154, 248, 264, 273, 274, 275, 278, 280, 283, 285, 287, 290, 292, 294, 295, 310

Gann, Ernest K., 331

Goodwin, Frederick Anderson, 335

Grange, Don, 151, 156, 157, 160

Grossman, Clive, 5, 175, 176, 198, 199, 230

Guy, James, 238

Guy, Jim, 238

Guy, June Elaine, 236, 237, 238

Haddon-Cave, Charles Anthony, 88, 89, 90, 91, 92, 93, 330

Hagon, John Graeme, 63, 64, 67, 68, 71, 73, 84

Hall, Richard, 330, 351

Hamel, Veronica, 319

Hampton, Jessica, x

Hardy, Mike, 327

Hayhoe, David, 329

Heron, Quentin, 148, 149, 279

Hie, Ricky, 85, 86

Hislop, Ian, 232

Ho, Ting Pong, x

Hoban, Kevin, 40

Holliday, Ailsa, 78

Hopkins, George, 331

Huggins, Adrian, 7, 8, 10, 11, 12, 13, 14, 15, 16, 17, 18, 19, 20, 24, 26, 29, 30, 31, 32, 34, 37, 38, 42, 52, 176, 177, 178, 179, 181, 182, 189, 193, 194, 195, 198, 199, 210, 217, 218, 219, 220, 221, 227, 230, 311

Hunsworth, Nicholas D., 154, 273, 311

Hunter, Malcolm, 153, 280

Hynde, Chrissie, 78

Joseph, Tara, 100

Keene, Brian, 7, 8, 9, 10, 11, 12, 13, 14, 15, 16, 40

Kelly, Christopher, 281

Kragt, Femmy, 167, 171

Kragt, Klaske, v, 1, 2, 3, 77, 78, 79, 80, 84, 85, 86, 136, 137, 139, 140, 142, 144, 164, 165, 166, 170, 171, 172, 201, 202, 207, 208, 234, 235, 238, 259, 267, 294, 298, 299, 300, 301, 302, 303

Kwan, Becky, 205, 206

Kwan, Shuk-hing Susan, 6, 8, 15, 17, 20, 24, 31, 194

Lam, Man-hon Johnson, 6, 194, 199

Lau, Jimmy, 58, 61, 68, 84, 270

Lau, Jimmy Senior, 58, 84

Lau, Lap-yan Martin, 57, 58, 59, 64, 67, 68, 69, 268, 271

Lawrence, Chris, 40

Lee, Cheuk-yan, 207

Lee, Martin, 151, 153

Lettich, Gerardo, 329

Leung, Chun-ying, 337

Leung, Mei-fun, Priscilla, 5, 37

Levitt, Martin J., 331

Lok, Frances, 151

Lowe, Christopher, 90

Ma, Tao-li Geoffrey, 175, 176, 179, 206, 214

Mahy, Martyn, 91

Mantegazza, Sergio, 339, 342

Maxwell, Ian Robert, 342

McEwan, Scott, 308, 309, 312, 313

McKirdy, Dave, 234

McLaughlin, Chris, 96, 98, 106

McLeish, Robin, 176, 198, 311

Meyohas, Marc, 342

Meyohas, Nathaniel, 342

Miller, Andrew L., 133

Moore, Patrick, 128

Morriss, Keith, 300

Neuberger, David Edmond, 175, 179, 183, 186, 206, 208, 214, 216, 217, 221, 223, 272

Nichols, Sandy, 84

Nipperess, Robert, 148, 150, 151, 152, 154, 273, 275, 278, 280, 283, 285, 287, 294, 306

O'Leary, Michael, 328

Oldfield, Richard, 90

Palmer, Imogen, x, 359

Patten, Christopher Francis, 338

Pearce, Rupert, 98

Pledger, Malcolm David, 89

Ponting, Ricky, 49

Prince, Eric, 91

Purcell, Dally, 133, 322

Rawlinson, Iain, 340

Reyes, Anselmo Trinidad, 5, 6, 17, 19, 20, 29, 34, 35, 36, 39, 42, 52, 53, 54, 176, 179, 197, 198, 205, 223, 230, 231, 248

Rhodes, Nicholas Peter, 9, 12, 13, 14, 27, 94, 95, 193, 315, 358

Richards, Keith, 165

Robinson, Jill, 46, 47, 81, 82, 83, 235, 259, 334, 347

Rodwell, Ian, 309

Sharp, Jonathan, 168

Siu, Phila, 315

Slosar, John Robert, 92, 304, 307

Smith, Adam, 331

Smith, Matthew, 299

Smith, Nicola Jane, 166, 167, 173

Smith, Terry, 331

Springsteen, Bruce, 170

Stock, Frank, 6, 53, 54, 194

Strauss, Andrew, 49

Suet, Wing Wong Isabella, 270

Sutch, Peter Dennis Antony, 304, 307

Sutcliffe, Peter, 232

Sutcliffe, Sonia, 232

Swaffield, Andrew, 341

Sweeney, Chris, 148, 277, 279, 286

Tang, Ching Robert, 175, 176, 184, 185, 220

Thompson, Anna, 330

Tiffany, Andy, x

Tremlett, Chris, 49

Turley, Alan, 322

Turnbull, David Muir, 94, 97, 261, 304

Tyler, Antony Nigel, 13, 15, 20, 23, 27, 92, 94, 95, 96, 97, 99, 102, 169, 176, 177, 180, 185, 186, 188, 189, 190, 191, 193, 218, 219, 220, 222, 304, 307, 330, 353

Vallance, Simon, 234, 235

Walsh, Frank, 89, 90, 328

Warham, James Stanley, 240, 241, 242

Warham, Joan Bertha, 239, 245

Warham, Richard Mark, 164, 167, 173

Waters, Malcolm, 329

Waterston, Douglas, 234

Watkinson, Mavis, 239, 240, 245

White, Tony, 72, 272

Wilkinson, David, 299

Winter, Johnny, 171

Woods, Alan, 298

Sources

[1] Michael Smith (2007-06-17). 'Blast fears as Nimrod planes leak fuel on spy missions'. London: *The Sunday Times*

[2] Sam Marsden, Press Association, *The Independent*, Tuesday 18 November 2014

[3] *Bloomberg Businessweek*, 21 November 2014

[4] www.ftejerez.com/multi-crew-pilots-license-mpl

[5] http://caeoaa.com/multi-crew-pilots-licence-training/#.VH0sScmVBOk

[6] en.wikipedia.org/wiki/South_African_Airways_Flight_295

[7] www.netdimensions.com

[8] www.*theguardian.com*/business/2013/nov/23/coop-scandal-paul-flowers-mutual-societies

[9] http://en.wikipedia.org/wiki/Bob_Diamond

[10] www.*independent.co.uk*/news/business/news/bob-diamond-no-apologies-no-restraint-no-shame-2182231.html

[11] www.*nytimes.com*/2013/05/05/magazine/robert-diamonds-next-life.html?pagewanted=all&_r=0

[12] www.*theguardian.com*/business/2011/dec/12/labour-regulations-city-rbs-collapse

[13] www.bbc.com/news/world-asia-china-29547860

[14] www.*wsj.com*/articles/hong-kong-leader-sticks-to-election-position-ahead-of-talks-1413817975

[15] wikipedia.org/wiki/United_Kingdom_general_election,_2010

[16] http://liamscheff.com/2011/10/hi-monsanto-you-evil-evil-evil-bastards/

[17] www.ibtimes.co.uk/monarch-restructuring-secretive-billionaire-mantegazza-family-behind-airline-1467206

[18] http://en.wikipedia.org/wiki/Iain_Rawlinson

[19] http://www.pensionprotectionfund.org.uk/About-Us/Pages/About-Us.aspx

[20] www.telegraph.co.uk/finance/personalfinance/pensions/11261370/Pensions-safety-net-Mine-was-cut-by-145000.html

[21] www.zoominfo.com/p/Marc-Meyohas/7738026

[22] https://municipaldreams.wordpress.com/2013/02/26/leeds-the-quarry-hill-flats

[23] www.*theguardian.com*/business/2014/mar/11/tesco-market-share-shrinks-lowest-level-decade-aldi-supermarket